GAUGUIN IN THE SOUTH SEAS

BY BENGT DANIELSSON

The Happy Island

What Happened on the Bounty

Love in the South Seas

Work and Life on Raroia

Forgotten Islands of the South Seas

From Raft to Raft

GAUGUIN
IN THE
SOUTH SEAS

BENGT DANIELSSON

ILLUSTRATED

1966
DOUBLEDAY & COMPANY, INC.
GARDEN CITY, NEW YORK

Translated from the Swedish GAUGUINS SÖDERHAVSAR
© Bengt Danielsson, 1964

Translated by Reginald Spink
French quotations translated from the original sources by
the author and the translator in collaboration
Color photographs by A. Sylvain, Papeete

LIBRARY OF CONGRESS CATALOG CARD NUMBER 65–12363
TRANSLATION COPYRIGHT © 1965 BY GEORGE ALLEN & UNWIN Ltd
ALL RIGHTS RESERVED
TEXT PRINTED IN THE UNITED STATES OF AMERICA
PHOTOGRAPHIC ILLUSTRATIONS PRINTED IN SWEDEN
FIRST EDITION IN THE UNITED STATES OF AMERICA

To My Helper Marie-Thérèse

CONTENTS

ILLUSTRATIONS

ILLUSTRATIONS IN THE TEXT

VOYAGE OF DISCOVERY

WHEN, in May 1951, forty-eight years after the death of Paul Gauguin almost to the day, I went ashore on Hivaoa, the island which was his last resting-place in the remote Marquesas, I had no other object in mind than anthropological studies. Although, of course, I had often heard Gauguin spoken of during my two earlier visits to Tahiti, the idea of writing a book about his life in the South Seas had never occurred to me. At that time, in fact, I would have regarded any such enterprise as totally unnecessary, since I took it for granted that all the biographical data had long been known and set down.

How wrong I had been was soon borne in on me by the surprising discovery, in the middle of the tropical forest on the southern shore of Hivaoa, only a few miles from Atuona where Gauguin had spent the last two years of his tormented life, of a large and well-stocked library. The impressive library belonged to a retired French schoolmaster, Guillaume Le Bronnec, who to judge from his overgrown copra plantation clearly preferred to cultivate his literary interests. Besides a good selection of French classics and several shelves of anthropological, historical, and other scholarly works, in French, English, and German, my friendly host possessed a surprisingly complete collection of books about Paul Gauguin.

Absently turning the pages of these books, I found that the former schoolmaster, following old-established habits, had made marginal notes and corrections, and it was plain to see that there was an astonishing number of quite elementary mistakes even of geography and ethnology. Monsieur Le Bronnec's explanation was simple: none of Gauguin's biographers had ever visited the South Seas. What is more, they had based their accounts almost exclusively on Gauguin's own letters and other written statements, which of course gave a highly fragmentary and subjective picture of events and affairs in the islands at the time.

Monsieur Le Bronnec—who a few years later at my insistence published some of his valuable notes—had never met Gauguin, having first arrived in the Marquesas in 1910. At Atuona, however, I met someone who had known Gauguin well—and considered it in no way a privilege. He was David Le Cadre, the Catholic bishop of the islands, who had gone there in 1900 straight from the seminary and remained true to the mission for the rest of his life. What Bishop Le Cadre and other elderly villagers, natives and Europeans, had to tell seemed to me so interesting and valuable that I included a chapter about Gauguin in my travel book *Forgotten Islands of the South Seas*. I need hardly say that this chapter I now find, thirteen years later, to be sadly deficient.

When I returned to Tahiti in 1953, I sought out, at Monsieur Le Bronnec's suggestion, a former interpreter and government official, by name Alexandre Drollet, who to my delighted surprise turned out to be a mine of information about Gauguin's early years in the South Seas. Monsieur Drollet, who had entered government service at the age of twenty, had met Gauguin a few hours after the latter's arrival in Tahiti in 1891 and later had seen him frequently in his own home, as his father, Sosthène Drollet, and Gauguin had been close friends. My interest was now definitely roused, and during the following years I devoted all the time I could spare from my anthropological researches to tracing other people who might have something to tell about Gauguin, his friends and enemies, and about life in the colony in his day.

The population of Tahiti and the Marquesas—and especially their European population—was extremely small at the turn of the century. Gauguin lived in the islands all told for ten years, and was a most original and striking personality. The memory of him therefore remained more vivid here than, for example, at the places in Brittany where he stayed, and where inquiries among the local inhabitants have been carried out with good results by French scholars. The names of the two dozen or so persons whose testimony proved reliable and valuable—about a tenth of the total number interviewed— are listed among my other sources. But oral traditions alone, no matter how carefully they are checked, do not provide a sufficient basis for a biography. For that reason I would never have embarked on the difficult task of trying to reconstruct Gauguin's life in the South Seas, if I had not in the course of time come across a large quantity of far more detailed and reliable information in various written or printed sources. This previously unknown, or at any rate unused, material consists chiefly of official letters and reports and court documents and records, located in the government archives at Papeete, articles and notices in local newspapers and missionary journals published in France, travel descriptions by occasional visitors, diaries and other family papers in private possession, and, last but not least, a number of new letters from, to, and about Gauguin himself. A full list of all the source material used will be found at the end of the book.

Stated more explicitly, my main purpose has been:

(1) to provide the most accurate and complete account possible of the last twelve years of Gauguin's life, of which ten were spent in the South Seas;

(2) to describe fairly fully the geographical, cultural, and social conditions in Tahiti and the Marquesas at that time;

(3) in every case to try to understand and explain Gauguin's actions, reactions, difficulties, griefs and triumphs, as the consequences of the interplay of a unique personality and a unique local environment.

I should like to point out immediately that I have been forced, to a far greater extent than I had thought necessary when I began my researches, to revise the previously accepted chronology. An unobtrusive figure refers to the relevant evidence in each case. Similarly, many of the more pathetic, romantic, and heroic episodes which figure prominently in previous accounts were not borne out by the evidence and have had to be dismissed either as misapprehensions or as pure myth. The loss is small; for Gauguin is great enough as an artist, and as a man both complex and extraordinary enough, to fascinate us even when deprived of his false halo.

With regard to Gauguin's artistic activities, I have abstained from all discussion of purely aesthetic and stylistic matters, for the simple reason that I am not qualified to discuss these, and have confined myself to the elucidation whenever possible of the sources of his inspiration and the meaning of the Tahitian titles of certain of his pictures.

Finally, a few words about the illustrations. These are of two kinds, but have all been chosen to conform with the general purpose of the book. Forty-five are monochrome photographs dating from the turn of the century and telling, better, in many cases, than would long descriptions, exactly what life was like in the islands in Gauguin's time. (The few exceptions among these are reproductions of paintings which are of particular interest in view of their subject-matter.) The rest are recent colour photographs of the places where Gauguin lived, or landscapes and scenes from native life of the kind which he loved to paint, and have been included in order to show how, and to what extent, he used and transformed reality.

In addition to the persons mentioned in the previous pages and in the list at the end of this book, I wish particularly to thank:

Father Patrick O'Reilly, Paris, and Mr Bjarne Kroepelien, Oslo, for generous help and free access to their splendid, unique collections of books, pamphlets and other documents relating to Tahiti and other islands in French Polynesia;

Dr Gerda Kjellberg, Stockholm, for the loan of important unpublished manuscripts dealing with Gauguin's life in Paris in 1893–95;

Mr Paul René Gauguin, Copenhagen, and Dr Guillot, Clohars-Carnoët, for their hospitality and assistance during my visits to Denmark and Brittany;

Mr Claude Gobert of the Compagnie des Messageries Maritimes, Paris, for information concerning Gauguin's many voyages on ships belonging to this company;

the art historians John Rewald, New York, Merete Bodelsen, Copenhagen, and Wladyslawa Jaworska, Warsaw, who have always readily replied to my many queries and repeatedly supplied me with material previously unknown to me;

the Tahitian scholars, Miss Aurora Natua and Mr Raoul Teissier, Papeete, whose profound knowledge has made it possible to solve many particularly difficult linguistic, ethnological and historical problems;

Mr Jirí Mucha, Prague, who kindly allowed me to profit from his own researches for a life of his father;

Mr Louis Grelet, Fatuiva, the only surviving friend of Gauguin in the Marquesas Islands.

GAUGUIN IN THE SOUTH SEAS

I

THE TROPICAL STUDIO

PAUL GAUGUIN and Tahiti have been closely connected in popular imagination for more than half a century. Although Tahiti has been visited and described at one time or another by many famous persons, among them Captain Cook, Herman Melville, and Robert Louis Stevenson, it is not these names but Gauguin's which at once springs to mind when the island is mentioned. Conversely, the name of Paul Gauguin has become a kind of watchword which always recalls Tahiti rather than Paris, Brittany, Martinique, Arles, or any of the other places where he also lived and worked. The only comparable case of such complete identification of a man with an island is perhaps that of Napoleon with St Helena. It is rather ironical, therefore, to have to begin a book devoted chiefly to Gauguin's life in Tahiti with the assertion that it was pure chance which took him there in the first place, and that the momentous journey was not even his own idea. That, however, is the case.

To discover the first link in the long chain of events which eventually led to this important turning-point in his life we must go back to the exceptionally cold winter of 1885–86, when Gauguin was trying unsuccessfully to support himself as a painter in Paris. The significant step from Sunday painter to full-time professional artist had been taken, more or less involuntarily, two years before, when he had lost his well-paid post as chief assistant to a stockbroker on the Paris Bourse, in a prolonged financial crisis due to a succession of scandals and company failures on a massive scale. Although he had painted industriously for nearly ten years in his spare time and had been praised by Manet, Pissarro, and Degas, he had by no means arrived at maturity as an artist. This alone should have made him pause. Even more, he should have reflected on the melancholy fact that there was no market for the kind of Impressionist pictures he was still painting at that time.

Gauguin had begun his long career on the Bourse with no other training than a few years of classical and theological studies at grammar-school level and five years of service at sea as a second mate in various merchant ships and as a conscript seaman in the Imperial Navy of Napoleon III. When his savings were spent by the spring of 1884, after a year of trying desperately to live by his painting, he thus lacked both specialized knowledge and an academic degree or diploma to fall back upon. His situation was rendered even more precarious by the fact that he had a wife and five children to support, the eldest of the children being only ten years of age. Having no better alternative, he took the advice of his Danish-born wife, Mette, and went to Copenhagen, where they hoped that her relations would help them. This turned out to be a great mistake. To all of his wife's relatives he was a good-for-nothing and it seemed useless even to try to help him; they strongly advised her to get rid of the wretched husband at the first opportunity. Mette, however, remained firmly convinced that her Paul had genius—for business. She therefore urged him to abandon his absurd ambition to become a painter and find employment with a large business firm or bank. Gauguin himself was no less convinced that it was only a matter of time before he would earn enough by his pictures to be able to maintain his family as before, and, mainly in order to escape from the persistent nagging that was depriving him of the ability to work, he returned, in June 1885, to Paris. To Paul as to Mette (who in order to support the children at once turned to teaching French and translating), it seemed no more than a temporary parting. Both were convinced that the other would soon see reason.

The ensuing winter, 1885–86, was the hardest period in all Gauguin's long and miserable life. That he survived at all was chiefly due to casual employment as a bill-sticker, at five francs a day. "I know what it means to be completely destitute; what it means to go hungry, cold, and so on," he recalled later. "It means nothing—or very little. You get used to it; and with a little self-mastery in the end laugh at it. What makes the hardship so terrible, however, is that it stops you from working, and your mind from developing. It is especially the case in Paris and other big cities, where the struggle for existence claims three-quarters of a man's time and half his energy. Yet the fact remains that suffering sharpens a man's wits. But sharpen them too much and he goes under!"

Yet even after this long winter of privations and humiliations Gauguin refused to accept Mette's terms for a reconciliation. But he was aware of the need to leave Paris if he was to come through at all. Where he went was immaterial, so long as the place was cheap and quiet. Strange to say, he seems momentarily to have had some vague plan then of going to the South Seas; for in a letter to his wife in May 1886 he said that he had been offered "farming work in Oceania." Unfortunately, he does not state who it was that had had the absurd idea of employing an artist and former Bourse employee on the land, nor does he mention the name of the island where the extraordinary experiment was to have taken place. However, he declined the mysterious offer, as it would have meant giving up his painting. That it was an effort to refuse an opportunity which would have ensured him a more dignified existence is clear from the ironic close of the same letter, in which he mentions a recent dramatic event in his wife's circle: "So Hermann has gone out of his mind. He's lucky to be cared for."

From a friend he heard of a boarding house in the village of Pont-Aven in Brittany, where the full *pension* cost only two francs a day. It was for this remarkably prosaic reason that Gauguin first went, in June 1886, to the place which also is chiefly indebted to him for its fame. The report proved correct, and Marie-Jeanne Gloanec, the good proprietress of the Pension Gloanec in the middle of the village, where Gauguin lodged, soon took such a liking to him that she often allowed him credit. From the start, Gauguin was fascinated by the bleak, austere landscape and the primitive old rural culture which still in those days distinguished the Bretons as a separate national group in speech, dress, and beliefs. But he soon realized that life in a Breton village had its drawbacks. For one thing, he felt a perpetual need to analyse, explain, and argue about art, his own in particular. In the summer months there were always some amateur painters or other visitors to keep him company in the evening and listen to his strange ideas. But when autumn and winter came round he found himself entirely alone in the cold and unheated boarding house. Had he only been able to find models on the many days when the weather was bad and he had to work indoors he would doubtless have endured the solitude rather better. But the bigoted and suspicious countrywomen and fishermen's wives of Pont-Aven could not be persuaded to sit for him, even when he allowed them to keep on all their embroidered jackets, shawls, starched bonnets, and other strange garments.

Gauguin had long been aware that there were many places where life was both cheaper and warmer, and where at the same time the people were more primitive and more amenable. It is doubtful how much he could remember of his earliest childhood, when with his mother and sister, Marie, a year older than himself, he had lived from the age of three to seven with distant relatives in Peru. But he would often recall with intense pleasure his other voyages to South America between the ages of seventeen and nineteen, as a mate's apprentice in several passenger ships. No wonder, then, that he now turned over in his mind the idea of going back there. There was a further reason for wanting to try his luck in that particular part of the world. A few years before, Gauguin's sister had married a Colombian, who had recently opened a store on the isthmus of Panama in the hope of making an early fortune by jobbing cheap wares to De Lesseps' canal-diggers at extortionate prices. After another miserable winter in Paris, Gauguin's mind was made up. He would go out to Panama, but would stay no longer with his sister and her husband than would be necessary to become self-supporting. He had already decided how that could be done. He would settle on the "almost uninhabited, free, and very fertile" little island of Taboga, on the Pacific side of the isthmus, and there "live like a savage." For company he resolved to take with him his most loyal admirer, Charles Laval, a painter barely out of his teens who copied Gauguin's style so exactly that unscrupulous art dealers have removed the signature from nearly all of his paintings and substituted Gauguin's considerably more valuable one. Where the two penniless travellers obtained their fare is a mystery, but they duly embarked for Panama in April 1887, travelling steerage in an overcrowded sailing ship.

Gauguin and his sister had never got on together, and he should have known in advance that she and her husband would do what they could to get rid of their unwelcome guests as soon as possible. What was worse, the island paradise of Taboga was already occupied by real savages—Indians—though they were civilized enough to take advantage of the boom and brazenly demand six francs a square yard for rough and stony ground. Gauguin had been no more than a month in Panama when he was already regretting that he had failed to disembark on the French island of Martinique, which nostalgically he called "a magnificent country, where life is cheap and pleasant." In order to raise enough money to return there, Laval began to paint portraits, while Gauguin, who in his own words was "unfortunately incapable of turning out realistic pictures bad enough to find clients," took a job as a navvy, working twelve hours a day canal-digging. He was discharged a fortnight later when the De Lesseps Canal Company found itself in financial difficulties. This probably saved his life; for, all unknowing, he had already contracted dysentery and yellow fever. As it happened, Laval and he succeeded in getting to Martinique at the last moment. Despite his serious condition, Gauguin with indomitable energy and will-power painted no fewer than twenty pictures in the four months which he spent on the island before being forced to return to France for medical attention.

Gauguin's Martinique pictures are better and more luminous than his earlier canvases, and he had good reason to be pleased with them. But other Impressionists had achieved far more brilliant landscapes in the meantime without leaving Paris. Gauguin's new pictures therefore met with no response and found no buyers. Deeply disappointed, he turned for asylum again to Madame Gloanec at Pont-Aven.

This time he stayed for nine months. On the surface his life there was dull and monotonous, but in terms of art it was the most eventful and significant period in his life. He had for long been dissatisfied with the Impressionist programme, which aimed basically at a faithful image of reality, even though it was reality seen from a new angle. Still less was he attracted to the attempt by Seurat and other Pointillists to turn painting into an exact science. The man who helped him to arrive at clarity and find the right path, strange to say, was a young painter of twenty, only half his own age, named Émile Bernard. In the summer of 1888 Émile was holidaying in Brittany with his mother and good-looking sister, Madeleine. He and Gauguin had become acquainted two years before, but it was only now that the two so unequal painters became sufficiently intimate to discuss art with each other seriously. It soon became clear that they had strikingly similar ideas. In the first place, they agreed that it was the painter's chief object to express intense visions and strong ideals, rather than to reproduce objective reality. Or as Gauguin formulated their new programme: "Do not paint too much from nature. Art is abstraction. Seek it in nature by dreaming in the presence of it; and above all think of the creation that will be the result." In close collaboration, they began to translate their theories into practice and evolve a new style. Slowly, the light and atmospheric perspective of Impressionism gave way in their pictures to more decorative compositions which were tapestry-like and two-dimensional. At the same time, all their figures and objects grew sharper in outline and more uniform in colour, until finally their pictures came to consist of large, clearly defined areas of colour. As they omitted all details and concentrated on the essentials, they called the new style they had arrived at Synthetist.

With the coming of autumn Émile returned to Paris with his parents, and Gauguin was alone once more in cold and rainy Pont-Aven. Once more his thoughts turned to the tropics. This time the van Gogh brothers, who were old acquaintances, took pity on him; Vincent by inviting him to sunny Arles, and Theo by making him a monthly allowance of 150 francs and promising to exhibit his work in his Paris art gallery. Having listened to the sun-drunk Vincent and relaxed in the warmth of Provence for a while, Gauguin made up his mind. Writing hopefully at the beginning of December 1888 to Émile Bernard, who had been prevented from going to Arles by military service, he said: "(Theo) van Gogh hopes to sell all my pictures. If I have that luck I shall go to Martinique; I am certain now that I can do good work there. And if I can lay my hands on a more substantial sum, I shall buy a house there and set up a studio, where my friends will find all they need for practically nothing. I am inclined to agree with Vincent that the future belongs to painters of the tropics, which have yet to be exploited, and that novel subjects are needed to stimulate the stupid picture-buying public."[1] Soon after, he announced his intention to leave in May 1889 and to be away for eighteen months.

As is well known, Gauguin's sunny existence at Arles was brought to a sudden tragic end when, in one of the most famous incidents in the history of art, Vincent cut off his ear in a fit of insanity and had

---

1. *Tahiti, the land of Gauguin's dreams and his destination in 1891, is like many another South Sea island the eroded summit of a long-extinct volcano which rises steeply from the ocean bed. The whole population live in the narrow, palm-grown belt along the shore of the lagoon, which is only partly enclosed by a coral reef.*

to be locked up in an asylum. Also, contrary to expectation, the picture-buying public demonstrated its extraordinary stupidity by failing to purchase any of the Provençal pictures in almost tropical colour which Gauguin submitted to Boussod et Valadon, the Paris art gallery managed by Theo van Gogh. Before he had succeeded in collecting the necessary fare, Gauguin had realized also that there were other tropical countries more interesting, and to an artist more promising, than Martinique, where for that matter the population, descendants of Negro slaves, lacked a native art or culture of their own. He made this discovery at the great Universal Exhibition of 1889 in Paris, where he showed seventeen of his pictures. Not, it is true, at the official salon; that was reserved for great, immortal (and now totally forgotten) masters such as Gérôme, Roll, Dagnan-Bouveret, and Cormon. But a shrewd friend from the Bourse, Émile Schuffenecker, commonly known as Schuff, and himself a spare-time painter, had found an unexpected way of entering the exhibition by the back door. Right in front of the official art pavilion was a smaller building which had been licensed to an Italian café proprietor named Volpini. There he had installed a restaurant called, of course, the *Café des Arts*, and had spared no expense to make it really luxurious and artistically attractive.

Among other fittings, Volpini had ordered some splendid wall mirrors. Unfortunately, however, the supplier had failed to deliver on time, a fact which Schuff had got wind of. When he astutely suggested that Volpini should allow him and some of his artist friends to clothe the embarrassingly naked walls with beautiful pictures he at once agreed. After all, it was the cheapest way of decorating the rooms. It would also assist the café to live up to its name. There were enough large bare walls to provide room for nearly a hundred paintings and drawings. The three sponsors who formed the self-appointed hanging committee—Schuff, Gauguin, and Bernard—therefore invited six other Synthetist and Impressionist painters to join them.

←—————————————————————

2. *Ever since its discovery in 1767, European visitors have praised the remarkable beauty of Tahiti and its women. Gauguin only became fully convinced that the eulogies were justified when he had settled in Mataiea, where this picture was taken from the shore looking towards Little Tahiti, the south-eastern peninsula.*

To ensure as large an attendance as possible at this unconventional gallery, the hopeful artists had a huge advertisement printed, and personally posted it up on the preceding days under Gauguin's expert supervision. For as a bill-sticker, too, he was the group's undisputed master.

While waiting for the stream of critics, collectors, and dealers to come pouring in, Gauguin strolled about the exhibition grounds, which were dominated by the newly constructed Eiffel Tower, the proud and audacious symbol of French industry and engineering. Gauguin found it hard to get interested in all the wonderful factory products and ingenious machines which filled most of the glass palaces and iron halls. What fascinated him more were the representations of Far Eastern sculpture, originals and replicas, which he saw for the first time in the French colonial section. He also studied the ethnological exhibition, called "The Evolution of the Dwelling," which included an impressively complete collection of bamboo huts, adobe houses, pile dwellings, tents, and shelters from all over the world. Another attraction which made a great appeal to him was a large Javanese village, where real temple dances could be seen, performed by graceful native women.

Each French colony of course had its own pavilion or section in the large central hall, but there is no documentary evidence to show that Gauguin took much interest in the Tahitian section. That, however, is not surprising, for it was quite unpretentious, its principal exhibits being a collection of plaited pandanus hats and a skull which was described, on very doubtful evidence, as an ancient drinking vessel.[2] The specimens of the celebrated species *Vahine tahitiensis* that were on display provided no greater attraction. The native women who had been imported from the legendary isle of love at great cost were not the young, beautiful, and seductive naiads one would have expected, but middle-aged matrons more remarkable for corpulence and ugliness than for anything else. The explanation of this rather odd display was that the Colonial Minister, anxious to avoid embarrassing scandals, had insisted that the Tahitians should be "married women of impeccable morals"—a stipulation which had greatly restricted the choice.[3]

To the mortification of the Synthetist and Impressionist painters, Volpini's string orchestra, which consisted of a dozen women violinists and a single male cornet-player conducted by a Russian princess, attracted far more attention than their pictures. If on rare occasions a member of the audience deigned to look at them it was only to make fun of them. Not one picture was sold. This annoyed Gauguin the more because he was now more eager than ever to set out for the tropics. His plans remained the same, except that he now proposed to travel east instead of west to Martinique. India, unfortunately, was British, and Java, sad to say, Dutch, so that it was most unlikely that French artists without means would receive any help or support there. Luckily, France a few years before had acquired a new colony, Indo-China, in South-East Asia, where ruins of great temples had been found at many points in the forests. Like many another adventurous young Frenchman at that time, Gauguin assumed that the authorities would gladly and immediately provide him with a free passage and a liberal monthly salary if only he took the trouble to submit an application to the colonial administration. What he had in mind, of course, was a comfortable post at some remote jungle station, without any superiors to interfere in his activities. Or as he candidly put it himself: "What I want is a good appointment in Tongking, where I can work at my painting and save money. The entire Orient and the philosophy inscribed there in art, in letters of gold—all this is worth studying, and I think I shall find renewed energies there. The West today is rotten, but a man with the character of Hercules can gain new vigour like Antaeus out there by touching the ground. And after a year or two one comes back strong and toughened up."[4]

As the boarding house in Brittany was the only place where he could still get credit while waiting for his appointment to the colonial service, he returned there once more. To his disgust, the Pension Gloanec at Pont-Aven proved to be full of trippers and academic painters. After a little searching, however, he found a small inn, which he and his disciples had all to themselves; it was at Le Pouldu, a solitary place among the sand-hills on the coast, which with its few scattered houses could scarcely lay claim to be called a village. Outstanding among these disciples were the following somewhat dissimilar persons:

Charles Laval, Gauguin's companion on the partly successful expedition to Panama and Martinique, now more subdued and melancholy than ever owing to his advanced tuberculosis;

Paul Sérusier, a respectable, well-dressed, and mediocre painter with some small private means and a firm belief in theosophy;

Charles Filiger, a timid homosexual Alsatian with a shady past, who chiefly painted madonnas and cubist chromatic pictures;

Jakob Meijer de Haan, a red-headed, hunchbacked, bandy-legged Dutchman, whose physical defects were outweighed by his generosity, manifested by his readiness to share with Gauguin the monthly allowance of 300 francs which he received from his family in Amsterdam.

The failure of the favourite disciple, Émile Bernard, to make the pilgrimage to Brittany that summer was entirely due to his long-suffering father, who wanted him to go into business and had forbidden him to have any more dealings with Gauguin and his misfit hangers-on.

The section of the Paris Universal Exhibition of 1889, at the Esplanade des Invalides, devoted to the French colonies. The central two-storey hall housed displays of typical products, ethnographical collections and photographs from the smaller colonies, among them Tahiti and the other islands of French Oceania. The more important colonies were represented by separate buildings, each in the style of its country. The building with the tall, pointed dome to the right of the central hall was a copy of the temple from Angkor Wat that Gauguin admired so much. The Javanese village where he frequently watched native dances was situated just beyond the last huts to the right, in a special section devoted to the Dutch East Indies.

The months went by and the heads of the Colonial Department seemed still to be unaware of the admirable empire-builder that could lie concealed in a Synthetist painter. Gauguin's wife, with whom he had continued to correspond during all these years, made another heroic effort to persuade him to abandon his hopeless attempt to win recognition. Although he suffered from their prolonged separation as much as Mette, Paul remained no less firmly convinced that "my business is art; that is my capital, my children's future, the honour of the name that I have given them. . . . So I go on working at my art, which at the moment has no money value (the times being bad), but which bids fair for the future. You will retort that it is a long way ahead, but what would you have me do? Am I to blame? I

am the one who suffers most by it."[5] The only short cut that he could
see to his objective was to attract attention by means of a series of
pictures with new and exotic themes. The suspense got on his nerves,
and he wrote disconsolately to Bernard: "I drag my old body about
on the sea-shore at Le Pouldu in the bleak north wind. Mechanically
I make a few studies. . . . But the soul in me is absent, mournfully
regarding the void which gapes before me—the void in which I see
my distressed family robbed of their parental support—and I myself
without a living soul in whom to confide my suffering. Since January
my sales have totalled 925 francs. To live on that amount at the age
of 42, buy colours, etc., would daunt the most hardened of men."
When the Colonial Department at long last acknowledged his application, the reply, to his unconcealed astonishment and intense disappointment, was "almost negative." The unfortunate reason, he now
realized for the first time, was that "usually the only people they send
to the colonies are persons who have misbehaved, embezzled, etc."

Gauguin now decided to go to Paris and lobby the responsible
authority in the Colonial Department. As so often before, the faithful Schuffenecker not only lent him the train fare but offered to provide board and lodging on his arrival. Packing will scarcely have
presented much of a problem, for Gauguin's entire worldly possessions
consisted of his unsaleable pictures and the clothes he stood up in:
a pair of shabby trousers, a greasy fisherman's jersey decorated with
Breton embroidery, and a seedy beige cloak of Spanish type. For head-
dress he had a beret, and for footwear a pair of clogs ornately painted
with flowers. To his great disappointment, his appearance in the offices of the Colonial Department, in February 1890, had only one result: the prompt rejection of his application.

Yet the visit to Paris was not without consequence: it gave him a
new and better idea. The man who unintentionally suggested it was
his old friend Odilon Redon, one of the few French artists of the
time who were thought even more eccentric and difficult to understand than Gauguin himself. Madame Redon came from the small
island of Réunion in the Indian Ocean and had visited Madagascar
several times on her way to and from France. The more she spoke of
it, the more firmly Gauguin became convinced that this old French
possession not only was as interesting, from the point of view both
of art and of folklore, as Indo-China, but would be an ideal place in
which to found a self-supporting colony of artists like the one he had
envisaged in Martinique. In Madagascar it was even possible to live

entirely without money—if you planted a few vegetables, kept a cow, and did a little leisurely shooting. Gauguin had already seen Malagasy huts at the Universal Exhibition the year before, and thought that it should be possible to erect one like them in no time.

But the voyage out would cost a fair sum of money. Moreover, he would want to take a little capital with him to buy land and get started. It was at this point that, through Schuff, he made the acquaintance of a Paris doctor and a man of parts, named Charlopin, who in his spare time was both an inventor and an art collector. Gauguin offered him nearly all his unsold works, totalling 38 pictures and five pieces of pottery, at the bargain price of 5,000 francs. Charlopin was ready to do a deal as soon as he obtained payment for one of his recent inventions. At the most it would take two months. In a considerably more cheerful frame of mind, Gauguin returned to Brittany and began to consider whom he should take with him on the expedition to Madagascar.

The first person to whom he offered a share in his grand existence was Émile Bernard, of course. An almost equally obvious choice was the affluent Meijer de Haan. The third man to receive the call was the faithful friend Schuff; for though Gauguin found him insufferably banal and officious, he would be a useful member of the new artists' colony because of his commercial bent—especially if he could be persuaded to sell a building site which he owned in Paris. After a little hesitation, Gauguin also decided to invite Vincent van Gogh. His hesitation in this case was due to the sad fact that Vincent was still in the asylum. But with Vincent to share in the tropical studio, his brother Theo could be relied on to promote sales of their work in his Paris gallery. With regard to the remaining disciples, it would be wise to await events. A request by Laval to join the party, however, would be refused; he had shown himself on the Panama adventure to be far too weak and soft to deserve consideration another time.

The one who displayed the greatest enthusiasm was Émile Bernard, who immediately replied: "Your letter fills me with joy, rapture, and renewed confidence. I want nothing better than to travel, to get right away, anywhere so long as it is somewhere unknown. Unhappily, however, there are two obstacles. The first is the question of money, the other that of working conditions out there. . . . But how glorious to get far, far away and escape from all cares! To abandon this loathsome European life; all these dolts, misers, and fat swindlers; all this pestilential scum. As for my fiancée (yes, I am in love,

and why not?), she will come after. If she really loves me, she is sure
to. Ah yes, ah yes; how grand to drink freedom to the full, to admire
the sea, imbibe the void. . . . Thank you for giving me such great
comfort; now I am so full of confidence."

If Bernard was rather more exalted and high-flown than usual, it
was not only because he was in love (to such an extent that he had
reluctantly accepted a post as designer at a textile mill in Lille in order
to afford marriage). His agitation derived even more from the fact
that he was beginning, for the first time in his life, to have all manner
of doubts, and was trying to cure them, as he said, by "an excess of
prayers, incense, and hymns." Gauguin's advice, though very sensible,
was a little too prosaic and practical for Bernard's taste. The gist of
it was that it would be both simpler and cheaper to find himself a
native woman in Madagascar, because in addition to the other advantages she would provide him with a free model. The money problem could easily be solved if Bernard were to work his passage as a
waiter.

By return post, Gauguin received an even more emotional letter in
which Bernard announced, quite out of the blue, that the remote
South Sea Island of Tahiti would be much more suitable for their
proposed tropical studio than Madagascar. With delightful candour,
he confessed that he had come to this conclusion after reading the
sentimental best seller, *The Marriage of Loti*. Pierre Loti described
life in Tahiti in the following alluring terms: "In Oceania toil is a
thing unknown. The forests produce spontaneously everything necessary for the nourishment of these carefree tribes; the fruit of the
bread-tree and wild bananas grow for everybody and suffice for all.
The years slip by for the Tahitians in utter idleness and perpetual
dreams, and these big children cannot conceive that there should be
so many people in our beautiful Europe who wear out their lives earning their daily bread." In another chapter he wrote: "One needs
neither weapons, supplies, nor money; hospitality is offered, warmly
and without charge, everywhere. And the only dangerous creatures
in the whole island are the European settlers, who are, moreover, few
in number, and practically all in the town of Papeete."[6] Gauguin
rightly objected that this was a novel, written by a naval officer during a brief shore leave, and asked Bernard to get further information
from a more reliable book. Bernard immediately sent him an official
handbook, published as recently as 1889, the year of the Universal Ex-

hibition, by the Colonial Department itself. One of the book's many contributors had actually visited Tahiti.

The pages which Gauguin read with the greatest interest were those dealing with the natives. The authors gave this positive and encouraging information about them: "The Tahitians, and the Malayo-Polynesians in general, are a magnificent race with beautiful figures. . . . With regard to the mental qualities of this race, it has produced in certain islands, such as Tahiti, a rather high level of culture, and is remarkable above all for its affability, gentleness, and hospitality. Theft and murder are in Tahiti almost unknown."[7] Referring to a publication by a French settler who had spent half his life in Tahiti,[8] they went on to say in the same style and spirit a page farther on: "A Tahitian woman is usually a perfect model for a sculptor. Her features can occasionally be a little too Malayan, but with her large, dark eyes, so wonderfully fine and clear, her almost excessively full lips, and her marvellously white and regular teeth, she looks so sweet and innocently voluptuous that it is impossible not to share in the general admiration which she arouses. Her long, jet-black hair is made up into two plaits or is left hanging loose over her shoulders, as suits her fancy. Her features are open and composed, with never a hint of worry or concern."

As for the problems of obtaining a living in Tahiti, these were incredibly simple, or rather they were non-existent: "Born where there is no winter, in a country where the soil is richly fertile, the Tahitians have only to lift their hands in order to harvest the bread-fruits and wild bananas which form their staple food. Consequently, they have no need to work, and the fishing which they carry on for the sake of a little variety in their diet is more a pleasure which they indulge in gladly."

In conclusion, the most expert contributor to this handbook, a botanist recently returned from Tahiti, sang the following paean of praise for this obviously perfect paradise: "While men and women on the opposite side of the globe toil to earn their living, contend with cold and hunger, and suffer constant privation, the lucky inhabitants of the remote South Sea paradise of Tahiti know life only at its brightest. For them, to live is to sing and love."

These passages confirmed Loti's statements in such strikingly similar words that one cannot help a feeling of suspicion that the compilers of the handbook had simply borrowed them from him. Gauguin, however, had no such suspicions, and he at once agreed enthusiastically with Émile that Tahiti was the ideal place for them.[9] Another advantage in switching the tropical studio to Tahiti was that there would be no need for them to work their passages as waiters; the passages could be obtained free. For the excellent handbook also contained the following gratifying information: "The French Colonization Society provides extensive assistance for farmers willing to settle in the South Seas. Its limited resources do not at present allow it to distribute free land in the eastern Pacific possessions, as will be done in New Caledonia. But the kind support given to the Society by the authorities makes it possible at least to arrange free passages for serious-minded settlers who are firmly resolved on emigration to a French colony." In Gauguin's view there was no question that they fulfilled the society's conditions; for surely they were both "serious-minded" and "firmly resolved?" A closer study of the handbook also revealed that it was even possible to make money in the South Seas, in a manner at once surprising and very pleasant. In the Tuamotu Islands, east of Tahiti, the natives dived for pearl-oysters, often finding large pearls in them. Gauguin wrote with enthusiasm to Bernard: "Without detriment to our free and wild life it is possible, indeed probable, that de Haan would do business with leading Dutch merchants in pearls."

At the same time, Gauguin sent a well-phrased letter to the economical Schuff giving word-for-word quotations from the handbook about the incredible ease of supporting oneself in Tahiti. Two further arguments that he knew his friend would appreciate were that "Tahiti is the healthiest country on earth" and that there was no future in "rotten Europe" for his children. The final appeal was: "Isn't this something to consider for a European who is dissatisfied with his existence?"

As Tahiti was such an earthly paradise, Gauguin also changed his plans in one other respect. The best statement of his intentions is found in a letter to another artist, the Dane J. F. Willumsen: "As for me, my mind is already made up. I shall soon be leaving for Tahiti, a small South Sea island where it is possible to live *without money*. I am determined to forget my miserable past, paint freely as I like without thought of fame, and in the end die out there, forgotten by everybody here in Europe."[10] In proof of the soundness of his decision he quoted almost word for word the inspired, and inspiring, lines in the handbook to the effect that to the inhabitants of Tahiti to live was to sing and to love. In similar terms he informed Odilon Redon of his firm resolve: "I am leaving for Tahiti, where I shall hope to end my days. My art, which I know you like, I regard as no more than a tender shoot, though one which I hope to develop into a wild and primitive growth, entirely for my own pleasure. What I need in order to achieve this objective is peace and quiet. The honour and respect of other people are now of absolutely no concern to me. The European Gauguin has ceased to exist and nobody will ever see any more of his works here again."[11] With regard to his wife and children, Gauguin hoped that they would eventually join him out there when he had properly installed himself and could offer them a more secure existence than they had so far experienced in Copenhagen.

Most likely it was at this period that he painted a little-known picture, signed and dated 1890, which reveals, even more clearly, what he expected to find in Tahiti (Fig. 6). The picture is of a nude Eve, preparing, with an air of complete unconcern, to pick a sinfully red fruit from an imaginary tree of the sort which up to then only Douanier Rousseau had painted. For years Gauguin had had to content himself with bought love and occasional liaisons with slatternly servant girls at Breton inns. At first sight, therefore, this picture seems merely to embody a banal erotic fantasy. In fact it is a sort of puzzle picture. Indeed, a perceptive American art historian, Henri Dorra, has recently pointed out that not only did Gauguin pose his Eve exactly like a Buddha on a Javanese temple frieze, which he saw at the Universal Exhibition in 1889, but that he gave her the head and features of his mother. Gauguin's beloved mother had then been dead for nineteen years, but he had a good photograph of her (which is still extant) and there can be no doubt that he used this as the model for his picture. The psycho-analytical interpretation of this astonishing loan given by the acute art historian provides a very good explanation of Gauguin's emotional make-up: "Here, as in the previous works, Eve stands primarily for the artist's quest for the primitive. Gauguin, whose social philosophy owes much to Jean-Jacques Rousseau, frequently juxtaposes in his writings the corrupt civilization of the West with man's primeval bliss. And when seeking inspiration from the 'types, religion, symbolism, mysticism' of primitive people he was looking for the traces of a distant and glorious past common to all humanity. What better symbol for this dream of a golden age than the robust and fertile mother of all races?

"Gauguin's Eve is exotic, and as such she stands for his natural affinity for tropical life. His was more than a passing taste for the sensuality of native women; of mixed origin—his mother had Peruvian as well as Spanish and French blood—he was deeply aware of his atavism, often referring to himself as a 'pariah' and as a 'savage' who must return to the savage.

"Besides being primitive and exotic, Gauguin's Eve is also a mother, and she stands for the emotional security which he had come to associate with tropical life through the circumstances of his own upbringing. The artist expressed this attitude with considerable feeling in a letter he wrote to his wife at the time of his departure to Tahiti, after he had been separated from her and his children for several years: 'What could make me unhappy (in Europe) would be to find myself isolated, without a mother, without a family, without children. . . . May the day come . . . when I shall go fleeing to the woods of an island of Oceania, live there off ecstasy, quiet and art, surrounded by a new family, far from this European struggle for money. There, in Tahiti, in the silence of the beautiful tropical nights, I shall be able to listen to the sweet murmuring music of my own heart in amorous harmony with the mysterious beings around me.' Paradoxical though it may seem at first, this attitude can be readily explained in terms of the artist's background. Paul Gauguin, whose father died soon after his birth, spent four years in Peru at an early age, living there in comparative luxury with his mother and his grandmother. From then on his life became much more difficult. When Aline Gauguin, his mother, returned to France with her children she found herself in straitened circumstances. And no sooner did the young Paul leave school than he enlisted as a seaman, to lead for several years the rootless existence of a sailor. Even his own marriage did not bring him the emotional satisfactions he had so far been unable to find, for his relationship with his wife turned out to be quite unstable. It would seem, then, that the years he spent in Peru as a young child were among the happiest and most secure of his existence.

"It is not unduly surprising, therefore, to find that Gauguin should have come to associate his quest for emotional security with his dreams of escape to the tropics; all through his adolescence the exotic lands he had visited must have become an imaginary refuge to which he could flee in times of anxiety. What is somewhat startling is the way in which he has combined the one with the other in our painting: the primitive and exotic Eve of his dreams has the features of his own mother, clearly derived from a photograph in his possession.

"Gauguin once wrote that he had gone very far back, beyond the horses of the Parthenon, to the rocking horse of his childhood. One might add that, subconsciously at least, his dreams of escape to the tropics went further back still, beyond his memories of childhood, to the comfort and warmth of prenatal bliss."[12]

The first disturbance of Gauguin's pleasant dream world came at the beginning of August 1890, with the brief message that Vincent van Gogh in another fit of madness had shot himself in the breast and had died soon after from loss of blood. With his customary candour Gauguin commented: "Sad though his death may be it does not unduly grieve me, because I foresaw it and knew what suffering the poor fellow endured in his struggle against his madness. To have died just now is a stroke of good luck for him, as it has put an end to his suffering; and if he experiences another life he will reap the reward of his good conduct in this (according to the law of Buddha). He takes with him the consolation of having never been abandoned by his brother, and of being understood by a few artists."

What Gauguin in his impatience found more insupportable than the knowledge that he would now have to manage without the impractical and unpredictable Vincent was the fact that, in spite of several reminders, Dr Charlopin had still failed to send him any money. This was the more discouraging because the French Colonization Society had shown surprisingly little interest in assisting the serious-minded emigrants to obtain free passages. The days grew shorter and wetter. From October, Gauguin and Meijer de Haan were the only residents in the cold inn at Le Pouldu. "Whenever shall I be able to start my life of freedom in the forest?" he bitterly complained. "God, what a time it takes! And to think that every day there are public subscriptions for flood victims. But painters! For them there is never any help. Nobody cares if an artist dies." However, when things were looking their blackest a miracle occurred. Gauguin received a telegram, which said:

PASSAGE TROPICS ASSURED. MONEY FOLLOWING. DIRECTOR THEO.

Clearly, Theo van Gogh had decided to honour his brother's memory by helping his friends to achieve the ambition they had in common. It was a noble and a glorious gesture. With the backing of Theo and his gallery all their financial worries would be at an end. But a few days later the miracle, like many before it, proved to have a natural explanation. Theo too had gone out of his mind, and had grown so apathetic after dispatching the telegram that he had lost all desire to live. Of course the art gallery disclaimed responsibility for his actions; least of all those which were connected with the mad idea of financing a costly voyage to the tropics for a party of unknown daubers.

To crown everything, Meijer de Haan's relations proved singularly reluctant to invest in a tropical studio. In the end they even threatened to stop his monthly allowance if he persisted in associating with Gauguin. Meijer de Haan agreed to meet them half way— by going to Paris in order to talk the matter over with them. But his precipitate departure in the middle of October may not have been entirely unconnected with a complication in his relations with Marie Henry, the landlady at Le Pouldu. At all events, she named him as the father of the child she gave birth to eight months later. Gauguin would have gone with his unlucky friend, feeling sure that his deal with Charlopin would soon be completed if only they could meet face to face. If not, he would persist until he had found another purchaser. Schuff, too, needed some shaking up. Unfortunately for Gauguin, he was detained by a little complication, rather different in character, in his own relations with Marie. He was forced to stay behind in pawn, for a debt of 300 francs which Meijer de Haan had been unable to pay for him. He was redeemed eventually by Émile Bernard, who achieved the incredible by selling five pictures for him in Paris at a hundred francs each.

II

SUCCESS AFTER SUCCESS

IT was November 7, 1890, when Gauguin finally arrived in Paris to fight the important battle that was to decide his future. As usual, Schuffenecker gave him board and lodging. But the good Schuff had not sold his plot of land, and seemed generally unwilling to give up his secure job of drawing-master in a grammar school. Nor had Meijer de Haan's negotiations with his hard-hearted and parsimonious relations led to the desired result. The hardest blow of all for Gauguin, however, was that Dr Charlopin, resisting every attempt at persuasion, refused finally to make the deal that would have been the most profitable of the century. (The thirty-eight pictures and five pieces of pottery which Gauguin offered him for 5,000 francs are now, at a conservative estimate, worth thirty million francs.) Gauguin transferred the offer to another private collector, the musician Ernest Chausson, telling him that he would be making a very lucrative investment. The suggestion was that Chausson should sell half the pictures singly at once to his many friends at double the purchase sum, which would have meant getting the rest for nothing.[18] It was all very ingenious, and the one thing needed for Chausson to take the well-baited hook was a liking for Gauguin's art. That, unfortunately, he lacked.

The art dealers to whom Gauguin now turned, in the hope that they would arrange a one-man show, were only a little more forthcoming. Actually, there were only two galleries where an attempt was worth making, and one of these was Boussod et Valadon, who already held a large stock of his paintings, dating from the time when

Theo van Gogh had managed the firm's branch in the rue Mont-
martre. Theo's successor, Maurice Joyant, who in his youth had been
a friend of Toulouse-Lautrec, was personally very well disposed. But
unfortunately the proprietors had given him the following precise
instructions on his appointment: "Our former manager, who was
as mad as his brother the painter, has accumulated a lot of atrocious
things by modernistic painters that are bringing the firm into disre-
pute. . . . You will also find pictures by a landscape painter, Claude
Monet, who has started to sell in America, but who unfortunately
turns out too many pictures. We are under contract to purchase his
entire production, and he is now unloading a mass of identical landscapes on to us. As for the other pictures, these, as we have said, are
appalling. Please clear matters up as soon as possible without asking
us for help. Otherwise we shall shut up the shop."[14] The worst of
these atrocious pictures, of course, were Gauguin's. The only way in
which Joyant could show his appreciation of them, therefore, was, in
spite of his employers' disapproval, to keep them and show them
discreetly on occasion to specially selected clients. Grateful though
Gauguin perhaps was for this help, it hardly assisted him to achieve
his ambition, which was to collect enough money as soon as possible
to take him to Tahiti. The other art dealer to whom he made a cau-
tious approach was Durand-Ruel, the brave champion of the Impressionists. But Durand-Ruel still had too many unsold pictures on his
hands to risk taking on an artist whose works were even more revolutionary. It looked as if the earthly paradise of Gauguin's dreams was
no easier to attain than any other paradise.

His one consolation was that a surprising number of young artists
knew of his work, wanted to meet him, and listened eagerly to what
he said. For this he could especially thank Paul Sérusier, his fellow-
boarder at Pont-Aven and Le Pouldu, who, acting as his apostle, had
preached the Synthetist gospel to the philistines in Paris. Many of
his friends, old as well as new, would often take an *apéritif* with a
group of authors, poets, critics, and journalists, who have won for
themselves a small but certain place in the history of French literature
under the name of "Symbolists." As in all literary movements, the
Symbolists were far more precise and explicit in indicating their dislikes than they were when trying to formulate programmes and aims
of their own. Fortunately, it is enough to note very briefly in this connection that what they despised most was the whole realistic and naturalistic tradition, which they wished to replace by a new literature—

the exact opposite of it. The only common denominator was a tendency to allow greater freedom to the spontaneous imagination; or, as one of the movement's prophets used to say, "to indicate, suggest, and stimulate," rather than describe and explain. One line of development led in time, therefore, to Surrealism. Highly revealing of the Symbolist ideology is the great interest which many members of the coterie took in theosophy, occultism, spiritualism, cabbalism, astrology, alchemy, and all the other obscurantist and pseudo-scientific doctrines so fashionable in Paris at that time. Politically, many of the Symbolists sympathized (from a safe distance) with the anarchists, who returned the compliment by agitating as fiercely for the new free verse as for the free new society.

One of the most cherished articles in the Symbolist faith was the theory that all the arts shared a common aim, and that poets, painters, dancers, and musicians, working along parallel lines in their respective media and idioms, could give expression to the same ideas, emotions, and moods. In the quest for a living proof of this article of faith the theorists had discovered a great poet, Stéphane Mallarmé, who often attended their café meetings. Also, they generously invited the weary, sick, and besotted Verlaine to their gatherings, hailing him as a symbolist pioneer, though often he would forget his lines and mumble, irritated: "I'm a decadent, I am." Among musicians, Wagner of course was the supreme master; it was from him that they had taken their doctrine of the unity of all the arts. But at the beginning of the 1890s they had still to find a great Symbolist painter. While some of them, to be sure, had the foresight to appreciate at this early stage the greatness of Odilon Redon, the latter unfortunately was too modest and retiring to serve as standard-bearer to the new movement. This left an awkward vacuum. When to their joy they found that Gauguin no more liked realism and naturalism in art and literature than they did themselves, they assumed that he was a Symbolist painter at heart without being fully aware of it. For his part, Gauguin believed as firmly as he had always done, and would do till he died, that all geniuses were unique and made their own laws. Incidentally, because of his limited knowledge and poor education he had difficulty in following the subtle aesthetic and philosophical debates which sounded in his ears, and occasionally applied to his new-found friends the irreverent name of "Cymbalists." But he was flattered by the respect and admiration which they showed him, and saw that they could do him many a good turn, especially those Symbolists who worked on the newspapers and for intellectual journals. Accordingly, he took care not to protest when they insisted on hailing him as the leading Symbolist painter.

The member of the Symbolist coterie whom Gauguin took to most from the start was a very handsome literary critic and poet, with Raphaelite curls, named Charles Morice, who was also a prominent lecturer, reciter, and orator. According to some contemporary statements, Morice was so eloquent that he not only bewitched his audience whatever the subject but would often become intoxicated himself by the flow of his own words and for long after would stagger like a man drunk. However, there may have been some confusion and misunderstanding about the reason for his intoxication, for Charles Morice in fact was very fond of the bottle. Furthermore, as befitted the popular image of a Paris Bohemian, he had a *penchant* for women, who for their part were attracted even more to him by his undoubted charms.

Like many another critic before and since, Morice had made his principal reputation with a book radically reassessing all the great writers of the previous generation. At the same time, this book had sounded a clarion call to the poets of the future; in short, the Symbolists. The whole school was convinced that Morice, who was only thirty, was in the highest degree a man of the future himself and soon, indeed very soon, would produce an immortal masterpiece that would make a great contribution to the final triumph of the Symbolist movement. Morice's achievements so far included the "discovery" of Verlaine and the subsequent campaign to make him known and appreciated. Morice gave further proof of his sound judgment by immediately appreciating the art of Gauguin, being intensely moved by it, and later springing warmly to its defence with perceptive and well-founded argument.

Correctly seeing another misunderstood genius in Gauguin, Morice watched his new friend and master closely and tried to remember his words and actions. The physical characteristics which struck him most at his first meeting with him were "a narrow brow and a nose more broken than curved or hooked, a mouth with thin straight lips, and heavy eyebrows which would slowly rise to reveal a pair of slightly protruding eyeballs with bluish pupils that rotated alternately to left and right, while he never troubled to allow his head or his body to keep company with them."[15] Another Symbolist of the cafés supplements this admirable but incomplete portrait with the details that

Gauguin's hair, "which had originally been chestnut tending to red, seemed bleached," and that he had a short moustache and a "curly but short and thin goatee beard."[16] It may be added that Gauguin was only five feet four inches tall, but muscular and powerfully built.

Despite his admiration, Morice confesses that at first he was shocked by Gauguin's "vivid but ungrammatical speech, full of seamen's expressions and studio slang, though he succeeded strangely enough in formulating ideas of rare sublimity and purity in it." The other Symbolist poet already quoted adds that Gauguin's voice was "thick and husky, due either to his congenital arthritis or the abuse of tobacco; for if Gauguin paused at any time in his cigarette smoking it was to put a clay pipe between his lips." The same informant also mentions the habit during his frequent visits to cafés of time after time "absent-mindedly filling up his coffee cup with poor brandy."

The most prominent feature of Gauguin's character, according to Morice, was "an aristocratic aloofness." Once again Morice was right; the words which recur constantly in every assessment of Gauguin's character are "superior" and "proud," and occasionally "arrogant." Even Gauguin's mother reluctantly admitted in her will: "As for my dear son, he will have to make his own way in life, for he has made himself so little loved by all my friends that he will soon find himself left to his own devices."[17] Gauguin's own explanation in a letter to Schuff, who had once ventured a mild rebuke, actually confirms the charge: "I am very surprised to hear that 'I do harm to myself by my superior attitude.' . . . The people who can be useful to me are not very numerous. I know who they are and don't think I have treated them badly. As for the individuals who can harm me—Pissarro and company—it is my talent, rather than my character, which makes them cackle so loudly. Whatever I do to compose my features, my face always gives the impression that I am condescending, and therefore I can't help it. But no matter! There's nothing to be gained by trying to ingratiate oneself with idiots—and I have reason for despising a large proportion of humanity."[18]

The ultimate reason for Gauguin's undoubted self-assurance, of course, was his absolute faith in his own genius and calling; his confidence in his greatness as an artist. In the light of history, one is inclined to agree with another of Gauguin's Symbolist friends, who said that his "intense egoism was justified, because it was creative egoism."[19] His great self-confidence well explains another prominent feature in his character: the incorrigible optimism which often made him act rashly and always led him into anticipating success. Thus his invariable failure was not the result of childish naivety, but to the fact that his contemporaries unfortunately did not share his own views of his greatness.

When Morice heard that Gauguin thought of going to the South Seas for good, he gave vent to his understanding and appreciation of this bold intention by declaiming the beautiful lines of Mallarmé:

> La chair est triste, hélas! et j'ai lu tous les livres.
> Fuir! là-bas fuir! Je sens que des oiseaux sont ivres
> d'être parmi l'écume inconnue et les cieux!
> Rien, ni les vieux jardins reflétés par les yeux
> ne retiendra ce coeur qui dans la mer se trempe,
> o nuits! ni la clarté déserte de ma lampe
> sur le vide papier que la blancheur défend
> et ni la jeune femme allaitant son enfant.
> Je partirai! Steamer balançant ta mâture,
> lève l'ancre pour une exotique nature!

Gauguin himself was far more practical and matter-of-fact; he promptly informed Morice of the cost of realizing his dreams of the South Seas, and confessed that he even lacked the money to buy food. But he added that luckily he had just thought of an easy way of raising the necessary funds for his passage. Gauguin's latest idea was to put up the best of his unsold pictures for auction at the Hôtel Drouot. For the venture to succeed, however, it was necessary for the leading newspapers and magazines to give the sale some publicity. It followed that he needed a well-placed contact and promoter, somebody with Morice's qualifications. Morice, to his credit, at once gave proof of his sincere admiration for Gauguin by assuming responsibility for this difficult essay in public relations. His first, very successful effort was to secure the support of the influential Stéphane Mallarmé.

As Gauguin became a well-known frequenter of the Symbolist cafés, his relations with his generous host and prospective travelling companion, Schuffenecker, became increasingly strained. The liberality with which Gauguin partook of his drinks and cigars, behaved like the master of the house, hung his pictures on every wall, and brought friends in with him at all hours of the day and night—Schuff had long become accustomed to and accepted with tolerant equanimity. Unfortunately, however, Gauguin now seemed to think that he had the same title to Schuff's beautiful and coquettish wife. That, at

least, was how Schuff came to see it, though without having any con-
clusive evidence to go on. The break came at the end of January 1891.
Even then, however, Schuff's unbounding admiration for Gauguin's
genius prevailed over his every other feeling; while evicting the artist,
he offered to take charge of his pictures. Another member of the great
expedition to the South Seas had thus dropped out.

Gauguin took a furnished room in the rue Delambre, between the
Luxembourg Gardens and the cemetery of Montparnasse, at eighteen
francs a month. The choice was doubtless dictated, in addition to the
low rent, by the fact that two blocks away, at number 13 in the rue de
la Grande-Chaumière, there was an extraordinarily cheap restaurant.
Called *Chez Charlotte* after the first name of its Alsatian proprietress,
Madame Caron, née Futterer, it drew most of its patrons from the
Académie Colarossi, a private school of painting across the street.
Gauguin was induced to become a regular patron by the further advantage that the proprietress would often allow poor artists to settle
their debts in pictures. As Madame Caron and her restaurant were to
play some part in Gauguin's life, the following description of the restaurant may be worth quoting:

"Right opposite Colarossi two large signboards painted on metal
caught the eye; one represented flowers, the other fruit, superbly
painted, perfect in composition and powerful in colour: the first was
by Alfons Mucha and the other by Wladyslaw Slewinski. Between
these signboards was the entrance to a small room, which looked
more like some shop of a Parisian *marchand des tableaux*, so full was
it of paintings of all sizes, right up to the ceiling. Some of these were
first-rate, others very interesting. . . . At lunch and dinner-time the
place was crowded and noisy. One could hear people talking in
French, English, Polish. Velvet berets of the Frenchmen mingled
with tired-looking Polish hats and, not infrequently, you would catch
a glimpse of the elegantly adorned head of a beautiful English girl.
. . . And there in the corner facing the door, behind the buffet, sat the
corpulent Madame Charlotte, dressed in a yellowy-orange gown with
a pink flowery pattern. *Ci-devant belle*, she had a luxuriant coiffure,
dark eyebrows and eyelashes, and light-cobalt eyes. She would greet
the arrivals with a pleasant smile; they were apparently all good, intimate friends. Above Madame's head hung her portrait, in which
she was seen wearing the very same gown—a beautiful pastel by
Wyspianski. . . .

"In the summer the whole company moved to the so-called little garden, enclosed all around by high walls. It was recognizable as such only by the sand under one's feet, a small fragment of sky, and a large landscape painted by Wyspianski—as if it were the background of a small stage—with adhesive paints on one of the walls. This fresco represented the Luxembourg Garden with its lawns, full of stone statues and ornamental balustrades against a background of spreading plane trees, and the façade of the palace. In the foreground, several girls dressed in Italian national costume, Wyspianski's favourite models."[20]

The furnishing of Gauguin's room in the rue Delambre was clearly in keeping with the rent, to judge from an account given by the Danish painter J. F. Willumsen of his first visit to it: "The studio was completely bare except for an iron bedstead which stood in the middle of the room, and on which Gauguin sat, with a woman on his knee, playing the guitar. The only work of art which I saw there was a small wooden figurine, just finished, on the mantelpiece. This represented an exotic-looking woman. Perhaps it personified one of the wish-dreams in Gauguin's mind. The leg was incomplete. Gauguin had called it *Lust*."[21]

The woman on Gauguin's knee was probably Juliette Huet, a pale, thin seamstress of twenty with straggling black hair whom he lived with at the time. With great difficulty he succeeded in persuading her to pose in the nude for a Symbolist painting. Gauguin himself called this strained declaration of solidarity with his new-found, useful friends *The Loss of Virginity*, but with an excess of prudery the title was afterwards altered without his knowledge to *Spring Awakening*. The picture shows Juliette lying on her back on a horizontal plane, half brown, half dark-green, holding in her hand a withered flower. A fox sits on her shoulder and a Breton wedding procession is approaching diagonally across the field in the background. To appreciate the symbolism it is necessary to know that the fox is a common symbol of physical desire and unchastity—in India. In short, the Symbolist message is scarcely more original than any simple folk allegory.

Gauguin soon moved into another furnished room which answered more fully to the name, and was in a house even more conveniently situated in relation to the *Chez Charlotte* restaurant—at 10 rue de la Grande-Chaumière, the address of the Académie Colarossi. He may have got the room rent-free, in return for giving a few lessons a week at the academy. The person who recommended him was an old friend and fellow-painter, Daniel de Monfreid, who also dined regularly at the *Chez Charlotte*.[22] Like Schuff, the honest and dependable Daniel was a man of limited talent, and like Schuff too would have given all he had for a spark of Gauguin's genius, which both men admired from the depth of their hearts. Yet Gauguin had thought highly enough of Daniel's pictures to include him in the ill-fated show in Volpini's café back in 1889. Like Gauguin, Daniel sought solace for the loss of an unappreciative wife, abandoned elsewhere. A further bond between them was their common interest in the sea. Daniel, whose parents were moderately well-to-do, owned a 36-ton yacht and would go for long cruises off the Atlantic coast or in the Mediterranean.

Meanwhile, the devoted Morice had gone the rounds of newspaper offices, soliciting articles and free publicity for the forthcoming auction. As a result of his eloquence and diplomacy, most of the art critics of the big dailies and magazines wrote articles about the sale and Gauguin's romantic flight from the evils of civilization, which were printed, in prominent positions, well before the event. The longest and most perceptive article was by Octave Mirbeau, a freelance writer of such great popularity that the dailies automatically increased by 10,000 copies their printing of any issue which contained one of his signed contributions. The most interesting passage for us in Mirbeau's, as always bright and well-written article, which appeared in the *Écho de Paris*, one of the largest papers, is his poetic account of the principal reasons for Gauguin's heroic decision: "The same need of silence, of meditation and absolute solitude which took him to Martinique takes him this time farther away to Tahiti and the South Seas, where nature comes closer to his dreams and where he hopes to find greater appreciation, like a prodigal son returning to the loving ancestral home." Outdoing himself, Mirbeau wrote another, somewhat shorter but even more laudatory article, which appeared two days later on the front page of the *Figaro*.[23]

Gauguin liked the articles so much that he asked permission to reproduce the longer one in the sale catalogue. But the man who was loudest in his praise of Gauguin's greatness, as was only right and natural, was the leading, almost prophetically acute Symbolist art critic, Albert Aurier. He concluded a fifteen-page laudatory essay in the *Mercure de France*, the movement's principal mouthpiece, with the following rousing blast:

"But disturbing, masterly, and wonderful as Gauguin's art is, it is as nothing when one thinks of the works which he might have achieved in any other civilization but ours. Let me say once again: like all ideist painters, Gauguin is essentially a decorator. In the limited confines of a canvas his compositions seem cramped. Sometimes they give the impression of being merely fragments of huge frescoes, on the point of bursting the frames which so narrowly enclose them.

"Indeed, we have so far had only one great decorator in this century, though it is already drawing to its close—two if we include Puvis de Chavannes! Yet our idiotic society, full of bankers and academic engineers, refuses this rare artist the smallest mansion or public hovel in which to spread the splendid mantle of his dreams, whereas the walls of our philistine pantheons are besmirched with the ejaculations of a painter like Lenepveu or of academic nonentities.

"If you powers that be only knew how posterity will execrate you, ridicule, and spit on you the day mankind begins to appreciate what is beautiful! Wake up; show a little common sense; you have in your midst a decorator of genius. Walls, walls; give him walls!"[24]

The pictures were available for public inspection in the sale room of the Hôtel Drouot on Sunday, February 22. Among the many visitors, Gauguin chanced to meet Émile Bernard, whom for some time he had neither seen nor heard of. Émile was obviously angry and bitter, and his pretty sister, who as usual accompanied him, openly accused Gauguin of "treachery," which she asserted had done Émile "great injury." Clearly, both she and her brother were mindful of the fact that none of the newspapers or magazines had mentioned the important part which Bernard had played in the origin of the Synthetist style. Bernard also seems to have expected that Gauguin would have invited him to participate in the sale. In either event, he forgot

--------------------------------→

3. *Although the Tahitians no longer have the time to splash and gambol for several hours a day as they did in Gauguin's time, they still bathe every morning and evening, at least, in the many rivers of cool, clear, and soft water which flow at close intervals down to the coast from the mountains in the interior.*

4. *On Saturdays, in the remote districts where the population still cling to some extent to their old customs, the men climb the steep mountain sides to pick the wild red bananas, returning with large bunches which, together with the fish they catch in the lagoon, will keep them and their families during the week.*

the regrettable fact, from his point of view, that none of his works could compare with Gauguin's. Bernard was clearly past reconciling or reasoning with. So without a word of reply Gauguin sadly turned his back on his one-time favourite disciple. Thus of the four companions he had originally contemplated taking with him to the South Seas only Meijer de Haan remained, and he was still having trouble with his unresponsive family.

For the rest, all went according to plan. Many people attended both the viewing and the sale the following day, and fortunately they were almost as interested in the pictures as in the painter. The bidding was brisk, and of the thirty pictures offered from Martinique, Arles, and Brittany, all but one were sold for substantially higher prices than the limit of 250 francs which Gauguin had placed. The most admired picture, *Jacob Wrestling with the Angel*, his great Synthetist manifesto of 1888, brought in the largest sum of all, 900 francs. Several others went for 500 and 400 francs. Allowing for the amount of 240 francs for a picture which Gauguin repurchased because it fell below the imposed minimum, the gross takings were 9,395 francs.[25] Even allowing for the auctioneer's fifteen per cent commission and the costs of framing, printing the catalogue, and other incidentals, the sale must have realized at least 7,500 francs—substantially more than the projected clearance sale to Charlopin would have given. Grateful to Morice for his assistance, Gauguin "lent" him 500 francs and appointed him his business manager during his absence in the South Seas.

It is not surprising that this success led Gauguin to believe in his imminent recognition. This would mean that at last he would be able to achieve his most ardent desire, which was to send for his wife, whom he had seen only briefly in 1887, and his five children whom he

---

5. *Gauguin in a characteristic pose, his eyes almost closed to the outside world, between two important periods in his life. Just back from Brittany, and still wearing a fisherman's jersey with its Breton embroidery, he was dreaming already of the South Seas when this photograph was taken in Paris is the winter of 1891.*

6. *What Gauguin dreamt of finding in Tahiti is well shown by this little-known picture of a nude Eve in a grand tropical paradise, which he painted in 1890 during the long interval of waiting* before leaving France.

had not seen for six years. But would Mette be willing to bring the children out to Tahiti, even supposing he had an assured income? Tenderly yet proudly, he inquired if he might come to Copenhagen to say goodbye. "I have so much to tell you," he explained; "things it would not do to put in writing. I realize the heavy burden which you bear, but there is always the future to look forward to and I believe that one day I shall be able to relieve you of all the burdens. The day will surely come when *your children* will be able to appear before any-body—anywhere—honoured and protected by their father's name." Mette, thinking there were children enough in the five that she al-ready had, replied that she would be glad to see him again but was afraid that their feelings would get the better of them and they would do something "foolish." When, rather hurt, Gauguin promised that in order to be on the safe side he would stay at a hotel, she told him that he was welcome. As a peace-offering she asked for a pair of Paris corsets.

Gauguin arrived at Copenhagen central station by the North Ex-press on March 7, and was met on the platform by his now rather greying wife and their two eldest children, Emil, aged 16, and Aline, 13. When he had left his luggage at a cheap hotel as promised, they proceeded to Mette's spacious flat at 47 Vimmelskaftet in the city centre, where the three youngest children were waiting for them. The latter—the boys Clovis, Jean and Paul, aged respectively 12, 10 and 7—knew only *bonjour* in French. The two eldest children knew very little more, and Emil was hostile to his father from the start. The only one of his children with whom Gauguin could make any contact, therefore, was the daughter, Aline. He was deeply touched by the in-tense curiosity which she evinced in his very romantic life and pro-fession, as they seemed to her to be.[26]

Neither husband nor wife has left any record of what they did and said during the week of that visit. But a letter from Paul to Mette, written a week later after his return to Paris, clearly indicates that she had fully agreed to a resumption of their married life but had refused flatly to engage in any South Seas adventure. Instead, therefore, he was ready to return to Europe when he had painted a sufficient num-ber of pictures for a one-man show. How complete their reconciliation was is indicated by the moving goodbye to his "adored Mette," as he now addressed her: "Now the future is assured, and I shall be happy —very happy—for you to share it with me. Though no longer stirred by passion, and with our hair growing grey, we shall still be able to enjoy a period of peace and spiritual bliss surrounded by our children, flesh of our flesh." The letter concluded: "Goodbye, dear Mette and dear children; love me well. When I return, we will begin a new marriage. What I send you today, therefore, is a betrothal kiss. Your Paul."[27]

During Gauguin's absence in Copenhagen, Morice had continued to act discreetly on his behalf. Through intermediaries, he had been endeavouring to persuade the Minister of Education that the much talked-of painter should be honoured with a *mission officielle*. Among others, the powerful Clemenceau had promised to put in a word for Gauguin, even though he did not know him personally. The high-sounding "official mission" was, and still is today, only a vaguely worded letter of recommendation, easily obtained by any "prominent intellectual" with the help of influential friends. But it is useful for a person visiting a French possession to hold such a letter because any governor, civil servant, gendarme, or customs officer is always impressed by documents which bear a minister's signature and will often grant special privileges to those who have them. On learning after his return from Copenhagen that the ground had been suitable prepared, Gauguin at once wrote off the following application, copying the obsequious tone and style usual in such letters:

Paris, March 15, 1891

Monsieur le Ministre!

I desire to proceed to Tahiti in order to execute a series of pictures of that country, the character and the lighting of which I have set myself to depict. Accordingly, I have the honour herewith, Monsieur le Ministre, to request that you grant me, like Monsieur Dumoulin, a *mission officielle*, which, while unremunerated, will, in the light of the other benefits which it will confer, nevertheless facilitate my studies and my voyage.

I remain, Monsieur le Ministre, your respectful servant,
Paul Gauguin.[28]

He even had the audacity to call with Morice on the leading promoter of the officially approved art he so deeply despised, the director of the Academy of Art himself. To tell the truth, it greatly depended on the opinion of that eminent person whether the Minister of Education would agree to the application. In deference to Gauguin's powerful friends rather than out of respect for his dreadfully unacademic art, the director graciously promised to ensure not only that Gauguin got his "official mission" but that the French Government purchased a picture for the sum of 3,000 francs when he returned. As he records in the book which he wrote on Gauguin shortly before he died, Morice was delighted by this fresh success and talked gaily of one thing and another as they made their way home.

"But Gauguin remained silent. I observed that his long period of painful struggle was over and that now, at long last, he could accomplish his task without distractions. Glancing at him as I spoke, I too in my turn fell silent, astonished by the despair on his face. His colour, naturally a leaden grey, had suddenly turned pallid; his features were distorted, his eyes unseeing, his gait shambling. I took him gently by the arm. He started, and pointing to the nearest café said:

" 'Let's go in there.'

"When we had seated ourselves in the darkest corner of the place—which was empty at that time in the morning—Gauguin rested his head on his elbows, and burying his face in his hands began to weep. I was more afraid than pitying. How could such a man weep?

"At length he raised his head a little, and murmured:

" 'I've never been so unhappy.'

" 'What? Unhappy? Today, when you are beginnning to be really appreciated and about to become famous?'

" 'Don't you see? I have failed to support both my vocation and my family. I chose to pursue my vocation, but I haven't even succeeded there. And today, when I have good reason for hope, I am more than ever tormented by the terrible sacrifice I have made and can never retrieve.'

"He spoke at some length of his wife and children, whom he had abandoned in order to devote all his energy, and all those years, to artistic creation, and whom he deeply loved.

"Suddenly he rose and said:

" 'Let me go! I need to be alone for a bit. I'll see you again in a few days' time.'

"And he added with a rueful smile:

" 'In time for you to forgive me for troubling you with my tears.' "[29]

In the presence of all his other Symbolist friends, however, Gauguin preserved his usual mask of optimism and self-assurance. For their part, they were now more eager than ever after these successes to count him one of theirs. They therefore declined to let him go without some solemn tribute to him and to their common ideals. The homage took the traditional form of a banquet, which was held on March 23 at their favourite haunt, the Café Voltaire, near the Place Odéon in the Latin Quarter. Although in no sense orthodox Symbolists, the two faithful companions, Paul Sérusier and Daniel de Monfreid, were both present. But there were two notable absentees; namely Émile Bernard and Émile Schuffenecker. As for Meijer de Haan, none of those who attended the dinner has troubled to record whether he was there or not. All we know of him for certain is that by this time he had finally abandoned the hope of getting any money for his passage from his unwilling relations. But as Gauguin now no longer intended to become a permanent exile, he had few regrets about travelling alone.

In the best traditions of France that important document, the menu, has been preserved for posterity.[30] Here it is in all its impressiveness:

Potages
Saint-Germain. Tapioca
Hors d'oeuvre
Beurre. Olives. Saucisson
*

Filet de barbue sauce dieppoise
*

Salmis de faisan aux champignons
Gigot d'agneau rôti
Flageolets maître d'hôtel
*

Fromage Brie
*

Corbeille de fruits
Petits fours glacés
*

Vin Beaujolais

The speeches were as numerous as the courses, and they too have been carefully recorded.[31] Fittingly, the first was by the evening's host, Stéphane Mallarmé, and was both clear and to the point:

"To cut short the preliminaries, let us drink a toast and wish Paul Gauguin a welcome return, while declaring our admiration for the superb dedication with which, at the zenith of his powers, he looks for renewal in distant lands and deep down into his own soul."

Then followed the toasting.

The next speaker was the now long-forgotten poet Eduard Dubus, who proposed a well-deserved toast for the authors and journalists who had arranged such excellent publicity for Gauguin's successful sale. He was followed by Charles Morice, who described in elegant verse the life of bliss which awaited Gauguin at the end of his long voyage. For in Morice's lyrical word-painting, doubtless inspired by Gauguin himself, Tahiti was a real paradise inhabited by "living statues from man's primeval age," who, "clad only in sunbeams" and full of "sweet desire," "walked always amid flowers."

The splendid verses were followed, of course, by more toasts—proposed by another Symbolist poet—not only for the Tahitian paradise and its new resident but for all the previous speakers. The next, and fifth, speaker was one of the youngest of those present, Julien Leclercq. His claim to the title of poet lay more in his personal appearance (a thin body, pallid complexion, tousled hair, and burning eyes) than in his slim little volume of laboured poems called *Strophe d'amant*. The difficulty which he must have felt in making an impression on the Symbolist coterie is painfully evident in the hackneyed phrases with which he proposed another toast for the guest of honour. He said:

"My dear Gauguin!

"To have made your acquaintance is not only to admire in you the great artist but also to esteem you warmly as a man; and to admire those one loves is always a great joy! During the three years of your absence, your friends will frequently miss their absent friend. Much will occur in those three years, my dear Gauguin. Those of us who as yet are very young—and I am one—will have grown up when you return, and those who are older will already have reaped the well-earned fruits of their labour. And as the future which has already begun to dawn will by then be even nearer, we shall all be able to praise your beautiful works with far greater authority."

The only interesting passage in this banal speech, of course, is the revelation that Gauguin now believed that it would require three years for him to finish his work in Tahiti.

Following another lyrical recitation, from Mallarmé's recent translation of Edgar Allan Poe's poem *The Raven*, succeeded by more toasts, the turn came at long last for Gauguin to express his thanks. Not surprisingly after this long succession of toasts, he could only declare, awkwardly and with the greatest difficulty: "I like you all and am much moved. I can therefore speak neither at length nor very well. Some of us have already created well-known masterpieces. I give you a toast for them and works still to come."

The first privilege accruing from Gauguin's "official mission" was a reduction of thirty per cent on all the steamship services operated by the French Government. This decided the question of his route. There were at that time four different ways of travelling to Tahiti from France.[32] The first, described with some technical justification as the only "direct connection," was also the slowest. The service was maintained by some ancient sailing ships which left Bordeaux three or four times a year, heavily laden with wine, brandy, liqueurs, preserves, cheese, and cloth, and which, all being well, arrived at Tahiti four months later after a rough and stormy passage via the Cape of Good Hope, Australia, and New Zealand. The fastest service was in the reverse direction, by boat, train, and boat again, from Le Havre via New York and San Francisco, and provided that no time was lost in waiting at intermediate points it was possible by this route to reach Tahiti in six weeks. The third and fourth routes were eastward through the Suez Canal and took the same course as far as Sydney. The services were maintained by the Compagnie des Messageries Maritimes, a Government-owned company, and ships left Marseilles at intervals of forty days. The onward voyage from Sydney was either by the same ship to New Caledonia, the largest French colony in the South Seas, and thence to Tahiti by another vessel, or alternatively by various smaller ships via New Zealand and Samoa.

To get the maximum advantage from his discount, Gauguin decided to go via New Caledonia. Wisely, he took a second-class ticket, which at the reduced rate cost exactly 805 francs. There was every reason to be economical. The loan to Morice, the journey to Copenhagen, food and lodging in Paris together with café visits, a hundred yards of canvas, oils, new clothes, and various other unavoidable outlays, had already depleted his funds. He had also had the misfortune to incur some additional, unforeseen expenses due to Juliette's pregnancy, of which he was the cause. To appease her—and at the same time divest himself of further parental responsibilities—he had been forced to present her with a small lump sum, install her in a room of her own, and provide her with a sewing-machine which would enable her to continue to work during her pregnancy. Thus of the net sum of 7,500 francs realized by the sale in February, only about half (if that) can have been left by the time he was ready to leave. Consequently, he was unable to remit any money to Mette, as he had somewhat rashly promised he would do while in Copenhagen. But it was an omission he would soon no doubt be in a position to make good; for in view of the successful auction there was a good prospect that the old pictures still remaining (which he had divided between the two galleries of Boussod et Valadon and Portier) would soon find purchasers. Moreover, he would shortly be sharing with Verlaine the proceeds of a special benefit performance at the Théâtre d'Art which his enterprising Symbolist friends had just decided to organize, with, as the main attraction, a great drama by Charles Morice.

Late in the afternoon of March 31, 1891, Gauguin took the train for Marseilles, the port of embarkation. Half-a-dozen friends saw him off at the Gare de Lyon and helped him with his bulky baggage, which included a shotgun, a French horn, two mandolins, and a guitar. The gun and the horn would enable him to keep down his expenses by hunting wild game in the Tahitian jungles. Musical instruments, of course, were even more useful and necessary in a primitive island where the inhabitants spent most of their time playing, singing, and loving.

III

AMONG COMPATRIOTS

GAUGUIN's ship, the *Océanien*, which sailed from Marseilles on April
1, 1891, was with her 4,150 tons rather smaller than most of the passenger vessels belonging to the Compagnie des Messageries Maritimes
which now operate the same service.[33] But she was new, spacious,
and luxuriantly appointed. Furthermore, she could make 15 knots,
which is a respectable speed even today. The *Océanien* passed through
the Suez Canal on April 7, and called four days later at Aden. There
Gauguin posted a brief letter to Daniel de Monfreid, in which he
stated that the third-class accommodation was nearly as good as the
second, and regretted his folly in needlessly paying the extra 500
francs. The regret suggests that his funds may have been even less
than the 3,000–4,000 francs which should have remained after deduction of all his known expenses from the receipts at the sale.

Well out in the Indian Ocean the ship soon changed course and
steered almost due south, the nearest ports of call being the Seychelles,
Réunion, and Mauritius. After passing Madagascar, Gauguin's originally proposed destination, the liner crossed to Australia through the
warm and beautiful region of the trade winds immediately south of
the Tropic of Capricorn. Like most travellers in the tropics who have
at length got under way after a long and cold winter, Gauguin relaxed
completely. If we are to believe his own statement, he spent most of
his time, indeed, "staring stupidly at the horizon." The only diversion
in his pleasantly idle life came when "occasionally porpoises shot up
from the waves to say good morning." Gauguin himself does not seem

to have said much more than "good morning" to any of his fellow passengers. Practically all of these were members of the French colonial service going out to new appointments, some in Réunion but most in New Caledonia. During the two years that had passed since he had striven to get appointed to the colonial service in Tongking, Gauguin's opinion of this class of people had clearly undergone a considerable change, for in his first letter to Mette he referred scornfully to them as "useless individuals," and thought it outrageous that the Government, that is to say the taxpayers, should have to pay for their "pleasure jaunts." He conceded, however, that "at heart they are worthy people, with only one fault, though that a fairly common one: they are every one absolute mediocrities." The contempt must have been mutual, for Gauguin confessed himself "so remarkably lonely" among all these respectable colonial officials and their families. A good reason for their avoidance of him, no doubt, was his singular appearance and dress. As if long hair which grew down to his shoulders and ill became his masculine features were not enough, he wore a brown velvet suit, purple shoes, and an artist's broad-brimmed hat.

After calling at Adelaide, Melbourne, and Sydney, all of which Gauguin found impressive but ludicrously unimaginative copies of English cities, the *Océanien* eventually anchored off Noumea on May 12. With great impartiality he wrote no less sarcastically of this typically French small town, in the 1890s a place of transportation almost as notorious as Guiana: "What a funny colony Noumea is! Both pretty and amusing! Employees earning 5,000 francs a year can ride with their families in their own carriages and keep their wives in expensive toilettes. Solve that riddle if you can! Impossible! The richest of them are discharged convicts and one day they will be on top. That tempts a man to swindle and cultivate the gay life; for if you are condemned you'll soon be very happy."

Gauguin had learnt to his dismay in the course of the voyage that there were only two or three sailings a year between New Caledonia and Tahiti, and that he would have to spend several months in Noumea if the worst came to the worst. But when immediately after arrival he inquired anxiously at the governor's office he was told, to his intense relief, that the next ship would leave in a week's time. The vessel proved to be a naval transport, the *Vire*, which carried civilian passengers when there was room. The fare was derisory—only 60 francs.[34] Thanks to his "official mission," Gauguin was quartered with the officers and allotted a place in the officers' mess. Yet the final stage of his journey was to be the most trying and uncomfortable. The main reason for this was that the *Vire* was a superannuated sailing ship, which should long since have been scrapped. Instead the parsimonious French Admiralty had fitted her with a 150-horsepower engine, which under favourable conditions gave her a top speed of six knots. In spite of the engine, the ship had been left with her three masts, which was fortunate as it turned out, for with the years the engine grew increasingly tired and unreliable, so that the commander had frequently to hoist sail in order to make port at all. The singular ship had another drawback. Although she had for years been used in the peaceful South Seas entirely as a troop transport, she still carried three heavy deck guns on either side, which gave her a heavy roll even in a moderate sea.

New Caledonia and Tahiti are situated at about the same latitude, in a region where the trade winds are easterly all the year round. The *Vire's* commander, therefore, familiar with her many faults, never attempted the foolhardy enterprise of turning her head on to the wind when eastbound, but instead, like generations of skippers before him, made for New Zealand waters, in order to get the benefit of the strong westerly winds which blow at this latitude. Although the distance thus covered was nearly twice as great as the straight course between Noumea and Tahiti, the voyage took less time, about three weeks—if nothing went wrong with the engine.

The *Vire* left Noumea according to plan on May 21, before the Australasian winter had really set in. Thus Gauguin can hardly have felt the cold when she passed the most southerly point on her semicircular route. But the ship was unbearably overcrowded; for Gauguin's fellow-passengers comprised thirty-five soldiers, three naval officers, a gendarme with his family, an infantry captain (with the un-French, probably Flemish, name of Swaton), and one poor Tahitian girl.[35] The passengers can have felt little desire to turn into their berths. This is how the accommodation is described by a French colonial official who made the same voyage a few years earlier: "I have my own cabin, situated next to the food store. But I spend as little time there as possible as it is pitch-dark even during the day and the ventilators have been screwed down, making it impossible to let out the stale air and foul engine smell. Yet up to now I have slept well, in spite of the countless numbers of giant cockroaches which crawl about my cabin and presumably come from the meat in the adjoining store-room. . . . However, time passes in one way or another. The best part of the day is the morning. As soon as day dawns, I rush joy-fully from my unhealthy cabin and ascend to the bridge, to fill my lungs with the fresh sea air."[36]

The weather was exceptionally good, and contrary to expectation the engine gave no trouble at all. In the early morning of the eight-eenth day after leaving Noumea Gauguin had his first sight of the first island in French Polynesia, or *Etablissements Français de l'Océanie*, as the colony was then called. It was the small, low-lying rocky island of Tupuai in the Austral group to the south of Tahiti, and the date was June 7. On that day Gauguin was 43, a very impor-tant birthday at a very critical stage in a man's life—especially if most of his work has still to be done. So it would not be too far-fetched to suppose that at that moment Gauguin felt very sensibly that he had reached a turning point in his life, and that his destiny would soon be decided once and for all in the island which lay ahead. It was still dark when, in the night of June 8–9, the *Vire* slipped into the lee of Tahi-ti's sister island of Moorea. The only visible signs that they had at last arrived at Gauguin's longed-for island paradise were some torchlights flickering and bobbing about on the water. These belonged to some native deep-sea fishermen, who were paddling up and down the west coast of Tahiti in outrigger canoes, luring flying-fish into their nets.

The entrance to the deep and safe lagoon on the northern side of Tahiti, where lay the colony's small capital, Papeete, was a danger-ously narrow gap in the coral reef with a strong current which it would have been too risky to try to negotiate in the dark. The ship's com-mander therefore reduced speed so as to arrive at daybreak. Yet when the cone-shaped outline of Tahiti with its 7,000-feet central peak be-came visible at half-past five in the morning of June 9, Gauguin was already too close for a proper view.[37] The right distance from which to see Tahiti at its most majestic is about ten miles. It also has to be seen on a clear day; for otherwise the view is restricted to the base of a blurred, bluish-grey volcanic mountain, veiled for the most part in a dense rain cloud. But in favourable conditions it is possible to distin-guish clearly from this distance every precipitous peak and deep, dark ravine which wind and water have carved out of the rock in millions of years of erosion. The desolate and primeval aspect of its moun-tains, together with their metallic blue or ashen tones, make Tahiti from a distance look like a lunar crater, which may explain why so many awe-struck travellers have recourse to adjectives like "ethereal" and "unreal" when trying to describe their first impression. As the ship draws nearer, the island slowly changes colour to a dark green, the mountains being not entirely bare but covered with a luxuriant carpet of tall ferns.

Nor did Gauguin obtain any impression of Papeete from the sea, though the *Vire* was only a few hundred yards from the shore when the sun rose and the pilot came aboard. The simple explanation in this case was that the town lay hidden behind a thick curtain of scarlet-flowered flame trees extending from one end to the other of the sweeping mile-long lagoon bay, where only one or two white schooners lying at anchor together with a few outrigger canoes indicated the presence of any human beings at all in the neighbourhood. It was only when the *Vire* had cast anchor, and her passengers had been rowed ashore to the grass-grown beach, that he could determine whether his preconceived picture resembled reality.

It was plain to see that it did not do so, for instead of a beautiful native village of thatched huts, he found a row of stores and taverns in ugly unplastered brick buildings, or even uglier unpainted plank houses with rusty corrugated iron roofs. Had Gauguin arrived at the time of Loti, twenty years earlier, he would have seen a slightly more beautiful sight, but since a fire had destroyed half of the town in 1884, the building of houses from palm-leaves, bamboo-canes, or similar highly combustible material had been prohibited. What was even more discouraging was that the few natives to be seen in the streets resembled by no means the naked Eves and savage Herculeses he had come half way round the world to study and paint. As regards the women, it was impossible to gain any impression at all of their figures, because they were completely hidden under wide, ankle-length dresses of a sack-like style encouraged by the missionaries. The equally decent clothing of the men was even more ludicrous, consisting invariably of a skirt-like loin-cloth of gaily printed cotton fabric, a white shirt, and a yellow straw-hat of the sort that Maurice Chevalier later made world-famous. The only visible respect in which the natives had resisted European fashion was in refusing, as a rule, to wear shoes.

For his part, Gauguin differed greatly from every other European the natives had ever seen by wearing neither a white linen suit, black frock coat, nor uniform, nor even a white topee. Since his hat and hair were both rather elegantly feminine, they promptly and fairly reasonably concluded he was a *mahu*, a certain type of male transvestite rather common in Tahiti and frowned on only by the missionaries. Actually, these deviates enjoyed marked respect and were much in

demand both as marriage partners and as domestic helps for their skill
in cooking and other domestic work.

As it was early morning and nobody in the town had observed the
Vire's approach, everyone in authority was conspicuous by his absence. There was no hotel in Papeete then, and Gauguin therefore
stood undecided on the quay, surrounded by a crowd of tittering natives. But it was not long before a breathless army lieutenant came
rushing up to welcome the most important personage on the passenger list, namely Captain Swaton, who had been posted to take over
the military command in Tahiti. As Gauguin was with Captain Swaton, he was courteously invited home by the young lieutenant, named
Jénot, who lived only a few hundred yards away by the shore. The natives soon congregated outside the garden gate, where they persisted
in staring so inquisitively at the European *mahu* that in the end Lieutenant Jénot had to drive them away.[38]

The most exalted person in the island was the native king, Pomare
V. But as Gauguin doubtless was already aware, or would soon be informed by Jénot, the real, and absolute, ruler was the French governor. Gauguin therefore went to his office as soon as it opened, in order
to present his letter of recommendation and find out the best way of
making use of it. Governor Étienne-Théodore-Mondésir Lacascade
proved to be a small man in his fifties with mutton-chop whiskers and
a somewhat dark complexion. His features were, however, entirely
European, and but for the fact that he had been born in the Negro
island of Guadeloupe, it would not have occurred even to his enemies
to call him a mulatto (Fig. 16). Unfortunately for Governor Lacascade, he not only had many enemies but was rather ridiculous in his
whole manner. An impartial witness, the American historian Henry
Adams, describes him in the following unflattering terms: "He was
very affable, and gave us all sorts of invitations which we could not
accept, jerking out his conversation with a sort of Japanese mixture of
deference, patronage, and suspiciousness."[39]

Henry Adams had visited Tahiti on a holiday voyage round the
world and had left Papeete only four days before Gauguin's arrival.
His travelling companion was his best friend, the painter John La
Farge, who in his lifetime with a certain amount of justification was
called "the American Puvis de Chavannes." Gauguin shared La
Farge's admiration for Puvis de Chavannes and would also have got on
very well with Henry Adams, for both men were at odds with civilization and dreamt of another and a better world. Both Henry Adams

and La Farge were extremely good observers and writers, and have left in their books and letters, for example, a most interesting account of Robert Louis Stevenson, whom they had met shortly before in Samoa. Had they stayed just a little longer, or arrived in Tahiti a little later, we should probably have what now we lack more than anything: an acute psychological picture of Gauguin and an expert account of his artistic theories and methods of work during his first period in Tahiti.

To return to Governor Lacascade: there can be little doubt that, for all his pompous manner, he was both efficient and knowledgeable. Originally a doctor and then for many years a bank manager, he had been elected a member of the French National Assembly before being appointed to a high post in the colonial service on the strength of his administrative and diplomatic gifts. It is indicative of the extraordinary confidence which he enjoyed that when Gauguin arrived he had already governed the French Oceanic Settlements for five years, whereas most of his predecessors had failed to last out their regulation three-year terms.[40] Lacascade had been informed of Gauguin's "official mission" a fortnight earlier, in a letter from the Colonial Department dispatched by the rather faster mail service via America. He was therefore extremely courteous and considerate, and set off a favourable chain reaction which ran right down the local hierarchy of officials. The problem of accommodation was solved immediately by the allocation until further notice of a room in one of the government buildings reserved for newly arrived officials. In his first letter to Mette, Gauguin reported with satisfaction: "I have been very well received by the governor and the head of the Department of the Interior, who is a splendid family man, as also by his wife and two daughters. I lunched with them and they are anxious to do all in their power to please me."

As a special favour, Gauguin was at once admitted to the Cercle Militaire, the exclusive club which was usually reserved to officers and senior officials. Matching the prominent part played by this club in the social life of Papeete, its premises were situated in the town's largest park in the centre, and in a giant banyan-tree ten feet above the ground had a refreshment balcony from where the members could look down condescendingly on the ordinary townspeople through the screening foliage as they drank their *apéritifs*. Here the two new members, Captain Swaton and Gauguin, were welcomed at the end of their first day in Tahiti by being garlanded in Tahitian fashion with flowers, and in the French treated to innumerable absinths.

Final confirmation of Gauguin's good connections came two days later, when the Government paper, the local *Journal Officiel*, carried a paragraph stating that the colony was honoured by a visit from "the picture-painter Goguin, here on an official mission."[41] The mis-spelling of the name went unnoticed, of course, as nobody in Tahiti had ever heard of Gauguin. But it was clear to everyone that he must be a very important person indeed, and there were many who suspected that his alleged artistic mission was merely a cover and that he had been sent by the Government in Paris to investigate the colony's affairs. (Such camouflaged inspections were not unusual at that time.) Consequently, Gauguin was everywhere received with the greatest respect, a fact which immediately encouraged him. Before long he had even convinced himself that the unexpected civilization of Papeete was an advantage rather than a fault. On June 11, the day of the newspaper announcement, he wrote to Mette: "I think I shall obtain some well-paid commissions for portraits: I am being constantly asked by all manner of people to paint them. At the moment I am making myself as difficult as possible (the surest way of getting well paid). At any rate, I think I shall be able to make money here, which I did not expect. Tomorrow I meet the entire royal family. It just shows the power of publicity. It's foolish, but I put a good face on it."[42]

But just before the time of the appointed audience the next morning the guns of Papeete began to boom out. As the unfortunate Gauguin was soon to learn with a shock, it was a salute of mourning and the occasion was the death of his intended patron, King Pomare V. Although the end had come suddenly, King Pomare had long been a doomed man, and the most surprising circumstance connected with him was that he should have lived to be 52. The primary cause of the king's demise was his huge thirst, which he had inherited together with a fortune big enough to quench it. To drink oneself to death, in fact, was a royal tradition. His great-grandfather, who at the end of the eighteenth century had made himself sole ruler of Tahiti after fierce fighting with rival chiefs; his grandfather, the bloodthirsty Pomare II, who had forcibly converted the entire population to Christianity; and his father, the insignificant consort of Queen Pomare IV, had all come to a sudden end in the same way. Pomare V, indeed, had scarcely been sober all his life. But he had only become a really chronic alcoholic after his voluntary retirement in 1880, when he had dedicated himself to the exacting ask of squandering the right royal pension of 5,000 francs a month which had been granted by the French Government as compensation. Even though the members of Papeete's two clubs generously helped him to drain the gigantic draughts of his favourite cocktail of rum, brandy, whisky, and liqueur which he used to mix, he inevitably contracted an incurable liver disease. But he had managed right to the end to keep upright, if mostly staggering, and Gauguin had therefore been justified in assuming that he would be received by him at the appointed hour.

But he could not have been more mistaken when he assumed that Pomare's unhappy release was a national tragedy, pathetically exclaiming: "With him the last remnants of the ancient tradition disappeared; with him Maori history came to an end. It was finished. The civilization of soldiers, traders, and colonial officials had prevailed. I felt a deep sadness." The sad but far less dramatic truth is that the civilizing processes had begun in Tahiti long before Pomare V had been born, and continued at the same steady pace during and long after his reign. As for the ancient traditions, King Pomare had never taken the least interest in them—unlike the queen, Marau, who after parting from her negligent husband rather early in their tempestuous marriage had devoted all her leisure to the task of writing down native legends, myths, tales, and chants.

The funeral arrangements were entrusted to the French director of the Public Works Department; and congratulating himself on his good luck in having an officially approved and sponsored artist available on the spot, he requested Gauguin to superintend the decorating of the great throne room, where the body of Pomare V had been laid in State, dressed in the uniform of a French admiral (Fig. 11). To his astonishment, Gauguin brusquely declined the honourable commission, on the singular ground that the queen and her suite of native women had more taste and could carry out the task more fittingly themselves.

Gauguin amply demonstrated that his refusal did not spring from any lack of respect for the departed monarch when on the day of the funeral, June 16, with several thousand natives and some hundred European civil servants and settlers, he followed the hearse on foot to the royal family's private mausoleum, which was situated on a beautiful spit of land three miles to the east of Papeete (Fig. 12). Gauguin called it "an indescribable monument," which "clashes glar-

ingly with the naturally decorative beauty of the vegetation and the
site." In fact the mausoleum can easily be described. It was a square
stone tower fifteen feet high, tapering slightly towards the top,
painted red, and with a corrugated roof. Long before Pomare's death,
the roof had been embellished, with unconscious symbolism, with
what was meant to be a Grecian urn but resembled a liqueur bottle.

A real delight to a newly arrived artist, however, was the sudden
sight of so many natives, so varied in type and in appearance, gathered
together at one place. While Governor Lacascade was reading a carefully prepared, bombastic speech, full of banal phrases such as "in
King Pomare you have lost a father, therefore draw closer to your
mother, France, the mother of us all," Gauguin took out his pad and
began to sketch. There was plenty of time; for Lacascade's speech had
to be translated into Tahitian, and he was followed by the royal
chaplain, who delivered a surprisingly long panegyric, considering the
late monarch's short list of virtues. The final speaker was the queen's
brother, Tati, a leading Tahitian orator, who never economized in his
oratory.[43] The ceremony over, everybody returned to the town in
what Gauguin considered was rather irreverent haste and disorder.
But then he must have been one of the few sincere mourners at the
funeral, since he mourned not only a good-natured and inoffensive
operetta king but also a lost patron and commissioner of pictures.
For that was how he had envisaged King Pomare V.

Still believing that there were many other personages whose portraits might profitably be painted and that it would be worth while,
therefore, to stay in Papeete for a time, Gauguin began, immediately
after the funeral, to look for a house. The only problem of accommodation in Papeete, it seemed, was that the houses there were like
wooden boxes, all identical except that some were square and some
oblong. In either case, they stood on boulders or tall piles so as to facilitate the free circulation of air underneath. This practice might
have had the desired result of keeping the rooms cooler if the roofs
had not invariably consisted of corrugated iron which turned them
into furnaces. Houses without ceilings were of course the worst. To
avoid being baked, the people of Papeete therefore spent most of the
day on their open verandahs, which extended along the front of every
house—unless the house was high enough off the ground for them to
recline underneath. Of course there was no sanitation, and water had
to be fetched by the bucket from one of the town's three taps. The

disadvantages were compensated for to some extent by the pleasant little garden which invariably surrounded each of these "villas."

Strange to say, a furnished house was unobtainable in Papeete then. When a suitable place had been found it was necessary to hire the furniture from a store. This inconvenient system doubtless owed its origin to the very diverse needs and habits of the tenants. Colonial officials liked to live in the European style, with their houses full of small tables, mirrors, tasselled curtains, and antimacassars. Many local French residents, on the other hand, were happy to live in the native fashion, with only a few plaited leaf mats to sit and sleep on and a large wooden chest to hold their clothes and other belongings. Gauguin furnished his newly rented house, at the rear of the Catholic church, fairly thoroughly: he procured a large double bed, two tables, four chairs, a chest of drawers, a couch, and a chest. The walls he decorated with art reproductions and a few photographs of Mette and the children.

In order to obtain clients as well as improve his knowledge of local conditions, he set about widening his social circle as quickly as he could. In his eagerness to become acceptable he even had his hair cut and took to wearing a white linen suit with a high-necked collar, as was the local fashion. (For the governor and certain other senior officials, the required everyday wear was a black frock-coat.) While far from ideal, this was not too unsuitable an attire in the tropical climate of Tahiti, particularly at the beginning of the cool, dry season—the time of Gauguin's arrival—when the temperature at noon seldom exceeded 85 degrees Fahrenheit and at night usually dropped to about 70 degrees.

As it was soon borne in on Gauguin, the 3,000 inhabitants of small-town Papeete were divided into a bewildering number of cliques and classes. At the top, of course, were the officials and military officers from France, who lived with their families and French servants. Usually, they were there for three years and were then transferred to other colonies. Altogether, this group in the 1890s did not exceed a hundred persons. They considered themselves not only a political but also a social and intellectual elite, as indeed to some extent they were. Many even bore aristocratic names. Consequently, they looked down on the French residents or settlers, nearly all of whom were ex-soldiers or former sailors who had married Tahitian women and had stayed on in the colony after completing their terms of service. Most of them had opened marine stores, shops, or taverns in Papeete,

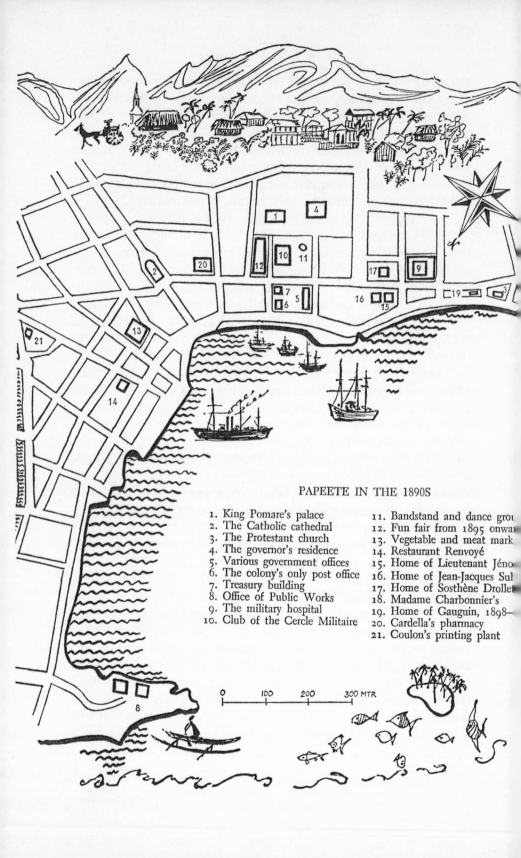

PAPEETE IN THE 1890S

1. King Pomare's palace
2. The Catholic cathedral
3. The Protestant church
4. The governor's residence
5. Various government offices
6. The colony's only post office
7. Treasury building
8. Office of Public Works
9. The military hospital
10. Club of the Cercle Militaire
11. Bandstand and dance grou
12. Fun fair from 1895 onwar
13. Vegetable and meat mark
14. Restaurant Renvoyé
15. Home of Lieutenant Jéno
16. Home of Jean-Jacques Suh
17. Home of Sosthène Droller
18. Madame Charbonnier's
19. Home of Gauguin, 1898–
20. Cardella's pharmacy
21. Coulon's printing plant

0   100   200   300 MTR

and many were well off. There were only two hundred of these settlers.
What the colonial officials disliked about them was less their coarse
speech and vulgar manners than their selfishness and meanness. The
settlers complained in their turn of the superior airs and supercilious-
ness of the civil and military officials—when they did not accuse them
of downright dishonesty. Furthermore, they all agreed that the officials sent out from France, who succeeded one another in quick succession, were grossly ignorant of local conditions and that, therefore,
the settlers were better qualified to govern the colony's 20,000 natives.
These matters apart, the settlers rarely agreed about anything, but
continually argued and quarrelled among themselves.

Intrigues and feuds were frequent in official circles as well. The
commonest causes of these disputes were potatoes and native girls.
The former article was chronically in short supply as it had to be imported, and soon went bad on the long voyage out. Since no official's
wife could ever contemplate the idea of profaning the sacred traditions of the French *cuisine* by replacing *pommes frites* with yams,
bread-fruits, sweet potatoes, or any of the other delicious Tahitian
vegetables, the battle for the few boxes of potatoes which at long intervals arrived unspoilt was bitter and ruthless. The problem of the
native girls was exactly the opposite: they were too plentiful, and the
officials were therefore inclined to turn to their arms for comfort and
relaxation from the frustrating potato wars. Social life among the official classes was an endless round of conventional dinners, the menus
and table plans of which would long be the chief topic of conversation
in the town. Between dinners the women would gossip over tea, while
their husbands gossiped, drank absinth, and played dominoes at the
Cercle Union. The dominant interest of both groups is shown even
more clearly by the fact that the only industries at that time in Papeete were rum distilling, brewing, and the manufacture of soft
drinks, chiefly Alka-Seltzer water.

Two or three times a year the officials and local French settlers
would meet at a reception given by the governor, and there with scant
success would endeavour to find neutral topics of conversation. During the rest of the year they would merely greet one another stiffly on
their evening or Sunday carriage drives along the main street and the
lagoon road. The only real bond between the two rival French groups
was their deep-seated suspicion of a third group: the three hundred
British and American businessmen and planters. Most of these had
been born in the island and had married into the best Tahitian fami-

lies, which made them, of course, still more dangerous and powerful as competitors. Later arrivals, forming a group disliked by both the French and the Anglo-Americans, were the Chinese, who also numbered about three hundred. They were former coolies, who had been imported twenty-five years before by a megalomanic Scot named William Stewart, in order to reduce the costs of running his cotton plantation, and who, willingly or unwillingly, had stayed behind when he had gone bankrupt. The occupations available to the Chinese, of course, were only the simplest and most poorly paid. Most were either tailors or pedlars. Others were butchers, or toiling market gardeners struggling to grow vegetables on artificially irrigated plots on the town outskirts. The most successful of the Chinese owned small general stores or simple eating houses patronized by natives and seamen. One or two had made enough money trading opium to enable them soon to achieve the highest ambition of every ageing Chinese—to return to China and afford an imposing funeral and tomb.

Finally, there was a large number—some 2,000—of more or less pure natives permanently settled in Papeete. Although they outnumbered the Europeans and Chinese together by two to one, they, unquestionably, formed the ethnic group which had least to say and were nationally the least conscious, so that it is logical to mention them last. About half of them were either women married to Europeans, or the children and relatives of these who had come to town with them. Very few native women, on the other hand, had entered into relationships with Chinamen, being unwilling to do so because the Chinese were guilty of the only two sins recognized by the Tahitians—dirtiness and stinginess.

The remaining natives in Papeete consisted of women, and a much smaller number of men, who had first come to trade, amuse themselves, and see the wonders of the capital. As frequently happens elsewhere, many of these country visitors had been so fascinated by the marvels of modern urban life that they had stayed and got themselves jobs, mostly as servants. The youngest, prettiest, and most enterprising of the women had of course soon discovered that there were plenty of French soldiers and sailors who, oddly enough, would compete to offer them drinks and gifts, or even money, asking no other favour in return than they would gladly have given to any unmarried man at home without payment. Looked after and shared out by the other ethnic groups, the natives to a large extent had forsaken their own ways and customs. But many continued in the Tahitian manner to bathe openly, morning and evening, in the Queen's stream which flowed through the town. And in the beautiful gardens which surrounded all the houses natives, men as well as women, would frequently be seen cooking the evening meal in Tahitian earth ovens.

Having particularly his own compatriots in mind, Gauguin summed up his impressions of the capital city of Papeete in the following harsh words: "It was Europe—the Europe I thought I had finished with—in a form even worse, with colonial snobbery and aping of our customs, fashions, vices, and crazes in a manner so grotesque that it bordered on caricature." Henry Adams had been only slightly more charitable, for he had written in a private letter on February 23, 1891: "Papeete is one of those ideal spots which have no fault except that of being insupportable. Stevenson warned us of its character, yet I am not sure but that, at some future day, when the halo of its distance again surrounds it, we may look back on our stay here with wonder that it bored us. The sun and moon leave nothing to desire. The mountains and the sea are fit for all the Gods of a Deological Cyclopaedia. The town is different from anything I ever saw in the long catalogue of towns I have met, and has an expression of lost beatitude quite symbolic of Paradise, apart from its inhabitants. As for its inhabitants, I cannot imagine why I should be so worried by them, but I am; and yet they are more amusing than we had a right to expect. My chief trouble is the pervasive half-castitude that permeates everything; a thickly whitey-brown, or dirty-white, complexion that suggests weakness, disease, and a combination of the least respectable qualities, both white and red. To be cooped up among two or three thousand such people, in a dirty shanty, with similar so-called cottages within ten feet on either side, makes one forget how exquisitely the morning sun filters through our vines and lights up our breakfast table, and how blue the sea is, before our gate, to say nothing of the tones of the mountains of Moorea, in the distance. Yet even when I forget the half-breeds and the cottages, and go swimming, so to speak, in the blue and purple light, I never lose consciousness of a sort of restless melancholy that will not explain why it should want to haunt a spot that by rights ought to be as gay as a comic opera."

As a newly arrived Parisian on an "official mission," Gauguin was at once taken up socially by the civil servants. Having spent the previous winter in the company of bohemians, he failed to strike the right tone, and moreover, as always, had great difficulty in concealing his thoughts. The only person he could endure without too great an effort was the amiable and helpful Lieutenant Jénot. Thanks to Jénot's friendly and unassuming character, two of his neighbours, though settlers and therefore members of the opposing group, associated with him, or at least occasionally looked in and joined him in an *apéritif*. One of these was Jean-Jacques Suhas, a male nurse, whose wife was a local beauty, the daughter of an Irishman and a native woman from one of the coral islands in the adjacent Tuamotu group. The other, Sosthène Drollet, a confectioner and jam-maker by trade, had lived in Tahiti since 1857 and knew all there was to know about everybody there. Gauguin met these useful persons at Lieutenant Jénot's house (No. 15 on the map on page 68), on one of his first days in Papeete, and later would often call on them for information about various matters. A son of Sosthène, the 20-year-old Alexandre, was already in spite of his youth one of the ablest of the Government interpreters. Gauguin was anxious to learn Tahitian, and like many another newly arrived European assumed it was an absurdly simple language because it was agglutinative and non-inflected. Alexandre Drollet generously gave Gauguin free lessons, but soon discovered that his pupil had no ear for languages. But he persevered in explaining the peculiar Tahitian manner of sentence construction by means of particles until, in sheer desperation, Gauguin gave up of his own accord.

Of course there were settlers with more money and influence than Sosthène Drollet and Jean-Jacques Suhas, and Gauguin tried hard to gain the friendship of the two biggest local bosses. One was François Cardella, Papeete's elected mayor, and a man who in his hands held many visible as well as invisible threads of the complex political machinery. The other was the island's leading capitalist, Auguste Goupil,

7. *The destination of Gauguin's voyage half round the world in 1891: the town and harbour of Papeete, here seen from the mountains.*

8. *The Vire, the creaky antiquated vessel in which Gauguin travelled the last lap of his voyage, anchored like all warships at a short distance from the shore.*

9. *To a seeker after paradise like Gauguin it must have been singularly depressing to land in this ugly little shanty town full of Europeans.*

10. *Proof that the natives were savages no longer was pitifully provided by the rifle practice of the men and the sack-like clothing worn by the women.*

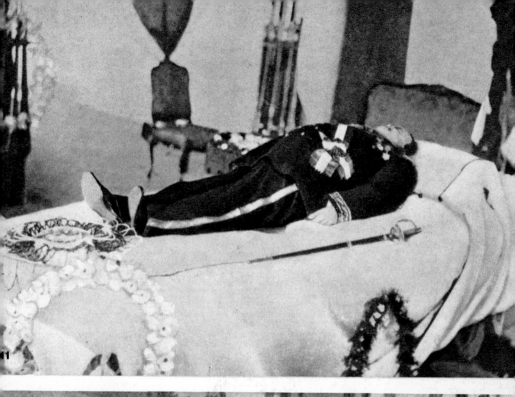

11

2

a self-taught lawyer and businessman, who boasted of having started his career not only empty-handed but barefooted, as he had been so poor when he had arrived in the colony twenty-five years earlier that he had not even possessed a pair of shoes. Thanks to his tremendous energy and great business acumen, he had soon made a fortune out of copra and desiccated coconut flakes, and for many years had occupied a splendid mansion outside the town. Goupil was also a gifted musician, as well as the only settler who took a little interest in art.[44] However, in the eyes of the settlers Gauguin belonged to the enemy camp because of his "official mission." Though correct and polite, neither Cardella nor Goupil invited him into their homes, and most of the other settlers as usual followed their example.

Because of the unresponsive attitude of the local French settlers and his own reluctance to share in the dreary round of dinners and parties given by the civil servants, Gauguin quickly gravitated to the perimeter of society. To his delight, he found life more interesting and entertaining there. For example, in the park where the military club with its mess and tree-top bar was situated, public dances were held twice a week (site 11 on the map of Papeete, page 68). The remarkable scene which he saw from that vantage point soon led Gauguin to drop his dominoes, put down his absinth glass, and descend a few rungs of the social ladder. The music was provided by an amateur band of horn-blowers, who took up their position, at eight o'clock every Wednesday and Saturday evening, in a small circular iron pavilion (which is still there) and for an hour and a half played gavottes, polkas, and waltzes. Those who attended were mostly natives and French soldiers, sailors, clerks, and domestic servants, but

---

11. *By the time Gauguin met his intended patron, the native ruler Pomare V, the King was dead and lying in state, dressed in the uniform of a French admiral.*

12. *Sadly, he joined the long funeral procession, walking behind the hearse drawn by mules and hung with saddle-cloths the three miles to the royal mausoleum.*

13. *Even in the country, the native women were surprisingly well dressed—at any rate when they went down to the coast road to meet the daily coach.*

14. *But most natives still lived in old-style oval huts with window-less walls of round bamboo canes and roofs of plaited pandanus or coconut palm leaves.*

government officials and local bigwigs might appear and display a little cursory interest from a distance without loss of face. Gauguin saw
no point in remaining an aloof spectator, and being a good dancer
was soon a much sought-after partner; for according to the charming
local custom, the women could also ask for a dance if they wished—
and they often did. Gauguin seems to have agreed wholeheartedly
with the delighted globe-trotter Pallander, who exclaimed: "Two hundred odd girls surround the bandstand, and amuse themselves by ca-
pering round in a circle. The colours! The dust! The enthusiasm! Let
us thank Heaven, or the French, that there is at least one little corner
still remaining in this hideously overgrown world where a man who is
satiated with civilization can lay his weary head and be lulled to sleep
in a whirl of tropical imagery. For years we have dreamed of such spectacles, and at last we have found one—in Papeete."[45]

A French writer who also visited Tahiti in the 1890s, has left a
rather more detailed description of these popular balls:

"On these occasions a score of vendors will install themselves about
the lawns, spreading their wares out on leaf mats or small tables in
the light of paraffin lamps and candles. The goods they have to sell
consist of fresh coconuts, Tahitian cigarettes (badly dried tobacco
wrapped in thin pandanus leaves), garlands of flowers, necklaces of
sweet-smelling tiare gardenias, artificial flowers made from thin strips
of leaf, glasses of beer, bottles of non-alcoholic beverages, and ice-cold
fruit juice.

"Strolling between the stands and the pavilion is a crowd of kanakas
of both sexes, for the most part rather dressed up, and also many Europeans, among them almost the entire crews of the ships in the harbour. The public, in short, is not very smart, but on the other hand
is very original.

"The big Tahitian children of nature, there to have a good time, are
extraordinarily affected by music, and the first blast of a trumpet pro-
duces a picturesque spectacle. Some natives begin to leap about clum-
sily in front of the pavilion. Their twists and turns are greeted with
taunts and laughter. Meanwhile, another group of dancers gallop
recklessly through the crowd of good-humoured spectators, singing
lustily. The whole happy crowd of people derive a great deal of innocent enjoyment and great fun from it, and even the violent collisions
are invariably greeted with jests and peals of laughter.

"Along the lawn, but at a safe distance from the dancers, many
more serious-minded persons will have seated themselves on mats and

cushions brought with them. These people consist of officers, members of the colonial service, and "female society"—that is, Queen Marau and her attendants, together with many other Tahitian and half-caste women. On all sides are also groups of native women in long white dresses, with thick black hair worn loose, eyes as dark as their hair, and sensuous, inviting lips. All wear a showy white gardenia in their ebony-black hair, and reclining comfortably on their mats fan themselves and smoke long cigarettes. Barely visible in the half-light, which lends itself so admirably to flirting and intimate talk, they receive the tributes, compliments, and jesting approaches of the men with a delightful charm peculiar to these tropical women, which always has a touch of piquancy owing to their immorality, incredible candour, and uninhibited *joie de vivre.*"[46]

Another French writer has left a rather less flattering picture of the Tahitian town girls, or rather street-girls, of Gauguin's day: "To satisfy them is impossible, for however generous you are they will always lack money. Many officers, for example, have given their mistresses the considerable amounts of several thousand francs on leaving the colony. All this they have squandered in a few days on sumptuous feasts, literally throwing away their money without the slightest hesitation or compunction. Thought for the morrow and feeling of gratitude are equally foreign to all Tahitian women. They live entirely for the moment, with never a thought for the future, any more than they remember the past. The tenderest and most compliant of lovers will hardly have gone before he is completely forgotten, almost from one day to the next. What these women chiefly desire, quite simply, is to intoxicate themselves with singing, dancing, drinking, and loving."[47] To which one might possibly reply, in Gauguin's own words, written appreciatively but without illusion: "All Tahitian women have so much love in their veins that it is always love, even when it is bought." Gauguin of course was using the always ambiguous word "love" in the sense of "erotic passion."

As early as half-past eight the band would bring the dancing to a close by playing the *Marseillaise.* But few people would go home so soon, according to the writer already quoted: "For the custom after the musical entertainment is to repair to the Chinese quarter for tea. Men and women go there in couples. To a Tahitian girl the acceptance of such an invitation is tantamount to agreeing to greater intimacy; for the free satisfaction of the instincts is thought in this hot and intoxicating country to be so natural that to refuse is an affront.

All at once, therefore, the Chinese quarter is invaded by an astonishingly mixed crowd of people who have only one thing in common: the determination to have a thoroughly good time. In view of the large numbers of people mingled here together, of different character and classes, it is remarkable that abuse is so rare and that joking seldom ends in quarrelling, though this may be because every Chinese café has its particular clientele."48

There was far less ceremony on the other evenings of the week, when the dance band in the central park did not play. On these evenings the rendezvous was the market-place adjoining the incredibly ugly market hall, built of grating and corrugated iron, in the Chinese quarter (site 13 on the map of Papeete, page 68). An outspoken member of the colonial service, who used to go there with Gauguin later on, has left this detailed description of it: "The market-place, where there are a few trees growing, is bounded by the rue Bonnard, the rue des Beaux-Arts (!), the town hall park, the premises of the Atwater firm, and the market hall. The only embellishment of the market-place is a small square fountain surrounded by an iron railing, from which a thin and almost invisible jet of water squirts into the air. At dusk, the old native women settle down with their backs to the fountain, light their reeking oil lamps, and spread out their tempting wares on a cloth or leaf mat: garlands of flowers, Tahitian cigarettes made from tobacco wrapped in pandanus leaf, and occasionally fresh fruit in the season.

"Alongside the market hall just opposite, sellers of oranges, watermelons, coconuts, pineapples, Tahitian chestnuts, sticky pastry, etc., install themselves, together with ice-cream vendors whose small machine with its ticking is a perpetual source of amusement to natives visiting the capital for the first time. The Chinese-owned, ill-lit taverns, small bars, inns, cafés, and shops in the surrounding streets will long have been packed with people, who are now spreading gradually across the market-place, presenting the usual spectacle.

"Groups of perfumed, barefooted natives of both sexes parade to and fro with wreaths of flowers on their heads, shaking hands and singing songs whose meaning can be easily understood even by those ignorant of the language. Among all these natives, who are lightly dressed—in some cases undressed—and all the women offering flowers, fruit, and themselves for sale, there are also many foreigners, chiefly seamen of all nationalities, French soldiers, shop assistants, and some government clerks, besides a few representatives of the cream of society, come, they will swear, solely out of curiosity or for study, but finding it difficult nevertheless to conceal the real object of their visit.

"At this 'Equality Fair,' with its absolute mixture of people, the most incredibly realistic scenes may be witnessed. Everything is for sale and everything finds a buyer in this cordial exchange, or 'flesh market' as it is appropriately called by the local inhabitants. While the general buying and selling is in full progress some of the natives will gather round the fountain, and quickly forming a choir will borrow an accordion or other instrument for accompaniment and join in a shrill and savage choral song in the midst of this strange and remarkable assembly. Not uncommonly the police—who on these occasions are always alert—are obliged to intervene to prevent scuffles, the occasional result of the inevitable difficulty in agreeing on the payment of certain commodities.

"Usually, the crowd disperses about eleven. As the custom is in other parts of the world, the courting couples steal off along the house walls, away from the light of street lamps and oil flares, the woman with a wreath of flowers on her head, the man carrying some titbit, a coconut, pineapple, or other fruit, for refreshment during their solitude later on. The sellers disappear on the heels of their last customers, and soon the market-place is hidden in the black veil of night. Only a single flickering lamp remains at the corner of the rue Bonnard. Sleep peacefully, dear inhabitants of Pepeete; the police are on watch. When a few hours later the market-hall gates are thrown open, there will be gossiping about the evening's and the night's events as the customer purchases melons and fish, and soon the gossip will have spread all over the town."[49]

The market life inspired one of Gauguin's best-known Tahitian pictures, *Ta Matete*, which is now in the Kunstmuseum at Basle. (The apparently Tahitian title—in which the first word should be the definite article *te*, and not *ta*—is actually a corruption of the English word "market.") This highly stylized picture shows some Tahitian *filles de joie* in the foreground, dressed in their best and waiting on a bench for customers, while in the background two men wearing short loincloths are heading for the market hall, carrying tunny fish on a pole. The stylization springs chiefly from the remarkable fact that Gauguin borrowed the poses and the gestures from an Egyptian tomb picture.

Gauguin was highly sexed and had usually had to repress himself. Now he could give free satisfaction to his instincts. After eight years of poverty and privation he also had a fair amount of money. Both his immediate future and the prospects which awaited him on his return to France seemed exceptionally bright. It is understandable, therefore, that he should now feel entitled to relax and enjoy himself. He must none the less have felt a slight twinge of conscience; for his next letter to Mette, written three weeks after his arrival, contained this piece of self-defence, which will have seemed rather mysterious to her: "Let me live for a time like this. Those who reproach me have no idea what an artist's nature can contain. Why do they try to force their demands on to us artists? We don't force ours on to them."[50]

Gauguin had good reason to plead continued indulgence in his habits; for his revelling and carousing was to culminate soon after in even greater festivity. The occasion was the biggest annual event in the colony, the French national day, which with admirable endurance and patriotism the natives, then as now, extended into a frenzied celebration lasting several weeks.[51] The first natives from the surrounding countryside and adjacent islands arrived in the capital in vessels carrying orange-coloured sails at the beginning of July, and in the next two weeks the population of Papeete was doubled. The celebrations opened officially with a salvo of guns at three o'clock in the afternoon of the thirteenth of July. After walking through the town in procession, the representatives of each district or island preceded by a flag and some drummers, the natives spent the rest of the day at the fun fair, with such simple fairground amusements as rifle-shooting, dart-throwing, shying at piles of tins, weightlifting, and eating doughnuts or candyfloss. Gauguin's contemporary, Pallander, gives the following amusing glimpse of the goings-on: "The short street leading past the *Faré Moni* from the quay to Pomare's palace gate is a sight for the gods. It is literally choked with booths of all kinds. Jugglers, gambling tables, ice-cream vendors, liquor sellers, and dealers in flowers have taken up positions at the sides of the road and are all talking at once. Some astonishing swindles are being perpetrated. Innocent lady passengers from the *Waikaré* are purchasing slices of watermelon at twenty-five cents apiece. Considering melons are only worth five cents apiece in Tahiti, the vendor makes a fair profit. The most atrocious liquors are offered for sale at the drinking-booths, the labels of some being enough to give one the cholera without tasting the mixture inside. At a table, raised slightly above the others, a splendid gentleman in checks, with a suggestion of artificial jewellery in his shirtsleeves and a decided dash of the tar-brush in his complexion, is spinning a wheel with gaudy-looking numbers gleaming round the circumference, and, to judge from the ceaseless jingle of money on the baize counter beneath him, doing a rousing business. Next door to him, behind a barrow laden with indigestible biscuits, a Kanaka of a musical turn of mind is courting the muse and custom by playing the flute. The street, with its seething exotic crowd, its list of weird articles offered for sale, is a Nijni-Novgorod fair in miniature. A mock perfumery store sports a pile of bottles filled with compounds which only Papeete slums could witness the boiling of. A pot of railway grease, flavoured with essence of cloves, is labelled 'Rimmel's Anodyne for the Hair.' Another bottle, which, from the smell, I should judge to be filled with alcohol and lavender water, is styled Eau de Cologne Jean Maria Farina."[52]

The fairground remained open all night. In the morning of the fourteenth, most of the revellers went straight from the fair to the *himene* or song contests on the lawn of the Cercle Militaire, which began at eight o'clock. Each district or island entered a choir of forty–fifty persons, who sang grand polyphonic chorales. This chorale singing, which according to his own testimony made a deep impression on Gauguin, was the most popular event of the festival at this time, since the famous Tahitian *upaupa* dances—which today are the main attraction —were still considered too obscene and undignified by the authorities to be included in a July 14th programme. "A South Sea *himene* in its highest degree of development is difficult to do justice to in print," says the author just quoted. He then proceeds to give the following excellent description of one such song contest: "It begins by the usual treble shriek pitched in any key which comes handy. Just as you are trembling for the girl's vocal organs the shriek loses its viciousness and modulates off into something—probably a tune—fitful enough to embarrass a phonograph. Apparently it is without rhyme or rhythm. But the chorus don't think so. The girl is working her way down step-fashion. As she sludders down comfortably into *mezzo* they chime in amicably one by one—some repeating the melody in fugue fashion, others improvising 'on their own;' others, the heavy swells of the entertainment, merely contenting themselves with growling a sort of ground-bass accompaniment.

"Very few of the rules regulating civilized choral music find echo here. Nothing forbids the intercrossing of the parts, and the bass gentlemen, if they be so minded, can blossom spontaneously into high-C tenors without infringing inter-island law. Certain harmonies, Chinese in colouring—to wit, the well-known 'Grail' harmony exploited by Wagner in the *Lohengrin* prelude—recur almost to weariness. Taking it as a whole, the result is strangely, uncouthly symmetrical. Who taught these people counterpoint? Certainly not the missionaries. They have never bothered their heads encouraging musical effort. Who taught them the art of modulation? Who showed them the precise point at which a ground bass must be altered to avoid cacophony? Is this wild Tahitian melody an arbitrary assortment of notes, or is it intended to be a painting in sound, a musical suggestion of the landscape it emanates from? Does not the droning sing-song of an Arab chant bear some resemblance to the desert? Is not the very form of Scotch music as written on paper a representation, in its jerky, irregular notchings, of the Scotch hills? Is it a mere coincidence that the *Ranz des Vaches* predominates in Swiss melodies, or the twang of the banjo in Negro ones? Does not this ebbing, swaying *himene*, with its growling substratum of male voices, signify the whistle of the tradewind in the palms and the roar of the reef? It is a problem worth investigating."[53]

At one o'clock came a long series of regattas in the sheltered lagoon harbour, with Tahitian outrigger canoes, ships' boats, and sailing cutters taking part. Meanwhile, other contests took place on shore, the most popular of these being racing on stilts for men (an ancient Tahitian sport) and climbing the greasy pole for women (a new French one). In the evening, competitors and spectators relaxed with a little dancing round the music pavilion before having another night out at the fair. Then on the fifteenth they walked in close formation to the racecourse in the Fautaua valley, where steeplechasing, flat racing, and trotting alternated with running for men and women, the foot races fortunately never exceeding 400 yards. The day ended in a Venetian regatta, so called, in which the various districts and islands competed to decorate a large double canoe with flowers and palm-leaves in the most beautiful manner. After another gay night, the fair closed for a while so that everybody could get some sleep, but only after the money prizes had been distributed.

The celebrations were not over even now; everybody went on playing, eating, and drinking to his heart's content for as long as any money remained to be spent. It was some time in August when the last bleary-eyed native sailed home with an aching head but with beatific smiles on his lips.

For Gauguin, the celebrations of the fourteenth of July were not only a further excuse for enjoying himself, they presented a unique opportunity for observing and sketching native types. At the time of King Pomare's funeral, to be sure, he had been able to draw more genuine natives than the ones who lived in Papeete. But the women had all worn long, loose mourning frocks and the men ill-fitting dark-coloured suits, and what is more had soon returned home. But now, all through July, there were plenty of much more lightly clad natives everywhere in Papeete, but especially in and around the encampment for the out-of-town visitors. When out walking Gauguin would often stop, and staring openly at a native tell the person to stand still while he made a sketch. Genial and affable as always, the natives would invariably respond, being only mildly put out when the remarkable stranger refused to give or even show them the finished "image."

While it was clearly possible to spend every day singing and loving, as Gauguin in France had looked forward to doing, he had realized by this time that it was impossible to do so without money. Certainly it could not be done in Papeete, where indeed the cost of living was higher than it was in Paris. A simple plank house like the one he had rented cost fifty–sixty francs a month. Two meals a day at Renvoyé's excellent French restaurant, where he used to eat, came to 150 francs a month. When there were guests, as there often were, the bill was even steeper. The many quayside shops were stocked with goods; indeed were stocked so well that clothes, fabrics, utensils and lamps hung from the ceiling and all the walls just as in an old-fashioned village general store, and occasionally even outside the door. To see such an array of tempting articles everywhere is before long to feel the need for some of them. Gauguin's Tahitian girl friends in particular had this feeling both daily and hourly, with the result that his funds drained away alarmingly. It was time to start on the lucrative portrait-painting.

To Gauguin's intense disappointment, neither the colonial officials nor the local magnates displayed any interest when at length he intimated his readiness to accept commissions. Probably they had concluded that a person so vulgar in his taste as to associate openly with Tahitian filles de joie, common shop assistants, sailors, soldiers, and clerks, could not possibly be a good painter. Either that or Gauguin had simply misjudged the initial situation and had based his optimistic hopes on mere empty courtesies and the intense curiosity which he had excited on his arrival. So instead of launching himself on a career as a society painter by painting the portrait of the governor, he had to content himself with an ordinary English cabinet-maker, Thomas Bambridge, as his first client. The cabinet-maker had no

fewer than twenty-two children, and for some reason wanted a portrait of the eldest, Susannah, by this time a sturdy matron in her
forties. Assuming correctly that the cabinet-maker would not easily
appreciate his Synthetist style, Gauguin produced an extremely realistic portrait of the middle-aged, faded and very corpulent Susannah,
adding the right finishing touch by imparting its authentic scarlet red
to the nose. The cabinet-maker of course regarded the picture as a
gross caricature, and would doubtless have destroyed it if he had not
already paid 200 good francs for it. In his grief he hid it instead in his
toolshed, where it was only rediscovered after Gauguin's death.[54] It
ended up in the Royal Museum of Modern Art in Brussels. The client's reluctance to acknowledge the picture has in a way survived him;
in practically every art book Susannah is wrongly named "Miss Cam-
bridge."

While few people in Papeete ever saw this "atrocious" picture, everyone learnt by circuitous means how shockingly deficient Gauguin was
in talent and tact. Consequently, no-one any longer had the slightest
desire to employ him as a portraitist—if anyone had ever seriously
thought of doing so in the first place. Furious at having wasted three
valuable months in Papeete, Gauguin decided without more delay to
go into the country, in order to achieve the ambition for which he
had come this long way, namely to study and paint the true, the unspoilt natives.

Thirty years before, Pierre Loti, whose novel about Tahiti was, as we
have seen, familiar to Gauguin, had been equally depressed by Papeete,
and had consoled any would-be followers in this lyrical vein:

"No. Those who have only lived among the half-civilized *filles de
joie* of Papeete and from them have learnt only the simple pidgin Tahitian spoken on the shore, only the ways and manners of the town;
who think of Tahiti simply as a place where all seems to have been
created for the pleasing of the senses and the gratification of the ap-
petites—these, I say, know nothing of what this island has to give.

"Neither do they—no doubt the majority—understand it who view
Tahiti from a worthier and a more decent standpoint, seeing it as a
poetic land of everlasting summer, full of flowers and beautiful
women.

"Its true charm lies elsewhere and is not open to all. To find it, one
has to go far away from Papeete to the parts where civilization has not
penetrated, where the villages, their huts thatched with pandanus
leaves, lie scattered under slender coconut palms on the edge of the
coral sea, by the boundless and solitary ocean."[55]

IV

AMONG NATIVES

LOTI was correct in saying that life in the remoter parts of Tahiti was much more primitive than in Papeete. But all things are relative; and compared with the ideal image Gauguin had formed before leaving Paris it was extremely civilized. The principal propagators of European civilization had been missionaries, sailors, and traders. As can well be imagined, the result was uneven and unsatisfactory. The most energetic civilizers of the Tahitians were of course the missionaries, and at the time of Gauguin's arrival the Calvinists had been at work for nearly a hundred years and the Roman Catholics and Mormons for fifty. Hence virtually nothing remained of the ancient Tahitian religion and mythology. Few natives even remembered the names of their old pagan gods and—owing to disparagement by the missionaries—were exceedingly ashamed of the ignorance and savagery of their ancestors. Instead they knew by heart an incredible number of biblical texts, prayers, and hymns. Regardless of sect, they all regularly attended church—at least once a day. Their Sundays were almost entirely devoted to churchgoing.

Furthermore, the natives often read to one another from the Bible when they gathered in the evening after work. The one thing which they failed to do was to understand the essence of the Christian message and doctrine. A French colonial official described a native Bible session which he attended against his will as follows: "Six or seven persons sat in Tahitian fashion (with crossed legs) on leaf mats, smoking and talking, while I sat a short distance away from them. One of the Tahitians was reading aloud to himself from the Bible. He read slowly, stumbling over the words, and did not seem to understand what he was reading. Another man, tiring of the monotonous sing-song, took the book from him and began to read from it himself. He must have been a deacon. Afterwards they all discussed the story of the expulsion of Adam and Eve from the Garden of Eden. Suddenly, one of them turned to me and asked:

" 'An apple; what is that?'

"After pondering the matter, I explained that an apple was like an *ahia*—a local fruit. I thought that would have disposed of the matter but was much mistaken, for another man proceeded to ask:

" 'Are you sure it was an apple?'

" 'Yes; everybody agrees that it was.'

" 'So God drove Adam and Eve out for the sake of an apple?'

" 'Yes.'

" 'Why?'

"I replied impatiently:

" 'If God had allowed them to stay, they would have eaten all His apples and there would have been none left for Him.'

"At this they all burst out laughing and laid the Bible aside."[56]

When it is known that the Bible was the only reading matter available in the Tahitian language at that time, one is even less inclined to ascribe the diligent scripture reading to true and genuine devotion. To understand the frequency with which they attended church and said their prayers it is also necessary to know that they honestly believed that so long as they fulfilled these obligations the divine powers were in no way interested in their behaviour at other times. Only foreign visitors saw anything incongruous in this attitude, as did, for instance, the two British travellers, Lord Albert Osborn and his friend Douglas Hall, who were "rather astonished" during a dance entertainment "to observe all the girls and men, who up to now had been singing love songs, with scarcely a break in the singing take off their crowns and garlands, and continue what seemed to us the same songs and tunes. On our asking Hinoi why they did this, he told us they were now singing their evening hymn. A moment later they put on their crowns, and the performance continued as before—if anything the dancing becoming a little wilder. Anything more incongruous I have seldom seen, yet all done quietly and naturally."[57] In short, like all true Polynesians, the Tahitians were still as little aware of a connection between religion and morals as they had always been.

Tahitian art, which was the cultural feature Gauguin chiefly

wanted to study at first hand, had in the past been largely religious.
(Most of the innumerable sculptures in stone and wood, moreover,
had been artistically very crude.) Native art had therefore died out
with the old religion at the beginning of the nineteenth century, and
the only place in the island where anything like a representative collection of Tahitian idols could be seen in the 1890s was the small museum of the Catholic mission in Papeete. Even this was much smaller
than the collections Gauguin could have seen in many an ethnological
museum in Europe.

The fine domestic arts and crafts met with the same fate when the
Tahitians began to receive factory-made goods, because the European
tools, implements, and utensils obtainable by barter, or purchasable
in the shops which soon spread over the island, were far more durable
and serviceable than the stone axes, bamboo knives, bone hooks, and
wooden bowls the natives had previously had to depend on. As regards dress, on the other hand, most country people in Gauguin's time
still wore light, cool loin-cloths in the Tahitian manner. Even so, the
material, which consisted of large-flowered cotton cloth, generally red
for women and blue for men, had for long been imported from Europe. Sunday clothes were of course grander and more becoming, being, as in Papeete, an ankle-length dress for women and an all-black
suit, usually woollen, for men. The only Tahitian domestic crafts still
practised in the 1890s were the weaving of mats and hats and the making of cloth from bark. Unlike the Hawaiian and Samoan women,
however, the Tahitian *vahines* seldom decorated their bark cloth; and
when they did, imparted only simple naturalistic patterns obtained
by dipping fern and hibiscus leaves in red sap and pressing them on
to the material by hand. Even this craft was declining, as the missionaries' wives encouraged the women to learn sewing. They applied their
newly acquired skill not only to making the few clothes which they
needed but to producing gay patchwork quilts—also to European patterns supplied by the missionaries' wives.

In religion, art, and home crafts the Tahitians had been offered
new, and it seemed infinitely better, goods in place of their old ones.
The changes had therefore been fast and far-reaching. The situation
in the case of music and dancing, however, was entirely different. Here
the missionaries had simply declared a ban without providing other
entertainments to take their place. The prohibition had consequently
remained ineffective and the natives had continued to sing their innocently frank songs and dance their undisguised erotic dances between

church services. The passage from the account by the two British travellers just quoted also contains this excellent description of a typical *upaupa* dance: "The Tahitian dance is very like most Oriental dances—that is to say, the main feature of it is a *danse du ventre*, the same one sees in Egypt and other Eastern countries. There is very little leg movement about their dancing at all. At this particular dance the dancers lined up in rows of about twenty, girls on one side and men on the other, with a space of about six feet between the two rows. The music is a monotonous drumming on native drums, or in the case of smaller dances they use a concertina. The best girl dancer and the best man dancer stood each at the head of their respective rows, facing us on the dais, and waved their arms and swayed their bodies in time to the music, each movement being copied by the dancers standing in line behind them. At this dance they went in for a good deal of gymnastic display—that is to say, one man would jump and stand on the shoulders of the man in front of him, then a man would leap on to another man's neck and they would simulate men on horseback. At intervals the premier *danseuse* would come out in front of the others, and dance in front of us; this would be entirely a *danse du ventre*, she wriggling and waggling about in front of us until we began to wonder if she was not made of india-rubber."

As hinted by the authors of this account the only change had been in the choice of musical instruments. Besides the traditional sharkskin drums and bamboo nose flutes there had long been one or more European accordions in every village band, while the Hawaiian guitar, which we now wrongly regard as the most typically Polynesian instrument, had yet to begin its triumphal progress. It is fair to say, therefore, that in taking a guitar and two mandolins with him to Tahiti Gauguin was before his time—from which it follows in turn that he can hardly have made much of a success of them.

In the political sphere, the changes appeared to be very great; for the old ruling families had given way in every district to democratically elected chiefs. Furthermore, the administrative and legal systems were entirely French. In point of fact, however, the reforms existed only on paper. Blissfully unaware of the orders and prohibitions decreed by the authorities in Papeete, whom they seldom saw, the natives in country districts continued to settle their differences in accordance with their old tribal laws. Incidentally, though French citizens, they were exempt from two of the least desirable burdens of civilized life, being liable neither to military service nor the payment of taxes.

The changes were even less thorough in the economic field, as all the natives who in Gauguin's time lived in country districts were self-supporting farmers and fishermen. Their chief crops were taro roots, sweet potatoes, and yams, and between these harvests they could pick bread-fruits from the trees which surrounded every hut and wild bananas in the hills. Usually, the only domestic animals were poultry, pigs, and dogs. All three were good livestock; for Tahitians have been very partial to dog-meat from time immemorial—understandably so, because it is a delicacy. The money which they earned by the production of copra and vanilla and by gathering wild oranges (Tahiti exported over three million oranges a year—chiefly to California, whose inhabitants in those days preferred gold-digging to fruit-growing) more than paid for the few garments and factory-made goods which they thought that they needed, but could if necessary do without.

Even more intact was the personality structure of the natives, to use a current term; for however civilized their clothes or frequent their attendance at church and their reading of the Bible, they had remained as cheerful, hospitable, carefree, and pleasure-loving as their forefathers. Charming scenes such as the following could still be seen, therefore, in every village: "In the shade of their bread-fruit trees outside the huts, sit picturesque groups of men and women, singing or talking together. If they are making bark cloth, the pounding of their mallets will always be accompanied by singing. Like fashionable ladies in Europe, the women spend several hours on their morning toilet. On waking, they plunge into the sea or the nearest river and dive, swim, and play tag in the water for hours at a stretch. When eventually they emerge from the bath they dry their bodies and their long, loose-flowing hair in the wind. They always devote the greatest care to their superbly beautiful jet-black hair. They do it up in two plaits, which they rub in *monoi*, a perfumed oil made from coconuts. Europeans at first dislike the pungent smell of *monoi*, but soon discover its special charm. To complete their toilets, the women gather wild flowers in the nearby woods and plait them into wreaths and garlands for their adornment."[58]

Finally, to round off this brief outline of cultural conditions in Gauguin's time, the Tahitian language had been extremely well preserved in every country district, for the obvious reason that the natives formed the overwhelming majority. French had not even become an auxiliary language, because, in spite of the heroic efforts of several generations of missionaries and schoolteachers, the children—who always among themselves and at home spoke Tahitian—forgot all they had learnt at school as soon as they grew up. Indeed, they seldom managed to learn more than a few prayers, paradigms, and fables of La Fontaine. A few unusually enterprising pupils might supplement their school knowledge with some French oaths and indecent expletives learnt in the bars of Tahiti.

The most melancholy fact, however, was not that 125 years of European influence had yielded such an imperfectly functioning semi-civilization, but that it had cost the Tahitians far too high a price. For their foreign mentors had brought besides bibles, tools, implements, utensils, and fancy goods, a fearful number of new diseases, which the natives did not know how to treat. As a result, even such comparatively innocuous maladies in the West as measles, whooping cough, influenza, and chickenpox often proved fatal. Still greater inroads were made in the long run, of course, by syphilis and tuberculosis, which had also been unknown to the Tahitians and other Polynesians before the arrival of Europeans. Furthermore, the natives not only began to drink alcohol but to distil it. Many of them soon followed the lofty example of the Pomare dynasty and drank themselves to death. The most popular beverage in Gauguin's time was rum, which was drunk either neat or diluted with strong beer. The great popularity of rum is easy to explain. It was the cheapest liquor available, as it was made in the island from locally grown sugar canes. The annual production in the early 1890s was about 45,000 gallons. French claret was almost equally popular, about 65,000 gallons of this being imported every year. Those who could not afford either rum or claret —or had already spent all their money on these—made fruit wine. Drunkenness culminated in July and August, when the wild orange-trees up in the hills were laden with fruit. "At harvest time the country becomes one vast tavern," an astonished eyewitness once wrote. "The population go in a body to some remote spot, where they gather oranges and, pressing the juice out, leave it to ferment for a while in casks, after which they go on to drink all through the night, indulging in indescribable orgies without once leaving the scene of the junketing. For some six weeks life for everybody else is intolerable."[59]

The disastrous results of disease and drunkenness are evident in the population statistics. At one time it looked as if the entire population would be wiped out, for in the thirty years after the island's discovery in 1767 it fell from 150,000 to one-tenth of the number. In the following thirty years it declined still further to a half of this sad remnant, or 8,000. Between the 1830s and 1891 the annual death rate was uncannily the same as the birth rate. The situation therefore remained very critical, and many well-informed observers were convinced that the Tahitians would eventually die out altogether.

To sum up, therefore, it may be said that Gauguin unfortunately had arrived at least a hundred years too late. Either that or he had chosen the wrong island. There were indeed various islands in the South Seas where the natives remained as yet uninfluenced by Western civilization and where conditions were nearly as paradisal as Gauguin had imagined them to be in Tahiti. It was some time before he discovered the true state of affairs, for several reasons. In the first place, his departure from Papeete was delayed by an extremely unpleasant occurrence: he had a violent haemorrhage and his heart began to give him trouble.[60] At the meagrely equipped military hospital, the only hospital in the colony, he continued to cough blood; "half a pint a day," he says. Gauguin does not tell us the diagnosis arrived at by the surgeon and general practitioner who were the only doctors at the hospital. But modern specialists whom I have consulted all agree that the symptoms are typical of syphilis in its second stage. If this is so, then Gauguin must have been infected for years. The hectic and far from healthy life he had led during the first three months in Papeete may have accelerated and aggravated the crisis. The doctors in the Papeete military hospital did what they could, but it was not much. They applied mustard plasters to his leg and cupped his chest. All that can be said in favour of this medieval treatment is that it did no harm, nor did it seriously hinder his natural resistance in checking the disease. Its chief drawback, as Gauguin saw it, was that the general hospital charges came to twelve francs a day. So as soon as the haemorrhage stopped he returned home.

Gauguin tells us that when he eventually recovered and could leave Papeete, some time in August 1891, he moved "to the jungle in the interior of the island." All his biographers have taken him at his word. This is how (to quote the most obvious example) his son Paul Gauguin, the Danish art critic, describes his father's return to nature, in his otherwise excellent book about the mutual relations of his parents: "He had first to follow the beaten track of his fellow-countrymen before arriving at the simple and primitive path which led to the jungle, where the last remnants of the island's original population continued to worship their pagan gods who controlled the mysterious forces of nature and primitive life."[61] That nowhere was there any pagan worship or primitive life in existence in Tahiti in the 1890s will have emerged clearly, I hope, from what has already been said. What is more, Gauguin could not have gone into the interior even had he wished to. Nine-tenths of Great Tahiti and Little Tahiti, as the barely connected parts of this twin island are usually called, consists of high, rugged mountains, not only uninhabited but uninhabitable and for the most part quite inaccessible. Even the approach to the lower slopes and plateaux is toilsome work which involves hacking a way through a forest of tall ferns ten to fifteen feet high. Most of the mountain peaks have never been scaled by either natives or Europeans. Only at one point is it possible to cross the island, and even there, for days on end, one must continually ford rivers full of slippery boulders, scramble up and down steep slopes, and swim across an icily cold mountain lake. The inhabitable parts of the double island are restricted to the narrow coastal strip, which is seldom more than half a mile in width. The only existing road hugs the coast. In Gauguin's time this was little more than a hilly bridle track along the east coast, and was only wide and smooth enough for wheeled traffic on the west and south coasts. Even there, the traveller had to keep a wary eye for treacherous tree-roots in his path and the boulders which hurtled at many points down the steep gorges.

In view of this peculiar topography, it is not surprising that Gauguin chose to travel in a comfortable barouche along the west coast, instead of trying to hew his way through the thicket of ferns to the interior. The owner and driver of the barouche was a new friend named Gaston Pia, who in spite of his unusual surname was in fact a Frenchman, a schoolmaster in one of the west-coast districts. As was his custom, Pia had driven in to Papeete during the summer holidays in order to attend the lengthy celebrations of the fourteenth of July, staying with a brother who like himself was an elementary schoolmaster, but at a school in town. It was during the festivities that Gauguin had made their acquaintance. The two brothers were keen amateur painters, Gaston being indeed so competent that, a few years later, he was appointed drawing master at the Protestant mission school in Papeete. Thus they felt a measure of professional solidarity with Gauguin, though they found it difficult to understand how an artist who was such a poor draughtsman and crude colourist had managed to get an "official mission." When preparing to return home at

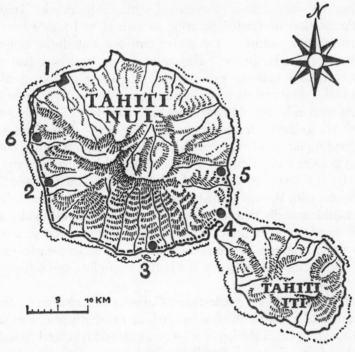

Map of Tahiti

1. Papeete, capital of French Polynesia
2. Elementary school and teacher's house in Paea
3. Gauguin's hut in Mataiea, 1891–93
4. Taravao, terminus of the Papeete coach
5. Teha'amana's two parent homes in Faaone
6. Punaauia, where Gauguin lived, 1895–1901

the end of the celebrations, Gaston was kind enough to invite Gauguin to go with him.[62] Like all elementary schoolmasters in Tahiti, Pia lived near his school, in this case in the middle of Paea, thirteen miles from Papeete. From the house, where another and far more convenient building now stands, Gauguin had a superb view of the steep mountains in the interior. On the other side it was only a hundred yards to the shore, but that was bordered by dense hibiscus thickets which screened the view of the lagoon and the sea. When, therefore, he wanted to enjoy the finest and most colourful view in the whole of the South Seas, the island of Moorea with the setting sun behind it, he used to follow the example of the natives and sit in the twilight on the soft sandy beach by the water's edge.

Otherwise, very little is known of this brief interlude in Gauguin's life, except that he started painting in earnest and finished at least two canvases: a picture of the native farm-hand at the school chopping wood and a landscape.[63] He cannot in any case have had much contact with the natives, because neither he nor Pia could speak Tahitian and the gregarious schoolmaster mixed chiefly with French settlers. As soon as he began to feel fit enough, therefore, Gauguin decided to look for a district farther away from Papeete, where there would be a greater chance of achieving his original ambition to live entirely among natives and as one of them. Perhaps his departure was hastened by the fact that a new school term began in the middle of September, with the result, first, that his host's time became fully occupied, and secondly that his peace and quiet were suddenly disturbed by a flock of noisy children. For practical reasons he was forced, unfortunately, to return to the point from which he had started, as Papeete was the only place which had both a post office and well-stocked shops.

During the national celebrations, Gauguin had also made the acquaintance of a native chief, a man whose original name was Ariioehau, though in the Tahitian way he had changed it several times. For the sake of simplicity, I will call him by the name by which he went in Gauguin's time, which was Tetuanui. He was the most pro-French of all the eighteen district chiefs in Tahiti, and the only one who spoke fluent French. As a reward for loyalty he had been given, among other privileges, a visit to the Universal Exhibition in Paris in 1889, at the French Government's expense.[64] Although in all probability Tetuanui had failed to see the Synthetist and Impressionist pictures in Volpini's Café des Arts, he and Gauguin nevertheless shared a number of memories and topics of conversation. It was therefore natural when Gauguin set out into the country again that he should reconnoitre his friend's district, which was Mataiea, on the south coast of Tahiti, more than twice the distance of Paea from Papeete.

On this occasion he borrowed a carriage from a drinking companion in the *gendarmerie*. As his fellow-traveller he took a half-caste girl whom he had picked up in some tavern or dance spot, and who answered to the nickname of Titi ("Breast"). To make the right sort of impression on the "rustics," she had put on her finest ball dress and church hat with artificial flowers and a chain of gold-painted sea shells. It was noon when the ill-assorted couple arrived at Chief Tetuanui's big official villa, which for all the world resembled a huge

Victorian folly. Tetuanui warmly welcomed his guests and proudly
showed them his domains. He had every reason to feel pride, for
Mataiea is one of the most beautiful parts of Tahiti, both because
the coastal plain here is exceptionally wide, so that the mountains are
not too near and can therefore be seen in all their splendour, and because the surf along the coral barrier which shelters the lagoon is
higher and more sparkling than anywhere else, owing to the ceaseless
south-east trade winds at this point. Furthermore, the lagoon is exceptionally beautiful by reason of its two palm-clad islets, which lend
a welcome perspective to the wonderful view of Little Tahiti twelve
miles to the east. Gauguin was so enchanted by the view that he at
once decided to settle in Mataiea without bothering to inspect any
other district.

The choice was not altogether a happy one. Mataiea, it is true, was
extremely beautiful. But unfortunately it happened also to be the
most civilized district. The difference was not perhaps so great or so
apparent, but a difference there certainly was. In the first place, this
was the only district in Tahiti with a Catholic-run primary school
where the teachers were French nuns. It had existed since 1854. More
than half of the local inhabitants, therefore, were Catholics, compared with only 15–20 per cent in other districts, and education there
was better. The head of the French Calvinist mission, bent on com-
peting with the Catholics, had appointed one of the ablest and most
zealous of his missionaries, Louis de Pomaret, instead of leaving a
native pastor in charge, as in other areas.

Exceptionally, too, the authorities in Mataiea were represented in
addition to Chief Tetuanui by a French gendarme. It was he who first
made Gauguin aware of his illusions with regard to Mataiea, by
threatening him, soon after his arrival, with a summons if he persisted
in bathing like Adam in his Eden. Another blessing of civilization, but
one for which both Gauguin and the natives were more grateful, was
the existence of a general store, run by a Chinese who kept open
round the clock and made good money selling preserves, coloured cotton fabrics, pots and pans, knives and fishhooks, on credit and at a
high rate of interest. As in every other district there were also a few
French settlers, though these were better off than most other white
settlers because they grew cane sugar which fetched fairly good prices
from a large rum distillery a few miles to the east of the Protestant
church.

Both Robert Louis Stevenson, who visited Tahiti in 1888, and

Henry Adams, who had just left it, had been more adventurous. But they had been better advised, and had had more helpful and powerful friends, than Gauguin. After travelling through every district on the west and south coasts, including Mataiea, they had both preferred— since they were looking for a genuinely Tahitian environment—to settle in Tautira, at the extreme north-eastern end of Little Tahiti.

On learning that Gauguin wanted to stay, Tetuanui showed him an uninhabited house in the district. It was a good two hundred yards from the shore and the view of the sea was hidden behind trees and bushes. But there was a fine stream, the Vaitara, for bathing in just outside the door, and beyond it a wide plain extending to the foot of the mountains in the interior. The owner of the house was an enterprising Tahitian who had earned good money gathering oranges, and so had been called Anani ("Orange"). Instead of squandering his money like most other Tahitian orange pickers, Anani had followed Tetuanui's example, and buying wood and sheet metal had built himself a two-roomed house with a verandah back and front. But as often happened, and still happens today, Anani when the house was finished thought it too fine to live in and so stayed in his old one, which was a traditionally built bamboo hut. Although this particular housing problem differed essentially from housing problems in other latitudes, Tetuanui was as anxious as any other public authority to solve it. He therefore suggested to Anani that he should rent the empty showpiece to Gauguin. But to the undisguised astonishment of both Tetuanui and Anani, Gauguin insisted on renting the simple bamboo hut instead.[65] After some hesitation, Anani agreed, and moved for the first time into his European-style villa. Whether Gauguin's choice was dictated by aesthetic, sentimental, or practical reasons, it was a very good one; for a bamboo hut with a roof of pandanus or palm leaves is easily the coolest and most comfortable dwelling in a tropical climate.

The bamboo hut was without rooms or partitions, and the sole "furnishing" was a thick layer of dried grass on the earthen floor. Not far away was a kitchen hut, where Anani's wife had done the cooking over an open fire or in a Tahitian earth oven. Much as Gauguin wanted to live in the native fashion, he at least needed some furniture and kitchen utensils. So when he went into Papeete to collect his things, he bought a bed, some chairs and a table, and a set of pots and pans. On the other hand, he no longer considered the dressy Titi a necessary, after seeing some of the women in neighbouring houses, and so he took this opportunity to get rid of her.

There were no villages in Mataiea; the 516 men, women, and children who comprised the total population in 1891 lived in about fifty huts and houses scattered among the palm-trees by the lagoon. Except for Anani and his family, Gauguin had no neighbours within sight, though there were some buildings within hearing. These were the Protestant church, school, and manse, which were so near that on days not too windy he could hear from his hut the hymn-singing in church and the patter of the schoolchildren. Nor was it very far in the other direction—a mile, to be precise—to the Catholic church. Thus every day he awoke and fell asleep to the sound of bell-ringing from two churches.

At first Gauguin was completely happy and contented with the change, and in the short period leading to Christmas painted some twenty pictures which powerfully express his joy in discovery. Most of these pictures depict simple scenes of everyday native life, such as two women plaiting leaf hats on the shore, some hungry children behind a table containing food, young people dancing at night round a bonfire in the palm forest, fishermen inspecting their nets, and muscular fruit-carriers meeting underneath a couple of decorative pandanus or screw-palms. Two are portraits of women belonging to neighbouring families and a few are landscapes, though never quite without human figures, horses, black Tahitian pigs, or lean mongrel dogs. Thus, as my brief sketch of conditions in the country districts, I hope, will have indicated, these paintings depict only the most beautiful, primitive, and idyllic aspects of life in Mataiea. There is no reason, of course, to criticize Gauguin because he painted what he found new and most attractive; clearly that would neither be missionaries, nuns, settlers, churches, plank houses, nor shops. But in view of the widespread misconception that Gauguin's pictures provide a complete panorama of life as it was lived in Tahiti in the 1890s, it is of interest and importance to point out that what he really gives us is only a very limited part of the reality.

It is a well-known fact that Gauguin, unlike such contemporary painters as Toulouse-Lautrec and Degas, was completely uninterested in catching the swift and fleeting movement. He gave best expression to his ideal in this advice to young artists: "Let everything you do carry the imprint of repose and tranquillity. Avoid, therefore, action poses. Every figure should be static." In Tahiti, Gauguin for the first time found people who embodied his stylistic ideal, for indeed the Tahitians have an astonishing ability to sit motionless for hours at a stretch, staring straight into the air at nothing. While many of the poses in Gauguin's pictures seem by Western standards contrived and unnatural, they are in fact very realistic, and hardly a day goes by in Tahiti but I "recognized" scenes from Gauguin's paintings.

On the other hand, he took great liberties with colours, as he had always done, and it was especially by means of his masterly choice of suggestive colours that he succeeded in investing everyday scenes with a mystical and mysterious character which they did not possess in real life. The only difference was one of degree. In his new environment, remote from Europe and European models, he felt even freer, and found it even easier, to go his own ways. Or according to his own statement: "It was so simple to paint things as I saw them, applying a red next to a blue without any special calculation. I was fascinated by golden figures in streams or on the sea-shore. Why did I hesitate to fix this glory of the sun on canvas? Because of the ancient European tradition. Because of the inhibiting fear of a degenerate people!" Gauguin's other piece of advice to his imaginary disciples is equally revealing of his own method of working: "It is very good for the young to have a model, but when they paint they should draw the curtain. It is better to employ a memory picture, for then the work becomes your own." In accordance with this advice, he generally did only sketches "from nature," using these to paint one or more pictures, which he would do in his large bamboo hut with its very good lighting due to the wide interstices in the walls of loosely connected bamboo canes.

To a painter of Gauguin's personality and artistic approach, the everyday life of Mataiea was not in the long run either adequate or satisfying in its range. In fact, he had looked forward to finding fresh inspiration in old Tahitian art, religion, and mythology. In view of the great extent to which the natives had become Europeanized and

---

→

15. *Gauguin's new home in Mataiea on the south coast can be seen between the trees in this picture. The small hut on the left was his kitchen.*

16. *Governor Lacascade (middle of the front row), whom Gauguin accused, among other things, of being a Negro, surrounded by his staff.*

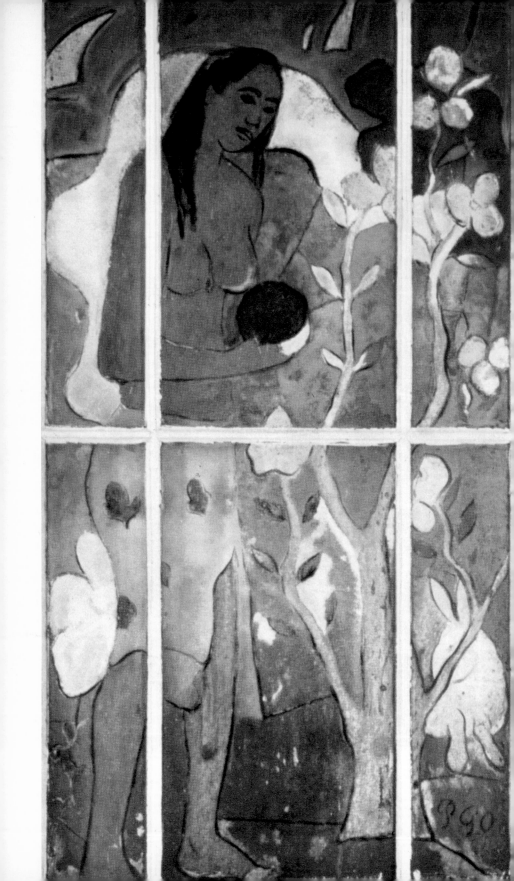

Christianized, it seems no more illogical that, turning from the world of reality for the first time since settling in Mataiea, he should have painted a picture with a biblical theme, depicting the Virgin Mary with the child Jesus, attended by three angels. Gauguin may have got the idea when visiting the nearby Catholic church, for he called it *Ia Orana Maria*—which are the first words of the Tahitian version of the very common prayer *Ave Maria*. All the figures in this picture have brown skins and Tahitian features, yet the chief source of inspiration was not the world he saw around him. As the French art historian Bernard Dorival has recently pointed out, all the figures assume Buddhist poses copied from a photograph of a Javanese temple frieze which Gauguin had obtained in 1889, the year of the exhibition, and is known to have taken with him to Tahiti.[66]

While gradually realizing how woefully little there was left of the ancient Tahitian culture, Gauguin at the same time experienced another deep disappointment. He had tried from the start to find a local girl who would live with him in his hut. Unfortunately, the plan proved very difficult to realize, mainly for the simple reason that there were very few unmarried young women available, Mataiea being a small district with only fifty families. The number of eligible females was further reduced by the fact that the prettiest used to go to Papeete and stay there. Moreover, the girls of Mataeia as a rule married early, with or without blessing of priest and chief. Gauguin solved his problem in the worst possible way, by sending for Titi. The experiment was doomed to failure. Titi was accustomed to the bustling life of the evening dances, the "flesh market," and the Chinese restaurants of Papeete, and loved every bit of it. Mataiea to her was boring, and the local inhabitants country bumpkins. For their part, Gauguin's neighbours found Titi altogether too conceited and affected and would have nothing to do with her. Reduced to Gauguin's company,

←————————————————————————————

17. A caricature of Lacascade, based on the double meaning of the word magot ("baboon" and "treasure"). The treasure alluded to by Gauguin was the fortune the governor was alleged to have amassed by means of bribes.

18. The new version of Eve in paradise, painted by Gauguin on a glass door in the house of his host Anani, who nursed him during his illness. Twenty-five years later it was bought by Somerset Maugham.

she soon made life unendurable for him by her constant chatter and extravagant demands on his attention. Worst of all, she interrupted his work. Finding himself unhappily obliged to choose either work or Titi, he had no hesitation in packing her off to Papeete where she belonged.

Even to find a girl willing now and then unfortunately was a problem. Gauguin's own excuse was that "the few girls in Mataiea without a *tane* (a man or husband) give me such frank, confident, and audacious looks that in fact I am afraid of them. I have also been told that they are sick; smitten by the disease we civilized Europeans have given them in gratitude for their hospitality." Gauguin's fear of becoming ill again was quite understandable. With regard to his alleged coyness with women, a characteristic that had never been very conspicuous in him, this is rather to be interpreted as an equally understandable fear of making himself look ridiculous. The risk was real; young unmarried people formed closed groups, and it was thought highly improper for middle-aged men to share in their mating games. In any case, it is very difficult for a European to preserve his dignity when courting a laughter-loving Tahitian girl, and having to do it in the language of signs.

It was a still greater disappointment to discover, contrary to all his expectations, that it was impossible to live without money even in the country. The authors of the fascinating handbook published by the Colonial Department had admittedly, in a way, been right; hunger and want were unknown among the Tahitians. But, unfortunately, the problem of getting a living was another matter in the case of a European who neither owned any land nor knew anything about Tahitian farming. Nor was Gauguin able to catch delicious fish in the lagoon like the natives; fishing, in Tahiti as elsewhere, being a difficult art which has to be acquired. As for shooting, the only game was wild boar; and this animal lived high up among the fern thickets in the cold, wet, and rugged mountains where hunting called for great endurance, besides well-trained dogs and a sound knowledge of the local geography. It goes without saying that wild-boar hunting was not a sport for a newcomer, least of all one who had recently risen from a sick bed.

The only other means of obtaining food free of charge was to gather wild bananas in the mountains. The Tahitians used to go out every Saturday, as they still do, to gather a supply of red mountain bananas for the following week. (For this reason, Saturday is known as *mahana ma'a*, or "food day"—a name Gauguin used as the title for a painting of a Tahitian carrying a banana, which is now in the Atheneum Museum in Helsinki.)[67] In this case, too, Gauguin was precluded from following the native example, for reasons easily understood by all Europeans who have tried to live in the Tahitian manner. Wild bananas grow so high up in the mountains that to reach them involves hours of arduous climbing. Every bunch weighs about twenty pounds. The roughly marked tracks follow narrow ridges, with precipices on either side. One such mountain excursion is more than enough for an untrained European, even supposing that he escapes breaking his legs and arms or plunging into an abyss on the return journey.

Gauguin realized that even if, by prolonged labour, he eventually succeeded in subsisting like the natives it would leave him no time for painting, and he therefore concluded that it would be futile to try. So reluctantly he solved the problem in an inglorious manner by becoming a regular customer of Aoni, the Chinaman whose simple village store was situated up the road. It goes without saying that Aoni's whole stock consisted of goods for which there was a demand in Mataiea, and that it did not include fruit, vegetables, fresh meat, eggs, or fish, because in these articles everybody except Gauguin was self-supporting. For the same reason there was no other shop or market in Mataiea which sold them. The logical step would seemingly have been to buy fresh meat, fish, and vegetables from the natives. But to trade in food was against their principles; and should a European be ignorant or ill-mannered enough to suggest such a deal, they would rather give it to him. To beg for food—which is what such a request would have amounted to—is a course which a European, and certainly a proud and sensitive European such as Gauguin, will rarely take as it is contrary to *his* ethics.

Gauguin thus found himself in the grotesque situation of living in a fertile and luxuriant country and subsisting almost entirely on tinned foods, white bread, beans, and macaroni. As all these had to be imported they were expensive. A tin of corned beef, for example, cost 2.50–3.50 francs, a kilo of preserved butter 4.50–6.00 francs, a kilo of cheese 1.75–2.00, a kilo of sugar 1.00, a kilo of rice or beans 1.00–1.50, and a kilo of flour 0.50 francs. Fresh milk was unobtainable. This, however, was a beverage Gauguin could do without. His usual drink, claret, cost 0.90 francs a litre, and his favourite, absinth, 7 francs a bottle. Beer sold at 9 francs the dozen bottles in the case of locally brewed beer and 20 francs a dozen when it was imported. Rum, the cheapest spirit, was 2.50 francs a litre.[68]

These unforeseen extras (on top of the inescapable monthly expenses of rent and tobacco) were extremely inconvenient, and by Christmas 1891 Gauguin's funds, which with a little economizing at the outset should have sufficed for a whole year, were almost spent. Disappointingly, he had not received a centime from the art dealers in Paris. Even his most assured source of income, as he believed it to be, the benefit performance at the Théâtre d'Art soon after his departure, had failed him. Instead of the estimated 1,500 francs, the performance had made a paltry 100 francs and this the sponsors had given in full to the other beneficiary, the even more needy Verlaine. The performance had also failed artistically. The principal item in the programme had been Charles Morice's long-awaited *magnum opus*, a three-act play entitled *Chérubin*, which, ironically enough, had for its theme the curse of money. It seemed as if Morice had abandoned himself to grief and despair at the play's hostile reception, for he had failed to write a line in the following six months and Gauguin had heard the shattering news indirectly. It is hardly necessary to add that in the circumstances Morice had been unable to repay the 500 francs borrowed in February 1891.

Luckily for Gauguin, he was on an "official mission" and the governor was therefore obliged to assist him. So at least Gauguin thought. He also knew exactly the sort of assistance he required. On a visit to town one day he had heard that the post of magistrate was vacant in the Marquesas Islands, and he realized at once that his every problem would be solved if he could obtain it. The salary of 500 francs a month would enable him to live not only comfortably but even royally. At the same time the appointment would, at long last, enable him to study the rich and flourishing art of the islands. Before leaving France he had cut out of magazines some reproductions of Marquesan tattoo patterns which had aroused his interest and admiration. Soon after his arrival in Papeete he had seen at the house of the chief of the *gendarmerie* a large collection of beautifully carved Marquesan stone statues, ornaments, battle clubs, and wooden bowls, bearing eloquent testimony to the skill and talent of the natives of these savage islands.[69] The Marquesas had the further important advantage of being so far away from Tahiti as to render the risk of intrusive inspections by senior government officials virtually non-existent.

Gauguin was undoubtedly right in his belief that the office of magistrate would have suited him very well; but it was questionable whether he was suitable for the office. He seems never to have been in any doubt about it himself, but he was less certain of Governor Lacascade's reaction. To make sure, therefore, he decided to start at the top and bring influence to bear on the governor's superiors in the Colonial Department in Paris. Writing to reproach Charles Morice for his long silence, he provided him with a good opportunity to atone for his negligence by paying another call on Clemenceau, as well as other influential persons who might be willing to testify to Gauguin's excellent qualifications for the post of magistrate in the Marquesas Islands. As it happened, Mette was in Paris early in 1892. She had gone there in an effort to collect some of the pictures left by Gauguin with Schuffenecker and the art dealers, hoping to obtain a little recompense for her husband's omission to send her a remittance before his departure for Tahiti. The enterprise proved fairly successful and made Mette feel rather conciliatory. She therefore promised to do what she could to help Morice to pull the right strings when Paul wrote saying, fairly enough, that most men, and particularly Frenchmen, are more easily moved by the pleas of women.

Although he had thus prepared the ground very carefully, he was unfortunately obliged by circumstances (that is to say, his increasingly disastrous lack of money) to approach Governor Lacascade before receiving any reply from Paris. His own magnificent version of the interview is as follows: "An honest magistrate (honest and for that reason doubtless ill-esteemed) became concerned about the difficulties I had in working, and advised me to request the governor for the appointment of magistrate in the Marquesas. He said that this office had long been vacant and had to be filled. The post had previously been held by a first-class incompetent nincompoop, and then by a favourite of the governor, who had appointed him in spite of opposition from the colonial Council and afterwards sent him back to France with an official rank and all the lavish treatment he could wish for. The costs had been covered quite illegally from funds drawn from God knows what source, and accounted for in the budget under heading X.

"It was almost an absolute sinecure, a pastime; and thus I should have been able to continue with my *useful work*. It was really like trying to tempt the Devil. So I declined to apply at once and requested a few days in which to think the matter over. A week later I had to go into Papeete again. The magistrate said to me: 'You must strike while the iron is hot. The public prosecutor has recently spoken to the governor, and the latter replied that he would be glad to be of service to you.'

"Without more ado I crossed the square (this conversation took place in front of Lacascade's palace) and walked into the residence. All the time I felt ashamed to come like a beggar to such a despicable and despised person. (Why is one dependent on despicable people?) The orderly took my card in to the governor and, five minutes later, asked me to go upstairs; the governor was ready to receive me. Sure enough, there was Lacascade, waiting at the top of the stairs for me. As always, he was well pomaded and dressed in a black frock-coat.

" 'Oh, is it you, Monsieur Gauguin?' he said. 'I had not expected to see you. What brings you?'

" 'I have come simply to make a request, Your Excellency. I am, as you know, an artist. I have concluded my studies in Tahiti and would like to go on to the Marquesas in order to continue them there. I have just been *advised* to apply for the long-vacant post of magistrate there.'

" 'My dear Monsieur Gauguin, what wild ideas! Where did you get them? You do not seem to be aware what special qualifications and previous studies are required to fill that delicate position. No, frankly, it is quite impossible to appoint you. It would make a very bad impression.'

"I could not help feeling great admiration for the genius of this humbug, who could conclude, after an examination lasting one minute, that I lacked all the qualifications, as also for the great civility with which he told me what a poor impression I should make as a magistrate."[70]

Little as Gauguin imagined, this sarcastic account clearly reveals his own bitterness and disappointment more than Lacascade's corruption and baseness.

The governor's categorical refusal to help him placed Gauguin in an extremely awkward and embarrassing situation. Even were he to write off immediately to his artist friends in Paris and by some miracle they were able to lend him a little money, it would take four months, at least, to get it. That was the shortest time in which it was possible to obtain a reply to a letter from Europe, and there was no telegraph cable to Tahiti. Even at that the mail service was well administered, letters and money orders being always dispatched by the shortest route via North America. The slowest part of the journey was the

3,660 miles between Tahiti and San Francisco, which was served by sailing vessels of 150–200 tons making the voyage once a month in each direction. The sailing day from San Francisco was the first of each month, from Papeete some time between the twelfth and the fifteenth, and the crossing took at least four weeks, sometimes much longer. The schooner which left Papeete on December 18, 1891, for example, carrying the important letters to Morice and Mette already mentioned, was driven right off course by strong contrary trade winds and took as much as 49 days to beat her way across to San Francisco.[71] This explains why there had been no replies when Gauguin called on Governor Lacascade.

In Mataiea, of course, there were no other available means of earning money. There were a few casual jobs in Papeete, but also plenty of distressed seamen and stranded natives of other islands in French Polynesia anxious to earn their passages home. Gauguin might have found employment as a schooner captain, or a bookkeeper in a business firm, as there was a shortage of people with specialized skills and he was better qualified than most of his compatriots who had gone in for these occupations. But it would have meant giving up his painting for good, and that was the last thing he wanted to do. As time passed and still no money arrived from France, therefore, he was forced to sell one by one all the possessions he could do without. Among the first to go was the immaculate hunting gun.

On top of his other troubles, it cost Gauguin 18 francs every time he went into the detestable town to raise money. Of course he could never afford a carriage of his own, like the settlers. His only means of travelling the thirty miles to the town, therefore, was by the ordinary public coach, which made a daily journey between Papeete and the village of Taravao, ten miles to the east of Mataiea on the isthmus between Great and Little Tahiti. As the journey took five and a half hours, 9 francs, for a single ticket, was not perhaps excessive. But the brave travellers who relied on this conveyance should in fact have been paid several times that amount for aches and pains received; for this is how the journey to Mataiea by coach is described by a contemporary traveller:

"The coach consists of an oblong and fairly wide open box which is furnished with three cross benches, each seating three persons if they sit close. The box is five feet from the ground and rests on three springs, two behind and one in front, the springs in turn resting on the two wheel axles. The front wheels are nearly the size of the rear wheels. On the left or right side, as it pleases the coachman, hangs a heavy and massive letter box, the strong hasps which hold it being frequently shaken off by the jolting of the coach.[72] Originally, a span of four horses had been used, harnessed two and two together, one pair behind the other. Often the rear pair would hold back when the front pair pulled and the coach would be kept waiting until they all agreed, which might take hours. Since people in Tahiti always follow new European trends with intense interest, they have now gone in for three horses, harnessed abreast of each other, and at many points this is all the road will allow room for. The improvement has resulted in a rather more regular service. These efforts finally culminated in the remarkable provision of a canopy, which enabled passengers to refrain from poking one another's eyes out with the ribs of their umbrellas. Guess what the first canopy consisted of! It was the bottom of a bedstead (fortunately, though, without springs), which rested on four poles. As the experiment proved successful, this model was at once adopted.

"The best seat is the one on the front bench next to the driver, because he likes to have only one passenger beside him, and also because the traveller is unencumbered by a lot of luggage under his feet. The rear bench is the right place for sanguine people who need a good shaking-up, which is unavoidable. For when the coach is full the rear springs are often pressed flat, and whenever that happens the passengers on this bench get a jolt, which is transmitted by way of the spine to the brain and thoroughly paralyses it."[73]

To complete the picture of Gauguin's hardships on the road, it is necessary to add that he made these visits to town in the middle of the rainy season. In this season, which in Tahiti lasts roughly from November to April, it is often extremely windy as well; and not even the best bedstead canopy in the world can afford shelter against a strong side wind.

The residents of Papeete, of course, saw no further reason to be friendly or well-disposed to Gauguin, now that the governor had convinced them all by his determined action that the man was a nonentity, in spite of the "official mission" he had so mysteriously procured. There were few exceptions to this rule. The most loyal of his friends proved to be the oldest; that is to say, Lieutenant Jénot and his neighbours, the confectioner Drollet and the male nurse Suhas. The first was ready at all times to put him up, and the others would often invite him to dinner. All three occasionally made him a small loan. Gauguin expressed his gratitude in the only way possible, which was to give them pictures. On one occasion he painted a portrait for the Suhas family. The occasion was an exceptional one; the reception was the same as always. The Suhas had an only child, a boy named Aristide, who when eighteen months old, at the beginning of March 1892, fell ill with some sort of gastritis. In the best—or worst—native tradition his mother went on feeding him. The end was sudden. When Gauguin, who happened to be in town, came "home" on March 5 he found Madame Suhas weeping bitterly at the bedside, where the boy had just died. Thinking, understandably enough, that a portrait of her son would be a reminder and a comfort to her, he at once took out his paints and a canvas, and working at top speed produced an oil painting of the dead Aristide as he lay with his eyes closed and a rosary clutched in his hand. But when he showed the finished picture to the distressed Madame Suhas she burst into an even more violent fit of tears, only interrupted when she sobbed in despair:

"But his face is all yellow. He looks like a Chinaman. . . ."

Gauguin made the polite excuse that the curtains by the death-bed produced a yellowish light, but Madame Suhas refused the gift and her embarrassed husband finally took it away and hid it.[74] In portfolios and studies of Gauguin's works it is stated almost without exception of this painting (which is now in the Kröller-Müller Museum at Otterlo in Holland) that it is a portrait of "Prince Atiti." There has never been such a prince in Tahiti, and in fact "Atiti" is merely the corrupt Tahitian form of the French name Aristide.

In spite of this further public failure as an artist, Gauguin, to his own and everyone else's surprise, was commissioned to paint another portrait only a fortnight later. The enterprising client was a notorious schooner captain by name Charles Arnaud, who like many another French settler could thank the Navy for his free voyage to Tahiti. After his discharge from the service, he had quickly risen to the rank of captain and somehow managed to buy a schooner, the *Mateata*, in which he cruised about the hundred-odd islands of French Polynesia, buying up copra and mother-of-pearl shells and selling poor-quality liquor, cotton fabrics, and flour at highly remunerative prices. Captain Arnaud went under the well-earned nickname of "The White Wolf," and by admiring colleagues was considered to be equally good at cheating the authorities as he was at cheating the natives. It was rumoured, for example, that he had more than once smuggled mother-of-pearl shells, which had been fished in prohibited waters, to America, and smuggled spirits in on the return voyages.

Gauguin had met Captain Arnaud for the first time at the house of their common friend, Sosthène Drollet, and the two ex-naval men, with many tales and recollections to swap, had soon become very good friends. In point of fact, they had much more in common than a long career in the French Navy; for both, in their different ways, were outsiders, contemptuous of established convention. Shortly after his return on March 18 from a trading expedition to the Tuamotu Islands, on which he must have done exceptionally good business, Arnaud commissioned a portrait of his wife and promised to pay 2,500 francs for it.[75] At least that is the sum Gauguin says they agreed on (though he states in one of his letters that it was "only" 2,000 francs). The probable truth is that Arnaud—who as a braggart as well had few masters—made the offer when in convivial mood at the bar and added a nought to impress the bystanders.

A disturbing aspect of the deal, as far as Gauguin was concerned, was that Arnaud planned to leave immediately on another trading expedition to the Mangareva Islands, a thousand miles away, and wisely, as usual, intended taking his pretty wife with him. This meant that the lucrative commission would have to be postponed until they returned some time in May. Gauguin would thus be obliged to live by favour perhaps for another two months, as not even the March mail ship, which arrived on the nineteenth, had brought either money or news from his business manager in Paris.

A few days later he complained bitterly of his troubles in a letter to his friend Paul Sérusier, the only person except Mette who had written to him by this mail: "Your letter arrives at one of those terrible moments in a man's life when he is forced to make a decision, even though he knows that, one way or the other, he will fail. To state my case briefly, I am broke, all because of Morice's perfidy, and the only thing I can do is to return home. But how to do so *without money*? Moreover, I want to stay. My work isn't finished yet; it has just begun and I am sure I can achieve something good. Yes, Morice has let me down; for if he has written twice by registered mail, as he says he has, I should have received the letters—all yours have arrived. And if I had another 500 francs (the 500 Morice owes me) I could manage. I have been promised a woman's portrait in May for 2,500 francs, though unfortunately I can't rely on the promise. But I shall do everything, including the impossible, to hold out till May. If I do get this commission—and the portrait will have to be a flattering one à la Bonnat—and get paid for it, I think I can get one or two more commissions, which would make me a free man again."

The most positive gain from Gauguin's enforced visits to town, paradoxically, was an extension of his restricted knowledge of Tahitian culture. The prosaic manner in which this at last was effected was by discovering and obtaining two well-known ethnological studies. He found one of these in the colony's official yearbook for 1892, which was published early in March and could be purchased for a small sum from the Government printing office. It contained, among ordinances, trade statistics, and civil service lists, a fifty-page article entitled *État de la Société Tahitienne à l'arrivée des Européens*, which had been reproduced from a review published in 1855 and long out of print. The author was a French naval officer named Edmond de Bovis, who in the course of a long period of service in the newly acquired colony during the 1840s had interviewed elderly chiefs and native historians. The article was comparatively reliable, but the picture which it gave of Tahitian culture was perforce very fragmentary. The other publication, one much more difficult to find, Gauguin borrowed from the wealthy businessman and lawyer Auguste Goupil, who also did him the good turn of buying his gun, probably at the same time. This book, in two thick volumes, is well known to anthropologists and historians, and had been published as early as 1837 under the poetic title of *Voyage aux îles du Grand Océan*. Its author was Jacques Antoine Moerenhout, a French businessman and later consul whose surname betrays his Flemish origin. This book, like the other, reconstructed the pre-European culture on the basis of interviews with elderly Tahitians. Moerenhout's stylistic ideal was the prose of Chateaubriand, of whom it has been aptly remarked that he had "great imagination and a brilliant style, combining impassioned eloquence with vivid milieu descriptions." The characterization applies equally to his admirer Moerenhout; and the book's style explains why Gauguin was carried away by it and accepted uncritically all Moerenhout's frequently false interpretations and ill-founded reconstructions of customs he had never personally witnessed.

It is worth mentioning that Gauguin could easily have borrowed from local residents many better works on Tahitian history and culture: for example, *Polynesian Researches*, by William Ellis of the London Missionary Society, who was stationed in the island from

1816 to 1822—not to mention Captain Cook's classical accounts, which contain many detailed descriptions of native customs written from first-hand experience. His imperfect knowledge of English would obviously prevent Gauguin from consulting these books.[76] What is more surprising is that he never discovered that, strangely enough, there were a few natives still alive who knew a good deal about the ancient lore. The most learned of these was Arii Taimai Salmon, the seventy-year-old mother of Queen Marau, who lived with her son, Chief Tati, in the neighbouring district of Papara, within six miles of Gauguin's hut. There is a good reason for Gauguin's ignorance in this case, however, in that Arii Taimai had been married to an Englishman, and both she and her children were very anglophile. Robert Louis Stevenson and Henry Adams had therefore been received with open arms by the whole Salmon family, and been told many of the legends known to Arii Taimai.[77] Gauguin, a poor and unknown Frenchman, would stand little chance of getting invited to a storytelling evening by Arii Taimai, especially since he had settled with Chief Tetuanui, who was Tati Salmon's greatest rival and opponent, in politics as in business.

Gauguin's most fascinating discovery in the works of both Bovis and Moerenhout, not surprisingly, was the accounts of the long-vanished Arioi society, which had practised, more fully perhaps than any other group of people before or since, the ideal of free love. Although every man and woman belonging to this respected society had the right to unrestricted sexual relations with every other, it was as efficiently organized as a religious order—which is exactly what it was, in fact. The Ariois believed themselves apostles of the god Oro, and endeavoured to spread his gospel by every available means. The most ingenious and celebrated of these were undoubtedly the numerous nude dances and exhibitions of sexual techniques with which unfailingly they drew large crowds to their revivalist meetings.

According to the Ariois, their society had been founded by Oro himself while on a visit to the earth, to which he had been lured by Vairaumati, a famous beauty. The first picture which Gauguin painted after his delighted discovery of the zestful Tahitian religion was based on this very episode, and depicts a native woman enthroned, like Vairaumati, in naked majesty on a couch of soft fabrics, with fresh fruit for her enjoyment on a small table standing at her feet. Obviously dissatisfied with the result, he painted another picture identical in theme. The first he called simply *Vairaumati Tei Oa* (which, correctly spelt, should be *Vairaumati Te I'oa*), or "Her Name is Vairaumati." The other, and far more successful, picture he called (reproducing Moerenhout's gross mis-spelling and plural "s") *Te Aa No Areois*, which means "Root of Ariois." The root in question is a coconut germ, which in the picture Vairaumati holds in her left hand. This apparently symbolizes the son whom Vairaumati had by Oro. However, to represent Vairaumati thus, as the principal figure at the founding of the Arioi society, is totally misleading; for according to the legend, the first Arioi was a chief from Raiatea, who was chosen by Oro.[78] By a grotesque chance, which would have appealed to Gauguin, the first picture has ended in the Hermitage Museum in Leningrad, while the second adorns the bar cabinet of an American multi-millionaire.

Gauguin was forcibly recalled from the splendours of the Tahitian past and his own beautiful dream world to the troublesome present at the end of April 1892, with the arrival of the next mail boat. Once more the few letters received did not include a money order. Nor had Captain Arnaud returned from his long cruise. Once more he called on the wealthy Auguste Goupil, who this time had only the humiliating offer of a casual job looking after some second-hand furniture. The furniture was the property of a Chinese country storekeeper in Paea, who had gone bankrupt through allowing the natives too much credit. His belongings had therefore been destrained and an auction announced. Meanwhile, Goupil, who was the liquidator, wanted a reliable caretaker. As nobody else had anything better to offer, Gauguin swallowed his pride and rode out to Paea. At least there was the consolation that he had a good friend there in the person of Gaston Pia the schoolmaster, who indeed gave him board and lodging. Eleven days later his casual job came to an end. The payment was 36 francs 75 centimes, which meant that his situation was very little better.[79]

Captain Arnaud was still not back from his cruise. All Gauguin could do, therefore, was to return to Mataiea and there continue to reflect on his dismal fate. He was worried now by the thought that after June 9 he could no longer count on repatriation at Government expense. That date was the anniversary of his arrival, and under current regulations a French citizen stranded in one of the colonies was entitled to a free passage home if he applied before the end of a year. If he voluntarily stayed longer, however, he ceased to be regarded as a distressed traveller and counted as a permanent settler. As it was far from certain that Arnaud would stick to his impetuous promise and it seemed increasingly unlikely that he would be able to earn enough money by occasional employment to keep himself, it would be no less than a disaster if he missed the chance of repatriation. An early decision had therefore to be made.

Altogether, he had painted about thirty-five pictures. (The exact number cannot be established but in any case can have been only a few more or less than this number.) With careful sifting, this would barely be enough for a one-man show, especially as he was dissatisfied with many of them himself. But he had hundreds of sketches, and with his method of working could continue to paint Tahitian pictures in Paris without difficulty. Indeed, he would no doubt be able to work even better and faster in Paris than in Tahiti, if staying there meant travelling to and fro between Papeete and Mataiea as during the last few months. How little time this had left him for work is shown by the fact that of the thirty-five pictures he had nevertheless succeeded in completing, the great majority had been painted in 1891 and only half a dozen in the first half of 1892. These were weighty considerations, and in the end they persuaded him to apply reluctantly for repatriation.

Besides the pictures which he had painted for exhibition and sale on his return to Paris, he had produced a work for himself alone. There was another respect in which this differed from the rest: it was a glass painting. A better name might perhaps be found for this work, which would avoid suggesting the leaded windows of churches, for this was of much simpler material; it was painted in oils straight on to the panes of the upper half of one of the doors in the house of his landlord Anani.

The unusual idea of creating such a painting on glass probably occurred to Gauguin towards the end of his first year in Tahiti, when he had been taken ill and his friendly host had put him to bed in his comfortable show house, which unlike Gauguin's bamboo hut was fully draught-proof. Though the temperature in Tahiti never falls below 65 degrees Fahrenheit at sea-level, the cold, humid night winds which sweep down from the mountains easily bring on chills and occasionally pneumonia. Anani's precautions were therefore wise. But Gauguin could never remain idle for long at a time, and after a few days, to his host's consternation, he hit upon this original means of satisfying his creative impulse.

At first sight, the glass painting on Anani's door (which Somerset Maugham bought from Anani's son in 1916)[80] seems rather commonplace, depicting merely a bare-bosomed Tahitian girl standing beside a bush (Fig. 18). It at once becomes significant, however, if we compare it with the picture of a nude Eve picking fruit from the tree of knowledge which Gauguin had painted in the autumn of 1890 in Brittany, when he had first begun to dream of his Tahitian paradise (Fig. 6). The glass painting is in fact a close counterpart, the only difference being that the second Eve is rather plumper and has a Tahitian figure. It is safe to say, therefore, that this glass painting, like the earlier painting in oils, reveals what Gauguin still missed and intensely longed for—a woman of his own.

This laboriously produced painting on glass is moving for yet another reason: it is a poor substitute for the sort of work he had long wanted to create. How painfully he himself realized this is evident from the reply which he wrote to Daniel soon after, when de Monfreid had said that he had begun to be interested in French church art: "A simple church window, fascinating because of its clearly differentiated colours and figures, is the most beautiful thing in existence, resembling in a way a piece of music. How bitter to admit that I was born to be an artist craftsman and cannot achieve my vocation. The fact is, I am far more gifted for making stained glass and ceramics, designing furniture, etc., than for painting in the strict meaning of the word."

It was when the mail boat arrived on June 1 and to his grief again brought neither money nor news from Morice that he finally decided to go into town and ask the governor for repatriation. The fact that at that moment his whole fortune amounted to 45 francs of course contributed to his decision.

With a heavy heart he crossed the open dance place opposite the governor's residence, where in the first blissful months he had spent so many happy hours, and entered the large gate on the other side. Mounting the steps which led to the governor's office, he found himself face to face with a thick-set, broad-shouldered man who was none other than Captain Arnaud.[81] The surprise was mutual.

"What the devil's brought you to this tack?" demanded the captain, who had returned two days earlier and evidently had more to answer for.

Gauguin's reply was in the same vein:

"The lousiest thing in the world. I've come to ask the governor for repatriation. I'm on my beam ends with my sails stripped."

Clearly stricken by his conscience, Arnaud promptly produced 400 francs, and pressing the money into Gauguin's palm said:

"Let me have a picture and we're quits."

It looked suspiciously like an attempt to back out of the hasty promise made two months ago. But a moment after Arnaud assured Gauguin that he still wanted him to paint his wife, while at the same time, casually and by the way, reducing the price to half. It also sounded suspicious when he confided that his wife was a little difficult to handle and still had to be persuaded to sit. However, the 400 francs and the vague new promise were enough to make Gauguin abandon his humiliating visit to the governor and decide to stay on in the island for the time being.

To let Arnaud know that he took their agreement seriously himself, Gauguin shortly afterwards gave him a realistic and easy-to-understand picture of two Tahitian girls plaiting hats on the shore of the lagoon.[82] (It is now in the Jeu de Paume annex of the Louvre.) On mature reflection, he took a wise precaution a few days later, intended to spare him from further visits to the detested governor. He wrote the following letter to his patron, the director of the Academy of Arts in Paris:

Tahiti, June 12, 1892

Monsieur le Directeur!

You did me the honour, at my request, to send me on an official mission to Tahiti, in order to study the customs and scenery of this country. I trust that you will appreciate my work on my return. Regardless of how economical one is, the cost of living here in Tahiti is high and travel extremely expensive. I therefore take the liberty, Monsieur le Directeur, to apply for repatriation to France, trusting that you will graciously grant me this favour.

I am, Monsieur le Directeur, your respectful servant,
Paul Gauguin.[83]

It would take four months to get a reply. But if he was as economical as he had just implied, the 400 francs he had received from Captain Arnaud would tide him over these four months. He was accordingly in better spirits than he had been for a long time when by the same post he wrote to Daniel de Monfreid, who had proved his most trustworthy friend, and recounted his adventures. "I still get a good laugh when I think of it," he declared. And he added with gay candour: "It has been like this all my life: I get to the edge of the abyss but never fall in. When (Theo) van Gogh at Goupil's gallery went mad, I thought that I was lost. And yet I came through. It only stimulated me to greater effort. Ah, well! My fate plays a strange game. But I have gained a further respite till my next disaster, and shall start working again."

V

THE MARRIAGE OF KOKE

DISAPPOINTINGLY Gauguin made slow progress at his work. Being
temporarily relieved of money troubles, he now had more time not
only for painting but unhappily for brooding, and sombre thoughts
engaged his mind. Once again he was and felt desperately lonely. After trying in vain to take a hold of himself and concentrate on his
work, he did the best thing possible and went looking for a "wife."
He does not put it like this in the account which he wrote after his
return to France but says that it was to find new themes and fresh
inspiration that he set out, at long last, to discover the more primitive
Tahiti beyond Mataiea. Yet his whole behaviour suggests that the
real impulse was his old desire for a Tahitian Eve.

He started his exploratory journey rather ordinarily by taking the
hated mail coach from Mataiea to its terminus at Taravao, ten
miles to the east on the isthmus between Great and Little Tahiti.
From Taravao two wretched carriage roads led to the smaller peninsula, while a third and even worse road, only a bridle track in fact,
turned back towards Papeete along the rough and rugged east coast of
Great Tahiti. In Taravao there was a Chinese storekeeper, who hired
carriages and horses at high rates to such few townspeople as ventured
in those days so far from Papeete. Fortunately, Gauguin was spared
this expense, as the French gendarme stationed at Taravao generously
lent him one of his riding horses without payment.

Clearly because this was supposed to be the most isolated part of
the island, where the natives must surely have preserved more of their

old customs, Gauguin took the route through the palm forests to the east coast of Great Tahiti. As he soon discovered, the most obvious difference was that there were more bamboo huts and fewer European settlers here than in Mataiea, while the natives were less careful about concealing their nakedness, as there were no resident gendarmes or missionaries to keep an eye on them. Old-fashioned, too, was the hospitality of an unknown native in the district of Fa'-aone, who invited Gauguin to enter his hut for rest and refreshment. As he had ridden five miles over steep hills and forded half-a-dozen fast-flowing rivers, and no doubt was as tired as his poor horse, Gauguin at once accepted the invitation. Inside the hut were several persons who sat or reclined in Tahitian fashion on the dry grass which covered the earth floor. While one woman went to get bread-fruits, wild bananas, and freshwater shrimps, another with understandable curiosity inquired the nature of his errand. Gauguin's non-committal answer was that he was going to Hitia'a, which was the adjoining district. Naturally, the woman wanted to know why he was going there. "I cannot tell," Gauguin declares, "what made me say it," but his reply was:

"To find myself a woman."

This spontaneous revelation of the true nature of his errand came as no surprise to his hosts; what they could not understand was why he was going on such a long journey for it. What is more, it was obviously felt as a slight on their local patriotism that he should seem to prefer the dowdy women of the next wretched district to the celebrated beauties of Fa'aone; for the woman immediately made the following offer:

"I can give you one if you like—my own daughter."

It was in the best Tahitian tradition for parents to arrange a match for their children; and the children usually submitted without complaint as they were seldom required to enter into any binding legal or religious pact and could therefore divorce each other whenever they wanted without formality. What is surprising in this case is that the mother should have offered her daughter to a complete stranger. The probable explanation is that Tahitians then were glad to marry their children to Europeans for the material advantages, as they are still. The women of Fa'aone could not know that Gauguin was neither as rich nor as influential as most other French residents were.

The enterprising mother was strikingly good-looking, and could not have been over forty. There was thus every reason for believing her when she said, in reply to Gauguin's question, that the proposed bride was both young and pretty. In high hopes, therefore, he told her to produce her daughter. After a quarter of an hour she duly presented the girl, who proved, by Tahitian standards, to be of marrying age— namely, thirteen. Teha'amana, as she was called, had like all true Polynesians a broad flat nose, very full lips, and powerful legs and thighs. She also had a catlike grace rare among Western women, a wonderfully soft skin, large expressive eyes, and jet-black hair which reached to her waist. The interval of a quarter of an hour had not been caused by any difficulty about persuading her; on the contrary, she had shown such alacrity as to start packing at once. Her whole trousseau was easily contained in a bundle which she held in her hand.

Gauguin was fascinated by her, and wooed her at once in the following, even by Tahitian standards, quick and matter-of-fact way:

"I greeted her. She smiled and sat down beside me."

" 'You are not afraid of me?' I asked.

" 'No.'

" 'Will you live in my hut for good?'

" 'Yes.'

" 'Have you ever been ill?'

" 'No.'

"That was all."

The most remarkable point about this account is that Gauguin says he conducted the entire conversation in Tahitian. Perhaps it is not too far fetched to explain this considerable linguistic feat by guessing that these were three useful standard questions which he had learnt long ago by heart. At the same time, he must have made some progress during the nine months he had spent in Mataiea. What is more, it is a well-known fact that it is easier to express a few simple ideas in a foreign language than it is to understand the answers. It is not surprising, therefore, that Gauguin should have made a mistake on a point of some importance when he took Teha'amana's parents to say that they came from the far-off Tonga Islands, on the other side of the Pacific. What they meant was that they had come originally from Rarotonga, which is what the Polynesians call the group situated to the east of Tahiti, which on European maps is marked as the Cook Islands. Before settling in Tahiti, they had spent some time on Huahine, another of the Society Islands, and it was there that Teha-'amana had been born.[84] The linguistic and cultural differences between the Cook and the Society Islands are so small, however, that the family had easily adjusted.

Although he had seen only a tiny part of the east coast of the main island and nothing of Little Tahiti, Gauguin now had no further wish to go on with his exploration, because he had found what he had really been looking for. To his great annoyance, however, Teha'-amana's mother and relations failed to understand his desire to be alone with her on their honeymoon, but started to follow them when they left by the shortest route back to Mataiea. Teha'amana, like a well-bred Tahitian wife, also walked behind Gauguin's horse. A few miles to the south, the whole troop came to a halt before another bamboo hut and invited Gauguin to enter. Inside, Teha'-amana to Gauguin's unfeigned astonishment introduced another couple to him as her parents. Before he could gain any explanation of this sudden increase in his family, the new mother-in-law started to interrogate him. Wisely and sensibly, she concluded:

"I want Teha'amana to come back here a week from now. If by then she is not happy, she shall not stay with you."

In his dismay at the disturbing turn which his wedding journey had now taken, Gauguin could not help reproaching the woman who in the first place had given him Teha'amana, unconditionally, as his wife, for having lied to him that she was the girl's mother. The woman, however, strenuously denied the charge, which she could do with a clear conscience. The misunderstanding had arisen because most Tahitians in addition to their real parents had foster-parents, a fact unknown to Gauguin. One of the objects of this custom, which is still widespread, was to strengthen the ties of friendship with rich and powerful families, a matter of particular importance in the case of recent immigrants, as Teha'amana's parents were. Assuming that their new son-in-law would hardly be so ill-mannered and ungracious as not to give each of them a wedding present, the entire party of parents and relatives conducted him, jostling and laughing, to the nearest store. The fact that this was five miles away at Taravao was no obstacle, for they were accustomed to long walks.

The Chinese storekeeper in Taravao also kept a restaurant (his son still does on the same spot), and it occurred to Gauguin now that it would be discourteous in the extreme if he neglected to return the recent hospitality of his in-laws by inviting them to a lavish wedding feast. As a result, his lean purse was even leaner when eventually he was able to board the coach with Teha'amana and take the bumpy road to Mataiea.

"There followed a week in which I was 'childish' as I had never been before," Gauguin says in his published account. "I loved her and told her so, and it brought smiles to her face." This public statement of his love comes strangely from a man so unsentimental as Gauguin. Much more characteristic of him is a later remark: "To make me say 'I love you,' you'll have to break all my teeth in." But there is every reason to believe that he was sincere in saying that he had fallen in love with Teha'amana, for she corresponded exactly to the dream picture he had formed of the Tahitian Eve. It was therefore with great reluctance and anxiety that he parted with her a week later, when she returned to Fa'aone in order to report to her shrewd second mother as promised. Gauguin, too, showed great shrewdness; for to consolidate the good impression he had made before, he gave her a little money and told her to buy a few bottles of rum for her many parents at the Chinese store in Taravao. But no doubt it was chiefly because of her own favourable report that Teha'amana alighted from the coach under the mango-trees near Gauguin's hut a few days later.

Gauguin's life had definitely taken a turn for the better. "I started to work again and my house was an abode of happiness," he says. "In the morning when the sun rose the house was filled with radiance. Teha'amana's face shone like gold, tinging everything with its lustre, and the two of us would go out and refresh ourselves in the nearby stream as simply and naturally as in the Garden of Eden, *fenua nave-nave*. As time passed, Teha'amana grew ever more pliant and affectionate in our day-to-day life. Tahitian *noanoa* imbued me absolutely. The hours and the days slipped by unnoticed. I no longer saw any difference between good and evil. All was beautiful, and all wonderful."

Teha'amana was unquestionably the right woman for him. Not because, by some lucky chance, she happened to be different and was unique in her personality, but on the contrary because she was in every respect an ordinary, typical Tahitian woman. Her need of money and gifts was small, her demand for romantic homage, compliments, and gallantries even smaller. Knowing by her simple upbringing in the country that men's and women's interests and work are different, she never interfered in, or even tried to understand, what Gauguin did, but let him paint in peace. Nor did it matter to her if he never kept regular hours, for she herself had never been used to them. Her habit of sitting quietly for hours at a time merely day-dreaming, when there was nothing else to do, also pleased Gauguin immensely after his wearing experience with the chattering Titi. Her perpetual gaiety and good humour were particularly pleasant and re-freshing to his mind. From a practical point of view, too, there were many advantages in having a woman like Teha'amana about the hut: she took over the washing, cooking, and all the other household chores as a matter of course from the start, and she could procure food by fishing and gathering wild fruits. But what appealed most of all to Gauguin, of course, was her physical charm, her youth, and her uninhibited sensuality. It is revealing that the words he most often used when speaking of Teha'amana were *noanoa* and *navenave*. The former means "fragrance" and bears an allusion to the sweet smell of home-made coconut oil perfumed with gardenia petals, called *monoi*, which, like all Tahitian women, Teha'amana regularly used to rub into her hair and body. *Navenave* is simply the Tahitian word for "sexual enjoyment." Gauguin was certainly right in the ironic com-parison which he drew between this full-blooded Tahitian woman of reality and the sentimental *dame aux camélias* described by Pierre Loti in his famous novel: "She is quite unlike the sweet Rarahu, lis-tening to the guitar-playing of the equally sweet Pierre Loti. Instead she is an Eve, who has shared in the Fall but still is able to walk naked and unashamed, as sensual and as beautiful as on the day of the Creation."

Unlike his predecessor Julien Viaud, who was to become Loti even to posterity, Gauguin had not been given a new name on his marriage, as old Tahitian custom required, because he had carried Teha'amana off in so much haste. Teha'amana kept her old name for the same reason; but instead of calling him Pauro, which is the Tahitian form of Paul, she and everybody else in Mataiea knew him as Koke, which is the nearest a Tahitian can get to pronouncing the difficult French name of Gauguin.

Incidentally, no other name could have suited Gauguin's new wife better than the one she already bore. It is formed from the definite article *te*, the causative particle *ha'a*, and the substantive *mana* ("strength"). It thus means "giver of strength," and as such is fre-quently met with in ancient prayers and mythological tales. What Teha'amana gave to Gauguin, as he gratefully acknowledged, was a new joy in life and new creative energy. No less valuable and impor-tant, she helped him to learn more of the life and customs of his Ta-

hitian neighbours. Because of this renewed and intensified interest in
the world about him, he returned to painting simple scenes of everyday life, as during the first months in Mataiea. At the same time these
new pictures clearly show that, by an inevitable process of identification, he now loved and idealized all Tahitians as intensely as he did
Teha'amana. Gauguin's own proud and conservative opinion was:
"I am rather pleased with my latest works. I feel that I am beginning
to master the character of the South Seas natives, and certainly what
I am doing here has never been done by anyone before, and nothing
like it is known in France. I hope that its newness will be to my advantage. Tahiti is not without charm, and though the women are not
in the literal sense beautiful they have some special fascinating quality, something infinitely mysterious."[85]

The finest picture among those which Gauguin painted during the
first happy months of his honeymoon rightly has Teha'amana for
its chief figure, and it was she who directly inspired it. This is the well-
known *Manao Tupapau*. Gauguin has himself described the genesis
of this picture: "One day I had to go into Papeete. I had promised
to return that same evening. About half-way home the conveyance
broke down, and I had to make the rest of the journey on foot. It was
one o'clock in the morning when I got home. As it happened I was
short of fuel oil in the house, and was about to get in a fresh supply.
The lamp was out and the room in darkness when I entered. I was
alarmed and extremely suspicious. Perhaps the bird had flown."

Striking a match, however, he caught sight of Teha'amana at once.
She was lying naked on the bed, face down, and rigid with fear. Gauguin did what he could to comfort and console, and so well did he
succeed that Teha'amana had soon recovered sufficiently to reproach
him as all Tahitian women will in similar situations:

"Never leave me without a light again. What have you been doing
in town, anyway? I expect you have been with those women who go

---

19. *Gauguin's thirteen-year-old* vahine, *Teha'amana (in his
    travel book* Noa Noa *called* Tehura), *who lived with
    him in Mataiea and Papeete for a year.*
20. *Photographs were a common source of inspiration to
    Gauguin. Charles Spitz, the only professional photog-
    rapher in Papeete, took this picture.*

drinking and dancing in the market and then give themselves to officers, sailors, or anybody."

Gauguin very wisely did not reply, but took her tenderly in his arms.

That he liked the picture less for sentimental reasons than because he thought it more than usually successful artistically is proved by the following analysis, which he recorded in his notebook soon after:

"A young native woman lies flat on her face. Her terror-stricken features are only partially visible. She rests on a bed, which is draped with a blue *pareu* and a cloth of chrome yellow. The reddish-violet background is strewn with flowers resembling electric sparks, and a rather strange figure stands by the bed.

"I am attracted by a form, a movement, and paint them, with no other intention than to do a nude. In this particular state the study is a little indecent. But I want to do a chaste picture, and above all render the native mentality and traditional character.

"As the *pareu* plays such an important part in a native woman's life, I use it as the bottom sheet of the bed. The bark-cloth has to be yellow, both because this colour comes as a surprise to the viewer and because it creates an illusion of a scene lit by a lamp, thus rendering it unnecessary to simulate lamplight. The background must seem a little frightening, for which reason the perfect colour is violet. Thus the musical part of the picture is completed.

"What can a nude Kanaka girl be doing on her bed in a rather risky pose such as this? She can be preparing herself, of course, for love-making. This is an interpretation which answers well to her character, but is an indecent idea which I dislike. If on the other hand she is asleep, the inference is that she has had intercourse, which also suggests something indecent. The only conceivable mood, therefore, is one of fear. But what sort of fear has possessed her? Certainly not the fear shown by Susanna when she was surprised (in the bath) by some old men. There is no such fear in the South Seas.

"No, it is, of course, fear of a *tupapau* (a spirit of the dead). The

21. *The pose of the water-drinking boy made such an appeal to him that he painted this picture,* Pape Moe ("The Mysterious Water"), *which closely resembles it.*

22. *When he ran short of paints and canvas, Gauguin made woodcarvings, including this one of the moon goddess Hina and the earth spirit Fatu.*

Kanakas are much afraid of them and always leave a lamp lit at night. Nobody will venture out on the road when the moon is down without a lamp—and even then nobody will ever go alone. As soon as this idea of a *tupapau* has occurred to me, I concentrate on it and make it the theme of my picture. The nude thus becomes subordinate.

"How does a native woman envisage a spectre? She has never visited a theatre or read novels. When she tries to imagine one, therefore, she has to think of some person she has seen. So my spectre is just like an ordinary little woman stretching out her hand as if to seize the prey. My feeling for the decorative leads me to strew the background with flowers. These are *tupapau* flowers (i.e. phosphorescent lights) and show that the spectres take an interest in us humans. That is the Tahitian belief. The title *Manao Tupapau* ("Thought or Belief and the Spectre") can have two meanings: either she is thinking of the spectre or the spectre is thinking of her.

"Let me sum up. The musical composition: undulating lines, harmonies of orange and blue connected by the secondary colours of yellow and violet, and lit by greenish sparks. The literary theme: the soul of the living woman united with the spirit of the dead. The opposites of night and day.

"I have set down the origin of this picture for those who must always know the why and the wherefore.

"But otherwise it is simply a nude from the South Seas."

Generally speaking, what Gauguin says of the superstition of the Tahitians and their firm belief in spectres is correct. But at the risk of seeming too punctilious it is necessary to take him up on two points. First, no Tahitian would ever imagine a *tupapau* as a harmless and very human little old woman in a bonnet; for they know from cruel experience that all spirits have a ghastly complexion, large bright eyes, and sharp fangs reaching from their upper jaws to their chins. Secondly, the title *Manao Tupapau* cannot have the double meaning Gauguin ascribes to it. Actually, it is made up of two root words without any modifying connective particle, the combination being as meaningless as "Thought Spirit," which in fact is the literal translation. While virtually all the Tahitian titles of Gauguin's pictures are just as faulty in their pidgin construction, mis-spellings, and incorrect syllabic divisions, it is fair to say that their meaning in the great majority of cases is never in doubt. It is hardly Gauguin's fault that many subsequent translations of these titles current in art books and exhibition catalogues are so wide of the mark.

Fascinated as he was by Teha'amana, Gauguin retained his old feelings for Mette and still planned to resume his relations with her and the children. Because the two women were in every respect so unlike, he honestly believed that his relations with the one were of no concern to the other. Also there was the fundamental difference that Gauguin's love of Teha'amana was what may be called anthropological. In other words, it was the sort of love which does not survive transference to another country or a different cultural environment. There was no question of Gauguin remaining permanently in Tahiti; something far more important to him than personal happiness necessitated his return to Europe: namely, his artistic career. Therefore, he never regarded his association with Teha'amana as anything more than a pleasant interlude in his life. But all this was difficult to put into a letter, and so he prudently refrained from mentioning Teha'amana in his correspondence with Mette. The risk of foolish jealousy had also to be taken into account in the case of Teha'amana. So when she asked him who the blonde woman was with the close-cut masculine hair whose photograph was on the wall, Gauguin played for safety and said she was his late wife.

By a curious coincidence, Gauguin's dual attachment was echoed by a popular Tahitian song, called *Oviri* or "The Savage," which must have appealed strongly to him, since he went to the trouble of writing it down in the original language.[86] In translation the verses read:

SOLO:
"Tonight, a fateful starry night,
My heart belongs to two women,
Who both sigh heavily.
My heart sings in tune with the flute.

CHORUS:
What is it he has in mind?
To play wild dance music on the shore?
What is it he has in mind?
Wild, too, are his self-absorbed thoughts.

SOLO:
My heart belongs to two women,
Who have both grown silent now.
My heart sings in tune with the flute.
Now very near, and now far away.

I think of those clear moonlit nights
When the beams shine through the crevices
And both are here in my heart.
My heart sings in tune with the flute,
Now very near, and now far away.

I have travelled far over the ocean
And have told my secret to the astonished sea,
Which roars all round the island—
But never gives an answer.
Now they are far, far away, those two women.
My heart sings in tune with the flute."

Thanks to a series of fortunate occurrences, Mette and Paul Gauguin in fact came closer to each other and their common ambition at this time. This was chiefly due to two Danish artists, Theodor Philipsen and Johan Rohde, who arranged not only for Gauguin to get invited to participate in the second "Free Exhibition of Modern Art," to be held in Copenhagen in the spring of 1893, but for a whole room to be reserved for works by him and van Gogh.[87] If he left Tahiti before the end of the year, he would arrive in Copenhagen just in time to supervise the hanging. Though Copenhagen was an unimportant backwater compared to Paris, it would at least give him the satisfaction of getting his revenge, in his wife's city, before her and all her relations, for the humiliations of eight years earlier. For whatever the critics might say, it was after all an honour and a triumph to take part under these conditions in an exhibition of such importance and significance. What is more, Mette's letter suggested that others in Denmark besides Philipsen and Rohde had begun to appreciate his work. For instance, she had managed to get as much as 1,500 francs for some old Brittany paintings which she had collected in Paris at the beginning of the year. She did not send him any of the money for the simple reason that she needed it even more than he did, but Gauguin was none the less delighted. "At long last a start to the harvest," he wrote to her. "So you see, all hope is not gone. You may remember what I said to you (about one customer bringing another). From every point of view, I am pleased with the result you have achieved with my canvases. First, it has brought some relief to you and assured you of a tranquil summer, and secondly it has given you some confidence. This wretched painting! How often you have cursed it—not the gift but the occupation."[88]

How little importance he really attached to his Tahitian "marriage" is shown by the fact that only three months after finding Teha'amana, he was already prepared to leave her without the least compunction to visit the Marquesas Islands and fittingly round off his stay in the South Seas before returning home by painting some pictures in a native environment really primitive. The tone in which he informs Mette of his plans is remarkably tender: "I am directing all my efforts to acquiring a thousand-franc note. If I succeed I intend to visit the small island of Dominique in the Marquesas, where there are only three Europeans and the islanders have been less spoilt by European civilization. Living here is very expensive and I am ruining my health by not eating. I can get food in the Marquesas, where the price of an ox is three francs or the trouble of hunting it. And I shall work. You ask when I mean to return. I long to see you all again and also need a little rest, but have to be sensible. A journey like this is no light undertaking, like an excursion. It must be complete, so that there will be no need for me to come again. After that my life of roving will be finished. Just have a little more confidence in me, Mette dear; it is for the good of us all."

But a thousand francs was a large sum of money, and when he wrote these lines at the beginning of September 1892 he was "broke" again. Soon after, his stock of canvas gave out. This time, however, he was not so disheartened. He had over fifty pictures in his locker and had practically finished in Tahiti. "I am studying with my eyes and my brain and resting a bit, which won't do me any harm," he wrote to Daniel de Monfreid. "Active people like me need to vegetate occasionally." [89]

However, it was not long before the enforced idleness began, as always, to get on his nerves. Fortunately he had his chisels, and luckily there were plenty of trees in the mountain valleys with dark mahogany-like or bright-red wood. With the same consummate skill with which he had previously painted oils and watercolours, made lithographs and etchings, modelled ceramics and carved marble, he now turned one block of wood after another into awesome Tahitian idols. At least that is what they have been called. Gauguin himself gave them the rather untranslatable name of *bibelots sauvages*, which is far more correct because they are all creatures of his imagination, entirely unconnected with the native art. He also made an extremely realistic mask of Teha'amana. [90] On the back of the block he carved with great justification, since through this girl his dream had now come true, a plastic counterpart to a familiar theme—a nude Eve in the same pose as his earlier paintings on canvas and glass.

Strangely, Gauguin succeeded in selling some of his woodcarvings in Papeete. This surprising success was in no way due to a sudden discovery by the local traders that they had a great artist in their midst. Their only reason for buying the sculptures after previously rejecting the paintings must have been that they regarded them as curios, for which, then as now, there was always a market, whether they were genuine or false, old or new. It is no less easy to understand why he sold only a few carvings. They were too artistic to find the approval of the great majority of tourists and other customers at the local curio shops, who always without fail chose, as they still do, the trash and the fake.

By turning to wood-carving and slackening his pace, Gauguin found more time to help Teha'amana obtain food. It was the right season, for deep-sea fishing, a pursuit traditionally reserved to men, begins every year in October. Gauguin's account of his first fishing expedition is full of apt observations conveyed in the vivid manner one might expect of an artist, and is interesting for other reasons as well:

"For about a fortnight, the flies which previously had been rare, had been appearing in swarms and were getting unbearable. This only pleased the Maoris, for it meant that the bonitos and tunny fish would soon be coming in from the open sea. They therefore began to look to the strength of their nets and hooks. Women and children helped to drag nets—or rather, long lines of palm-leaves—along the shore and across the coral sea-bed between the beach and the reef. In this way they manage to catch a kind of small fish of which the tunny are very fond.

"Then one day the men launched a large double canoe, which in the prow had a long rod that could be raised quickly by means of two ropes attached to the stern. With this gear the fish can be rapidly pulled up and hauled aboard when it bites. Putting off through a gap in the reef, we proceeded far out to sea. A turtle watched us go by. We arrived at a spot where the sea is very deep. This is known as the tunny hole, because it is down there in the depths that the tunny spend the night sleeping, out of reach of sharks. A cloud of sea-birds were keeping a look-out for tunny, and whenever a fish surfaced would dive and rise again with a strip of flesh in their beaks. We were in the midst of a bloodbath. . . .

"The skipper of the boat deputed one of the crew to cast the hook.

Time passed; not a tunny would bite. Another man was designated. Now there was a bite by a magnificent fish which bent the rod. From the stern four strong arms tightened the rope which was attached to the rod, and the tunny began to approach the surface. At that moment a shark pounced on the prey. A few snaps of its jaws and all that remained for us on board the boat was the head. The fishing had started badly.

"It was my turn to try now, and soon we caught a big tunny. A few sharp blows on the head with a stick were enough to make the irridescent, glittering body writhe in its death throes. We were equally successful a second time. There could be no doubt about it; the Frenchman had brought good luck. They all began shouting that I was a good fellow; and proud to be praised I did not contradict them.

"We fished until evening. By the time that our supply of bait began to run out, the sun had already set the horizon ablaze with red. We prepared to return home. Ten fine tunny fish overloaded the canoe. While the men were busy arranging the gear, I asked a youth why they had all laughed and whispered so much together when my two tunny fish were hauled aboard. He would not reply; but knowing a Maori's weak resistance when pressed, I persisted. He then told me that when the hook is fixed in the fish's lower jaw it means that your *vahine* has been unfaithful to you while you have been away fishing. I smiled sceptically.

"We returned. Night falls fast in the tropics. Twenty-two strong arms dipped their paddles into the sea at once, the strokes called by excited shouts. The phosphor in our wake gleamed like snow, and I had the feeling of taking part in a wild race, watched only by mysterious creatures of the deep and the shoals of inquisitive fish which followed us and from time to time broke the surface.

"After two hours of paddling, we arrived at the gap in the reef, where the surf breaks with great force. It is a dangerous place to pass because of the sill formed by the reef. You have therefore to steer your way in with the canoe's prow head on to the breakers. The natives are skilful, but it was not without some sensation of fear that I watched their manoeuvres, which, however, they performed very well. The shore ahead was illumined by moving lights, consisting of huge torches made from dried palm-leaves. In this flood of light, which lit up both sea and land, we were awaited by our families. While some sat motionless, others, chiefly the children, ran to and fro, hopping about and crying shrilly without pause. A vigorous spurt and the canoe slid high up on to the sandy beach.

"The whole catch was now spread out on the sand. The skipper shared it out in equal portions among those who had taken part either in fishing for the large fish or catching the small bait, without distinction of man, woman, or child. There were thirty-seven portions.

"My *vahine* was not slow to seize an axe, chop some wood, and make a fire. Meanwhile, I cleaned myself up and put on some warm clothes as protection against the cold night. My fish was roasted, but she ate hers raw. After a thousand questions about the fishing, it was time for bed. I was burning to ask her a certain question. Would it be of any use? At last I asked it:

" 'Have you been good?'

" 'Yes.'

" 'And did you have a nice lover today?'

" 'I have not had a lover.'

" 'You are lying. The fish has spoken.'

"Her face took on an expression I had never before seen there. She appeared to be praying. . . . Then she came to me and, resigned and with tears in her eyes, said:

" 'You must beat me; strike me hard.'

"But her resigned face and wonderful body reminded me of a perfect statue, and I felt that were I to lay hands on such a masterpiece of creation I should be for ever damned. She was a beautiful, golden-yellow flower to me, full of fragrant Tahitian *noa noa*, and I worshipped her as an artist and a man.

" 'Beat me, I tell you. Otherwise you will bear me a grudge for a long time, and the grudge will make you ill.'

"Instead I embraced her. After a tropical night came a radiant morning. Mother-in-law brought us some fresh coconuts. She looked quizzically at Teha'amana. She knew her secret. Slily she said:

" 'You went fishing yesterday. Did all go well?'

"I replied:

" 'I hope I can soon go on another fishing trip.' "

Both Gauguin and the tunny spoke the truth. In the first place, there was, and still is, a deep-seated superstition of the kind referred to, which goes back to pre-European times when complete abstinence was required of men and women, for magical reasons, both before and during a fishing expedition.[91] Secondly, Teha'amana had many lovers, whom she used to meet in the thickets of the palm forest when

Gauguin was under the impression that she was gathering food or gossiping with friends.[92] That the honeymoon was now definitely over is also indicated by another detail in Gauguin's narrative. I refer, of course, to the presence of his mother-in-law in the hut. There may even have been more than one mother-in-law there.

Although he had realized by this time that there were certain drawbacks to a native-style marriage, Gauguin was the first to admit that Teha'amana remained remarkably unaffected and uncomplaining when she became pregnant, as she soon did. There were good reasons why she did not take the mishap as seriously as, for example, the unfortunate seamstress Juliette had done in Paris. It was the simple truth, and not, as it might seem to be, a case of cynical wishful thinking, when Gauguin declared that "here a child is always welcome, and is often stipulated in advance by the relations. In fact, they will actually compete in order to become the adoptive parents, a child being in Tahiti the best possible gift."[93] But if, on the other hand, a pleasure-loving Tahitian girl thinks that pregnancy will keep her too long from sharing in the gay parties and mating dances, then everyone —except missionaries and gendarmes—will regard it as her private affair should she prefer an abortion. Teha'amana seems to have decided on the latter course, for she never gave birth to this child.

As calculated, Gauguin at the beginning of November received a reply to the application for repatriation which he had posted to Paris four and a half months earlier. It was, however, an indirect one; for, in accordance with protocol, it was addressed to the governor, who informed Gauguin soon after the arrival of the mail-boat and requested him to attend at the Government office in Papeete. At the same time, the miracle he had waited sixteen weary months for came to pass: he received a small sum from Paris in payment of a picture which had been sold. The person who sent it was neither Morice nor either of the art dealers, Portier and Joyant, who represented him; it was Daniel de Monfreid, who, assisted by Maillol, had persuaded a British collector, Archibald Aspol, to buy an old Breton picture for 300 francs. It was enough to pay for a short visit to the Marquesas. But on reflection, Gauguin decided to abandon this plan and return as quickly as possible to France, by a ship which was due to leave Papeete in January 1893.

The main reason for this change of plans was the poor state of his health. "I have suddenly aged quite astonishingly," he confided anxiously to his friend Daniel. His heart had also begun to trouble him again. The one reassuring circumstance was that the violent palpitations were not succeeded by haemorrhages, as they had been the year before. Gauguin himself blamed the "insipid and deficient" native food he had been eating since Teha'amana had taken over the house work. He was not the first Frenchman to cherish a blind faith in the superiority, therapeutic as well as gastronomic, of the French *cuisine*, and to suffer grievously in Tahiti from a shortage of *bifteck* and *pommes frites*. Yet neither he nor anyone else has satisfactorily explained why the natives were so wonderfully fit and healthy and possessed dazzlingly perfect teeth when Tahiti was discovered, though they lived chiefly on vegetables, fruit, and fish, and why they grew sickly and toothless when they began to eat European food. It should also be remembered that Gauguin, for financial reasons, had been unusually abstemious in the use of spirits, wine, tobacco, and coffee for a whole year, and moreover had lived an open-air life. His health should thus have been better rather than worse. The only possible reason why it was just the reverse must therefore have been that unfortunately neither the mustard plasters nor the cupping in the hospital at Papeete the year before can have cured the syphilitic infection from which he was suffering.

Believing in the correctness of his own diagnosis, he spent his remittance on a plentiful supply of tinned goods and other civilized food, plus a no less necessary roll of best-quality copra sacking, which would enable him to paint some pictures he had long had in mind. As there was an interval of at least two months before his departure, he concentrated on the pictures and did not trouble to go to town and call on the governor until the beginning of December. Governor Lacascade, instead of handing him a free ticket and with a wry smile wishing him a pleasant voyage, launched into a lengthy explanation. Slowly it dawned on the miserable Gauguin that he had completely misinterpreted the situation. True, the Colonial Department had requested the governor to furnish him with a free passage home. But, Lacascade explained, a request was not an order. Everything depended on the availability of the necessary funds. Having carefully considered the matter, he had been driven to the conclusion that unfortunately the colony lacked the means with which to defray the costs of Gauguin's repatriation. Unknown to Gauguin, a new director had been appointed at the Academy of Art since he had left Paris. Being reluctant to spend his allocations on an enterprise so manifestly wasteful, he had tried to evade further responsibility for the troublesome *protégé* he had inherited from his predecessor by passing Gauguin's application on to the Colonial Department. There they had followed the same procedure, and passed the application on to Tahiti.[94] Given a little good will, the governor should certainly have been able to provide the trifling amount in question. But Lacascade was far from well disposed towards Gauguin, for, since their earlier clash, Gauguin had maliciously caricatured him in a number of drawings which were well known in Papeete (a specimen is reproduced as Fig. 16). Gauguin had no choice but to swallow his rage and politely request the governor to send the application back through the same slow official channels, in the hope that the new director of the Academy would have more sympathy with him next time.

Gauguin had the consolation that the majority of the French settlers now hated Governor Lacascade as intensely as he did, and listened readily to the recital of his grievances. The swing in public opinion had been brought about by a decree, issued a few months before, which had suddenly imposed a tariff on all imports, and for which, rightly or wrongly, the settlers had held Lacascade responsible. The governor had in vain sought to justify the measure by pointing out that there were neither income nor property taxes in Tahiti, though the administration and policing of the colony, its health service, road and bridge constructions, harbour facilities, and so on, cost over half a million francs a year, which so far had been included in the French metropolitan budget. Indignantly, the settlers retorted that they paid twenty-four francs a year for the upkeep of roads and nearly the same amount in sundry stamp duties, angrily declaring that the unnecessary new tariff could be dispensed with by cutting administrative costs and shipping useless and superfluous colonial officials back to France. Why not begin, for example, with Lacascade himself? The following editorial in one of the local newspapers is typical of the attacks that were being made on Lacascade at the time:

"When in biblical times God wanted to punish His chosen people, He inflicted on them the disasters we know as the ten plagues of Egypt.

"Could this be the reason why the Colonial Department has sent and left with us Monsieur Lacascade and his *alter ego*, Monsieur Ours, who have once more blatantly demonstrated their indifference by certain recent statements which are manifestly scandalous?

"Since the motherland has clearly desired to punish us by allowing officials whom everyone would like to see the back of to stay on in their posts, the question which arises is what crime have we committed?

"Our patience is getting exhausted and we have already suffered enough; for as one of our friends has wittily observed, palm bugs, caterpillars, cockroaches, wasps, rats, mice, floods, tidal waves, hurricanes and cyclones, these plagues are not even annual, whereas *administrative misrule* is a disaster of almost daily occurrence which threatens to ruin the colony and finally lead to the death of us poor people."[95]

While these acrimonious attacks on Lacascade must have given Gauguin a good deal of malicious pleasure, the fact remains that ultimately they were the main reason why the governor had so categorically refused to help him. Under vicious attack from all his enemies, Lacascade was afraid of giving them further grounds for criticism, which he would obviously have done had he spent public money on repatriating an individual whom the settlers regarded as a worthless dauber.

Of the 300 francs which Gauguin had received a month earlier, only 150 remained. To maintain himself during the four or five months he now had to stay in Tahiti was a serious enough problem in itself. But his position would be disastrous if the reply to his second application when it arrived was another refusal. In his distress, he wrote an anxious letter to Paul Sérusier, in which he asked him to get the right people to put in a word on his behalf at the Academy. Had Charles Morice been rather more forthcoming, Gauguin would have preferred to approach that more skilled and experienced contact. But Morice had just demonstrated his slackness by filling his first letter for eighteen months with complaints about Gauguin's silence! Realizing even as he wrote that Sérusier was scarcely equal to the task, Gauguin followed up with a letter by the same mail to Schuffenecker, asking for a loan which would enable him if necessary to pay for his own passage. In his desperation he went to the extent of offering an interest of twenty per cent. Finally, he wrote both to Joyant and Portier for more information than the lax Morice had provided. Perhaps, after all, there was a little money due to him there?

The saddest result of the distressing postponement of his return to Europe for another four months was that it would now be quite impossible to get there in time for the important exhibition in Copenhagen. The canvases could of course be sent as parcels, but postage was expensive and the state they would arrive in uncertain. Helpful as ever, Lieutenant Jénot sprang to the rescue by arranging for another officer, named Audoye, to take a small number of canvases with him when he returned to France at the completion of his term of service in the colony.[96] The drastic limitation which this involved, while it annoyed Gauguin, had the extremely interesting result of providing us with certain knowledge as to which of the fifty pictures painted up to that time he regarded as the most successful and representative. They were the following eight (the present owners being given in brackets):

Parau Parau (J. H. Whitney, New York)
Eaha Oe Feii (The Hermitage, Leningrad)
Manao Tupapau (C. Goodyear, New York)
Parahi Te Marae (R. Meyer de Schauensee, Devon, USA)
Te Faaturuma (Art Museum, Worcester, USA)
Te Raau Rahi (The Art Institute of Chicago)
I Raro Te Oviri (Institute of Art, Minneapolis)
Te Fare Maorie (M. Roniger, Switzerland)

The priorities of these eight pictures are clearly indicated by the prices which Gauguin fixed at the same time. It comes as no surprise to note that he thought *Manao Tupapau* worth more than twice as much as the rest: namely, 2,000 francs. Next in order came *Eaha Oe Feii*, 800 francs, and *Parahi Te Marae*, 700 francs while for each of the rest he asked 600 francs.

Just as at the beginning of 1892, when he had also suffered from the malignity and indifference of the society in which he lived, Gauguin again in this new difficult period turned to the past, and started on a new series of pictures based on themes from Tahitian religion and mythology. As before, his sources were the books of Bovis and Moerenhout, though by now he had probably returned the borrowed copy of the latter, after copying out the most interesting passages in a notebook, which he inscribed *Ancien culte mahorie*. (Of all the many misspellings of the word *maori* by Gauguin this easily takes the prize.) The Tahitian legend which fascinated him most on this occasion was one about the moon goddess Hina, who, being the only female divinity in the Polynesian Parnassus, had perforce to serve as the mother of practically all the gods. Since to the Polynesians there was no essential difference between gods and men, she was also believed to be the ancestral mother of the human race. As to which of the gods was the supreme father and original begetter, there was no general agreement among the various tribes, of whom the Tahitians alone allotted the important role to Ta'aroa. Moerenhout's brief passage about Hina is, if anything, even more confused and incomplete than his accounts of the other Tahitian gods, being confined almost entirely to a fragment of an apocryphal legend telling how the moon goddess tried to persuade her son, the earth genie Fatu, to bestow eternal life upon human beings.[97]

These deficiencies, however, were of little concern to Gauguin, who was looking primarily for a pictorial symbol of the earthly paradise he imagined Tahiti to have been in pre-European times. There was no book—by Moerenhout, Bovis, or any other author—which contained a picture of Hina, for the simple reason that the Tahitians, unlike, say, the Greeks, never created realistic individualized images of their gods. Gauguin had therefore to rely on his own superb imagination when he embarked on a series of paintings of Tahitians dancing round a gigantic massive statue of Hina in a peaceful arcadian landscape (Fig. 24). Possibly a few lines in Moerenhout's book about the giant statues of Easter Island, which Gauguin copied in his manuscript *Ancien culte mahorie*, provided the initial inspiration. But for a real model of the huge stone image in such pictures as *Hina Maruru*, *Matamua*, and *Pastorales Tahitiennes*, we have to look far beyond the South Seas, for more than anything else it resembles a Buddha or an enthroned Egyptian pharaoh.

The supreme liberty with which Gauguin borrowed, reshaped, and fused elements from the most diverse sources is particularly well illustrated in another picture with a mythological theme painted at this time: the little-known *Pape Moe* (now in the Bührle Collection at Zürich). Gauguin translates the title as "The Mysterious Water," apparently in allusion to the well-known Tahitian and Polynesian myth of the magic water (actually flood of light) of the god Tane, which among other things imparts new life to Hina, enabling her (i.e. the moon) to be reborn every month. The picture, which shows a young Tahitian boy (or girl) in a magical landscape, quenching his thirst from a jet of water (Fig. 21), has certainly an aura of mystery which justifies the title. But it can easily be demonstrated that Gauguin copied the entire scene, down to the smallest details, from a photograph (Fig. 20) taken by Charles Spitz, a French Alsatian businessman of Papeete, who was so skilled as a photographer that he had won an award for views used in decorating the Tahitian section of the Universal Exhibition of 1889.[98]

Even the most realistic of the pictures which Gauguin painted in this period, the farewell portrait of Teha'amana, dated 1893 (Fig. 19), contains many mythological and anthropological features. As a reward for posing so often and so patiently, and in all manner of positions and strange attire, she was allowed on this occasion to sit in the way every Tahitian woman likes to be portrayed, seated stiffly on the edge of a chair, full face and in her best churchgoing clothes. Yet Gauguin managed to include in the background not only a pattern composed with characters in Easter Island script (which he had doubtless seen in the museum of the Catholic mission in Papeete, where there were several specimens of this writing), but also a pair of spectral heads of his own design and a Hindu female deity. In fact, the sole Tahitian element in the picture is the plaited palm-leaf fan which Teha'amana is holding in her left hand. This may well be taken as a mark of gratitude to her by Gauguin, because in former times a fan of this kind was the principal attribute of a great beauty. The Tahitian title of this picture, *Merahi Metua No Teha'amana*, clearly visible in the bottom left-hand corner, has given rise to more misunderstanding and misinterpretation than the titles of most of Gauguin's other paintings, which is saying a good deal. Even the least inaccurate rendering of the title, "Teha'amana has many ancestors," does little to make its meaning clear. The correct translation is "Teha'amana has many parents." At first sight this may not seem to carry much more sense; but if we bear in mind the manner in which Gauguin obtained her, and of how he won the favour of two mothers-in-law, then the title becomes not only intelligible but very witty.

With the help of this certainly identifiable portrait (which all who knew Teha'amana say is an excellent likeness) it is tempting to try to determine which other pictures she posed for. But the result of such an investigation, as might be expected, is both unsatisfactory and unreliable, because Gauguin was seldom interested in producing photographically accurate portraits. The only exceptions, indeed, seem to be this very picture and the wooden mask of Teha'amana, previously mentioned, which tally feature by feature. It is characteristic of this sort of guessing game, incidentally, that the number of pictures in which scholars have believed they have identified Gauguin's *vahine* corresponds to the number of all the female pictures painted by him during the whole of his first period in Tahiti.

The harvest and fishing season enabled Gauguin to make his 150 francs last him for over two months, and so to finish his work. By February 1893, when his supply of canvas ran out, he had done in all "sixty-six more or less successful canvases and some ultra-savage carvings," which he justifiably regarded as "enough for one man." His return to the world of reality on this occasion proved a great shock, for it was at this time that he received from one of the Paris art dealers the account which he had requested. It showed that Joyant, of Boussod et Valadon, had sold several pictures as long ago as May 1891, when Gauguin was still on the way to Tahiti, and that his agent, Morice, had drawn the proceeds, 853.25 francs. It was only too obvious that he had spent it all.

Gauguin, with every justification, called Morice a bare-faced liar and thief, and vowed that he would have no mercy on the scoundrel when he returned to Paris. The same mail brought him a gloomy letter from Mette, who as usual took a pessimistic view of things, though she had succeeded in selling another picture. Gauguin began his reply in a manner which was hardly calculated to cheer her up: "And what am I to say? I have now lived for nine years without seeing my family, without a home, often without anything to eat. For two months I have had to manage without spending anything at all on food. Day in and day out I live on *maiore*, an insipid fruit like bread, and a glass of water. I can't even treat myself to a cup of tea, owing to the expense of sugar. I endure it all stoically, though it is affecting my health, and my eyesight, on which I am dependent, is failing rapidly. If you had sent me the money you got for the last picture you would have saved my life."[99] At the same time he atoned for all his faults, including the blatant lies about his terrible sufferings, by agreeing to a sacrifice of the sort Mette would most appreciate. This is how he described his surprising new plans: "What I want is not easy to get but is not impossible. In the Paris schools there are a number of drawing inspectors. They have little to do and are well paid at the rate of 10,000 francs a year. Reganey, who once had an official mission, is an inspector now. So I am asking friends in Paris to do what they can to get me such a post. Puvis de Chavannes, who is a member of the Institute (which appoints the inspectors), is favourably disposed to me. They may write and ask you to see Pasteur's son, who is on very good terms with Bonnat. With these members of the Institute on your side, there should be a chance. I have no illusions, but the thing must be tried and I hope you will do all you can in this matter. It would mean, my dear Mette, being happily reunited, you and I and the children, with assurance for our old age. No more uncertainty."

Probably, Mette found these plans rather less promising and practicable than her husband did, especially as their realization chiefly depended on her.

To dispel the gloom and while away the final month of waiting, Gauguin began to jot down his thoughts, ideas, and recollections in a notebook. He aptly described these jottings as "scattered notes, like dreams without logical arrangement, and like life itself without uniformity." Of course many of the notes had to do with art, including the following piece of advice, which is at the same time an excellent statement of his own methods of working:

"Never try unduly to perfect your work. The first impression is a delicate one, and the results fall off if you go on trying to improve the details. That way you cool the seething blood-red lava into lifeless stone. Throw such stone away without scruple, though it looks like a ruby."

In other notes he summarized his views on love and sexual relations. Two typical aphorisms clearly project his experiences in Tahiti:

"Women want their liberty. They have a right to it. But they are not prevented from getting it by men. The day they cease to site their virtue below their navels they will be free. And perhaps healthier."

*   *   *

"In Europe men and women have intercourse because they love each other. In the South Seas they love each other because they have had intercourse. Who is right?"

Even more revealing of his own situation and character are the following reflections:

"Isn't it bad management to sacrifice everything for the children, and doesn't it lead the nation to sacrifice those achievements which its most gifted and energetic members could attain? A man sacrifices himself for his children, who when they grow up sacrifice themselves for *their* children. And so on. As a result everybody sacrifices himself. And the lunacy knows no end."

*   *   *

"The man who is always confident only suffers when his hopes come to nothing. The man who is always despairing suffers constantly because of this very trait. The same with the man who is always pessimistic."

As both a former stockbroker's assistant and an ex-canal-digger, Gauguin not unnaturally took an interest in the Panama scandal, which was fully reported in the Papeete newspapers in March 1893, and for once placed on record his somewhat anarchistic ideas on politics and economics:

"Apropos Panama, what a disaster! What a lot of people ruined, etc.

"I do not share this opinion, and consider that if the scandal had not taken place one like it would have had to be invented. The share-holders, they say, are to be pitied. All right. But poor people who un-successfully try to get work, are they not also to be pitied?

"Most shareholders are mean, not to say miserly, individuals; if not, they belong to the very large body of speculators who concern themselves very little with what happens to those who risk their lives travelling far from home and toiling in an unhealthy country.

"Ministers, members of the Chamber of Deputies, and financiers, they have all filled their pockets with their dishonest gains. Yet at the same time they have put this money back into circulation and pro-vided work for others. Can one be sure that the money invested by the shareholders has been honestly earned?

"Still, business has been furthered, many orders placed, and many fees paid; and there, across the ocean, the canal has really been started. All this is a worthwhile achievement. With regard to the morals. . . .

"For morals to be respected, it would be better to abolish the Bourse and speculators. But the Bourse and speculators are the foun-dations of our modern financial system. So why do we take such a poor view of a fool who spends what he has stolen on buying a ribbon?"

* * *

"My political opinion? I have none. But there is universal suffrage, so I suppose I ought to have one.

"I am a republican, because I believe in social peace. Most people in France are undoubtedly republican. I am, then, a republican. Actually, so few people care for the things that are great and sublime that we need a democratic government.

"Long live democracy! There is nothing any better. . . .

"But I am for sublimity, beauty, taste, and the old motto 'Noblesse oblige.' Also I am for the good manners and indeed the courtesy of Louis XIV.

"Thus (instinctively and not knowing why) I am an aristocrat—as an artist. Art is a minority interest and must therefore be aristocratic. Incidentally, the only people to patronize art have been the aristocracy, who have commissioned great works of art. Whether they have done so spontaneously, from a sense of duty or perhaps out of vanity, is of no consequence. Kings and popes have treated artists almost as equals.

"Democrats, bankers, ministers, art critics put on patronizing airs but patronize nobody. On the contrary, they haggle like customers at a fish market. And you would have an artist be a republican!

"That is all my political opinion. I believe that every member of society has the right to live and enjoy a standard of living in accordance with his labour. An artist cannot live. Therefore, society is badly and criminally organized.

"It may be argued that the artist does work which is useless. A workman, a factory-owner, anybody who makes something for the community which has a value in terms of money, enriches the nation. I would even go further and say that only he enriches the nation. What is valuable in his work remains even after his death. Which is certainly not the case with the money-broker. A hundred francs, say, circulates in a number of currencies. The money-broker makes the same sum change owners a number of times and then end up in his own pocket. The nation still owns a hundred francs and not a centime more. An artist, on the contrary, is like a workman; if he makes a picture which is worth, say, ten francs, the nation is ten francs the richer. Yet he is supposed to be a useless creature!

"Good God, what calculations!"

Gauguin's little book of confessions has been rather inaptly called *Cahier pour Aline*, because it is inscribed with a dedication to his daughter in which he says: "These ruminations are reflections of myself. She, too, is a savage; she will understand me. . . . But will my thoughts be of use to her? I know that she loves and respects her father. . . . At any rate, Aline, thank God, has a head and a heart sufficiently uplifted not to be scared and corrupted by contact with the demoniacal brain nature has given me." Yet it is doubtful whether Gauguin meant to send Aline these notes, which were hardly suitable for or even intelligible to a conventionally educated girl of fifteen, and in fact he never did send them to her. The surprising dedication may therefore be interpreted simply as yet another moving indication of Gauguin's intense nostalgia for his family.

The first mail-boat which could possibly have brought a reply from Paris to his new request for repatriation arrived on March 5 but without any such reply, though unexpectedly there was a remittance of 300 francs, as before from Daniel Monfreid, in payment of a Breton picture which he had succeeded in selling to the same British collector. The blunting of a man's perceptions which can result from the continued disappointment of his hopes is shown by Gauguin's acknowledgement, which merely said: "Your 300 francs comes most conveniently, at a time when I am right out of money and have no means of earning any."

On March 21, the next mail-boat anchored in the harbour of Papeete after crossing from San Francisco in twenty-two days, the fastest passage in living memory. Once more the ship brought no news either from the Academy or from the Colonial Department; but again, as at the beginning of the month, Gauguin's scant mail included a pleasant surprise. Mette had sent him the large amount of 700 francs from the proceeds of pictures sold in the recent months.[100] The only thought which detracted from the pleasure was that had he received the money only a little earlier he could have paid a visit to the Marquesas, which, as he told Mette and Daniel, would have been "immensely useful," leading to even better and more interesting work.

Shortly afterwards, the authorities announced the departure of a troop transport, the *Durance*, for Noumea on May 1. This fitted in with his alternative and far more sensible plan of returning as soon as possible to France, which after all dominated his thoughts at this time. Even if the next mail-boat brought news of the rejection of his application for repatriation, he would now be able to go home, because the steerage passage, less the reduction to which he was entitled, cost only half the thousand francs he had just received. Once again, therefore, Gauguin, to quote his own words of the year before, had been saved on the brink of the abyss at the last moment.

Yet when the *Durance* left according to plan on May 1, Gauguin was not a passenger. The obvious deduction would be that he had still not received any news from the Academy of Art and that, obstinately and unreasonably, he still hoped for a free passage. It certainly seems strange that he should have abandoned his plans to travel by the *Durance* on such slender grounds, especially since ships for Noumea were few and far between and a prolonged stay of several months in Tahiti would have cost him as much as he might have saved by getting a free passage, which was still far from certain. However, a study of the local press reveals that, as luck would have it, another warship was scheduled to depart for Noumea only a month later.[101] In the light of this knowledge Gauguin's action becomes more readily intelligible, the risk he took considerably less. The vessel concerned was a cruiser, the *Duchaffault*, which was due to call at Tahiti *en route* from San Francisco to Noumea. Gauguin could safely assume that it would carry civilian passengers, since all warships did so, there being no other services between these French possessions in the South Seas.

In order to be nearer to the post office and administrative offices, Gauguin moved into Papeete with Teha'amana, and, in the area where his friends Lieutenant Jénot and the Drollet and Suhas families lived, rented a house, which with a little good will could be called furnished. The enterprising and business-like lady who had recently gone in for renting houses in this new way was a Madame Charbonnier. She had arrived in the island in a rather unusual manner. Some time in the 1860s, when still very young, she had been picked up by the *police de moeurs* of Paris in a street of ill repute. With many of her unforunate sisters, she had been deported "for rehabilitation" to the penal colony of New Caledonia, where there was a chronic shortage of women among convicts. On the voyage out, however, she had shrewdly decided that it would be better to be rehabilitated somewhere else, and she had managed to get ashore in Tahiti. The change of environment, together with her energy and initiative, had produced such remarkable results that in course of time she had acquired a valuable plot of land in Papeete. On this she built five small houses, with two rooms and a verandah, which she rented out, mainly to government officials and army and navy officers—that is, to persons with a steady income. Few people knew anything about her background, and in Gauguin's time she was a very respectable as well as respected widow of long standing, dressed always in a long black dress with a high collar. On the psychological plane, however, the transformation seems to have been far from complete, for to Gauguin's annoyance he found her one day—or perhaps night—peeping into his bedroom through the

glass of the verandah door. So taking out his brushes, he quickly
blocked out the panes with a painting of Tahitian women, animals,
and flowers, which, to be frank, was more successful from the practical
than from the artistic point of view.[102]

Gauguin had calculated correctly. The next mail-boat from San
Francisco arrived before the cruiser, bringing, at long last, a letter from
the Colonial Department which instructed the governor to repatriate
"the destitute and distressed artist," the costs to be paid from Paris.
The reason for the long delay in replying was that the reluctant director of the Academy of Art had once more remitted the whole matter,
this time to the Home Office, where there was a special repatriation
department. For some reason, the Foreign Office had also become involved in this unimportant case. Thus no fewer than four different
ministries had been obliged to inform one another of their intentions
and actions, or lack of them. The final result of this paper-chase was
that the announcement of the decision missed the schooner which
left San Francisco on May 1 by, perhaps, only a few days, which meant
that the delay was long enough for the beneficiary to be kept waiting
in great distress for another month. The Home Office, unlike the
Academy of Art, had never assumed any obligation towards Gauguin
or awarded him any official mission, and consequently it granted him
free repatriation on the same terms as any other distressed citizen; that
is to say, the cheapest.[103] But what were the cheapest terms on a
naval vessel such as the *Duchaffault?* This was a delicate question,
and the ministries in Paris had not provided any answer to it. As narrowly interpreted by Governor Lacascade, the instructions left no
doubt that Gauguin was to be quartered with the crew in the fore-
castle, or at best with the boatswains. Gauguin protested, pointing
out that on the *Vire* he had travelled with the officers, and regarding
Lacascade's declaration as an act of mean revenge.

That may well have been so; but if it was, the wretched Lacascade
had already suffered more than enough through an act of vengeance
directed at himself. With the May boat he had also received a brief
letter from the Colonial Department notifying him of his transfer to
the island of Mayotte, in the Indian Ocean, which, as this colony was
much less important than Oceania, meant degradation. This ignominious end to his long and meritorious administration of Tahiti and
its dependencies was due entirely to the bitter campaign which had
been waged against him by the settlers and their influential representatives in Paris arising from the dissatisfaction with the new tariffs he

had imposed. Well aware of this, Lacascade, very understandably, had no wish to remain among his malevolent slanderers until the arrival of a successor, but instead left by the first ship to call at Papeete. It was the British steamer *Richmond*, which maintained a regular service between Tahiti and New Zealand. Most of the settlers were callous enough to gather on the quay when Lacascade embarked on June 4, and to take leave of him with whistles and catcalls.[104]

Gauguin won another and more honourable victory over his arch-enemy when he embarked on the *Duchaffault* on June 14; for not only did the ship's commander welcome him affably aboard, he even gave him a separate cabin and a place in the officers' mess.[105] The leave-takers on the shore this time consisted mostly of Tahitian women, who had spent a couple of wonderfully happy weeks with the ship's officers and men, and who were now, as Tahitian etiquette required, weeping their eyes out as they wished their generous friends *bon voyage* by flinging wreaths of white flowers into the lagoon. One of the girls at least had come specially for Gauguin's sake; for there, sitting on a boulder at the water's edge, dangling her bare foot in the sea and gazing if possible even more tearfully than her fellows towards the departing ship, was Teha'amana. Here and there among the colourful groups of natives were black-and-white patches formed by well-dressed Europeans, several of whom had also come chiefly in order to take leave of Gauguin. These, of course, were Lieutenant Jénot and members of the Drollet and Suhas families, and in traditional Tahitian style they stood and waved until the *Duchaffault* had manoeuvred her way slowly through the narrow gap in the reef.

Thanks to her powerful engines, the *Duchaffault* never had any need to make wide detours in order to find favourable winds, as the old tub the *Vire* had been forced to do. Furthermore, the trade winds gave good backing on a voyage between Tahiti and New Caledonia, and it took Gauguin only a week to reach Noumea. As a matter of fact, it would have suited him better if the passage had taken as long as the outward voyage on the *Vire* had done; for he now found himself waiting no less than three weeks at Noumea for the connection to France, during which time, of course, he had to stay at a hotel and eat at restaurants. To a "destitute and distressed" traveller this was a heavy blow, as Gauguin ruefully observed. When the homeward-bound passenger steamer of the Messageries Maritimes, the *Armand Béhic*, at last arrived, the steerage-class dormitory to which he had been assigned was packed with troops and the outside deck had been converted into a shelter for sheep and cattle. Gauguin's lower-class life became even more intolerable when among the luxuriously berthed and punctiliously attended first-class passengers he happened to notice his old bugbear Governor Lacascade, who had managed to pick up an immediate connection from New Zealand so as to arrive in Sydney just in time to catch the *Armand Béhic*. Although he could scarcely afford it, Gauguin at once paid the difference and transferred to second class.

As a result of these various unforeseen expenses, when he arrived at Marseilles on August 30 he had only four francs left of the 650 francs he had possessed when he had embarked at Papeete.[106] However, he was in good heart and full of confidence, knowing that among his baggage he had sixty-six splendid pictures which would surely help him to achieve the ambition for which he had fought so long—recognition as the great artist he knew himself to be and the assurance of a comfortable existence that at long last would enable him and his family to be reunited.

23. *Gauguin in his studio in the rue Vercingétorix at the beginning of 1894. Standing on the left are his neighbour William Molard and Anna the "Javanese."*
24. *Many woodcuts as well as paintings are dominated by such figures of huge idols, all of which are creatures of Gauguin's imagination without counterpart in Tahiti.*
25. *After Gauguin's return to Tahiti, Anna continued her career as an artist's model and posed in Paris with great success for Alphonse Mucha (among others), who took this photograph of her about 1898. The photograph has been kindly lent by his son, Jiri Mucha, Prague.*

VI

THE TURNING-POINT

GAUGUIN appears to have foreseen additional expenses on the home-ward voyage, for he wrote both to Mette and to Daniel before leaving Tahiti and asked for money to be sent to Marseilles. But the shipping agent who boarded the *Armand Béhic* when it docked had neither money nor letters for him. The train fare to Paris cost about twenty francs—five times the amount he possessed. To stay on the ship was not permitted. His only alternative was to put up at a cheap hotel and wait there until it pleased somebody to ransom him.

The person supposedly more interested than anyone else in rescu-ing him from this predicament was Maurice Joyant, the manager of Boussod et Valadon's art gallery, which had everything to gain from a successful exhibition of the new Tahitian pictures. He therefore sent Joyant a telegram, doubtless for obvious reasons a short one.

---

26. *This wonderful view of the sea and the island of Moorea is exactly as Gauguin saw it in the six years of 1895–1901 during which he lived on the west coast of Tahiti. Other artists now often set up their easels under the iron-trees and the coconut-palms on the same spot.*

27. *Preparing the evening meal of fruit and bread outside the kitchen hut—a simple scene of everyday native life such as Gauguin went on painting with obvious pleasure to the end of his life, alternately with mythological sub-jects and numerous still lifes.*

Immediately thereafter he had the good idea of inquiring at the general post office if there were any letters awaiting collection. There was one from Daniel. It contained the brief information that Sérusier had agreed to lend him 250 francs, which could be collected at a certain stated address in Paris. After spending his last remaining cash on another telegram, requesting the immediate forwarding of this sum, Gauguin can have had nothing else to do but spend a few hours strolling about the city, looking at the shops (especially the food shops and the restaurants and cafés), before going to bed at his cheap hotel on an empty stomach.

Fortunately, the 250 francs arrived the next day, and the same evening he arrived by train in Paris. It was the holiday season, and moreover a Friday, with the result that all his friends were out of town and there was nobody at the station to meet him. Worse, he had nowhere to leave his bags, rolls of pictures, and carvings. On the off-chance, he called a cab and drove to Daniel's studio, where after some arguing he persuaded the *concierge* to let him in.

The first visit, of course, was to the Galerie Boussod et Valadon; but if on the way there he tried to phrase a few home truths about Joyant's slackness and apathy the effort was wasted. Joyant had fallen out with the proprietors six months before and was no longer employed by them. As nobody else at the gallery had been willing to handle Gauguin's unsaleable pictures, Joyant on leaving had returned them to Daniel. The other dealer whom Gauguin had relied on— Portier—had long ago resigned his thankless commission, as Gauguin had probably learnt before his departure from Tahiti.

Disheartened though Gauguin was at the sudden and abrupt end to his business connections with the Galerie Boussod et Valadon, it was in certain respects an advantage, because it meant that he would now be free to arrange a one-man show at a larger and more distinguished gallery. In spite of the rejection of a similar request which he had made in the autumn of 1890, he decided to make another approach to the famous dealer Paul Durand-Ruel, who after a long and uphill struggle had finally succeeded in creating a public demand for Impressionist pictures. On this occasion he had better luck; Durand-Ruel *père* was on his way to America and his two sons, who were looking after the gallery, were far more responsive, the more so since Edgar Degas, who was himself one of the chief suppliers to this gallery, had warmly recommended Gauguin.[107] But the Durand-Ruel *fils* were not so responsive as to be ready to defray all the costs themselves. Consequently, Gauguin by some means or other had to raise the sum of 1,000 francs, the cost of framing the pictures, advertising the show, and printing posters, programmes, and invitation cards.

Still, this partial success led him, when he left the Galerie Durand-Ruel, to rent a room in the rue de la Grande-Chaumière, *numéro* 8, which was next door to the Académie Colarossi where he had lived before going to Tahiti. Money for a quarter's rent in advance was lent to him by his old benefactress, Madame Caron, the owner of the restaurant *Chez Charlotte* across the road, who also solved another serious problem for him by allowing him to eat there on credit until further notice. That he chose this time to live at No 8 was due to the generous offer made by one of the most faithful frequenters of the restaurant, the Czech painter Alphonse Mucha, of the use of his studio there.[108] Gauguin had assumed that Mette would have sold enough pictures during the Free Exhibition of Modern Art in Copenhagen to cover all his expenses. Much to his annoyance, she had not yet replied to the letter he had sent her immediately after landing at Marseilles, and he therefore wrote to her again. The second letter had barely been posted when he received from her a telegram, informing him of the sudden death at Orleans of his only relative in France, a 75-year-old uncle.

Before leaving for Orleans, he dashed off a short letter to her which began angrily as follows: "I really understand less and less. You must have my address because you have sent a telegram to me at my new lodging. Yet you have not gone to the trouble of sending me a line." The sting in the tail was even sharper: "Good God, how hard it is to do anything when all those you rely on leave you in the lurch—one's wife above all. Tell me candidly what the matter is. I want to know where I stand. Why have you and Emil not come to Paris to welcome me? It wouldn't have killed you. But enough of that. Write *long letters* for my information, and reply to all the questions in my earlier letters."[109]

On returning from the funeral, he found a week-old letter awaiting him—proof that Mette had not been as passive as he had thought. In fact, she had replied immediately to his first letter, but for lack of any other address had sent it to Schuffenecker's in Paris. It had been forwarded on from there, first to Dieppe, where the Schuffenecker's were spending their summer holidays, and thence to Daniel's country estate in the Pyrenees, before finally reaching its destination.

The delayed news was very disheartening. The Copenhagen exhibition, it is true, had been well attended and Gauguin's and van Gogh's pictures had attracted more attention than all the rest put together.[110] But the demand by buyers had been very poor and the few pictures which Mette had succeeded in selling had realized only a few hundred kroner, which she had already spent on food and clothing for the children. "So you will have to fend for yourself," was her uncompromising conclusion. Luckily, Gauguin's uncle had left both securities and cash, and Gauguin's share in these might be 10,000 francs or even more. He made no disguise of his satisfaction that his uncle "had had the excellent idea of dying" so conveniently. The only annoying thing connected with it was that the legacy was to be shared with his sister Marie in Colombia, and the lawyer in Orleans who had charge of the estate required her authorization before he could make payment, and it would take several months to get it.

In his excitement, Gauguin put the following proposal to Mette: "In November I shall strike a big blow which will decide our whole future, and judging from what I have already been able to sense in the course of my approaches, I think that all will turn out well. There is not a minute to lose, therefore, and, as you will realize, I can't leave Paris before the exhibition, before, that is, the end of November. As you have some time to spare, why not come to Paris with little Paul? It would make rather a rest for you, and I should be delighted to embrace you again. We should be able to talk things over, which is necessary (but impossible to do by letter). I have a fairly well furnished studio, so there would be neither trouble nor expense, and from every point of view it would be very useful. If you can find the money for the fare it will be reimbursed in two months at the most. In the house there are two Danish ladies whom you know, and one of the children might sleep with them. We would make some useful visits together, and would later reap the fruits of this little expense. Don't raise a lot of fuss and objections; make your arrangements and COME as soon as possible."

Although he ardently implored her to relax and allow herself for once to be governed by her feelings instead of her reason, Mette could not act against her nature any more now than before—or for that matter any more than anybody else. In her sober judgment, Paul's suggestion was a dangerous attempt to anticipate success. After all, it was only two months to the exhibition at Durand-Ruel's which, he assured her, would bring his final success. As they had already waited for each other eight years, it should not be difficult to wait for another two months. In any case, Mette could not afford the trip to Paris. It so happened that Gauguin's suggestion, unknown to him, came at a most inconvenient moment, when their eldest son, Emil, had just passed his university entrance examination and Mette was struggling to raise the money for him to continue his studies. Neither had she the slightest faith in Paul's ability to keep his promise of repayment, even if she did manage to raise the fare to Paris, which seemed unlikely. In fact, everything went to show that he was still the same old spendthrift he had always been. Had she not, at some sacrifice, sent him 700 francs just previous to his departure from Tahiti? Yet he had arrived without a centime and had immediately asked her not only for more money, but to involve herself in much unnecessary expense. To crown all, he had not even troubled to apologize for his recent abusive letter, accusing her unjustly and offensively of being a bad correspondent.

Believing it futile to try to convince Paul of his bad behaviour, she gave vent to her bitterness at his conduct in a long letter to Schuff, who had often had occasion to complain of the same injustices himself. "He is completely hopeless," she wrote. "He never thinks of anything but himself and his own convenience, and is full of self-satisfied admiration of his own greatness. The fact that his children have to get their daily bread from his wife's friends is of no concern to him at all and a fact he dislikes being reminded of. Therefore he doesn't know! Yes, this time I'm indignant. You probably know what has happened. A week after his arrival our uncle in Orleans died, very conveniently for Paul, who will inherit 15,000 francs. . . . You and I know that he went off on his little jaunt to Tahiti with *all* the proceeds of the sale. In spite of all that I said nothing. Now he hasn't as much as hinted at sharing the 15,000 with me, as I have taken the liberty of pointing out to him. To cap all, he wants me to find money for a trip to Paris. It is even more necessary that I should stay here now than it was before: I can't just go away and leave the five big children, who have *only me* to depend on. If he wants to see us he knows where to find us. I'm not such a fool as to go roaming the world at random!"

Gauguin, for his part, made no further attempt to persuade his "hard" and "calculating" wife to visit Paris, and wisely concentrated on the preparations for the exhibition at Durand-Ruel's, which if it proved as successful as he expected would solve his marriage problems with the rest. All hope of drawing the legacy before the show being now in vain, the first requisite was to raise money, by one way or another, as soon as possible. Although the new director of the Academy of Art, Roujon, had clearly demonstrated his dislike by repeatedly refusing to pay his passage home, Gauguin nevertheless decided to call on him, in order to remind him of the promise to purchase a picture, made two years before by his predecessor when granting him the "official mission." Heartily sick of all the trouble he had already had on Gauguin's behalf, and bent on getting rid of the pesterer once and for all, Roujon replied with brutal candour immediately:

"I cannot support your art, which I find revolting and unintelligible. Were I, as director of the Academy, to back such revolutionary art, I should create a scandal, and all the inspectors are of the same opinion."

When with ill-concealed anger Gauguin retorted that he did not presume to ask that the board of the Academy should like his art, but only that it should keep its promise, Roujon smiled ironically and brought the discussion to a close by asking:

"Have you got it in writing?"

Gauguin had not, and so had no alternative but to retire, richer by yet another unpleasant experience but in cash as poor as before.

According to his own statement, he eventually succeeded in borrowing nearly two thousand francs from friends as, one by one, they returned from their holidays. On this occasion they incurred little risk, for it was only a matter of time before Gauguin would get his legacy.

The importance of publicizing a sale in the right manner had been brought home to Gauguin two years before, when Morice had so effectively aroused interest in the auction that it had realized nearly ten thousand francs. But who would assist in providing publicity on this occasion? The only person who could have replaced Morice as Gauguin's public relations manager was Albert Aurier, the art critic of the *Mercure de France,* who had so unreservedly proclaimed his greatness in two long and enthusiastic articles, but he had since died of typhus. So when at this critical moment "that miserable thief and liar," Charles Morice, wrote remorsefully and persuasively asking for a meeting that would "put an end to the painful situation which has arisen," Gauguin sent him a most conciliatory reply. He may have sincerely hoped that Morice was ready to purchase indulgence by the immediate repayment of his debt. If so, he was soon undeceived, for Morice if anything was poorer than ever. Following his humiliating failure as a playwright in the spring of 1891, he had fallen back on occasional reporting and linage for the boulevard papers, and had frequently gone both cold and hungry in the two years of Gauguin's absence. Yet he was now happier than at any time in his life, having fallen wonderfully in love with one of his many conquests, a widowed countess, who was a few years older than he and had a daughter aged ten. That the attachment was sincere as well as mutual had been shown by her readiness to share in his poverty. Touched a little by Morice's misery and by his happiness, Gauguin promptly forgot his resolve to exact payment of every centime which his friend owed him. It was obvious, moreover, that the only way in which Morice could settle his debt was by journalistic assignments like those which had given the successful publicity campaign two years before.

Another friend of the winter before his departure for Tahiti whom Gauguin now resumed relations with, more or less involuntarily, was Juliette. She had the strangely naïve idea that if she went to live with him again he would win custody over their two-year-old daughter, Germaine, whom she loved as only a mother can. Glad to escape from both onerous duties and noisy crying, besides complications with Mette which would be highly unwelcome, Gauguin was careful not to disabuse her. But whenever possible he gave her a little money, which sufficed to induce the grateful Juliette to pay him an occasional visit.

As if he had not enough already to engage his mind, Gauguin at once began writing a book about his Tahitian journey. His decision to embark on such a difficult enterprise at a time when he already had his hands full can have only one explanation: namely, that like every other beginner he grossly underestimated the toils and labours of authorship. The principal inducement, it would seem, was the prospect of earning a little urgently needed money. *The Marriage of Loti* had been an immediate best seller and was frequently reprinted. Since Gauguin had lived far longer in Tahiti than Pierre Loti, and had had far more interesting experiences, it seemed reasonable to suppose that his account would sell likewise.

As he should have known at the start, it soon proved quite impossible both to write a book and at the same time organize a large one-man show, all in the course of two months. A particularly arduous and protracted task, as it turned out, was the stretching and framing of the canvases, which were of varying sizes. The difference in many cases will have been only a few centimetres, but it was enough to render serial production of the frames impossible. For this and other reasons, it took Gauguin all his time to get everything ready for viewing day, even when that was postponed from the fourth to the ninth of November.[111] As before, Morice had prepared the ground thoroughly in advance. All the leading art magazines carried articles or announcements long before the event. Between visits to editors, Morice had also managed to write an excellent foreword to the catalogue. Furthermore, he not only sent invitations to every important figure in the world of art but in many cases made sure they came. The result was all that could be expected; well before two o'clock, the time indicated in the invitations, the carriages began arriving in front of the Galerie Durand-Ruel in the rue Lafitte.

Gauguin had very carefully sifted his material, and included only forty-one of the sixty-six pictures and two of the dozen or so "ultrasavage" woodcarvings he had brought back with him.[112] To emphasize the continuity in his work as well as its development, he also included three earlier pictures painted in Brittany. Practically all the pictures exhibited on this occasion now occupy prominent places in famous museums all over the world, and every history of modern art published in recent years has contained one or more reproductions of them. Works like *Ia Orana Maria* (which Gauguin placed first in the catalogue), *Manao Tupapau, I Raro Te Oviri, Nafea Faa Ipoipo, Vahine No Te Tiare,* and *Te Aa No Areois,* are well known and admired not only by specialists but by millions of ordinary art-lovers. Gauguin thought as highly of his art as posterity, and was certain that the forty-one Tahitian pictures which glowed and sparkled from the gallery's walls in colour combinations never before seen would ultimately convince his contemporaries of his greatness. How sure he was of himself and his approaching triumph comes out most clearly in the final ironic sentence of his last letter to Mette before the show: "Now at last I shall know whether it was *foolish* to take myself off to Tahiti."

He knew a few minutes after two o'clock. The indifferent, derisive, or puzzled faces which he saw on all sides told their own unmistakable story. He had failed. But let Charles Morice take over, for he was at Gauguin's side during the viewing: "Gauguin's great projects had all been put to shame. But what hurt his pride more than anything was that he had been forced to admit to himself that he had miscalculated in a number of respects. Had he not dreamt of appearing as a prophet? Had he not gone to a distant land when the mediocrities had refused to recognize the genius in their midst, in order to stand in his right perspective and seem even greater when he returned? 'My flight may be a defeat, but my return will be a triumph,' he had said. Instead, his return had cruelly magnified his earlier defeat.

"The fear which must have clutched at his heart at that moment can easily be imagined. But to use a metaphor of which he was naively fond and quoted frequently, he patiently endured his torments like an Indian, smilingly. Yet never once, faced with the combined antipathy of everyone present, did he for a moment doubt that he was right. And to stand firm was the conviction to which he clung. For what did the incredible misjudgment of his contemporaries matter when posterity would prove him right?

"As soon as he had realized that they were judging him without troubling to study and discuss his art, he adopted an air of supreme indifference, smiling without betraying the effort which it cost him, quietly asking his friends their impressions, and discussing their replies coolly and dispassionately without trace of bitterness.

"When, at the end of this ill-fated day, he accompanied Monsieur Degas to the door, he remained stubbornly silent in spite of the latter's praise. But as the famous old master was leaving, Gauguin took one of the exhibits, a stick he had carved, from the wall and handed it to him, saying:

" 'Monsieur Degas, you have forgotten your stick.' "[113]

One painter who did not share the high opinion of Degas was Gauguin's old friend and teacher, Camille Pissarro, who has left this account of his visit to the exhibition:

"I saw Gauguin. He told me his theories about art and assured me that the young would find salvation by replenishing themselves at remote and savage sources. I told him that this art did not belong to him. That he was a civilized man and hence it was his function to show us harmonious things. We parted both unconvinced. Gauguin is certainly not without talent, but how difficult it is for him to find his own way! He is always poaching on someone's ground; now he is pillaging the savages of Oceania."[114]

The newspapers were only a little more positive.[115] As before, the highest praise came from the ardent supporter of the Symbolists, Octave Mirbeau, who, with great insight, wrote: "What he sought in

Brittany he has finally found in Tahiti: a simplification of his forms and colours and a decorative balance and harmony." Still more interesting for us, who entirely agree with his judgment, are the passages in Mirbeau's review describing Gauguin's life in Tahiti, based, of course, on first-hand information: "Gauguin does not tarry in the towns. Immediately upon his arrival he chooses a house in the mountains, far from the villages and the European way of life. He lives exclusively among the natives, and in their manner. He eats their food, dresses like them, follows all their customs, and approves of their games, pleasures, and traditions. In the evenings he joins their gatherings. He listens to the tales of the old men, fills himself with sublime, poetic legends, and sings a part in their improvised choir. . . . Through these tales, this music . . . the past of this marvellous land of laziness, grace, harmony, strength, naivity, greatness, perversity, and love is gradually conjured up. The myths take shape, the monstrous divinities with blood-stained lips who kill women and devour children rise up again, inspiring the same powerful fear as in ancient times. . . . So intimately has Gauguin shared the life of the Maoris that their past has become for him his own. All he had to do was to interpret it in his works. And here they are, these works, radiating a strange beauty whose existence Pierre Loti did not for a moment surmise." Apart from Mirbeau's review, which was published in the *Echo de Paris*, the few other articles to appear were in this style: "I can think of nothing more childish than this reversion to whimsy primitives, from whom he has taken only the faults without having either their naivety or their readiness to do their best." Another critic called the pictures "delusions of a sick mind, grossly insulting to art and nature;" while a third affirmed briefly and maliciously: "To discuss this exhibition would be to attach unwarranted importance to a farce." A fourth wrote: "We are completely unmoved by this evocation of Tahitian legends, this *Ave Maria* that is just a picture in the style of Bastien Lepage, for which no native Gounod has troubled to compose any music. . . . We now await the arrival in Paris of a Tahitian painter who will exhibit his works at Durand-Ruel's or somewhere, while living in the Botanical Gardens. In short, we await a real Maori."

The show was fully appreciated, as would seem logical, by only the gossip-writers, who above all made fun of Gauguin's yellow seas, purple trees, pink fields, and other "unnatural" colours. One of the most popular stories, which unfortunately happens to be true, concerns an

Englishwoman, who at the sight of the red dog in the *Hina* sequence of pictures on viewing day could not repress a terrified yell. One of the brighter gossip-writers must have thought his compatriots more shock-proof, for he gave this advice to his readers: "If you would like to entertain your children, send them to the Gauguin exhibition. The attractions include coloured images of ape-like female quadrumanes stretched out on green billiard tables." The allusion was to the magnificent nude, *Otahi*.

Also financially the show was of course a dismal failure. Degas bought one of the *Hina* series on the first day. A Russian purchased another. A French collector, after long hesitation, took *Ia Orana Maria* on hire purchase. An unknown young art dealer named Vollard, who had recently opened a small gallery in the same street as Durand-Ruel's, bought one of the more conventional pictures, depicting a fully clad Tahitian woman sitting in a rocking-chair. Only eleven of the forty-four pictures were sold. After paying the expenses and his debts, Gauguin had barely enough left to keep him going till he drew his legacy.

To resume his family life with Mette and the children was now out of the question; for she had made this conditional on his having a regular income and being able to support them. In his shame and despair at the disastrous result, he put off telling her about it for as long as possible. When at length she wrote asking impatiently when he proposed visiting Copenhagen, he foolishly tried to assure her that the exhibition had been "a very great artistic success," that the press had been "sensible and laudatory," and that "many people" considered him to be "the greatest of modern painters." But he reluctantly admitted that from a financial point of view the show had "not really given the expected result." With regard to their future, therefore, he could only suggest that they should meet in the summer of 1895, during the school holidays. With the obvious idea of avoiding any embarrassing questions from Mette's relations, he proposed taking a cottage on the coast of Norway.

The attempt to deceive Mette was doomed of course to fail. In the first place, she kept in touch with events in Paris through the French newspapers, and, in the second place, she had many friends who sent her cuttings. The most informative and revealing article was one by Morice in the December issue of the *Mercure de France*, which began in this original manner: "Two important artistic events have taken place simultaneously, as if by intention: the day of the Paris première of Ibsen's *An Enemy of the People* was viewing day for the exhibition of pictures and sculptures brought home from Tahiti by Paul Gauguin.

"At the Théatre de l'Oeuvre and at Durand-Ruel's the same play was enacted. Dramatically and with a simplicity previously unknown, Ibsen shows us a man who suffers for truth in an environment new at any rate to us Frenchmen. Gauguin is the author as well as the principal protagonist of a similar tragedy. The country, the people, and the environment where he has chosen to proclaim his artistic truths, to give free and magnificent expression to his beautiful visions, are similarly unfamiliar to us here in the West. His setting, on the other hand, is even simpler than the dramatist's, and the liberties he takes are undoubtedly bolder and more deeply stamped with his personality.

"But is it really so difficult to understand him and his bold simplifications? The sole requirement is that in approaching the work of any artist and poet we should grant him his creative freedom and allow him to forget the patterns and models set by every previous great master, as also, of course, the irritating conventions of all minor artists. But nobody has been willing to take the trouble. Here it is not so much public opinion I have in mind—for, in spite of all its prejudices it can be shaped and directed—as the so-called experts, artists, critics, and some journalists and other contributors to the newspapers. Here malice and stupidity have conspired together on a grand scale. What absurd opinions we have heard, overtly or covertly, in the gallery in the rue Lafitte these last few days. To say nothing of the ones expressed, by all sorts of writers, in the best-informed daily papers!"

Morice also told his readers:

"Gauguin dwells sadly on his happy time across the seas, when he worked with the blessed creativity of an inspired poet on these pictures so far removed from our decadent society with all its cliques and intrigues. Perhaps he will return there. If so, we shall have driven him away. He is already saying:

" 'I don't want to see Europeans any more.' "

After analysing and explaining some of the more important pictures of the exhibition, Morice concluded by quoting Wagner's famous credo, which Gauguin had long since made his: "I believe in the sanctity of the spirit and in the truth of art one and indivisible. I believe that this art springs from a divine source and that it lives in the hearts of all men, illuminated by the celestial light. I believe that the man who has once tasted the sublime delights of this great art will be for ever dedicated and devoted to it, unable to deny it. I believe that with its help we can all achieve bliss. I believe in a last judgment when all who have dared to traffic here on earth in this pure and sublime art, who have sullied and degraded it in their base desire for material gain, will be condemned to an awful punishment. I believe that the faithful servants of the same great art will in turn be glorified, and that, surrounded by an aura of celestial radiance, scents, and melodious music, they will be received back and will dwell for ever in the divine source of all harmony."

According to Morice, Gauguin's friends did what they could to dissuade him from yielding to his understandable impulse to return immediately to the South Seas. One of their strongest arguments was that leaving Paris again he would become completely forgotten and sacrifice his last chance of success. Their arguments must have made some impression on him, for even before the close of the exhibition he was busily engaged in further attempts to win public favour indirectly. He had deduced, no doubt correctly, that those who saw the show were puzzled and bewildered less by his bold use of colours and revolutionary new style than by the strange and incomprehensible themes. The basic obstacle, in short, was that, unlike scenes from Greek mythology, which were admired and applauded in every official salon, his Tahitian gods and goddesses failed to evoke associations in the viewer's mind. It followed that what was needed was a popular account of Tahitian culture and mythology. Optimistic once more, he resolved to complete his book about Tahiti, and to alter its entire plan so as to make it principally a commentary on and an explanation of his work. For this purpose, he thought that the book should be illustrated with some reproductions.

Morice had meanwhile come to the same conclusion, except that he considered himself better equipped to expound Gauguin's art than Gauguin. He therefore suggested a collaboration, each to be responsible for alternate chapters. Gauguin's share would be that of providing the cultural background by relating his experiences in Tahiti, while Morice would describe and explain the pictures. Morice generously offered in addition to polish Gauguin's style. Morice had provided ample proof that he understood and sincerely admired Gauguin's art. Gauguin in turn just as sincerely admired his friend's florid and inflated style, and by now had realized that the writing of a book entailed far more effort than he had envisaged when he had made the first abortive attempt. So it is not nearly so surprising as it has seemed to some biographers that he so promptly and gladly agreed to Morice's suggestion, though perhaps he should have thought twice about his collaborator's idea of contributing some of his material in verse.

Since it would now be necessary to spend the winter in Paris, Gauguin moved into more spacious lodgings. They belonged to the landlord of the house at No 8 the rue de la Grande-Chaumière, and probably cost very little more to rent than the tiny place he had hitherto occupied.

The new lodgings were in the rue Vercingétorix, on the other side of the Montparnasse cemetery, and consisted of two large rooms in a ramshackle wooden house which looked like a barn and was built of inferior timber which the owner had bought at spot price when the pavilions of the Universal Exhibition were demolished in the autumn of 1889. As a further measure of economy, the house had only one staircase, so that the top-floor tenants at the opposite end of the house could reach their rooms only by means of a narrow balcony which extended along the entire front of the house. Gauguin's flat was at the far end of the balcony, farthest from the staircase.[116]

Gauguin bought a second-hand bed, which he placed in the smaller room, where there was a stove. He furnished the larger room with some equally old chairs and a dilapidated sofa. He borrowed a carpet from Daniel to cover the unpleasantly cold floor. For some unknown reason, and by unknown means, the simple furnishing was completed with a piano and a large camera on a tripod. The biggest problem with regard to decorating the walls was the reverse of that of furnishing the floors: it was to find room for all the unsold pictures. To provide a better background to them, he first painted the walls chrome yellow, and here and there among the pictures, for variety hung some Tahitian spears and Australian boomerangs which he had brought back. He also tacked up some reproductions of favourite pictures by Cranach, Holbein, Botticelli, Puvis de Chavannes, Manet, and Degas. Fortunately, he still possessed originals by the artists he rated highest —van Gogh, Cézanne, and Odilon Redon—which Schuff or Daniel must have stored for him during his absence. Over the bed, hung two sunflower paintings, a purple landscape and a portrait by van Gogh.[117] Disliking the sight of large rectangles of white in the midst of so much brilliance, he finally painted the window-panes and the panels of the balcony door.

The house walls were so thin and badly sound-proofed that it was important to have tolerant and friendly neighbours. In this respect

Gauguin was lucky. What is more, some of his neighbours, and in particular the young married couple on the floor below, William and Ida Molard, immediately took a liking to him, entertained him with their company, and introduced him to their numerous interesting friends. William Molard's one absorbing interest was music, and he spent his leisure composing great symphonies which suffered from the single fault of being unplayable. Consequently, he could no more live by his art than could his neighbour in the rooms above, though unlike him he had reluctantly stuck to his ordinary work. This was neither exciting nor very rewarding, for after long service he was still only an ordinary clerk in the Ministry of Agriculture. Molard's mother was Norwegian and he spoke that language fluently. His wife Ida, *née* Ericson, was a sculptress and by birth Swedish. In her youth she had studied at the Royal Academy of Art in Stockholm, and as might be expected her portrait busts and statuettes were extremely conventional. Yet in her private life she had been anything but conventional. A Swedish friend of the family, who often used to visit the house at 6 rue Vercingétorix when a student in Paris before the turn of the century, has told this amusing story of Ida's youth: "Ida was awarded a travelling scholarship by the Royal Swedish Academy of Art, but for an extraordinary reason never received it. In the scholarship year, on February 17, 1881, she gave birth to an illegitimate baby by the opera singer Fritz Arlberg, and had it christened Judith. Proud and happy, she wrapped a shawl round her treasure and went off to see the director of the academy, then Count George von Rosen, to thank him for the scholarship and allow him to admire her baby. The unexpected consequence was that the academy in moral indignation cancelled the scholarship. 'If only she had not shown me her baby!' Count von Rosen later said to an acquaintance of mine. A further consequence was that one Mrs Bonnier gave Ida from her own pocket the equivalent of the scholarship. . . . With this money Ida went to Paris, where she married and spent the rest of her life."[118]

Dr Kjellberg describes Ida Molard as "a small and extremely coquettish lady, blonde and plump, and dressed in frills and laces," and she gives the following glimpse of her life in the rue Vercingétorix which provides a good idea of her character: "The Molards had rented their rooms while the house was still under construction and the landlord had allowed them to dispense with the partitions in their flat, which had originally been planned as three rooms and a kitchen, plus two small alcoves for beds a few steps above the floor. Ida could thus do her cooking while conversing animatedly with visitors, who streamed into the hospitable home at all hours of the day, but chiefly in the evening when there was a party on." Ida Ericson-Molard was particularly hospitable and generous to neglected children, lost dogs, and failed artists. Thus Gauguin easily qualified for her motherly attentions.

Her daughter Judith, then nearly thirteen, also took to Gauguin in her way. As often happens in such cases, she had formed an idealized picture of her father, and judged her stepfather in the light of it, with the result that nothing he could ever say or do appealed to her. The absolute rejection of her stepfather was reflected in her feelings for her mother, whom she was continually trying by acts of defiance to pay out for the "betrayal" of her real father. As also happens in such cases, she transferred the love and affection which she withheld from her parents to her teachers. A painter, and one whose career had been so romantic and adventurous as Gauguin's, was of course an even more interesting and worthy object of her devotions (especially since she had already decided she would be a painter herself), and she worshipped him from the start. As for Gauguin, Judith to some extent took the place of his adored daughter, Aline, and he was deeply touched by the girl's devotion to him. But if we are to believe Judith's unpublished memoirs, written in later years, his feelings for her do not appear to have been only fatherly, but often suspiciously like those he had recently cherished for another thirteen-year-old, Teha'-amana in Tahiti. This is how Judith describes the ambiguous relationship: "There was no need for me to look in the mirror (which in fact was forbidden) in order to know that my hair was blonde and curly. I also knew that other forms, firm and round, had been added to the curves of childhood. . . . Without the least feeling of surprise, I allowed Gauguin's fine plump hands to touch these forms, which they did as if caressing a jug or a woodcarving."

An even better impression, both of the ambiguous attraction of Gauguin and Judith for each other and of his relations with the rest of the Molard family, is conveyed by this recollection of Judith:

"'Go and fetch William,' Mother said.

"William was sitting for a *Portrait of a Musician*. It seemed to me as if Gauguin's idea was to paint a portrait of a blissful imbecile. Mother did not like William to stay behind after the sitting. She was afraid that he would be unfaithful to her in his thoughts, as he talked to Gauguin about Negresses.

"I went upstairs. It was growing dusk. William was sitting at the piano, energetically pounding out a blatantly false potpourri of all Wagner's operas, which would occasionally be broken by a chord struck several times in succession. Each time he would say:

" 'That's beautiful, that is!'

"It was Sieglinde quarrelling with Tristan, on a Venusberg turned into a madhouse.

"I went quietly up to Gauguin. He slipped his arms round my waist, and laying his hand like a shell round my budding breast repeated in his gruff voice, which was barely audible:

" 'This is mine, all this.'

"Everything was his, indeed: my affection, my as yet unaroused sensuousness, my whole soul. I stood up on tiptoe and raised my lips towards his cheek, but met his lips. I offered him my whole soul, as I offered him my lips, and all he had to do was take it."

But to poor, highly strung Judith's disappointment, Gauguin fell right out of the sentimental and heroic role for which she had cast him; for when he spoke, it was to say, very prosaically:

" 'Come and have an absinth, Molard?'

"But Molard was deaf; he was still taking it out of the piano. 'If only I could prolong this minute,' I thought. 'If only Tristan would go on with his infernal apprentices' dance, the whole world could go under for all I cared. I would give my whole life for that one minute.' But they left. I watched them go from the balcony. What an odd pair they were, just like Don Quixote and Sancho Panza: the slight round-shouldered figure of Molard following Gauguin, his dog in turn following him. He tripped pinch-toed along in his pointed boots, the pug limping behind on three legs. Gauguin, however, moved with all the lithe suppleness of a dancer, as if floating on water and never for a moment off-balance. His overcoat, which was turned in at the waist, fluttered behind him like the tails of a Japanese carp. As always it was unbuttoned. A high-collared jacket was visible beneath, and over this was a loosely tied scarf. His head-dress was an ordinary felt hat, worn at a rakish angle. Hanging from a leather strap round his wrist was a carved iron-wood stick.

"They went off to drink their absinth.

"And it was a very small girl who went downstairs, to be scolded because William had gone off drinking."

At the Molard's, Gauguin met a number of musicians, poets, and painters, French and Scandinavian, and they soon got into the habit

of mounting the steep stairs for a chat with him whenever they visited
No 6 rue Vercingétorix. Gauguin was clearly in his glory with so
many friends about him after the two lonely years in Tahiti, and it
was not long before he began to follow the Parisian fashion and hold
a weekly "at home" every Thursday. The refreshments, surprisingly
enough, were limited to tea and cakes, which were handed round by
Judith. But of course they had the important advantage of being
cheap. The entertainment on such occasions was no less cheap and
simple, consisting of interminable discussions, solos on the guitar and
the piano, song duets, and charades, the last arranged by the life
and soul of the party, one Francisco Durrio, a dwarf-like Spanish
sculptor, who was nicknamed Paco, or Paquito. Occasionally, Gauguin would contribute to the entertainment himself by reading a few
newly written pages of his book on Tahiti. Once, in a particularly gay
mood, he dressed up as a cannibal chief from the South Seas.[119] His
old friends, Schuff, Daniel de Monfreid, Sérusier, and Morice, all of
whom were married and serious-minded men, naturally felt out of
place in this rather undergraduate atmosphere and the intervals between their visits grew gradually longer. (De Haan had long ago returned to Holland to obtain better treatment for his consumption,
though to no avail for he was slowly dying.) The one former friend of
sorts who attended the Thursday parties regularly was Morice's
shadow, Julien Leclercq, who after publishing his savagely attacked
collection of poems, Strophes d'Amant, had taken up palmistry and
the study of physiognomy.[120] Another faithful attender was Juliette,
who though still refusing to live with Gauguin felt a strong proprie-
tary right in him and would often be unreasonably jealous.

When reports of the merry parties reached Copenhagen in somewhat embroidered form, Mette grew deeply suspicious. She soon became firmly convinced that Paul had drawn the legacy and was busy
squandering it. His imagined offence seemed to her particularly vile
because he had long ago promised that any money which might come
to him from his uncle would be spent on the children's education. So
she lost no time in reminding him of the promise, which she happened
to have in writing. It was clear from her angry letter that she did not
believe him when he declared that the estate had still to be wound up.
Gauguin, who owed money right and left and had succeeded only with
difficulty in getting an extension of his credit at the Chez Charlotte
restaurant, was deeply offended by Mette's false suspicions and lack
of confidence in him. He therefore at once sent her a statement of his

expenses, totalling 2,490 francs, together with the following tart comment: "It's extraordinary that I should have to render you an account and prove to you I can't live in the street, and that returning ill from the tropics I can't walk about naked and live without heating." He also asked her to render him an *exact account"* showing, "without *cheating,"* how many pictures she had sold and what she had got for them. The phrase "without *cheating"* was inspired by reports from friends that in fact Mette had sold two pictures at 1,000 kroner each during the Copenhagen exhibition; that is to say, about ten times as much as she had stated. Instead of complying, Mette counterattacked, wondering how Paul could find it in him to charge her with *cheating* when at the same time he cheated grossly himself by including the expenses of the show at Durand-Ruel's in his accounts but not the income.

Only a personal confrontation, which would have forced them both to listen and reply, could have removed the mutual misunderstandings and recriminations. But Mette had no more inclination to leave Copenhagen, or means with which to do so, than before. Gauguin was far from finishing his book, and would have had great difficulty in borrowing the fare to Copenhagen even had he wanted to go. Thus they continued to write letters which became increasingly abusive and acrimonious, and as time went on contained fewer and fewer explanations and more and more angry accusations. The useless and distressing correspondence, which slowly poisoned both their minds, had the worst possible outcome, for it was brought brusquely to a close by the following lines from Gauguin, written in January 1894: "The accident I had in Tahiti nearly finished me. The privations and afflictions had a bad effect on my heart and the spitting of blood was only stopped with difficulty. The doctor's advice was that a recurrence would be fatal, and so in the future I must be careful. So if you intend to go on writing letters of the kind you have sent me since my return, I must beg you to desist."[121]

When Gauguin eventually obtained his long-awaited legacy, amounting to no less than 13,000 francs, at the beginning of February 1894, he got his own back on Mette very effectively by sending her only 1,500 francs. His promise of more if and when she needed it can hardly have been cheering to her, for it was plain to see that it was a promise he had no intention of keeping unless she kissed the rod. To friends in Paris he was far more generous. When a few days later he left on a "grand trip" to Brussels, to see an exhibition of modern art which included a few works of his own, he took Julien Leclercq with him and paid all his expenses. To Daniel, an older and even more loyal friend, he wrote at this time: "The lawyer has at last delivered the cash into my chaste hands; I hereby inform you of this in order that you may not hesitate to beg a consideration."[122]

Thanks to his unusually full purse, Gauguin was able on his return to obtain what he missed most of all: a regular female companion who would help to pass the time more quickly and more pleasantly while he finished his book and waited for Mette to simmer down. The new art dealer, Vollard, who had demonstrated his exceptional flair, alone among all the dealers, by buying a picture at the show at Durand-Ruel's, had meanwhile come increasingly to realize that it would be a good long-term policy to stick to Gauguin. At a chance meeting at this time, therefore, he immediately tried to curry favour with him. How he did so, Vollard relates with his usual candour in his rambling memoirs: "An opera singer, Madame Nina Pack, was a particularly good friend of a rich banker who had business dealings with merchants from the (East Indian) islands. The singer happened to remark in the hearing of one such merchant: 'I should love to have a little Negress.' A few months later, a policeman presented himself to Madame Pack with a young half-caste girl, Indian and Malay, who had been found wandering about alone in the streets. Round her neck was a label inscribed: 'To Madame Nina Pack, rue de la Rochefoucault, Paris. Consignment from Java.' The child was given the name Anna. Some time later, after a quarrel with her mistress, she was dismissed. So she came to see me (she knew me from my visits to her mistress) and asked if I could find her another place. Her talents for domestic work seemed to me very indifferent and I felt that she might make a better model. When I mentioned the matter to Gauguin, he said:

" 'Send her to me, and I'll see what she's good for.' "[123]

Anna's false certificate of origin must have called forth pleasant memories of the Universal Exhibition in 1889, when Gauguin had paid frequent visits to the Javanese village there. Even more attractive was her age, which was thirteen—exactly the same as Teha'amana's, which continually recurred in the nostalgic account of his happy life in Tahiti he was then working on so busily. There, however, the resemblance ended; for not only was Anna too lazy and apathetic to cook, so that Gauguin had to eat out with her, but also—and worse— she was talkative, inquisitive, and intruding to a degree. Nevertheless she amused and entertained him sufficiently for him to want to keep her, dress her, and as far as possible satisfy her whims, even to the extent of getting her a monkey for a pet.

Juliette found out upsettingly what had happened when, on entering the studio one day, she came upon her already domesticated rival face to face. Equally surprised, Anna was for once struck dumb. Assuming from this that the Negress, as she called her, was ignorant of French, Juliette called her all the names she could think of, none of which was at all flattering. Anna got her own back by quietly waiting until Juliette paused to draw breath, when with icy politeness and in perfect French she inquired:

"Has Madame finished?"

This had the intended effect of infuriating Juliette even more and making her regret that she had come without her seamstress's scissors. Tiring of abuse at last, she abruptly left the house, and never set foot in Gauguin's studio again or even communicated with him.

As for Judith, she seems to have preferred the new rival, who, unlike Juliette, at any rate took a childlike pleasure in playing with her. Yet she, too, was capable of being jealous of Anna. In her memoirs there is the following malicious description of a visit to the two rival spring salons, on the Champs de Mars, which she made with Gauguin's coterie: "Like an explorer who takes with him a collection of knickknacks when he goes off to meet a tribe of savages, Gauguin had brought home various things made by the orphan children of the Catholic convent schools (in Tahiti). When showing them to us, he said with a laugh: 'You've no idea what can be got in the islands in exchange for such articles as these.' Among other things, he had some incredibly fine-plaited leaves for making hats. Anna and I were both given such plaited-leaf rolls. A hatter made a hard straw hat, in the style later made famous by Maurice Chevalier, for Anna. A milliner made a girl's hat with a stylish emerald-green band for me. . . . At the opening of the spring show we were dressed differently; for though Anna, like me, was only thirteen, she had rigged herself out in grand style, while I wore a short dress. We had arranged to meet outside the entrance to the Palais des Beaux-Arts, as we were two to a ticket. The odd crowd which gathered round Gauguin consisted of a 'bodyguard' of thin men—Morice, Leclercq, Ranson, Roinard, and Monfreid—and a troupe of little people—my mother, myself, the Maufras, Paco, and Anna. We cannot have averaged more than five feet in height.

"Once through the turnstiles, each followed his own glittering lodestar; some beginning to look round for useful acquaintances, others trying mainly to attract attention, the rest bent on discovering the latest masterpiece by Rodin, Besnard, or Gauguin. Anna looked as if she meant to lay the world at her feet, walking determinedly erect with her head in the air and thrusting out her little pointed chin over her stiff, embroidered collar. Her straw hat rested at the back of her head on a great knot of blue-black hair and so inclined at an angle of forty-five degrees in the direction of her nose, which was as flat as that of a baby chimpanzee. She was wearing a tight-fitting blouse of checked silk with puff sleeves and ample decorative folds and a long gown with a train which she held at waist height in her silk-gloved hand."

Because of his wide social activities and his unaccustomed and thus laborious writing, Gauguin understandably painted few pictures that winter of 1893–94. Three at least were of Tahitian subjects, the rest being self-portraits or portraits of friends. The Tahiti canvases were almost all of the same high quality as the pictures painted in the island, which confirms his frequently repeated statement that he obtained the best results when he painted "from memory" rather than "from nature."

Two of his self-portraits in one way or another bear witness to his close connections with the Molard family. One of these was done on the back of the oil-painting of William Molard which Judith, not without some reason, thought resembled a "blissful imbecile." The other was an outline portrait engraved on a plaster plaque. It was the only time in his life that he used this material, and the idea occurred to him one day when he was sitting for Ida Molard, whose main artistic output consisted of realistic plaster busts and reliefs. To see himself in profile, of course, he had to use two mirrors. The Tahitian title that he gave to this masterly portrait was *Oviri* ("Savage"), which was the title of the song he had copied down during his stay in Mataiea.[124] A no less interesting and important portrait was a full-length nude of Anna (with the monkey at her feet), in a pose which recalled the similarly naked Arioi beauty, Vairaumati, in one of Gauguin's mythological pictures of 1892. Gauguin not unnaturally connected and contrasted Anna with Judith (as doubtless he would often do in his thoughts) when he gave this picture its rather scabrous title in pidgin Tahitian. This is *Aita Parari Te Tamari Vahine Judith,* and it means "The Child-woman Judith is not yet breached."[125] Fortunately, the Molards were ignorant of Tahitian.

But his most remarkable productions at this time were the ten woodcuts which he made to illustrate his book, *Noa Noa*, and which an engraver named Flouquet, who lived in the same block, helped him to print.[126] Six of them were copies of oil paintings which had been shown at Durand-Ruel's. Of the other four, three were imaginative renderings of the Tahitian myth of the creation, and the last, *Te Faruru*, the finest of all, just a picture of a pair of lovers without mythological associations of any sort. These woodcuts only partly achieved their purpose, which was to popularize the pictures. They also had the major disadvantage, from a practical point of view, of being far too large (14 × 8 inches) to serve as book illustrations. These faults were compensated for many times, however, by their artistic merit. A leading specialist has said:

"They are his greatest prints, and in the whole history of print-making there is nothing to compare with them. They may be said to have brought about both a revival and a revolution in the wood-block medium. At the time, the woodcut had fallen into neglect. Wood engraving, so popular for illustration and reproduction, had arrived at a final stage of virtuosity, as in the works of engravers like Auguste Lepère and Timothy Cole, which seemed a brilliant but losing fight with the cheaper and more durable success of photo-mechanical methods. In Gauguin's hands the medium received unusual treatment. He made of it an ideal instrument for his peculiar spatial expression, which made no attempt to suggest depth and atmosphere, but achieved something of the character of bas-relief. The finished blocks, apart from the impressions taken from them, are independent in their sculptural effect. Before they were worked upon they were the same as those used for wood engravings, consisting of small sections of the hard wood fitted together, cut against the grain. Gauguin's method was to engrave lines of the composition into the surface with a burin, instead of cutting away the wood so that the lines for printing stood above. He then gouged out other portions in varying depths. . . . With all their evanescent quality these compositions stand with Gauguin's highest achievements: they are imbued with the same mysterious contemplation, the fatalistic, silent terror and vague melancholy which are his personal attributes as an artist and which free him forever from his wretched existence."[127]

Unfortunately, it is not possible to feel the same enthusiasm for the narrative which Gauguin, with the help of Morice, eventually completed. Poor Morice is generally blamed for the many inaccuracies and exaggerations which it contains. Since the chance discovery of Gauguin's first draft of Noa Noa, however, it has now become possible to apportion the responsibility, and a comparison of this and the final text makes it clear that Morice went no further than he was meant to do, which was to polish Gauguin's style and fill in certain gaps as instructed.[128] It is certainly true that the style of the revised version is far too precious, meandering, and elaborate for modern tastes. But having said that, we must in all fairness bear in mind that Gauguin was a great admirer of his collaborator's style and personally approved all Morice's "corrections" and "improvements."

Actually, the most serious faults are not so much of style as of matter. The renaming of Teha'amana as Tehura—perhaps because the authors thought the real name too long and difficult to pronounce in French—is of minor importance. (To be exact, there is a double mistake in the "cover" name by which Gauguin's vahine has been known all these years, the correct spelling being Teura or Te'ura—without an "h.") A far worse fault is that Gauguin the author is only a little more realistic and objective than Gauguin the painter. The general impression conveyed by the book is that life was still extremely primitive and idyllic in Tahiti in the 1890s. The only exception, Gauguin suggests, was Papeete, where the Europeans to a man were mean and ridiculous (the "Negro" Lacascade of course being the worst), whereas all the natives in the "jungles of the interior" were unspoilt children of nature, almost Rousseau-esque in their nobility and goodness. Of his own troubles and financial embarrassments Gauguin says nothing. On the contrary, he asserts in all seriousness that not only did he live in the same superbly simple manner as the natives, but that "mentally" he soon became "a true savage, a genuine Maori," on moving from the civilized plague-spot which was Papeete and settling in Mataiea. In most cases Gauguin's falsifications were probably unconscious, for

---

28. *At odd moments of the day most women, those of mature years at any rate, work at a typically Tahitian craft, the weaving of elegant Sunday hats and huge sleeping-mats from soft yellow pandanus-leaves.*

29. *In the broad lagoon inside the sheltering coral reef there are not only delicious fish in abundance but quantities of fine clams, which the Tahitians gather and open on the shore before returning home.*

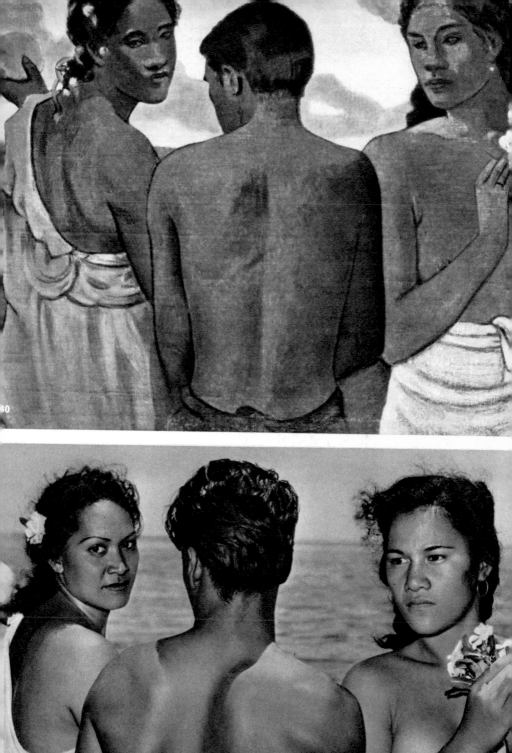

3

there are many statements which suggest that to a large extent he believed in his own idealization.

But in one important respect, at least, he was less than innocent; this was in his barefaced assertion that he got all his information about Tahitian religion and mythology from Teha'amana-Tehura. "She knows all the gods of the Maori Olympus by heart," he affirms, and adds that she gave him "a full course in Tahitian theology," on moonlit nights when they rested side by side in their bed, gazing up at the starry sky through the lattices of the bamboo hut. It can easily be shown that the entire chapter on Tahitian mythology is no more than a careless compilation of excerpts from Moerenhout's book.[129] The absurdity of Gauguin's assertion that a thirteen-year-old girl as late as the 1890s knew the theology and religious rites which always in pre-European times had been withheld from women will have been made clear, I hope, in chapter four of this book. It is also worth noting that the much criticized Pierre Loti, who had a similar love affair in Tahiti *twenty years before Gauguin*, confessed that his *vahine* "knew nothing about the god Ta'aroa, or the many goddesses in his train; she had never heard of any of the figures in Polynesian mythology."[130]

Noa Noa, the title which Gauguin had chosen for his half-finished book—Morice had scarcely started on his separate contributions—was a common Tahitian term meaning "scented" or "fragrant." The substantive *Fenua*—"land" or "island"—is implied. Thus the correct translation is "The Fragrant Isle." While it is true that there are many deliciously fragrant flowers (as well as women) in Tahiti, Gauguin's choice of title only becomes fully comprehensible if, following his ex-

---

o. One of Gauguin's best-known pictures, painted during his second period in Tahiti, whose three figures recur in many other compositions.

1. A photographic reconstruction of the painting, especially made for this book, shows how well Gauguin was able to render the Tahitian race type.

2. The daughters of Auguste Goupil, waiting in front of their father's grand country villa in Punaauia for the arrival of their drawing master, Paul Gauguin.

3. The unpretentious post office at Papeete, to which Gauguin often drove in a horse-drawn carriage of just this type in order to inquire after money or letters.

ample, we turn to Moerenhout's classic description of how in ancient times the Tahitians envisaged their Paradise: "They had a celestial abode, called *Rohutu noanoa*, where there was a radiant life of pleasures far surpassing those of the Greek Elysium, the Mohammedan Heaven, or any of the delectable places devised by the founders of the world's religions. The sun shone (in the Tahitian Paradise) with extraordinary brilliance, the air was full of sweet smells and ever pure; disease, pain, and sorrow were unknown; flowers were always fresh, fruit always ripe, delicious food abundant. Singing, dancing, and feasting succeeded one another without end, and there was a diversity of the most delightful pleasures in the company of perpetually youthful and eternally beautiful women."[131]

The title was more apt than Gauguin imagined; for now, in the light of all his trials and tribulations since returning to France, he obviously saw his experiences in Tahiti in transfigured form, and sincerely believed that life there was nearly as perfect and delectable as in the celestial paradise of *Rohutu noanoa*.

VII

ON THE WRONG TRACK

THE illustrations and the narrative chapters of *Noa Noa* completed, there was nothing to detain Gauguin in Paris any longer. Thanks to his legacy, he was free for once to do exactly as he pleased. Thus the opportunity had come for visiting Copenhagen and having a heart-to-heart talk with his wife. Had he done so, a reconciliation would doubtless have been the result. But unfortunately he still could not bring himself to make the first move. Or he may have decided to postpone his pilgrimage until the summer, when the children would be on holiday and he could take the whole family to some beautiful and quiet resort far from Copenhagen and Mette's embarrassing relations. What his real intentions were we cannot tell. What we do know is that when he left Paris at the beginning of May 1894, after urging Morice to expedite his lyrical and critical contributions to *Noa Noa*, it was to go, not by the North express, but to Brittany. What is more, he stupidly took Anna, who in turn took her monkey.

Gauguin expected that Marie Henry, his former landlady at Le Pouldu, would welcome him as warmly as she had done before. But he found on arrival that she had sold the inn, married, and moved to another village. When he looked her up in order to revive old memories and collect the pictures and sculptures which he had left with her on his hasty departure in November 1890, she flatly refused to surrender these works. Remarkably, her husband had decided that they had, or would have in the future, a money value.[132] Incensed by this downright dishonesty, Gauguin threatened to take legal action, which he did shortly after when she refused to budge.

The last of his old friends now living in the district was Charles Filiger. Still painting his madonnas and chromatic cubist pictures, he had
become such a recluse that he only rarely ventured out of doors in the
daytime. Nor, indeed, was there accommodation for sudden guests in
his squalid little bachelor's room on a remote and desolate farm. After lodging for a while with a Polish painter named Slewinski, one of
his many fellow-diners at the *Chez Charlotte* restaurant, who had
rented a cottage for the summer at Le Pouldu, Gauguin proceeded to
Pont-Aven. Madame Gloanec, who in the meantime had enlarged and
modernized her boarding house, gave him a much better welcome,
and friendly as ever did all she could to make both him, Anna, and the
monkey feel at home. Most of the guests who were on full board were
as usual artists, with or without their models or wives, and before long
Gauguin was surrounded by a band of curious fellow-boarders, eager
to hear his gospel. The most interested listeners among his new audience were two artists from across the Channel, Mortimer Menpes and
Roderic O'Conor, and a young French engraver named Armand
Séguin.

Menpes has described himself thus: "Painter, etcher, raconteur,
and rifle-shot, inartistically born in Australia. Education: nominally
at a grammar school in Port Adelaide, but really on a life scheme of
his own. His career as a painter began when he was one year old; he is
still a painter. He has held more one-man exhibitions in London than
any other living painter, among them 'Beautiful Women' and 'Beautiful Children.'"[133] A daughter of Menpes gives us the following account of life at Madame Gloanec's *pension* at this time: "The artists
allowed their hair and beards to grow. Day after day they wore the
same old paint-stained suits of corduroys, battered wide-brimmed
hats, loose flannel shirts, and coarse wooden sabots stuffed with straw.
. . . In the *salle à manger* . . . rough men sat on either side of a long
table, serving themselves out of a common dish, and dipping great
slices of bread into their plates. . . . For the three years that he (Mortimer Menpes) remained on this battlefield of creeds conflicts of opinion raged constantly. Everyone was frantically devoted to one or
another of the dominating principles of the moderns. . . . The Primitives afforded joy. Their distinctive mark was a walking stick, carved
by a New Zealand Maori, which they carried with them. It gave them
inspiration."[134]

Roderic O'Conor, of course, was an Irishman, of the same age as
Menpes, both having been born in 1860. His history and personality

can be summarized as follows: Partly educated in England, he went to Antwerp in 1881, where he studied for two years before he moved on to Paris. There he first studied under Carolus-Duran, but soon came into touch with the Impressionists and to a large extent adopted their style. In 1889 and 1890 he exhibited at the *Salon des Indépendants*, showing no less than ten works the latter year. By the early nineties he was in Pont-Aven every summer. Although highly gifted as an artist, he lacked power of expression, a fact of which he was tragically aware himself. O'Conor was cultivated, had read widely in French and English, and was conversant with the Latin masters. He was also an avid book collector, a discriminate buyer of modern French paintings, as well as Japanese and Indian sculpture, and a music lover who played the violin—but not very well. He clearly had a private income which enabled him to indulge his dislike of picture dealers. A great favourite of the ladies, he went from mistress to mistress, but always reserved the privilege of separate lodgings and the freedom to go out alone with his friends.[135]

Somerset Maugham, who knew O'Conor well, described him in *The Magician* as "a tall, dark fellow with strongly marked features, untidy hair and a ragged black moustache," and used him as a model for Clutton in his novel *Of Human Bondage*. This little glimpse of his character is particularly revealing: "He sat quietly, with a sardonic expression on his gaunt face, and spoke only when opportunity occurred to throw in a witticism. . . . He seldom talked about anything but painting, and then only with the one or two persons whom he thought worthwhile." Though not named, it is obviously to Gauguin that Clutton-O'Conor refers when he calls one of the painters he met in Brittany "a queer fellow who had been a stockbroker."

It is easy to see why Gauguin preferred the Irishman, and why O'Conor for his part was so appreciative that he soon became as constant a companion as Séguin, of whom we know little other than that he was extremely precocious, gifted, sensitive—and poor.[136] Thus O'Conor and Séguin resemble in a remarkable degree Meijer de Haan and Émile Bernard, those two former favourite disciples, so much so as to be almost their doubles. On the surface, therefore, Gauguin's life at Pont-Aven was little different from the life he had led in Brittany on previous visits. But in fact everything had changed, because of his misfortunes and problems. He therefore painted little, and that badly, and spent most of the time roaming indifferently about the fields and roads.

On May 25, he went on an excursion to the small fishing port of Concarneau, ten miles farther along the Breton peninsula, with Séguin, O'Conor, and a fourth painter whose name was Jourdain—accompanied by their women. The residents of Concarneau were not so familiar with the sight of eccentrically dressed painters and models as the people of Pont-Aven were by now. It was not long, therefore, before the four couples had a train of grinning urchins at their heels, and as the party passed by one of the quayside taverns along the fishing harbour some sailors made loud and scornful remarks. Jourdain suggested taking another route. Gauguin, pointing to a narrow alley, said derisively:

"Go that way, if you're afraid."

It sufficed to silence Jourdain.

The youngsters soon grew bolder and more aggressive. Anna may have upset them more than was necessary by sticking out her tongue at them or thumbing her nose, the way she used to do when annoyed, for suddenly they began to throw stones. Séguin seized one of the young louts and pinched his ear. As bad luck would have it, the boy's father was sitting in one of the taverns, and with misguided parental zeal rushed out and laid into Séguin. Without the slightest hesitation, Gauguin sprang to his friend's aid and knocked the big man down with a well-aimed punch. The man's drinking companions, feeling an equally strong sense of solidarity with a friend in distress, then joined the battle. Séguin, who lacked by a long chalk Gauguin's muscular strength and boxing skill, took such fright at the turn of events that he dived headlong into the harbour fully dressed. But Gauguin, O'Conor, and Jourdain made a powerful counter-attack, and would doubtless have carried the day but for the arrival of reinforcements from the taverns. These new assailants also went for the screaming Anna, though the other women nobly did their best to shield her. Suddenly Gauguin tripped and fell. A moment later he was being kicked by sabots. Strangely, he made no effort to rise. Eventually, the attackers realized they had gone too far and made off.

Gauguin still lay in the same position when the gendarmes arrived, but though faint was fully conscious and able to tell what was wrong with him. He had broken his right leg; so badly indeed that the shinbone protruded just above the ankle. Both O'Conor and Jourdain had been badly mauled. Séguin's mistress had an injured rib. The other women had escaped with a fright, thanks to the strong protection of their whalebone corsets.

Borrowing a gig, the sorry bloodstained company drove their fallen chief back to Pont-Aven. The doctor whom they called in could only bandage the leg and advise a few months of complete rest. But before long Gauguin had to send for him again and ask for a morphine injection to still the aching pains which prevented him from getting any sleep. He had to deaden the pains with morphine and alcohol practically every day for over two months, and even so managed to get only a few hours sleep at a time.

On August 23, running the risk of opening up the wound, he made the twenty-mile journey to Quimper, where sentence was passed on the assailants by the district court, though, strangely, the police had discovered only two, Sauban, a pilot, and Monfort, a fisherman. The court records have been preserved, and the charge sheet (with a customary mis-spelling of Gauguin's name) reads: "Wilful assault on Monsieur Paul Gauguen, leading to bodily injury and incapacity for a period of more than twenty days." Gauguin asked for 10,000 francs in damages, but to his extreme surprise and disgust the amount was reduced by the court to 600 francs—which was less than the medical and legal costs. In addition to these trifling damages, Sauban was sentenced to a mere eight days' imprisonment, "as it had not been fully proved that Sauban was responsible for the serious fracture of M. Gauguen's leg." Montfort was acquitted.[137]

Gauguin was justified in describing the sentence as "absurdly mild," and in a letter to Molard a few days later he alleged that the magistrates' leniency sprang from the fact that "the scoundrels of Concarneau are voters, and my assailant is a friend of the republican authorities." As the only way to get his revenge he urged Molard to ask Julien Leclercq—who occupied his studio in the rue Vercingétorix rent-free and thus had a fair-sized debt of gratitude to repay—to persuade the editor of the *Écho de Paris* or some other large daily to publish "a stinging article about the district court at Quimper."

Gauguin informed Molard in the same letter that he had finally made the decision which his friends had long foreseen and feared: "In December I shall return (to Paris) and exert myself to sell all my belongings, either *en bloc* or piecemeal. With the necessary capital in my pocket I shall return to the South Seas, this time with my two companions here, Séguin and an Irishman. It is no use objecting. Nothing will stop me going, and it will be for good. What an idiotic existence life is in Europe!"[138] His announcement of the news to Daniel de Monfreid is even more revealing both of his desperate mood and of his pathetic illusions: "If all goes well I shall leave in February (1895). Thus I shall be able to end my days a free man, peacefully, with no concern for the morrow, and no more battling all the time with imbeciles. . . . No more painting, apart from any I may do for my own amusement. My house will be of carved wood."[139] To a certain extent, Gauguin's hopes of finding a real paradise on earth were justified on this occasion, for he now contemplated going to Samoa where the natives still lived in the ancient Polynesian way, and where he should have gone in the first place instead of to Tahiti.[140]

But he said nothing to Mette about this important decision, which was to change her whole future as well as his, his only feelings for her now being those of bitterness and rancour. The chief reason for this was Mette's silence during his long and painful convalescence, though she was well aware of what had occurred. It could be said in her defence, of course, that in ceasing to write at the beginning of the year she was doing only what she had been told to do. Moreover, Paul's escapades with Anna had come to her ears, and had angered her just as much as the non-arrival of a further share in the legacy. Nevertheless, it was definitely her turn to make a move towards a reconciliation after the misadventure at Concarneau, and Paul would doubtless have been mollified by a few tender and cheering words from her. Unhappily, she could no more forget her pride now than before, and thus she lost her last chance of repairing their marriage.

For two reasons, Gauguin did not leave Pont-Aven immediately; for one thing he was still too weak and exhausted, and for another he wanted to see his second case, the one against Marie Henry, through the courts. For Anna, however, the prospect of another month or two in this dull little country town was too much; she had long since wearied alike of the monotony and of her duties as a nurse. Gauguin was no less tired of her sulks and tantrums. When, therefore, she asked him for her train fare to Paris he gladly gave it to her, relieved to be rid of her so easily and cheaply.

The district court at Quimper finally passed judgment in his case on November 14, and as in the previous one showed an outrageous bias in favour of the local electors by rejecting Gauguin's claim for damages and even ordering him to pay the defendant's costs. The reason adduced was his neglect to obtain a written receipt from Marie Henry before leaving Le Pouldu in November 1890, a neglect which, in the opinion of the court, could have only one meaning: he was no longer interested in the works of art he had left behind.[141] Angry and dejected, Gauguin took the first train for Paris. What he found when he entered the studio in the rue Vercingétorix was not calculated to cheer him up; Anna had been there already and made off with all his valuables—everything, that is, except his pictures. Another disheartening piece of news was that Morice had still to complete his contributions to Noa Noa and was very vague about when he would be able to do so.

So as to leave as quickly as possible, Gauguin decided to sell off his whole stock of pictures by auction, as he had so successfully done before his first departure for Tahiti. While Morice once again embarked on the difficult task of persuading his friends and colleagues of the press to provide the free publicity, Gauguin began to cast around for a known and influential person who might lend some of the lustre and distinction of his name by writing a preface to the catalogue. He eventually found the right man among the many friends of William and Ida Molard, in the person of the Swedish writer August Strindberg. Strindberg had arrived in Paris in August 1894, and after the *première* of *The Father* in the middle of December (which Gauguin had attended) had become one of the most talked-of and controversial authors in the French capital. The Parisians were even more fascinated than they had been before when they learnt that he was an alchemist, and when he published, in *La Revue Blanche*, a long study entitled *A la zoologie de le femme*, in which he "proved" with copious quotations from learned works and much ill-concealed venom that women are the inferiors of men in intellect. On his first visit to the Molards (he and Ida had known each other in Stockholm) Strindberg had been mistrustfully on his dignity and had asked his hosts to explain to all those present that he knew no French; but before long he had followed Gauguin upstairs and there recovered his speech. Strindberg's fame reached its climax soon after, when he published his even more violent anti-feminist tract, *A Fool's Speech in His Defence*, in the middle of January 1895. It was just then that Gauguin wanted his preface, as the date of the sale had been fixed for February 18. During most of January Strindberg was undergoing treatment for a disease of the skin in a Paris hospital, but the day on which he was discharged, January 31, Gauguin invited him to a party in his studio and at the appropriate moment asked for his help. The next day Strindberg wrote him a long letter,[142] which began in this none too promising manner:

"My dear Gauguin,
"You insist that the preface to your catalogue should be written by

me, in memory of our stay here in the winter of 1894-95 behind the Institute, not far from the Pantheon, and in particular near to the cemetery of Montparnasse.

"I should have liked to give you this token of remembrance to take with you to the South Seas, where you are going in search of space and a setting in keeping with your powerful stature; but I feel that I have been placed in a false position from the outset and so I am replying at once to your request with an 'I cannot,' or more brutally 'I will not.'"

Strindberg's no less candid reason was as follows:

"I cannot understand your art and cannot like it. (I have no comprehension of your art, which is now so entirely Tahitian.) However, I know that this admission will neither surprise nor offend you, as you seem rather to be fortified by other people's hatred, at the same time as your personality, concerned to remain free, thrives on it. Probably you are right; for as soon as people begin to appreciate and admire you, follow your example, and group and classify you, a label will have been affixed to your art—a label which in five years' time will have become to the young an epithet for an obsolete art, which they will do all they can to make even more old-fashioned.

"I have myself made serious efforts to classify you, to fit you as a link in the chain, in order to understand the history of your evolution —but in vain."

After a brief account of his much more successful attempts to comprehend the new Impressionist art during previous visits to Paris Strindberg went on:

"But in the death agonies of Naturalism there was one name which all spoke of admiringly, namely that of Puvis de Chavannes. Alone and unlike anyone else he painted with a believer's conviction, while taking the contemporary liking for allusiveness into account. (Nothing was yet known of Symbolism, that unfortunate term which is now applied to the ancient phenomenon of allegory.)

"It was to Puvis de Chavannes that my thoughts turned last night, when to the southern sounds of the mandolin and guitar I studied the sun-drenched pictures on the walls of your studio, and the memory of them pursued me all night in my sleep. I saw trees no botanist would ever find, beasts Cuvier would never have dreamt of, and people you alone could have created. I saw a sea which appeared to flow out of a volcano, and a sky inhabitable by no God. 'Monsieur,' I said in my dream, 'you have created a new earth and a new heaven, but I do not feel easy in your new universe; for me, a lover of the *chiaroscuro*, it is too ablaze with sunlight. And in your paradise dwells an Eve who is not my ideal; for I also have a feminine ideal—or two!'

"This morning I visited the Luxembourg, to see Chavannes' work, to which my thoughts continued to revert. With great sympathy I saw *The Poor Fisherman* intent on seeking the fish that will bring him the love and affection of his flower-picking wife and idle child. It is beautiful! But then at once I was put off by the fisherman's crown of thorns. Because I hate Christ and crowns of thorns! Monsieur, I hate them, do you hear? I totally reject this pitiable God who acquiesces in blows. For a divinity give me Vitsliputsli, who eats human hearts in broad daylight.

"But Gauguin was not made from Chavannes' rib, nor from Manet's or Bastien-Lepage's.

"Then who is he? He is Gauguin the savage, who hates civilization's restrictions; rather a Titan, jealous of the Creator and wanting in his leisure to make his own little Creation. He is a child taking his toys to pieces to make new ones, rejecting and defying and preferring a red sky to everybody else's blue one.

"Upon my word, it looks as if, working myself up while writing, I begin in some measure to understand Gauguin's art!

"A modern author has been reproached for not painting real people, but *quite simply* inventing his characters. Quite simply!

"*Bon voyage*, master! But come back again and look me up. Perhaps by then I may have learnt to understand your art better, which will enable me to write a real foreword to a new catalogue in a new Hôtel Drouet; for I, too, begin to feel a great need to turn savage and make a new world.

August Strindberg."

This was not exactly what Gauguin had expected. But Strindberg's reply was both interesting and amusing, and his fame was at its height. Gauguin therefore printed the letter in full in the sales catalogue, together with a short reply. The next step was to get the catalogue to the press in good time before the sale. Several of the leading newspapers, as expected, reproduced the highly original preface.

But one clever publicity gimmick was hardly enough to persuade those who only eighteen months earlier had ridiculed and rejected his "barbarous" and unintelligible pictures to start bidding briskly for them now. *Noa Noa*, the book which would supposedly give the background to the Tahitian paintings and explain Gauguin's art, still had to be completed. Moreover, the fact that an artist disillusioned with civilization was about to abandon it for ever could hardly be expected to arouse the same interest a second time as it had done the first. Added to this, in the winter of 1894–95 the Parisians had precious little time for or interest in art shows or other cultural events. In the first place, the anarchists, who the summer before had succeeded in assassinating the French President, Sadi-Carnot, were at this time terrorizing the capital as thoroughly as the SAO terrorists have done more recently. Secondly, the Panama scandal continued to develop apace, leading to as frequent changes of government as in the years preceding General de Gaulle's accession to power. Thirdly, an event occurred which shook the nation and split it into two opposing camps exactly as under Pétain; this was the harsh sentence passed just before Christmas 1894, on very doubtful evidence, in the Dreyfus case. The prospect of attracting a large number of ready buyers to Gauguin's sale was therefore very slim indeed. In fact, attendance at the sale, on February 18, 1895, was small, and the bidding slack. Gauguin made a reckless attempt to boost the market by making bids himself through agents. The attempt was a disastrous failure, most of the items being knocked down to them, with resultant bigger commission to the auctioneer. Only nine of the forty-seven pictures offered went to genuine buyers, two of them to Degas.

As usual, Mette was well informed about her husband's activities through newspaper reports and letters. The only piece of information which she did not get was the one that four-fifths of the sales had in fact been re-purchases. As she had still received only 1,500 francs from the legacy, she could contain herself no longer, and wrote a sharp letter reminding him of her troubles in providing for the children. The result, of course, was the opposite of that expected. Instead of admitting that her complaint was fair and reasonable, Gauguin fastened on to the bitter fact that when Mette at length broke her year-long silence it was to ask him for money. In a sudden wave of anger, he replied brutally:

"Now, let us talk things over. Nobody would deny that a man who has gone through what I've gone through since I came back must have reflected sadly on life, the family, and everything else.

"1. You write: 'You must fend for yourself.'

"2. The children write—nothing.

"3. My ankle was broken and it's ruining my health; not a word did I receive from my family.

"4. The winter has been terribly long and in my solitude I have tried in vain to nurse a *chronic* bronchitis. I literally cannot live without sunshine.

"In these circumstances and because of the enemies my painting has made for me, I must take all sorts of precautions in order not to fail. I *will not* descend into abject poverty at the age of 47, and yet I am very near to it. If I am thrown down, *nobody* in the world will help me on to my feet again. Your words, 'You must fend for yourself,' contain deep wisdom. I shall observe them."

Yet it suggests a guilty conscience that in this parting letter he furnished Mette with false information about the proceeds of the sale. He told her there was a net *loss* of 464.80 francs. But if his figures are checked against the accounts, which have been preserved, it becomes clear that he made a *profit* of 1,430.02 francs.[143]

As he still possessed a large proportion of his legacy he should have been able to leave for the South Seas once the sale was over. Indeed, the sooner he did so the better, because every day spent in Paris ate into his capital, which would be sorely needed in Samoa. Yet he allowed the weeks and months to slip away without making the slightest preparations for his departure. The reason for this strange behaviour—which has escaped the notice of most of his biographers because of Morice's mis-statement that Gauguin sailed "in the early spring of 1895"—was that just before the sale he had fallen ill again. This time he had eruptions all over his body, and everyone, including Gauguin, agreed that they were syphilitic.[144] As in those days the methods of treatment were not very effective it was several months before he ventured to book his passage. Concern for his health may also have caused him to abandon his plan of going to primitive Samoa and decide instead to return to Tahiti, where there was a European hospital. The fact that O'Conor and Séguin were either unable or unwilling to leave with him immediately may have been a further reason for deciding against a quite unfamiliar island, where most of the few white residents were British or German.

He spent the interval of waiting in producing a stoneware sculpture, two feet high, which he called *Oviri*, after his favourite Tahitian song. The title is much more appropriate to this sculpture than to the previous self-portrait in plaster, for it represents a nude female with a gruesome round-eyed death's head, standing on a she-wolf and crushing the life out of a whelp against her side. This sculpture, which a leading authority has called his "supreme achievement as a ceramist," Gauguin submitted to the spring salon of the Société Nationale des Beaux-Arts—only to have it promptly rejected.[145] He responded by writing two open letters to *Le Soir*, in which he sharply attacked the Society, the Academy, and the new director, Roujon.

Far more interesting than these polemics, however, is a long interview with Gauguin which was printed in the *Écho de Paris*. The interview is worth reproducing in full, not only because it has never previously been reprinted but also, and especially, because it provides an excellent insight into his personality and artistic theories. This is what the paper's star reporter wrote in the issue of May 13, 1895:

"The Art of Painting and the Painters

M. Paul Gauguin

"He is the wildest of all the innovators, and of all the 'misunderstood' artists the one least inclined to compromise. A number of his *discoverers* have forsaken him. To the great majority of people he is just a humbug. Yet he calmly goes on painting his orange rivers and red dogs, and for every day which passes adheres more and more to this personal *manner*.

"Gauguin is built like a Hercules: his greying hair is curly, his features are energetic, his eyes clear; and when he smiles in his characteristic way he seems alike gentle, shy, and ironical."

" 'What exactly does it mean, this expression "to copy nature?" ' he asks me, stretching himself defiantly. 'Follow the example of the masters,' we are advised. But what for? Why should we follow their example? They are masters for the sole reason that they refused to follow anybody else's example. Bouguereau has talked of women glowing in all the colours of the rainbow and denies the existence of blue shadows. One can just as well deny the existence of brown shadows such as he paints; what cannot be denied is that his canvases are devoid of any glow. He may have glowed himself when he painted his pictures but it was with sweating to make slavish copies of objects as they appear to be, and striving for success in a field where, in spite of his exertions, he is surpassed by photography. A man who sweats smells, and his tastelessness and incompetence smell a long way off. After all, it matters little whether blue shadows do or do not exist. If a painter tomorrow decides that shadows are pink, or violet, there is no reason why he should have to defend his decision, assuming that his work is harmonious and thought-provoking.'

" 'Then your red dogs and pink skies. . . .'

" '. . . are deliberate. Absolutely deliberate. They are necessary. Every feature in my paintings is carefully considered and calculated in advance. Just as in a musical composition, if you like. My simple object, which I take from daily life or from nature, is merely a pretext, which helps me by means of a definite arrangement of lines and colours to create symphonies and harmonies. They have no counterparts at all in reality, in the vulgar sense of that word; they do not give direct expression to any idea, their only purpose being to stimulate the imagination—just as music does without the aid of ideas or pictures—simply by that mysterious affinity which exists between certain arrangements of colours and lines and our minds.'

" 'These are rather novel theories!'

" 'They are not at all novel!' Monsieur Gauguin exclaimed emphatically and with some feeling. 'All great artists have always done exactly the same. Raphael, Rembrandt, Velasquez, Botticelli, Cranach, they all distorted nature. Go to the Louvre and look at their pictures and you will see how different they are. According to your theory, one of them must be right and the rest wrong. Unless they have all been deceiving us. If you demand that a work should be true to nature, then neither Rembrandt nor Raphael succeeded, any more than Botticelli or Bouguereau. Shall I tell you what will soon be the most faithful work of art? A photograph, when it can render colours, as it will soon be able to. And you would have an intelligent being sweat away for months to achieve the same illusion of reality as an ingenious little machine? It is the same with sculpture. It is possible already to make perfect casts. A skilled moulder can make a Falguière statue for you with ease whenever you like.'

" 'So you do not wish to be called revolutionary?'

" 'I find the expression ridiculous. Monsieur Roujon has applied it to me. I told him that all artists whose work differs from their predecessors' work have merited it. Indeed, it is for that reason alone that they are masters. Manet is a master, and Delacroix. At first their work was considered atrocious, and people laughed at Delacroix' violet horses—which, incidentally, I have looked for in vain in his pictures. But such is the public. I have become reconciled to the idea that I shall remain misunderstood for a long time to come. If I only did what others have already done before me I should in my own estimation be just a worthless plagiarist. But whenever I strive to conceive something new I am called wretched. In that case I would rather be a wretch than a plagiarist.'

" 'There are many cultivated people who think that, as the Greeks achieved sculpture of ideal perfection and purity and the Renaissance did the same in painting, nothing now remains but to emulate their works. The same people would even say that the plastic arts have exhausted their potentialities!'

" 'That is an absolute mistake. Beauty is eternal and can have a thousand forms. The Middle Ages had one ideal of beauty, Egypt another. The Greeks strove for complete harmony of the human body, and Raphael had very beautiful models. But you can equally well produce a valid work of art from a model that is as ugly as sin. There are plenty of such works in the Louvre.'

" 'Why did you make your journey to Tahiti?'

" 'I had once been fascinated by this idyllic island and its primitive and simple people. That is why I returned and why I am now going back there again.[146] In order to achieve something new, you have to go back to the sources, to man's childhood. My Eve is almost animal. That is why she is chaste for all her nakedness. But all the Venuses in the Salon are indecent and disgracefully lewd. . . .'

"Monsieur Gauguin fell silent, and with a rather ecstatic expression on his face turned to regard a picture on the wall of some Tahitian women in the jungle. A few moments after he continued:

" 'Before leaving, I shall publish in collaboration with my friend Charles Morice a book about my life in Tahiti and my views on art. Morice comments in verse on the works I have brought back with me. In short, the book will be a statement about why and how I made the journey.'

" 'What will be its title?'

" 'Noanoa—a Tahitian word meaning "fragrant." In other words, the book will be about what Tahiti exhales.'

Eugène Tardieu."

But in spite of constant proddings, Morice had not yet delivered more than a fraction of his contributions to Noa Noa, and it was obvious that the book could not appear before Gauguin's departure. He therefore copied out the completed parts, in order not to waste the results of his efforts during the previous winter, should Morice mislay the original manuscript after his departure, as he might well do. It would also be useful to have the copy in Tahiti in case Morice were to suggest changes and improvements in the completed half of the manuscript.[147] Morice to some extent tried to make up for his negligence by publishing a long, last-minute farewell article in *Le Soir* on June 28. The article was prophetic in several respects. This is what he wrote under the unsensational heading *"Departure of Gauguin:"*

"Had we not made it a habit—and how deep-seated the habit is—of turning everything upside down and with diabolical obstinacy doing exactly the opposite of what both justice and reason require, more people would be thinking now of this artist who is about to flee from our civilization voluntarily and for ever, rather than gossiping about the latest adventure of Mademoiselle Otero.

"Yet I am charitable enough to believe that there are still some passers-by of the frivolous nightly gatherings in Paris who are prepared to give five minutes' thought to serious matters, and I have at least the excuse that what I have to report is of immediate concern.

"Tomorrow a great artist will leave Paris and France without hope of returning; a great artist who is nauseated by 'the air full of gas and treacle' (to quote Théophile Gautier) which we in the West have to breathe. . . . Whatever those excellent people may think who have such great admiration for the wonders of modern life and who grow ecstatic at the mention of the word 'progress,' it is nevertheless a fact that, in line with the rule indicated at the beginning of this article, namely that at all times and in all circumstances we behave contrary to the dictates of intelligence, it is almost impossible for persons with native talent and with ambition and a creative urge to fulfil their natural function in our society. Everything presents obstacles, including the animosity of the authorities and the hatred of the mediocre. . . . Why, therefore, should we expect that he (Gauguin) should continue to tolerate these unfair and unjust conditions if he can avoid them? Since he cannot expect help from society, well disposed as it is to the rich alone, he for his part cannot serve it. For the truth is that he is excluded from every official exhibition in advance and no one will ever employ his creative genius. So what use is it to stay?

"Out there (in the South Seas), on the other hand, where a man can live on little money and material and space costs nothing at all, he will be able to erect great monuments, which astonished travellers will perhaps some day discover; so that it will one day be necessary to fetch his works from the square of some Tahitian village, by the shores of a sea bordered by surf-sprayed coral reefs, and ship them at great cost home to France, the land which has denied to one of the most outstanding French sculptors of the century his right to produce those very works. . . .

"In spite of the personal sadness which this departure causes me, I am happy to record the lesson that this event teaches us, the warning which it gives to the official arbiters of the world of art. It is an important episode in the merciless war that has been declared by true artists on those who trespass against art and those who—with what right—rule over them.

"When you see that an artist such as he has to go so far off in order to live and be free, will you persist in remaining deaf to the protest made along with him by the whole younger generation against the men and the works that you applaud? Do you know that this younger generation, which one day will hurl at you the charge that you so richly deserve, *has ceased even to laugh* at Bonnat, Gérôme and Bouguereau?"

With his usual dislike of sentimental and theatrical scenes, Gauguin forbade his friends to see him off at the station. Not even Morice, who had rendered him such great service, or his devoted disciples Séguin and O'Conor, who were soon to follow him to Tahiti, were excepted from this prohibition. As for that most loyal and trustworthy friend, Daniel de Monfreid, he had left Paris in the middle of May. Gauguin was determined that his last Thursday "at home" should proceed as usual, which indeed it did except in one particular, as indicated by the following passage in Judith's memoirs:

"Dressed in one of my gowns, powdered with flour, and with his large eyes made up with coal, Paco gave a last plaintive rendering of some languishing songs of Malaga. He sang, but his singing was more like incense rising from a censer. His lavender-blue eyes glistened with tears, which made them resemble amethysts. They were fixed all the time on Gauguin, who stood in front of the open fireplace, fingering the oily astrakhan facings of his jacket, while a slight tremor passed through the arch which was formed by his eyebrows.

"While with death in my heart I served tea and slices of sweet cake on large mother-of-pearl shells, for the last time, Gauguin was overwhelmed by his savage instincts, and anticipating the joy of soon being back once more in his right element he danced an *upaupa*:

Upaupa Tahiti
upaupa faaruru
e—e—e!"

To show Judith his gratitude and give her a last well-deserved remembrance of him, Gauguin took her to the Montparnasse Theatre to see *Les Cloches de Corneville* the night before leaving Paris. After this obvious demonstration of the special place which she held in his affections, it was of course impossible to deny her the right to see him off at the station the next day. Inevitably, this meant that her mother and stepfather had to go, too. Paco, who turned up at the last moment, was prompted by this to follow at his master's heels, which he did with his usual dog-like devotion in spite of Gauguin's furious protests. Contrary to his desire and determination, therefore, Gauguin had in the end to endure a long sentimental scene of farewells on the platform, to the accompaniment of tears, embraces, and banal talk.

In short, his departure was as much a failure as the whole of his long stay in France.

VIII

REPEAT PERFORMANCE

GAUGUIN left on this occasion without an "official mission" and so he could not claim a reduction in the fare on ships of the Government-owned Messageries Maritimes company. Nevertheless he travelled, as he had done four years earlier, via Suez and Australia, because it was cheaper, and not by the shorter, quicker, and more interesting route via America. But instead of going on to Noumea, where, as he now knew, there was a risk of being delayed for weeks and even months waiting for a connection, he wisely disembarked at Sydney when his ship, the *Australien*, arrived there on August 5. From there he was able to proceed immediately by another ship to Auckland, the port from which the small New Zealand steamer the *Richmond* departed once a month on the round trip to Samoa, Rarotonga, and Tahiti. Unfortunately, however, this had just left, so he had to wait rather more than three weeks in Auckland. The interval of waiting was rather unpleasant, since August is the coldest month in the New Zealand winter and, in true British tradition, none of the hotels or houses was well heated. Knowing nobody and speaking barely enough English to make himself understood in even the simplest of situations, Gauguin was lonely and isolated. But the passage to Tahiti, when at length he embarked on it, turned out to be even worse, for exactly the opposite reasons: the badly ventilated, iron-built *Richmond* was unbearably stuffy and confined, and moreover pitched and rolled as violently as that other old tub, the *Vire*. Her only advantage was that she was faster than the *Vire*, and could do eight knots. So, after only eleven days of beating against the trade winds, the *Richmond* slipped into Papeete harbour on September 8 and berthed—like all merchant ships but unlike naval vessels—alongside the small wooden jetty at the eastern end of the bay.[148]

Contrary to his first arrival in 1891, Gauguin aroused no interest when he stepped ashore this time, as he was already well known, and what is more had been spurned by the European residents. But even if he had been an absolute newcomer they would doubtless have ignored him just the same, because the previous ship to arrive had brought with it another Frenchman whom everyone wanted to meet and invite, as their guest of honour, to their house parties. This celebrated and sought-after person was a former governor named Isidore Chessé, who had been honoured with the newly invented title of Commissioner General and as such sent out on an important special mission to Tahiti.[149] The mere acceptance of this commission almost warranted the grandiloquent title, for it was an extremely difficult one, which entailed solving, quickly and pacifically, a problem which had defeated a long succession of governors, among them the able Lacascade. This problem was how to persuade the natives of Raiatea, another of the Society Islands, about 120 miles north-west of Tahiti, to recognize French supremacy. These natives, aided and abetted by Nonconformist British missionaries, who had converted them, had persisted for two generations in flying the Union Jack and singing "God Save the Queen," though the British Government in a formal treaty with the French had renounced their claims to the island in return for concessions elsewhere in the South Seas. To the embarrassment of the French, the pro-British sentiments of the Raiateans remained unaffected by this repudiation. But the situation had only become a positive nuisance when, in 1892, the French had introduced in Tahiti the import tariff mentioned earlier, and enterprising Anglo-American businessmen had started to use Raiatea as a commercial free port, to the great detriment of French merchants in Papeete. Being still reluctant to occupy the island by force, the French Government had decided in 1895 to make a final attempt at reaching a peaceful solution and to this end had deputed Chessé, who as the colony's governor fifteen years before had shown great diplomatic skill in persuading King Pomare V to renounce his powers in return for the generous pension that had enabled him to drink himself to death so soon after. When Gauguin arrived, the commissioner general had been in Papeete only a month and was still making the round of welcomes and celebrations.

From past experience, Gauguin knew that the residents of Papeete had small regard for artists, and he was neither surprised nor disappointed when they omitted to invite him to their parties. But he could scarcely fail to be both disturbed and distressed by the numerous fresh signs of advancing civilization—or decadence, according to whether the point of view was European or Tahitian—which were visible on all sides. The most striking innovation was the electric lighting, which after nightfall shed a yellow glow on the open-air dance floor, the market and several streets, making everybody look like Chinese. The noisiest novelty was a huge steam-driven merry-go-round, which an enterprising businessman had been allowed to install in the park outside the now vacant royal palace. A contemporary visitor much less sensitive to ugliness had this to say of it:

"The thing itself is a poor contrivance enough, with steam gearing and mottled wooden horses, whose unnaturalness sets the pre-Raphaelite masters at zero. Watch the people though. The trading schooners have swept them together from the funniest out-of-the-way islands. Just imagine the pride of a mother in some lost coral dab, who after a year's 'screwing' takes her family of daughters to be 'finished' in this giddiest of baby capitals. Queer notions of civilization the poor things must get! Here on the grass you can see a bevy of timid brown things stand and gaze pensively at the merry-go-round. If you want to have some fun, buy a few tickets and distribute them among the innocents. The wooden horse is very tame. He won't either bite or kick. Like as not, if the girls come from some very small island, they will have never seen a horse or any beast larger than a pig. Never mind, start them on the machine. Off they go—to a jingling tune from *Madame Angot*, with shrilling whistle and panting steam-pipe. Horrors! one of the beauties has been ill-advised enough to jump off, and goes rolling over on the grass, a mass of flashing brown limbs and flying hair. Two more hang on with faces deathly pale. A fourth, the youngest of the bunch, has started sobbing and calling for mamma. The machine is stopped and they are let down, pleased but shaken. The amusements of the white *Faranis* are as awful as their wickedness."[150]

An equally ludicrous nuisance was the many cyclists, chiefly Frenchmen in sports clothes but including some Tahitian women with flowing robes and hair, who wobbled along the pot-holed and unsurfaced streets. On the lawns surrounding the governor's residence, colonial officials now eagerly went in for another new but more gentlemanly sport, that of tennis, which the enterprising new head of the Department of the Interior, Gustave Gallet, had introduced. There was even progress in art and culture, as was indicated by a regular advertisement in the four-page weekly, *Le Messager de Tahiti*, which read as follows:

"THE FINE ARTS IN EVERY HOME!

"We have pleasure in offering our readers *four* superb oleographs of J. F. Millet's famous paintings, *The Angelus, The Gleaners, The Sower*, and *The Shepherdess and Flock*, which depict rural life in masterly style against a background full of sound and healthy poetry.

"The long travels of *The Angelus*, first to America, where a fortune in gold was offered for it, and then back again to France at a cost of over 700,000 francs, are familiar to everyone. Everyone, therefore, will wish to have a real *facsimile* of this and the *three* other pictures, which though less well-known are nevertheless worthy to set beside it.

"The reproductions are works of art in themselves and will attract just attention anywhere. They are 42 centimetres high and 52 centimetres long, and will be sent post free in return for payment in advance at the price of three francs per picture, five francs for any two, and nine francs for all four pictures."

As the advertisement appeared regularly week after week, the enterprise would appear to have been worth while, suggesting that Gauguin had found a serious rival in the task of catering for local artistic needs. For who would be so foolish as to pay several hundred francs for an original painting by a dauber when such excellent reproductions of recognized masterpieces could be had for as little as three francs each?

Whether it was because he was disgusted by all this "progress" in Papeete or because the plan had been slowly ripening in his mind on the way out, Gauguin resolved almost at once to achieve his old ambition of going to the more remote Marquesas. That he was sure of finding there the paradise which had made him return to the South Seas is made plain by the manner in which he announced his decision to William Molard in a letter written a week after his arrival: "Next month I shall be in La Dominique, a delightful little island in the Marquesas, where living costs next to nothing and I shall be free from all Europeans. With my small capital and a well-equipped studio I shall live there like a lord."[151]

While waiting for a ship to the Marquesas Islands Gauguin lodged in one of Madame Charbonnier's furnished bungalows. His best friend, Lieutenant Jénot, had long ago been transferred to another colony. But two of his nearest neighbours at Madame Charbonnier's were newly arrived magistrates, both bachelors, who happened to be interested not only in *ava, vahine e upaupa,* or "wine, women, and song," but also in art and literature. In fact one of them, Édouard Charlier, was a spare-time painter, while the other, Maurice Olivaint, wrote florid and vaguely Symbolist verses, which in due course were published in book form, besides a bizarre novel, *Sur les coraux,* in which the principal character is a cruelly persecuted bigamist who flees to the South Seas and there eventually finds happiness by becoming a polygamist.[152] Gauguin was not long in the company of these pleasant and hospitable neighbours before he was tempted to join them on their evening rounds of the taverns, the evening dances and the "flesh" market.

Charlier and Olivaint introduced Gauguin to a third government servant, a man he felt drawn to from the start but for quite different reasons. He was a hot-blooded Corsican, named Jules Agostini, who since 1894 had been director of public works in the colony. Agostini had two hobbies, both of which interested Gauguin. In the first place, he was an enthusiastic amateur photographer and owned a large and clumsy camera he could neither carry nor mount without help, which Gauguin was willing to provide. And, secondly, he was an amateur anthropologist of no little accomplishment and was busily collecting material for some interesting papers, which he published after

---

→

34. *Gauguin's new house and studio in Punaauia, photographed in 1897 by his friend Jules Agostini, and showing the statue of a nude woman which upset the Catholic priest of the district so much.*

35. *Where do we come from? What are we? Where are we going?—the picture which Gauguin called his spiritual testament—photographed in his studio on June 2, 1898, by Lemasson the postmaster.*

36. *Whether this photograph was taken by a friend or he bought it in Papeete, Gauguin was fascinated by the appearance and poses of these women.*

his return to France in various scientific journals. Gauguin was delighted to have, at long last, a friend with whom he could discuss Tahitian anthropology and mythology. Then, at the beginning of October, a young new postmaster, Henry Lemasson, arrived, also bringing a large camera, and soon the three were going on photographic expeditions together into the surrounding country.[153]

The first connection to the Marquesas after Gauguin's arrival in Papeete was a small schooner, of only forty-three tons and very much the worse for wear, which was scheduled to leave on October 28. Passengers slept without cover on deck in all weathers, along with pigs, goats, and hens. Gauguin therefore had a good excuse for not taking this boat. Another vessel, of 127 tons, which by local standards was fairly large, was due to depart on November 15, and this had a number of berths below deck with only the minor inconveniences of cockroaches, rats, and the stench of copra.[154] But once more Gauguin failed to embark for his ultimate paradise, and instead began to look around for a convenient place to build himself a hut in Tahiti.

There is no documentary material to explain this sudden change of plans. But it is reasonable to suppose that there had been a further deterioration in his health and that he was aware of the need for hospital treatment, which he could only get in Tahiti. The melancholy fact that Séguin and O'Conor had neither followed him out nor written to say when they would be doing so will no doubt have contributed to the decision. We now know for certain that neither Séguin nor O'Conor had ever seriously contemplated following Gauguin to Tahiti. The brief but revealing explanation which Séguin gave shortly before his death was that Gauguin was too autocratic.[155] O'Conor's reason may also be ascribed to incompatibility, for this is how Alan Brook relates a conversation he once had with him about a letter from Gauguin: "It was too scatalogical for publication—details of the ideal

---

37. *The result was this greatly stylized double portrait with a quite different background and decorative flowers.*

38. *Another French painter, Le Moine, who arrived after Gauguin, was given a well-paid sinecure by the governor. But then he painted pretty pictures such as this.*

39. *As the editor of Les Guêpes, Gauguin took the opportunity to insert free advertisements for his own hectographed and illustrated monthly, Le Sourire.*

position in sexual intercourse—and I lost the letter when the Germans pillaged the house; but an interesting feature of the letter was that Gauguin urged O'Conor to accompany him to the South Seas. I thought this wonderful and asked: 'Why didn't you go?' O'Conor, snuffling indignation: 'Do you see me going to the South Seas with that character?' "¹⁵⁶ It is quite likely that Gauguin in his heart of hearts had realized how unrealistic his hope had been, and that on mature reflection he shrank from isolating himself for ever in the remote Marquesas Islands where there would be nobody with whom to discuss art. With his well-known need of company he may have reasoned that, thanks to his many new friends, he would now be much more at home in Tahiti.

Gauguin abandoned his idea of the Marquesas but not his dream of a life in paradise. He set out to realize this by copying as closely as possible the pattern of his happy life with Teha'amana in Mataiea, in 1892–93, though this did not mean that he had to return to Mataiea. In fact, there were at least two reasons for not going back there. One was that it was a long way from Papeete, and he had unpleasant memories of the expensive and uncomfortable five-hour journey by coach. The other was that it was exceptionally rainy as well as civilized in Mataiea. The district Gauguin chose when he came to leave Papeete, in November 1895, was Punaauia on the west coast, a region he already knew fairly well as he had often driven through it on the way from Mataiea to Papeete. It was a good choice, and many Europeans in Tahiti today have followed his example.

Gauguin decided this time to build a house of his own and so avoid having to pay rent for the rest of his life. Like every European settler before or since, he soon found that all the land in the district unfortunately was collectively owned by some native kinship group, and that there was always somebody who either opposed the deal or was inaccessible when there was a plot he would have liked to buy or lease. But in the end he managed to find a site on the shore eight miles from Pepeete (site 6 on map 2, page 91) which belonged to a Frenchman, who was willing to lease it on very reasonable terms.

To find a few Tahitians anxious to earn a little extra cash for wine and beer by building a house for him was a far easier matter. Gauguin ordered an oval hut with walls of unsplit bamboo canes and a roof of plaited palm leaves, very like the one he had rented from Anani in Mataiea. It can hardly have taken the natives a week to finish it. Gauguin improved the hut inside by dividing it into two

with a curtain he had brought from the studio in the rue Vercingétorix, furnishing one half with a bed and in the other setting up his
easel. Enough light would normally have filtered through the wide interstices between the bamboo canes to make windows unnecessary,
but surrounding iron-wood-trees, which Gauguin did not wish to fell
or was not allowed to, cast such heavy shadows that he had a window
put in the roof of the studio half. He also, to some extent, realized
his old dream of having "a house of carved wood," as he made several
large panels, which he hung on the wall, and with great care transformed two of the posts into forbidding idols. A fact connected with
the house which he probably found less attractive was its situation
mid-way between the district's Protestant and Catholic churches.
But a distinct advantage was that the Chinese store was much nearer
than the store in Mataiea, only just across the road.

As soon as the hut was ready, Gauguin sent for Teha'amana. When
he had left in 1893 she had at first worked as a servant for Chief Tetuanui in Mataiea, but had soon married a young Tahitian boy,
named Ma'ari, from the adjacent district of Papara. This did not prevent her from immediately taking the coach for Punaauia when
summoned by Koke. But the new honeymoon came to an abrupt end
only a week later, and probably she would have gone home even earlier had not Gauguin generously given her a number of beautiful bead
necklaces and shining brass rings. What frightened Teha'amana away
and made her remain reluctantly faithful to her husband was the
discovery on the first day, or night, that her Koke was covered all over
with running sores.[157] At a neighbouring hut Gauguin eventually
found a girl who was less particular. Gauguin himself says that his
new *vahine* was only just over thirteen, the same age as Teha'amana
when he had first met her. In fact, she was fourteen and a half when
she moved into his hut in the New Year of 1896; her birth certificate,
which I have traced, gives her date of birth as June 27, 1881. Gauguin, being still unable to hear the difference between an aitch and
the Tahitian glottal catch, calls her in all his letters Pahura. Her full
and proper name was Pau'ura a Tai.

Attempts to turn the clock back are always hazardous experiments
and even at best never fully succeed, since no person can experience
exactly the same feelings or react in precisely the same way twice; for
though the stimuli may be identical, one's personality changes over
the years. In Gauguin's case, of course, the difference was that in his
association with Pau'ura and other natives of Punaauia he could not

experience a second time the same joy of discovery and delighted surprise which had made his life in Mataiea so fascinating and pleasurable. What is more, Pau'ura was in every respect inferior to Teha'amana, the general consensus of opinion (which includes Gauguin's) being that she was stupid, lazy, and slovenly. There was another important difference, which Gauguin only found out gradually: Pau'ura was not so dependent on him for company as Teha'amana had been. The reason for this was that the natives of Mataiea, being staunch local patriots like all the natives, had regarded Teha'amana, the girl from Fa'aone, as an outsider, not to say foreigner, which had induced her to draw closer to Gauguin. But Pau'ura, who had been born in Punaauia, not only had her parents but many other relatives and friends near at hand, and continued to spend a good deal of her time with them, even after she had "officially" moved into Gauguin's house.

The single respect in which Gauguin's life exactly repeated his life in Mataiea was, ironically, the fact that he had to contend with the embarrassments of poor finance and bad health which he desired at all costs to avoid. The similarity was particularly marked in the case of money. Before leaving Paris he had followed the procedure of 1891 and shared out his unsold pictures between two little-known dealers, Lévy and Chaudet, whose clientele and turnover were alike small. With the same incorrigible optimism he had expected them to do big business and quickly send him money. The result was no less discouraging. In the case of Lévy it was disastrous; the only letter Gauguin received from him, soon after his arrival, contained instead of money a notice to terminate their contract.

Gauguin had also managed before leaving Paris to persuade some more or less reluctant private collectors to accept pictures, totalling an amount of 4,300 francs, under a hire-purchase arrangement. As his agent and authorized collector of payments he had appointed William Molard, Morice having proved himself unreliable while the able Daniel de Monfreid unfortunately was seldom in Paris. But Molard's many excellent qualities did not include either a good head for business or great initiative, and his task was rendered even more difficult by the fact that most of the clients had quickly regretted their hasty purchases. So instead of the regular instalments Gauguin had confidently looked forward to, each mail-boat brought ever more gloomy reports from the unhappy Molard.[158]

As in 1891, Gauguin had taken with him a substantial sum of

money which must have totalled several thousand francs. A bamboo hut of the sort he had had built cost about 500 francs. He is known to have spent about 300 francs on a horse and trap to make him independent of coaches. The removal to Punaauia, however, including renting of the land could not have cost more than 1,000 francs altogether. And though the cost of living had risen since 1893, it was still possible for a single man to live well in Papeete on 250 francs a month, and on half that amount in Punaauia. Gauguin's capital should therefore have lasted him a year at least. Yet, exactly as during the first period, he had spent it all within a few months of his arrival, and in the same way—by squandering it. For once he admitted this himself in a letter to Daniel which, together with a series of angry complaints about the laxity of dealers and the falseness of friends, contained the following candid confession: "When I have money in my pocket and hopes of getting more, I always spend it recklessly, believing that thanks to my talent all be well in the future—with the result that I am soon at the end of my tether."

The astonishing rapidity with which Gauguin spent his badly needed starting capital no doubt had something to do with his close proximity to the town. It was too easy for his new friends to visit him. Gauguin frequently invited them to dinner, and this could not be done without money. His method of making friends with and influencing the natives in Punaauia proved also to be rather expensive in the long run. Every inquisitive caller was liberally treated to claret from a 200-litre cask which stood inside the door and was replaced as soon as empty.[159] As claret cost a franc a litre and the Punaauia natives were always thirsty, a good deal of money must literally have flowed in this way.

The main difference as far as his health was concerned was that he experienced both more and worse symptoms than during the previous period. There had been serious eruptions after his arrival in Tahiti. But it was only when his bad ankle began to be painful again in February 1896, just when he had started painting, that his situation became desperate. Time after time he had to lay aside his brush and palette, take pain-killing drugs, and lie in bed. The artistic results suffered, for in his own words he had a temperament which forced him to paint his pictures "feverishly at one go." Yet the few which he succeeded in completing at this time included one which he regarded as "the best I have ever painted." It was a nude of Pau'ura, shown reclining on the ground in a Tahitian landscape in almost the same pose as Manet's *Olympia*, a picture Gauguin rated very highly and had a reproduction of. In a sort of mock homage, he gave this picture of the extremely plebeian Pau'ura the title *Arii Vahine*, which means "The Queen" or "The Noblewoman." (It is now in the Pushkin Museum in Moscow.) While convinced that this was his best picture, he wondered if it would be any use sending it to Paris, "when there are already so many others which are unsaleable and make people howl. This would only create still louder howls. So I am condemned to taking my own life if I am not to die of starvation."

As usual, Gauguin was grossly exaggerating, for there was no real risk of his dying of starvation. In the best Tahitian tradition, Pau'ura's many relations were always ready to give their new son-in-law a basket of vegetables or a fish freshly caught in the lagoon. A settler named Fortuné Teissier who had taken a liking to him occasionally gave him a French meal. But it is fairly certain that Gauguin at least was undernourished, and that he often went hungry rather than humble himself to beg when, because of his illness, he should have been taking particular care of himself. However, the most serious consequence of his shortage of money was that he could not afford medical attention. In his distress, he wrote in quick succession to his three closest friends —Émile Schuffenecker, Charles Morice, and Daniel de Monfreid—and pleaded movingly for their help. The help which he hoped to obtain from them was carefully specified and adapted to each.

To the sentimental and rather naïve Schuff he wrote, in April: "I already owe 1,000 francs in Tahiti and have no idea when I shall get any more. I have a bad foot and my far from invigorating diet consists of water, with bread and tea for dinner, to keep my expenses down to 100 francs a month. . . . In the struggle which I have now been waging for years I have never had any support. I am already fifty and already done for, without strength and without hope. . . . In any case I have lost all my pride. Nobody has ever given me patronage because everybody has always thought me strong. But I am weak and in need of patronage."[160] The "patronage" Gauguin had in mind was a regular monthly allowance from a wealthy count, known to Schuff, who for years had paid Charles Filiger and Émile Bernard 100 francs a month in return for first refusals of their best pictures.

The letter to the ever dilatory Morice was even more gloomy, being written a month later, when Gauguin's condition had taken a turn for the worse. "I am laid up," he wrote, "with excruciating pains in my broken ankle. Deep sores have appeared and I am unable to get better. This is robbing me of my energy, which I now need more than ever to cope with all my other vexations. . . . I would have you know that I am on the verge of suicide (a ridiculous act, no doubt, but inevitable). I shall make up my mind in the next few months, depending on what replies I get and whether they are accompanied by money." Knowing Morice's financial difficulties as well as he knew his own, however, he did not pursue this line further than to inquire how things stood with *Noa Noa*, and to remind his partner to remit half the proceeds of the book to its principal author. The letter concluded with this grim exhortation: "Bear all this in mind, Morice, and reply with action. There are cruel times when words cannot charm."

Finally, in June, Gauguin requested the reliable and methodical Daniel de Monfreid for assistance in the realization of a project which had slowly taken shape during many sleepless nights. Basically, the scheme was simple and realistic. He wanted Daniel to start a sort of purchasing or subscription society, consisting of fifteen art collectors who would undertake to buy one picture a year from him at the very reasonable price of 160 francs. To make the idea even more attractive, he suggested that the members should pay their annual subscription in quarterly instalments of 40 francs. The pictures were to be allocated by lot. The chief advantage of this scheme from Gauguin's point of view was that the society could start at once; Daniel had only to distribute the pictures returned by Lévy and collect the first instalments. He undertook to continue supplying pictures for annual distribution in advance. With justified irritation, he added: "Damn it, I'm not being extortionate! I should only be earning 200 francs a month (*less* than a workman gets), though I'm nearly fifty and have a fair reputation. I hardly need to say that as I've never sold rubbish before I don't mean to begin now. All pictures sent will be exhibition standard as before. If I resign myself to a life of *poverty* now, I do so simply because I want to work entirely for my art."

Postal services between Tahiti and Paris were still as slow as ever, the connection between Papeete and San Francisco being maintained, as before, by a sailing ship, which made a monthly voyage in each direction. Before Gauguin received the replies to his letters, his sufferings had grown so unbearable that he went into hospital in Papeete, though he knew that he could not pay the 9.90 francs a day which it would cost. His stay in hospital coincided with the celebrations of the fourteenth of July, and the laughing and screaming on the dance ground and in the fun fair nearby were so audible in the general wards as to disturb the patients' sleep. Gauguin had come to the bottom of his health curve, which had fallen steeply since he had entered with such gusto into the gay celebration of the fourteenth of July in 1891. The measures taken by the hospital doctors to put him on his feet again are and will remain a mystery. But so well did he feel a fortnight later that he submitted with rather shameless good humour to the superintendent's abuse when he left the hospital without paying.

He had good need of his restored strength, for when the replies to his three cries of distress finally arrived they were extremely discouraging. Schuff had completely failed to convince the noble art collector that Gauguin's pictures were in the same class as Filiger's and Bernard's, and he had confined himself to the charitable gift of a few hundred francs. With the best of intentions, Schuff had tried to compensate for his failure by drafting a public petition for a Government pension and persuading prominent artists and writers to sign with a view to submitting it to the Academy. The same idea had occurred to Morice, though he had boldly approached the director of the Academy, Roujon, himself. Although Gauguin's bitter newspaper attack on him in the previous spring must have been fresh in his mind, Roujon promised, remarkably enough, to do what he could—and sent a money order for 200 francs as an "encouragement." In shame and anger at this humiliating public begging, Gauguin at once returned the money to the Academy. When Daniel's letter at length arrived, it turned out that he, on the other hand, had been wanting in initiative and so far had failed to enrol a single member for the projected subscription society, and even doubted if the idea was at all feasible.

As in 1892, therefore, Gauguin had no alternative but to try to raise money in Tahiti. The prospects were no better now than they had been then, unless he abandoned painting and took some minor employment in a business firm or government office. That was the last thing he would do, and so in spite of his earlier rebuff he decided to call on the well-to-do lawyer Goupil and again try to persuade him to commission a portrait. That year Goupil had reached the climax of his successful career, had done exceptionally good business and been appointed honorary consul of the united kingdoms of Sweden and Norway. He ought, therefore, to be in an exceptionally generous mood. Another reason for appealing to him first was that he happened to be a neighbour. The splendid country residence where Goupil lived in state and luxury was situated in the northernmost tip of Punaauia, less than three miles from Gauguin's simple bamboo hut.

It stood in a large park of European style, with trimmed hedges and well-kept lawns, which was embellished with some huge casts of Greek statues. (The house with its statues, though derelict, is still there.)

As was obvious from the statues in his park, Goupil's taste was classical, and it was with considerable hesitation that he finally yielded to Gauguin's entreaties and agreed to have a portrait painted. But afraid of getting a caricature which might make him a laughing-stock, he gave the sitting to his youngest daughter, Jeanne, who was aged nine and so was too young to realize the dangers. Contrary to Goupil's fears, however, the commission resulted in a charming and extremely lifelike portrait. It was set against a flat background of the same colours, pink and purple, which Gauguin had used in his nude of Anna, in 1894. (The picture is now in the Ordrupgaard Museum near Copenhagen.) Goupil was so pleasantly surprised that he appointed Gauguin drawing-master to his four daughters, for whom he was anxious to provide a good European education. In those days, of course, that meant lessons in drawing and watercolour painting, piano-playing, and foreign languages. It was not exactly the sort of patronage Gauguin had hoped for, but it had its advantages and the girls were nice and well-behaved. The eldest, incidentally, was called Aline like Gauguin's own beloved daughter, and was of the same age—eighteen.[161] The principal advantage to Gauguin was that he became a frequent guest at Goupil's table, where even on ordinary weekdays an astonishing number of delicious dishes and wines were served.

Although the fine food and wine absorbed a good deal of Goupil's attention, he managed nevertheless to carry on an animated conversation with his guests. But it would frequently become very one-sided because of his tendency to long monologues when the topic was a favourite subject of his, as this account by another fortunate dinner guest shows: "Over dessert he thus declaimed: 'Three primary duties pertain to man while here on earth on the physical plane. *Passez le vin; merci bien!*' All were attention.

" 'Enumerate them, please, *père avocat-général*.'

" 'Well, to begin with, a man must be a *father*. Fruitless bachelors deserve extinction. I would place a stiff poll-tax on every man exceeding twenty who cannot claim either son or daughter. *Secundus*, his business is to till the ground, to turn the soil and make it yield; just, in a word, to plant trees. Look at me! I've planted this garden and watched the things grow from infancy to age, and the doing of this duty strengthened the brain for professional work. Thirdly and lastly, he should write a book, the product of mature thought in ripe age, setting forth his knowledge and the fruits of experience in some form or other that will benefit *posterity*, for which all men should have most sacred regard. And if I were to add a fourth,' said the learned counsel, as he helped himself to a glass of *vin blanc* and passed the bottle, 'I should say, travel. Seeing the world is a grand education; it ennobles the mind, widens the understanding, and poisons prejudice. It presses home the axiom that, despite all creeds, colour and caste, the *genus homo* is ONE; and all should strive for the common good. Well, sir, I've travelled—I have been to South America, and farther too; once ran away in an open boat—and now that my hair is turning grey, I wouldn't leave Tahiti for the mines on the Rand.'

" 'And what are the duties of woman?' we ventured to ask.

" 'To look after the house, sir, and mind the children; to be good wives, good mothers; to leave politics alone and darn the clothes.' "[162]

Gauguin's views roughly coincided with Goupil's on almost every one of these points and he answered fairly closely to the lawyer's image of the ideal man. But he was accustomed to being the focus of attention in any company himself and had the utmost difficulty in submitting to the humbler role of attentive listener and punctuating "yes-man" which was now assigned to him. Especially when Goupil began to hold forth on matters of art, he found it impossible to remain silent and soon was committing the even more unpardonable sin of contradicting. Inevitably, Goupil's friendship cooled and Gauguin gave in his notice.

Perhaps because he had been able to eat all he needed, his health had shown a steady recovery in the two or three months of his employment by Goupil, and by the end of October 1896 complete recovery seemed only a matter of time. With health and strength his spirits also revived and with them his creativity, to which he gave expression in an unusual way by modelling several statues in clay and, in mock emulation of Goupil's aristocratic pretensions, erecting them in his garden. But there every resemblance ceased, for Gauguin's sculptures were far from classical. The most successful depicted a running female nude and a lioness playing with a cub. These two statues aroused great interest in Punaauia, for different reasons. While the natives came from far and near to see the strange unfamiliar animals, Father Michel, the Roman Catholic priest of Punaauia, had eyes for only the nude woman. Before taking holy orders, Father Michel had been in his youth an army NCO, and was still a very militant man.[163] He threatened to destroy the statue with his own hands unless Gauguin removed or at least draped it. For once, Gauguin was glad there was a gendarme in the area, and he sent for him. This rather embarrassed man could only explain to the irate Father Michel that Gauguin was within his rights and could sue him for trespass and breach of the peace if he took the threatened action. From that time, Father Michel missed no opportunity of condemning Gauguin's sinful ways and ungodly example. As an obvious consequence, many Catholic natives in the district were afraid to have further dealings with Gauguin. Fortunately, Pau'ura was a Protestant.

Gauguin's high spirits were not noticeably affected by the fact that Pau'ura had long been pregnant, and for some mysterious reason was intent on having her baby. The birth took place just before Christmas, but the baby girl was so delicate that she died a few days after.[164] The only effect on Gauguin was artistic; the birth must have inspired the two very similar nativity pictures, dated 1896, both of which depict a Tahitian mother with her new-born baby in a crib. (One of these is now in the Bayerische Staatsgemäldesammlungen in Munich, while the other is in the Hermitage Museum in Leningrad.)

It is worth recalling at this point that Gauguin had painted a picture with a Christian theme transposed to a Tahitian setting in Mataiea, the famous *Ia Orana Maria*. The main difference is that in the later pictures he included two cows, taken from a painting by Tassaert, and several Maori designs from New Zealand, which he had seen in a museum when waiting for his connection in Auckland, while in the earlier picture he employed decorative features taken from a Javanese temple frieze. A close study of these nativity pictures reveals the additional interesting fact that Gauguin's knowledge of Tahitian was as deficient as ever. It was so rudimentary that he confused two such common words as *tamaroa* (son), the singular form, with *tamarii* (sons), which is the plural form. Thus he made the mistake of calling one of the pictures *Te Tamari No Atua*, which means "God's sons," when he obviously meant "The Son of God."

The arrival of the Christmas boat on December 27, 1896, was a lucky event, because it brought both a money order from Chaudet for 1,200 francs and a letter which promised another and a larger remittance shortly. In a letter to Séguin, dated January 15, 1897, which has hitherto remained unpublished and unknown, Gauguin wrote happily: "I will send you a photo of my studio as soon as I have taken one, showing the polychrome wooden panels, the statues among the flowers, etc. Just to sit here at the open door, smoking a cigarette and drinking a glass of absinth, is an unmixed pleasure which I have every day. And then I have a fifteen-year-old wife who cooks my simple everyday fare and gets down on her back for me whenever I want, all for the modest reward of a frock, worth ten francs, a month. . . . You have no idea how far 125 francs will go here. I can ride or drive round in a trap as often as I feel like it. The horse and trap are my own, like the house and all the rest. If I could sell 1,800 francs' worth of pictures I would stay here for the rest of my days. I want no other life, only this."[165]

In another letter to Charles Morice, sent at the same time, he gave even more original proof of his high spirits. Commissioner-General Chessé's diplomatic mission, which had begun auspiciously with so many splendid house parties, had ended in ignominious failure. At his wit's end, Chessé had even persuaded the British consul to make an attempt. "The British consul went down on a French man-of-war to the island," reports the indignant Douglas Hall, "and explained to them (the natives) that they must accept French rule, and told them to haul down the British flag. They refused; and the consul returned from the rebel camp to the man-of-war, and said that he regretted he could not induce them to comply with his request. The French captain made a polite bow, and said his instructions were to fire on the British flag unless it was removed in a quarter of an hour. Needless to say, this was not done, and the man-of-war fired fifteen shots before they shot away the flagstaff, the British consul remaining on board the whole time. Personally, I cannot imagine an Englishman sitting quietly by while his country's flag was shot away, however unlawfully it had been hoisted; but, in conversing with the consul, I could not get him to accept this view. His contention was rather a lame one; that it was not a British flag, but only a counterfeit of it unlawfully hoisted."[166] The attempt was to no avail, for undaunted the natives soon after hoisted their tattered Union Jack again.

Owing to their failure, both Chessé and the governor had eventually been recalled. The task of converting the obstinate natives of Raiatea from treasonable British royalists into well-behaved French loyalists had then passed to a man of an altogether different stamp, namely the tennis-playing Gustave Gallet, head of the Department of the Interior, who had given proof of his drive and resourcefulness during the clashes between natives and French settlers in New Caledonia, in 1878. To show that he meant business, Gallet had mounted an expedition consisting of two warships and two companies of troops. One of the latter, comprising Tahitian volunteers, was led by Gauguin's old friend, Chief Tetuanui of Mataiea. (The Tahitians and the Raiateans had been bitter enemies from time immemorial.) But even this show of force had failed to convince the stiff-necked natives, and when Gauguin was writing his letter they had taken to the mountains and were entrenching themselves. Gauguin ingeniously suggested that Morice should write, in his name, a concocted interview with a native warrior chief of Raiatea and get it published in a left-wing Paris newspaper.[167] As Gauguin candidly admitted, his suggestion sprang not from any anti-colonial sentiments, but from a purely egoistic desire to show the disdainful settlers in Tahiti, who still ignored him, that he had powerful friends in influential positions in Paris and was a bigger man than they took him for! Very revealingly, Gauguin at the same time kept close and intimate company not only with Tetuanui but also with the officers of the two French warships, when the military expedition a few weeks later returned to Tahiti after putting down the native resistance.

One of the warships, the *Duguay-Trouin*, was a cruiser, which had been ordered especially for this campaign from Paris, and Gauguin was on the quay to take leave of his friends when the ship left Papeete on March 3 homeward bound. He had reason to be grateful, for the ship's surgeon had kindly agreed to take with him his latest eight pictures. They included two of his best works. One was an alike sensuous and spiritual nude of Pau'ura, a counterpart to *Manao Tupapau*, his earlier nude of Teha'amana. The title he gave to it was *Nevermore*, the refrain of Edgar Allan Poe's poem *The Raven*, which Stéphan Mallarmé, it will be remembered, had read in his French translation at the farewell banquet in March 1891. Gauguin himself, however, says that the terrifying bird in the background is not that of Poe but the even more satanic raven of the French poet Leconte de Lisle. The other painting depicts two squatting Tahitian women and a baby, in a room with imaginary wall decorations, and a door open to the mountains in the interior of the island. Gauguin's deliberately enigmatic commentary was: "All is dream in this picture. Is it the baby, is it the horseman on the path, or merely the painter who is dreaming? Some people think it is immaterial. But who knows? Perhaps it is not." In view of the meditative peace and tranquillity which pervades this picture, the Tahitian title of *Rereioa* which Gauguin gave it (spelt correctly in a letter but wrongly on the picture) is not a very apt one, for to the natives the word means a special kind of dream, namely a nightmare. By a lucky chance these two pictures, painted at the same time, have been reunited; both hang in the inner room of the Courtauld Institute in London.

Like the two previous periods of relative happiness experienced by Gauguin in the fourteen years of trying to live by his painting, this period, too, came to an abrupt end. The turning point was reached already in April 1897, and was caused by two unexpected deaths. He learnt of one of these in a short letter from Mette, which in matter-of-fact tones reported the sudden death on January 19 of their nineteen-year-old daughter Aline, as the result of pneumonia brought on by a ball. "At first I felt nothing at all, used as I was to constant misfortune," he recorded. "But my brain gradually began functioning again, and the pain sank deeper every day that passed, so that now I am completely depressed. It really looks as if somewhere up there in the higher regions I have an enemy who never for a moment will leave me in peace." This did indeed seem to be so; for that very same month he also learnt that the French settler from whom he had leased his land in Punaauia had died suddenly, and had been so heavily in debt that his heirs were obliged to sell his property at once. The new owner of the plot wanted it for his own use, and as Gauguin had neglected to obtain a written contract covering the lease he had perforce, to his extreme annoyance, to move immediately.

To avoid any recurrence of this upsetting experience in future, Gauguin naturally thought of buying a piece of land. It is also easy to understand that after so many years of incessant moving he wanted a house which would be more like a real home than the bamboo hut had been, especially as he now contemplated staying in Punaauia for good. But what is less easy to understand is the reckless expenditure he incurred in realizing this ambition. True, he had just received 1,035 francs from Chaudet, and the excellent piece of ground covering two and a half acres on the shore between the road and the lagoon a quarter of a mile farther south, which the widow of a French settler agreed to sell him, cost only 700 francs.[168] But instead of waiting for his next payment before beginning to build, he applied for a loan to the Caisse Agricole, at the time the only bank in Tahiti. The main object of this bank was to assist enterprising planters to buy land and extend their cultivation. There were some hundred coconut palms on Gauguin's new plot, and he intended to plant a little vanilla. By a rather elastic interpretation of definitions he thought, therefore, that he could claim recognition as a planter and thus obtain a loan. Unfortunately, the member of the bank's board best known to him, Sosthène Drollet, had recently died. However, he had at Drollet's house met most of the other members, and this nodding acquaintance sufficed to get him a loan of a thousand francs at ten per cent interest, repayable within a year.

Gauguin at once set about building a house which was so large and luxurious that the loan proved far from adequate. For the wall and floors, for example, he used planed planks, a very expensive material which, in the absence in those days of both suitable timber and a sawmill in Tahiti, had to be imported at great cost from North America. Moreover, the house measured 63 feet by 25 feet. In fact, he built two houses: the dwelling, which stood on three-foot piles and had an open verandah on either side; and, connected with it, a studio, which was fitted with sliding doors and had a floor of compacted earth (Fig. 34). From the house itself, as from the studio, there were magnificent views of the mountains in the interior, the sea, and the nearby island of Moorea, eight miles to the east (Fig. 26). In the end, Gauguin only got his great house finished by obtaining credit from the builders.

His personal contribution to the structure consisted of some more wooden panels, which he nailed to the walls of the bedroom and studio together with the ones that had previously decorated his hut. According to Lemasson the postmaster, who remained one of Gauguin's closest friends and often visited him in Punaauia, the house on the other hand was sparsely furnished, with ill-assorted pieces. Visitors, however, had to exercise the greatest care when moving about it, owing to the quantities of paints, brushes, rolls of canvas, books, clothes, musical instruments, and other miscellaneous objects which lay scattered about in the greatest confusion. Thanks to Lemasson's memoirs, we also know exactly what Gauguin looked like and how he dressed at this time. "He was powerfully built, with blue eyes, a high complexion, a slight tan, and chestnut-brown hair and beard—thin imperial, to be exact—which were already greying. At home he invariably dressed in native fashion, wearing a cotton tunic and a loincloth . . . and always bare-footed. But when visiting Papeete he wore European clothes: a high-collared jacket and white, or more often blue, linen trousers of Vichy fabric, white canvas shoes, and a broad-brimmed hat of plaited pandanus leaves. Because of his unhealed leg ulcers—evidence of his impaired health—he had a slight limp and supported himself by a stout stick."[169]

The justified pleasure of having at long last a house of his own was soon dissipated by the renewed financial embarrassment due to the building of it. Contrary to what he had optimistically expected, no more money arrived from Chaudet. His debtors in France did not even answer his letters, and meanwhile his creditors in Tahiti pressed him more and more. As in the previous year, his health declined with the same diabolical rapidity as his finances. To begin with, the eruption in his injured foot spread up the leg, and then suddenly to the other leg. He rubbed the legs with powdered arsenic and bandaged them to the knees, which strangely enough stopped the "eczema" (as Gauguin always called the eruption) from spreading. He then caught an inflammation of the eye which, though he was assured by the doctors that it was not dangerous, of course had the distressing consequence of preventing him from painting. When the doctors eventually got the better of this infection, the ankle which had been broken in 1894 began to give such intense pain that he could no longer put any weight on it and had to lie down and take pain-killing drugs, which had the effect of stupefying him. Attempts to get up led to giddiness and fainting fits, and he also had bouts of fever. In August he sent Molard the following sad report:

"I would have written to you last month when I received your letter, but (and it is a big 'but') I was physically unable to do so. I was suffering from a double conjunctivitis, from which I have still not entirely recovered. Alas, my health is worse than ever. After a real improvement, I suffered a serious relapse; the disease has spread over a wide area and I am now prostrate for twenty out of the twenty-four hours, yet get little sleep. I have painted nothing for two months. I have had no letter from Chaudet for five months, and not a centime. All credit has been stopped; I owe 1,500 francs and have no idea how I am to live, though my diet is austere." After exhorting Molard to do all he could to recover some of his claims in Paris, he concluded his short letter with these anguished lines: "Bad luck has dogged me since childhood. Never any luck, never any joy. Always adversity. And so I cry: 'God, if You exist, I charge You with injustice and malice.' You know, on hearing of my poor Aline's death I could not believe in anything any more and laughed in defiance. What is the use of virtue, work, courage, and intelligence?"

The natives of Punaauia and his few friends among the colonial officials and settlers were firmly convinced by this time that Gauguin suffered not only from a common syphilitic infection but something far more malignant and dangerous, namely leprosy. The suspicions which many of them had long held were encouraged, more than anything else, by Gauguin's sudden concern to keep his legs so carefully bandaged. The only sure means of protection against leprosy known in the island at that time was to avoid any contact with the miserable sufferers from this dread disease. (The victims were invariably driven ruthlessly into the mountains or deported to a remote island in the Tuamotu group.) On top of all his other troubles, therefore, Gauguin now found himself all at once very lonely, just when he had most need of company, comfort, and help. The only person who dared to enter the house was Pau'ura, but she was not always there when he wanted her most. The common misconception that Gauguin had leprosy was taken over, incidentally, by Somerset Maugham in his novel *The Moon and Sixpence*, which is loosely based on the life of Gauguin, and its fame has helped to establish this unfounded belief in Europe and Tahiti.

Unable to paint and having no friends to talk to, Gauguin turned in his solitude to recording the thoughts which occupied his mind. As he wrote, his notes grew into a long religious essay on the meaning and purpose of life, *The Modern Spirit and Catholicism*. Gauguin himself was convinced that this long essay, running to more than seventy large foolscap pages, was his best and profoundest piece of writing to date.[170] In this he was quite mistaken; what strikes the patient reader of this hitherto unpublished manuscript most of all is his unoriginal ideas, muddled thinking, scant documentation, and tortuous, almost unintelligible pseudo-scientific jargon. All that emerges clearly, in fact, is that its author was a very sick man, and that he was deeply concerned with metaphysical questions.

Gauguin stated his purpose at the outset in these fairly comprehensible terms: "We have undoubtedly arrived at the period of scientific evolution foretold in the Bible, where it says: 'For nothing is secret, that shall not be made manifest; neither any thing hid, that shall not be known and come abroad.' (St Luke). Confronted with the problem that is posed by the questions *Where do we come from? What are we? Where are we going?* We must ask ourselves what is our ideal, natural, and rational destiny. . . . In order to neglect nothing which is involved in this problem of nature and ourselves, we must consider seriously (if only summarily) this doctrine of Christ in its *natural*

and rational sense, which, freed from the veils that have concealed
and distorted it, thus appears in its true simplicity but full of splendour, throwing a bright light on the problem of our nature and our
destiny."

Two categories of people were responsible for this distortion of
the truth: "The divorce between modern society and true Christianity rests entirely on a misunderstanding due to the falsification and
blatant fraud of the Catholic Church, a fact which it is important
to make clear, especially since the true doctrine of Christ is so much
akin to and in harmony with the principles and aspirations of modern
society that the former is bound to fuse ultimately with the latter to
form a higher organism." But at the same time Gauguin contended:
"The materialists, left behind by the continuous advance of modern
science (influenced, it must be said, by suspicion of and aversion to
Catholic theological and theocratic mysticism and dogmatism), content themselves—as do the Catholics with their dogmas—with vulgar,
primitive, and traditional notions, not realizing that by going too far
in the other direction one can steer from Charybdis into Scylla."

Whereupon Gauguin bravely endeavoured to show, by means of a
wealth of quotations from various works on astronomy, physics,
and physiology, that "the history of the atom and the soul" is the history of "one and the same being at two different stages." His conclusion (slightly clarified in the arduous process of translation) was as
follows: "This moment, when the first nebulous agglomerations (of
atoms) have formed, then becomes the point of departure of a geometrical progression—a point to which the infinitely small, infinitely
slow reason can perhaps return—the first stage which may be regarded
as zero in relation to something which is infinite, having no beginning."

Clearly a little dissatisfied with the results of his labours so far,
Gauguin then launched into a completely different kind of "investigation" and made a rapid survey of the world religions to prove the
basic similarity and unity of their fundamental creeds and myths.
(Here it may be recalled that his friend Sérusier had zealously prop-
agated this article of the theosophical faith.) The truly amazing number of parallels between the Christian faith and Egyptian, Persian,
Hindu, Chinese, and even Tahitian and Maori beliefs, were "proved"
by means of copious quotations, taken mainly from the French translation of a book by the British poet and spiritualist, Gerald Massey,
with the impressive title A *Book of the Beginnings, containing an*

attempt to recover and reconstitute the lost origins of the myths and mysteries, types and symbols, religions and languages, with Egypt for the mouthpiece and Africa as the birth-place.

Gauguin summed up this equally unconvincing chapter in the following equally obscure words: "The various quotations in the preceding chapter are in our opinion more than sufficient to establish that the Jesus of the Gospels is none other than the Jesus Christ of the Myth, the Jesus Christ of the astrologers."

He devoted the last third of the essay, rather surprisingly, to a renewed and far more virulent attack on the Catholic Church (though in the light of the boorish behaviour and oversimplified teachings of his arch-enemy, the village priest Father Michel, it may not be so surprising after all). Here are a few excerpts: "How has it come about that the Catholic Church has succeeded in distorting the truth right from the start? This only becomes understandable when it is realized that the sacred books were kept out of circulation. . . . But what is really incredible is that even today, when the truth is plain to all who can see and read, there should be *intelligent and cultivated* people who still adhere to the Church. Can we regard them as men of good faith without accusing them of insanity? The most likely explanation is that it is a question of commercial interest. . . . And this infallible authority which the Church arrogates to itself it pretends to have received in order to make *dogmatic* decisions, contrary to true sense, regarding all biblical texts, to dogmatize on all religious doctrines, including those concerning the presence of the body and soul of Christ at the Eucharist, the Immaculate Conception, the miracles of the relics, and so on. . . . The Catholic Church, in doctrine and in practice, represents that pharisaical apostasy referred to in the Bible as the principal expression of the Anti-Christ, first set on the false path of the supernatural and then involved, entangled, and in the biblical expression taken in the net, one made specially for the purpose, from which she can only escape in *confusion*, finally unveiled and unmasked, and despised by all."

Before he could complete the essay, his heart, which had given him no serious trouble since 1892, collapsed under the strain. Attack followed quickly after attack, each more violent than the one before. The end seemed to be near. Or as Gauguin expressed it: "God has at last heard my voice, praying, not for a change, but for complete deliverance. My heart, which has been continuously assailed and repeatedly mishandled by heavy blows, is greatly affected. And with this illness have come daily suffocating fits and bouts of blood-spitting. The carcass has so far held out, but soon will surely crack. Which, for that matter, is better than being forced to take my own life, which I would be driven to do by lack of food and the wherewithal to obtain any." Yet, contrary to what he seems sincerely to have wished for, he survived; the heart attacks ceased after a few weeks as suddenly as they had started. But this time he did not allow the apparent improvement to deceive him. He knew he had only gained another respite. He might live on for years yet. But what sort of life would it be if for long periods he were unable to paint? Where would he get money to live on, even if he was well enough to paint?

His only hope was that the doctors in Papeete might work another miracle, if he went into hospital for a longer period. It would cost several hundred francs, but he convinced himself that a substantial sum could well arrive by the next mail-boat. He had written a persuasive letter in July to Chaudet, in which he had explained his desperate plight in detail and had begged him to do everything he could to sell more pictures. At least there should soon be a reply to that. But when the long-awaited mail-boat arrived at the beginning of December, it brought neither money from Chaudet nor any news. As a poor consolation there was the October number of the literary monthly *La Revue Blanche*, which surprisingly contained the first half of his narrative text of *Noa Noa* and five lyrics by Charles Morice.

The contrast between the ecstatic descriptions of the Tahitian paradise in the narrative and his miserable life as he absently turned the review's pages could hardly have been greater. Moreover, Morice had neglected to send him his share of the fee. Once more Gauguin's thoughts turned darkly on suicide. But meanwhile he had realized by now that he was more qualified to express his thoughts on life and death in images than in words. Before his departure there therefore remained one final picture to be painted, a great composition which, in his own words, would be his "spiritual testament." His supply of canvas had long since run out, but for this problem he had an old solution. Taking a piece of the ordinary coarse jute material which in Tahiti was used for making copra sacks, and which came in rolls four and a half feet wide, he cut off a portion a little more than thirteen feet in length and, with trembling fingers, made a wooden frame on which he laboriously stretched out the fabric. Then seizing his brushes and paints, which had remained untouched for six months, he started work, oblivious of his pains and weariness.

In its great size and complex design, comprising a dozen figures arranged in four groups with the sea and the island of Moorea for background, the picture which slowly emerged between bouts of dizziness and excruciating pain comes as closely as may be to the sort of monumental fresco which Gauguin had dreamt all his life of painting (Fig. 35). Its message must be read in reverse order, the logical starting point being a baby and a group of Tahitian mothers in the bottom right-hand corner. As Gauguin explained it, "they simply give themselves up to the joy of living." The eye should then move on to the middle figure, an almost naked man who is picking fruit from the tree of knowledge. To the right of this tree two troubled figures in long mantles can be seen. Still according to Gauguin, they represent the unhappy ones who have eaten of the tree of knowledge and so cannot refrain from pondering on the mysteries of life. Sitting at their feet is another man, who, in amazement at the strange questions which he hears them discussing, raises his hand above his head as though to ward them off. To the left of the central figure and turning away from it, a small boy plays happily between a goat and two cats, also representing innocence. To the left of this well-defined group a woman stands with her back to a large idol, "whose mysterious and rhythmical motioning of the hands seems to point to the beyond." The last group, to the left of the idol, comprises a young woman and an old woman sitting resigned, her head in her hands. Finally, in the bottom left-hand corner of the picture, a strange bird holds a lizard in its claw, a symbol, Gauguin says, of "the vanity and futility of words." The title of the picture is inscribed in black letters on a gold panel in the top left-hand corner. It is: *Where do we come from? What are we? Where are we going?*

Gauguin's spiritual testament is thus seen to be pessimistic. All who persist, as do rational Westerners, in trying to understand and analyse everything, including the problems of life and death, inevitably grow unhappy, while animals, children, and "savages," among them the Tahitians, are happy for the very reason that it never enters their heads to reflect on metaphysical problems to which there are no solutions. Although "savages" by no means form so uniform a group as Gauguin believed, he was certainly right in thinking that the Tahitians are little inclined to metaphysical speculation. To one who has lived for a long time among them, indeed, their most striking characteristic is their extraordinary stoicism, not to say indifference, in the face of death. But try as he will, a white man cannot shed his cultural heritage and in this respect emulate the natives, as Gauguin was well aware from his own experience when he painted this picture.

Being a rational Westerner, Gauguin of course seriously reconsidered his situation after finishing his great painting, which was some time about Christmas 1897. The next mail-boat was due in a few days' time. Suppose it brought a large remittance from Chaudet or Molard? Fate had played enough tricks on him already for it to win such a spectacular one in the end. A few more days of waiting before the contemplated suicide hardly mattered. It was on December 30 that the mail-boat anchored in Papeete harbour, and in all probability the mail was distributed as usual the next day—when, once again, Gauguin was to learn that there was no money order for him.

With the courage of despair, he put a box of powdered arsenic into his pocket and limped off in the direction of the mountains.[171] The path leading to the foothills was lined for the first 200 yards of its course by native huts. From all sides came the sound of laughter, of music and singing, from the boisterous New Year parties which would continue until Twelfth Night. It was high summer in Tahiti and all the shrubs and trees alongside the narrow path were a mass of blossom, filling the air with its fragrance—*noanoa*. But, blind and deaf to the world about him, Gauguin walked straight on, through the fields of yams and sweet potatoes beyond the huts, and panting began to climb the first steep hill.

As always, it was wonderfully still and peaceful in the mountains. At the first plateau there were no longer any trees to conceal the magnificent view of the shore, the lagoon, and the sea. The ground was covered with ferns. Slumping on to the soft bed of leaves, he took out the box of arsenic and swallowed its contents. He must have taken an overdose; for after a while, when he had already dropped off into a merciful sleep, he suddenly began to vomit and threw up all or most of the powder. Too exhausted either to go back for more or try other means, he lay there helpless in the pitiless heat of the tropical sun. His bowels burnt like fire and his head ached and throbbed without ceasing. The approach of evening brought temporary relief. But it was not long before the cold and damp night wind began to sweep down the mountain sides, bringing fresh and almost unendurable torments. It was well after sunrise on the following day, when the rapidly increasing heat was once more becoming his worst problem, that he eventually managed to gather his last remaining strength and stagger slowly down from his Hill of Calvary back to the coast and to life.

IX

HUMILIATION AND REVENGE

THE logical step after an unsuccessful attempt at suicide is obviously to try again with more care. But like most persons in the same situation, Gauguin was too bewildered either to act or to think logically when he arrived home weak and exhausted from the mountains. What he did was to lie flat on his back and give way to weariness. Although he gradually recovered to a surprising extent and even at times was free from the depressing ache in his leg, he felt "like the living dead." Lacking energy and will-power, he deferred making decisions and concentrated on gaining a little respite and time to reflect.

Unlike their fellow-unfortunates at rest under the earth, the living dead, alas, need food, clothes, and somewhere to live. Gauguin's case was even more urgent: he needed, as soon as possible, 2,500 francs with which to pay his debts. Eventually, at the end of January 1898 700 francs arrived from Chaudet and 150 francs from Maufra, one of his debtors. But this was the amount he needed to prevent the Chinese grocer in Punaauia, who supplied nearly all his food, from suspending his credit. Thus not a centime remained for paying the largest of his creditors, the Agricultural Bank, whose manager undoubtedly would foreclose and sell off his fine house without compunction when the next payment fell due in May.

For the first time since leaving the Bourse in 1883, Gauguin was prepared to abandon his painting, and the way in which he endeavoured to solve his problems when he could again leave the house, at the end of March 1898, without risk of immediate giddiness and

fainting fits, in fact was to go back fifteen years. It so happened that
at this time the post of secretary-treasurer in the Agricultural Bank
fell vacant. As a one-time stockbroker, Gauguin was fully justified
in regarding himself as the best-qualified man in the colony for the
job. As a prominent member of the bank's staff, it would of course be
easy to obtain a deferment of his loan. A very brief postponement
in any case would be enough, for the annual salary of the secretary-
treasurer was 4,000 francs, plus a guaranteed minimum sum of 6,000
francs in perquisites. As the latter usually amounted to more, the
lucky holder of this key post could easily make about 1,000 francs a
month.[172]

The appointment to the post of secretary-treasurer to the bank, like
all other important appointments in the highly centralized colonial
administration, was made by the governor. In spite of his earlier unhappy experience, therefore, Gauguin harnessed his horse, and driving
into town handed in his card at the governor's office with a request
for an interview. Since February 1898, the office of governor had been
held by the blunt, forceful, and outspoken former head of the Department of the Interior, Gustave Gallet, who had been promoted for
his successful "pacification" of the anglophile natives of Raiatea. Unfortunately for Gauguin, Gallet found it hard to believe his uncor-
roborated statement about his previous financial experience. And,
understandably enough, he considered it a very poor recommendation
that Gauguin had failed to repay his loan in the prescribed period.

However, Gauguin looked so wretched and in such genuine despair
that Gallet in the end was prompted to offer him another, more suitable post. It was a minor appointment as draughtsman in the Public

---

40. *"A corpulent robot with a stupid countenance" was Gauguin's malicious description of Gustave Gallet, the forth-
right and energetic governor who was his archenemy and
special scapegoat in the period 1899–1901.*

41. *The martial figure of Gallet was succeeded in the gover-
norship by Édouard Petit, a mild-mannered lawyer who
usually dressed in civilian clothes and often travelled
with his family, driving the trap himself.*

42. *With twenty-six other passengers, Gauguin on September 10, 1901, embarked in Papeete harbour on the fast
luxury steamer Croix du Sud, to settle for good in "a
primitive cannibal island" in the Marquesas group.*

41

Works Department, at a salary of six francs a day worked. This meant that not only Sundays and public holidays were unpaid but also, as a precaution against shirking and too many unwarranted sick leaves, all other days which were not worked. The monthly salary thus amounted to about 150 francs, which would just enable Gauguin to live but would leave nothing over for payment of debts. As if everything had conspired to make the appointment disagreeable, Gauguin's good friend Jules Agostini, long the director of the Public Works Department, had obtained his transfer to another colony only two months earlier.[173] Yet strangely enough Gauguin accepted the job—though all things considered, his decision may not have been so strange as at first sight it seems. It may well be that it was precisely the prospect of complete self-effacement and oblivion which appealed to him. There is a very well-known parallel, for example, thirty years later, when Colonel T. E. Lawrence enlisted as a private in the Air Force under an assumed name. That this can be the only possible explanation is confirmed by the fact that Gauguin adhered to his decision even when, immediately after, he received 575 francs from Daniel de Monfreid in payment of pictures and also obtained a prolongation of his loan on very favourable terms. As he rather belatedly realized, he had given himself a good deal of unnecessary concern; for, as the owner of a property worth between three and four thousand francs, the Agricultural Bank's regulations allowed him to convert his one-year security loan at 10 per cent into a mortgage at 6 per cent, repayable over a period of six years.[174]

Driving eight miles a day, there and back, between his home in Punaauia and the Public Works Department in Papeete on a gravel road which was full of potholes was too time-wasting and exhausting.

---

43. *The supreme achievement of the 200 years of civilizing Tahiti: a contented housewife of Papeete sits in a rocking chair in a beautiful cement-built house with flower-patterned linoleum on the floor, sewing an unnecessary quilt for the unused sofa show-piece.*

44. *A Tahitian family on their way to service in the Calvinist church of Paofai in Papeete dressed in their Sunday best. The woman in the middle, having suffered from sore feet before, has this time left her leather shoes at home, while the men in a true spirit of penitence are wearing their thick woollen jackets in the tropical heat.*

So Gauguin locked up his large studio villa and taking Pau'ura and a few other necessaries with him moved into a small two-room house in the western suburb of Paofai, which one of his new fellow-workers, Victor Lequerré, had agreed to let to him very cheaply. Lequerré's great helpfulness was due to the intercession of his new bride, Teraiehoa, a girl from Mataiea who had been Teha'amana's best friend.[175] Within a circle which was less than a hundred yards in radius, Gauguin not only had his old friends, the Drollets and the Suhas, but also his new friends on Madame Charbonnier's little estate (map on page 68). It was just as near to the hospital—which was a great advantage because he would now be able to obtain regular and thorough treatment as an out-patient. It was a good deal farther, about three-quarters of a mile, to his work, the Public Works Department being then situated at the extreme tip of Fare Ute, the narrow peninsula at the eastern end of the lagoon. This, however, cannot have mattered very much, as Gauguin had his trap. He also had another means of getting to his office, one which he often availed himself of because it provided him with the only physical exercise he could still practise; this was to paddle across the lagoon in an outrigger canoe, which he usually did with his colleagues and landlord, Victor Lequerré.

The work was as dreary as Gauguin had expected. The life of a civil servant in the mid-1890s, sixty years before the first air-conditioning plant was installed in Papeete, has been well described by Jules Agostini, the former head of the Public Works Department, who had long first-hand experience of it: "The day begins at dawn, at four o'clock in the morning, when the inhabitants go to buy food in the covered market opposite the Town Hall. . . . Shops and offices open between six and seven. The staff usually begin by questioning one another about the *parau api* (or latest news), leading on to juicy and smutty stories which a girl, servant, or friend has heard in the market hall. The stories help to while away the stipulated hours, though work is sometimes neglected. . . .

"Towards ten o'clock when the sun is fast reaching zenith, making the wooden buildings terribly hot, the conversation languishes and at length stops altogether. However, by now it is time for officials and staff to leave their offices, shops, and warehouses, and go off into the town. Some stop at one of the clubs, while others will go straight home to lunch with their families.

"Shops reopen to the public at twelve o'clock, an hour earlier than the administrative offices. Work now is even more painful than in the

morning, as it has grown hotter; and what with the heat and the processes of digestion the staff are more inclined for a siesta than to
measure cloth or deal with something which can wait, and indeed
will almost be the better for waiting. At long last, five o'clock brings
the hour of release. Without stopping to waste a single minute, everybody—heads and staff, senior and junior—hurry off at such a rate it
might be supposed they had been long incarcerated in prison and
were at last being released. But of course they have had an intoler-
ably long and arduous day!

"Everybody hurries off to enjoy himself as he chooses. To many
this means an outing to Faaa or Fautaua, where there will be every
kind of vehicle, gay athletic horsemen, and charming beauties riding
bicycles, moving slowly and calmly or racing along at breakneck
speed. To others it will mean a game of dominoes, preceded and
followed by the customary *apéritifs*. A few old hands, taking no
thought for the morrow, may indulge in a pipe of opium.

"About an hour is set aside for the evening meal, after which one
leaves the table for the club again, or strolls yawning along the
streets, which by now are almost deserted."[176]

Gauguin described his new life as "unapt" and his work as "not
very intellectual," which was certainly an understatement. In addition
to the office work, which chiefly consisted of copying building designs
and plans, his duties occasionally included road inspection, a task
which he found even more tedious and boring. There was some
change of work when the ill-tempered artillery sergeant, who had been
acting Director of Public Works, abandoned the impossible task of
instilling some discipline into the staff and in May 1898 returned to
barrack duties. The new deputy for the permanent director, who had
yet to arrive, was a humble technician from the embryonic Munici-
pal Works Department of Papeete named Jules Auffray, who had the
opposite fault of being too easy-going. Auffray happened to be a very
competent amateur painter who in his youth had studied at the Academy of Art in Paris in the hope, soon disappointed, of becoming a
great artist. But he could find no better use for Gauguin's special
talents than his predecessor; or rather, did not think that he had any
talent—a fairly logical conclusion considering that Auffray judged every
work of art by the academic standards which he had learnt to admire
in his youth, and still admired. On the other hand, the new deputy
director was glad to have a man in the office who had the intellectual
talents and the scholarship to assist in the correspondence, which

though not very extensive posed many a problem both of drafting and of spelling. He readily excused Gauguin, therefore, when the latter happened to arrive late at the office or for some incomprehensible reason—to him—suddenly lost his temper and showed it by slamming the doors.[177]

During all the years of his life in Tahiti before taking this employment, Gauguin had remained an outsider, belonging to no established profession, class political party, or religious body. He had often suffered from his isolation and the consequent lack of help and support. But at the same time he had avoided getting involved in the fierce battles which were continually fought among the different groups, and especially between settlers and civil servants. The few people with whom he had voluntarily mixed irrespective of class, race, or group affiliation, had both regarded and treated him as an equal—when they had not, exceptionally, looked up to and admired him, as Lieutenant Jénot, the Drollets, and the poetic magistrate Olivaint had done. But when he became an assistant draughtsman in the Public Works Department, he suddenly found himself labelled and classified. From that moment, his old friends among the settlers ceased to have anything to do with him, because as they shortsightedly saw it he had now joined the enemy. At the same time, his status among the civil servants was the lowest in the hierarchy. Consequently, the magistrates, heads of department, captains and lieutenants, who had freely associated with Gauguin the artist, now thought it beneath their dignity to have dealings with Gauguin the office worker. Some of them even looked embarrassed the other way if they chanced to encounter him when supervising a gang of native workmen in the street or the town approaches.

A fact which greatly aggravated Gauguin's solitude and irritated him was that his low rank debarred him from election to the Cercle Militaire, the public servants' club to which he had been temporarily admitted in 1891, thanks to his "official mission." The minimum qualification for membership of this club was the rank of second lieutenant or equivalent civilian status. Of the low-grade officials who could and would have anything to do with him there were only three who made any appeal to Gauguin. One of these was Victor Lequerré, the colleague already mentioned, but being only twenty he was too young to serve as anything more than a useful help and general messenger. A no less devoted but more interesting companion—"friend" is hardly the word in either case—was a Breton ex-soldier named

Pierre Levergos, who had participated in the campaign against the anglophile natives of Raiatea and been wounded in the hand by an enemy spear. On demobilization shortly after, he had been rewarded for gallantry with both a medal and a comfortable sinecure as orderly in the governor's office. What particularly appealed to Gauguin in Levergos, of course, was that he always found an attentive listener when he talked of Brittany—as he did with great nostalgia fairly often. The most intellectual and favourite among the three new companions, however, was François Picquenot, a government clerk whom Gauguin had known during his first visit but had had little to do with.[178] It was an important bond of sympathy between the two men that they had both seen national service in the Navy.

Gauguin's life became even more cheerless and lonely a few months later when Pau'ura left him. Koke's position now as a low-grade draughtsman had no connection with her departure. She may even have been too simple and ignorant to realize that he had changed his work; after all, he still spent most of his time "making pictures," as she always in the native way described Gauguin's artistic activities. The only difference she will have been conscious of was that Koke now did his work away from home, leaving her all day alone in a strange place, and this was a difference which she strongly disliked. If only he had given her money to enjoy herself with she might have borne her fate with more equanimity. But unfortunately Koke had less money to give away now. So before very long poor, idle and lonely Pau'ura began to grow homesick for Punaauia and her friends and relatives there. One day she could stand it no longer, and quickly packing her few belongings into a bundle she took the coach. Her decision may have been hastened by the fact that in August 1898 she was pregnant and, unlike Koke, wanted to keep her baby again.

Gauguin made several journeys to Punaauia to persuade her to return, but she stuck to her decision to stay where she belonged. At the same time she still considered, with some justification, that she was entitled to live in Gauguin's luxurious house and make use of his domestic utensils and tools when she wanted. Gauguin took the opposite view, turned her out, and made the doors and windows more secure. Finding on his next visit that with the help of friends she had broken in, he availed himself of this excellent opportunity to get his revenge by summonsing her for housebreaking. A search revealed that she had committed the further offence of taking a ring, a coffee mill, and a copra sack. In spite of her protests that she was still Koke's *va-*

hine and that, therefore, they were accusing her absurdly of breaking in on herself, she was sentenced to a fine of fifteen francs and a week's imprisonment. A legally minded neighbour, disapproving of Gauguin's methods, helped her to lodge an appeal with a higher court, which acquitted her.[179] This verdict may well have been connected with the fact that the procurator and head of the colony's judicial system was now Gauguin's gay companion of 1895–96, Édouard Charlier, who knew all that Pau'ura had meant and done for Gauguin.

Gauguin could not afford a replacement for Pau'ura. Even an occasional visit to the popular evening dances and the "flesh market," where he had had so much fun during the first happy months in Papeete in 1891, required a thicker purse, as well as better legs, than he could now command. Thus his only alternative when his solitude got the better of him was to go for an absinth or a beer at one of the town's seven low-class taverns, which were mainly patronized by sailors, soldiers, servants, shop assistants, and natives. According to many eye-witnesses, he seems on such evenings to have drunk heavily, and to have shown an unfortunate tendency to argue, quarrel, and fight on the slightest pretext or provocation.

When at length he took out his brushes and palette one Sunday morning it was simply to earn a little extra money and lead a rather quieter life by paying off some of his more pressing creditors. One of these, Ambroise Millaud, actually commissioned a picture. Monsieur Millaud managed one of the town's two pharmacies, and may have felt that common decency required him to lend a helping hand to one of his biggest customers, for he actually agreed to pay a far larger sum than the amount Gauguin owed him. He stipulated in return that Gauguin should produce a "comprehensible and recognizable" picture.

Gauguin tried hard to fulfil these conditions, and indeed the picture which he presented some time afterwards, *The White Horse*, is one of his most popular and easily appreciated works. Nevertheless, Millaud when he saw it was indignant and exclaimed:

"But the horse is green! There aren't any such horses!"

With the utmost dignity and self-control, Gauguin replied:

"My dear Monsieur Millaud, have you never observed how green all things look in the late afternoon, when with your eyes half-open you lean comfortably back in your rocking-chair on the verandah, admiring the play of light in nature?"

Millaud's sarcastic retort was that when he paid several hundred francs for a picture he wanted one he could appreciate at *any time of the day*, without having to sit half-dozing in his rocking-chair. So there was no deal, and the picture eventually found its way to Daniel de Monfreid's studio in Paris, where so many other unsold pictures by Gauguin were stocked.[180] There it stayed until de Monfreid sold it in 1927 to the Louvre, where it now occupies a prominent place in the Gauguin room in the Jeu de Paume annexe.

Another of the two or three pictures dating from this period, when Gauguin had become a Sunday painter as in his Paris youth, has long occupied an equally prominent place in the Tate Gallery in London—*Faa Iheihe*. Because of the fresco-like character and the bright and gay colours of this painting, it is usually regarded as an optimistic counterpart to the tragic painting *Where do we come from? What are we? Where are we going?* The title (which should be spelt *Fa'ai'ei'e*) confirms this interpretation, for the meaning of this common causative verb is "to beautify, adorn, embellish, or glorify." It need hardly be said that Gauguin did not find a purchaser for this picture in Tahiti, any more than he did for *The White Horse*.

The choice of subject and the general character of these paintings suggest that Gauguin at this point had concluded that life after all was worth living. He certainly had good reasons for looking forward to the future with somewhat greater confidence than he had had at the beginning of the year. Chaudet had excelled himself and in quick succession sent him two money orders totalling 1,300 francs. Furthermore, Daniel had made up for his failure to organize a subscription society a year earlier by private sales to the value of 600 francs. Thanks to these unexpected windfalls, Gauguin was able in August 1898 to make a first repayment of 400 francs to the Agricultural Bank, and in September to re-enter hospital.[181] In three weeks he had made such rapid progress towards recovery that he thought that, given continued nursing, he would soon be fit again. Of course it was a vain hope. A study of Gauguin's long record of bad health shows that painful attacks alternated with improvements at astonishingly regular intervals, and that neither careful nursing nor gross neglect affected the cyclic changes very much. Each period of reasonably good health and of intense suffering usually lasted from six to eight months.

He had barely made up his mind to resign his job when, in accordance with this diabolical pattern, he began to have such violent pains

in his badly healed ankle that the only relief he could get was by taking morphine—and even that was effective for only very brief spells.
Thus he found himself in December 1898 in exactly the same situation as barely a year earlier, and in despair he asked himself and Daniel: "Isn't it a hundred times better to die, if I can't get well again?
You reproached me for my stupid act (the attempted suicide), considering it unworthy of Gauguin. But if only you knew the mood I
am in now after three years of suffering! If I am to be prevented from
painting, which is now all I care for in life (my wife and children
being of no further consequence to me), there is nothing left in my
heart but emptiness." At the same time he gave the answer to his
question in the same illogical manner as before: "Thus I am condemned to live, though I no longer have any spiritual reason for doing
so." When in January 1899 a further sum of 1,000 francs arrived from
Daniel, at least he was able to make things a little more tolerable for
himself by quitting the dreary office in the Public Works Department
and returning to his house in Punaauia.

To his great astonishment and satisfaction, Pau'ura immediately
returned to him as though to do so was the most natural thing in the
world, and quietly helped him to clean up and repair the house and
clear out the rats and termites. Her conduct is quite understandable,
however, when it is remembered that it was chiefly the life in town,
and not Koke, that had dissatisfied her and caused her to leave him.
She was five months pregnant; and it was her turn to be astonished
when Gauguin seemed genuinely pleased and grateful at the prospect
of soon becoming a father again. His own explanation was: "It is a
happy event for me, because the child perhaps will lead me back to
life, which at present I find so unbearable." When on April 19 Pau'ura
presented him with a baby boy, he was still so pleased and interested
that he named him Émile, like the eldest son of his marriage with
Mette.[182] As at Christmas 1896, when Pau'ura had had her first,
short-lived baby, Gauguin painted two very similar pictures; or rather,
two versions of the same picture. Although the theme and title are
Maternity, Pau'ura's place in the composition is much less prominent
than in the previous nativity pictures. In fact, both versions are dominated by two standing native women, one wearing a red and the other
a blue loin-cloth, while Pau'ura squats humbly at their feet, breast-
feeding her baby. As with many another pair of pictures by Gauguin
with the same subject, one is now in Russia, while the other is in the
United States.

However, it was not the pleasures of parenthood which gave a new direction and fresh purpose to Gauguin's life; it was an unexpected opportunity for sweet revenge for many humiliations. It all began when he found that in addition to the things which Pau'ura had taken from the house during the ten months of his absence, many more articles had disappeared. What is more, the burglars had formed the habit and were still paying occasional nocturnal calls. But the only intruder whom he succeeded in catching red-handed, as it were, was a woman (probably a friend of Pau'ura's, or perhaps one of his own former girl friends) whose only offence, as trivial as it was odd, consisted in "going about in the night with an ordinary house broom and sweeping among the bushes in the grounds, which were enclosed by a wooden fence." In order to make an example of her and put a stop to such visitations, Gauguin notified the police. As neither the native police nor the French *gendarmerie* took the trouble to make any inquiries, he drove into Papeete and called on the procurator, his former friend Charlier. The latter bluntly informed Gauguin that he had thrown the complaint into the waste-paper basket out of kindness for him, as he thought that he had made himself look ridiculous enough by his previous complaint about Pau'ura. Moreover, Charlier said, a person whose only offence had been to sweep the shrubbery with a broom could hardly be charged with housebreaking. Infuriated, Gauguin sought to convince the procurator, statute book in hand, that there were plenty of charges that could be preferred against the woman. Angered by this insinuation that he did not know his job, Charlier at once turned Gauguin out.

Unluckily the burgling and stealing went on, for the obvious reason that the culprits had not been punished. Gauguin lodged more complaints and paid further visits to the procurator, who finally remitted the case to the native police officer in Punaauia with a request for a full investigation. When the native policeman, as usual unwilling to side with a European, procrastinated week after week, Gauguin lost his temper and wrote a long letter of protest to Charlier.[183] But instead of posting it to the procurator, he sent it to the editor of *Les Guêpes* (The Wasps), a new monthly paper in Papeete which flaunted the proud motto: "Right is stronger than might." The editor published the letter in the June issue, while carefully pointing out that he took no responsibility for its contents. Gauguin could not have chosen a more appropriately named paper, feeling waspish him-

self and determined to sting Charlier sharply. The tone was set in the
first lines of the letter, which began:

"Monsieur Charlier,

"I do not know whether our Government has created and organized
our colonies for the purpose of settling them. But I do know—in spite
of my ignorance in many respects—that there are men with the courage to become settlers. As a settler, I pay, every year, a good deal of
money in taxes, and as a settler, too, I demand to be left in peace on
my property by intruders, since under the law I not only have duties
but also the right to its protection.

"It may be that the colony's resources do not suffice to prevent
fraud and theft, or to investigate them when that becomes necessary.
But the settlers of Tahiti will be surprised to learn that you refuse
to prosecute the thieves whom we catch in the act. This procedure
introduced by you may be brilliant from your point of view, but it has
very damaging consequences as far as we are concerned. Thanks to
your protection, the natives rob us and go scot-free. . . . It is common knowledge in this district that I can be robbed and attacked,
and the sanction is exploited every day. Tomorrow the authorities
will be guilty of aggression, and I shall have to pay for it.

"The confidence which I repose in the good sense and the power of
the general public leads me to speak out in these pages, because I
would have the law protect me just as I would have it punish me if I
cease to be honest. I can handle both pen and sword, and I demand
that everyone, including the procurator, should pay me due respect."

After recounting the broom-sweeping episode and an equally mysterious affair of a vanished key to a letter-box, Gauguin repeated his
challenge in even more insulting terms, clearly in order to make sure
that it would be accepted:

"How can settlers continue to feel safe in this district, subject as
they are to the obvious bias of native chiefs and your arbitrary and
autocratic rulings? You have no such rights, but you do have duties.

"Where it concerns my rights I am adamant, for it also concerns my
dignity. That is why I have just requested you to inform me whether
you behave to me as you have done in order to satisfy an absurd desire
to tread on my toes (which are in poor condition). I mean whether
you behave in this way to make a fool of me? If that is so, I shall have
the honour to send my seconds to wait upon you.

"Alternatively, as the more probable explanation, you must admit your inability to administer the law . . . and to being always impelled by vanity and stupidity; otherwise you would never for one moment have persuaded yourself that you are a person of consequence. Furthermore, you seem obviously to be convinced that your protectors will always manage to get you out of the scrapes into which your blunders constantly lead you.

"If this is the case, I will request the Government to recall you to France, so that you may start your law studies again and learn the rudiments of your profession.

With my compliments,
Paul Gauguin,
Punavia."

To press home the procurator's laxness and inefficiency, Gauguin proceeded to urge settlers in the district who had similar complaints to write a collective letter at once to the governor. Since their literary ability was not all that it might have been, he tried to facilitate their task by furnishing a model letter, which ran as follows:

"Monsieur le Gouverneur,

"We herewith have the honour to inform you that letters of complaint addressed by us to the *gendarmerie* and forwarded by the latter to the procurator have so far been without result.

"As this silence is highly detrimental to us settlers, and as we assume that the law exists for our protection, we beseech you to see what can be done in order to remedy this sad state of affairs in Tahiti.

Yours respectfully,
(Signatures)"[184]

Whether from charity or because he felt that that was the shrewdest tactics, Charlier ignored the attack. Gauguin, who appears to have genuinely believed that he was waging an honourable war in a just cause, and in the meantime had drafted a seven-page speech in his own defence, was greatly disappointed. "The result nil as far as I am concerned; neither duel nor prosecution," he wrote. "What rottenness there is in the colonies!" But it had done him good to give vent to his spleen; and going on where he had left off, he wrote a long article for the July number of *Les Guêpes*, attacking in the same libellous manner another person who had treated him condescendingly, Governor Gallet. The final sally well sums up the contents of this article:

"The colony's affairs are no more important or difficult to handle than those of a business firm of the tenth order. . . . One cannot help doubting the ability of the civil servants to appreciate the colony's needs, the requirements of its people, when one reflects that they are only temporary visitors and are not interested in anything which does not have to do with their emoluments and their own security." The unavoidable conclusion is: "The administration is the enemy of colonization."

Stimulated by the interest aroused by these attacks, Gauguin then decided to make revenge doubly sweet by getting paid for it. He accordingly started a four-page hectograph monthly, of course illustrated, which he called *Le Sourire* (The Smile). The bulk of the first issue, which appeared on August 21, 1899, was devoted to an attack on a third person whom Gauguin thought had treated him badly—the lawyer Goupil. There was a good pretext to hand; for Goupil was trying to form a vast company with the object of realizing an old ambition, which was to build a railway from Papeete to Mataiea. Not only to Gauguin but to many other citizens in the colony it looked as if the principal purpose of the projected railway would be to transport the desiccated coconut flakes produced at some factories on this side of the island, all of which belonged to Auguste Goupil. Gauguin's attack therefore took the form of an ironical description of an imaginary trip on the new railway on the opening day. To his feigned surprise all the stations where the train stopped during the triumphal journey turned out on closer inspection to be coconut flake factories. The principal junction seemed very familiar to Gauguin and with good reason—it was Goupil's splendid country estate. Although he did not name the owner, he described the estate in this easily recognizable manner: "It is situated at a curve, and looks like a pile of sardine tins arranged in storeys, as if a carpenter had wanted to copy a castle. In civilized manner, exactly as at Versailles, statues decorate the garden. There are also gates, and wonderful vases of false metal on columns containing thin aloe plants of zinc! Looking through the door, I thought I saw at the other end of the estate a pair of hands playing a guitar. I thought also that I heard a sweet refrain, 'I love this money. . . .'" At the terminus all the VIPs on board were invited by Goupil to a magnificent banquet, whereas the vulgar crowd, including Gauguin, was fed, at their own expense, in the station buffet—with desiccated coconut flakes.

The person who most appreciated Gauguin's writings was Goupil's chief rival, François Cardella, the mayor of Papeete, a fact of which Gauguin must have had some presentiment, for he sent him a personally inscribed copy of the first issue of Le Sourire.[185] Cardella had been born in Corsica, and had the hot temper and hot-headedness that are usually attributed to Corsicans. While still a medical student, he had been mobilized and drafted to Mexico as an assistant surgeon during the French intervention of 1863. From there he had been sent as a ship's doctor to Tahiti, which he had found so much to his liking that he had decided to stay there after completing his period of service, like many another before and since. Without wasting any more time on study, he had opened a pharmacy, which in Gauguin's time, as already stated, was managed by his friend Ambroise Millaud, a former government clerk. The business had been a profitable one for Cardella, but he had only become really rich when he had managed to obtain a monopoly in the growing of opium poppies in the colony and had also established himself as a butcher. One of the few men in the colony with ample time and money, he devoted most of his maturer years to politics and had been the elected mayor of Papeete since the granting of corporate rights in 1890. However, Cardella was usually to be found, not at the town hall, but on the verandah of his centrally situated pharmacy (site 20 on map 2, page 68), and it was there that Gauguin had got to know him on his many visits for medicine. It was at the pharmacy, too, that he had first met the editor of Les Guêpes, a watchmaker and printer whose name was Germain Coulon.[186]

Cardella was the leader of the political party which called itself the Catholic Party, the majority of its members being at least nominally Catholic. The opposing party was naturally called the Protestant Party for the contrary reason; it was led by Goupil and two Calvinist missionaries. These two parties, neither of which had any fixed programme or established organization, had originated when the colony had been granted limited self-government in 1885, and since then had contended fiercely for the eighteen seats in the General Council, as the diminutive local parliament was called. Members were elected by general direct vote, but there the resemblance to a modern democracy ceased, because only those persons who could read and write French were eligible for election. The qualification excluded practically all the natives from election, but they did not consider this a serious injustice; on the contrary they were glad to vote for any French candidate so long as they remained exempt from taxation and were left in peace between the infrequent elections, as indeed they were.

The mouthpiece of the Catholic Party was *Les Guêpes*, Cardella and another wealthy businessman, Victor Raoulx, being the proprietors.[187] The opposition party controlled two papers, *L'Oceanie Française*, which was owned by Goupil, and *Le Messager de Tahiti*, which belonged to another lawyer, Léonce Brault. The remarkable thing about these political papers was not their contents, which were invariably confined to dull and petty local feuds, but the fact that their publishers, with immense labour deserving of a better cause, succeeded in getting them set up in type and printed on their incredibly primitive presses.

Although they fought each other valiantly for the honour of controlling the General Council, the Chamber of Commerce, or the Chamber of Agriculture, the French merchants, bar owners, and planters, who formed the compact majority in each party, were unanimous on one point: that they were infinitely better qualified to administer the colony than the civil servants who were sent out from Paris. The most violent clashes always occurred in the General Council, because this was the only mixed body where representatives of the two groups met. The French settlers held overwhelming numerical power in the council, where the local administration was represented by only the head of the Department of the Interior; but in reality the administration held all the trumps, because the governor or the Colonial Minister in Paris could veto the council's decisions. The following quotation gives a fair idea of the colony's parliamentary life and traditions:

"The meetings of the General Council form a welcome diversion for the inhabitants, who lack entertainment. In a room thick with the smoke from paraffin lamps about a dozen citizens sit arguing under the chairmanship of an honourable merchant. The head of the Department of the Interior is also present. The public are freely admitted to the room and talk familiarly with the people's representatives. These come from all trades: joiners, bakers, watchmakers, wine merchants, grocers, butchers, etc. The professions are represented by two or three self-taught lawyers, men who have scraped through their entrance examinations with difficulty but who behave like leading counsel, and there are also two or three naval officers who have settled in Tahiti after reaching retirement age.

"There is much merriment. The baker asks permission to speak.

Holding a copy of the colony's budget, he sadly notes that the revenues fill two pages while the expenditures take up twenty-eight. General laughter. A question is then asked about the elegant silver-braided uniform worn on official occasions by the head of the Department of the Interior. He does his best to justify his disguise. Soon after, sharp attacks are made on the administration and police force, and in the midst of all this there is a sudden shout of:

"'Abolish the whole system of foreclosing!' "[188]

The Catholic Party had been in office since 1890, and still held a comfortable majority of eleven seats in the council as against the seven of the Protestant Party when, at the end of 1899, something quite unexpected occurred. At the beginning of that year, Governor Gallet had paid a visit to Paris, and had persuaded the Colonial Department to introduce a reform, which was promulgated on August 10 and announced in Papeete two months later.[189] Under this reform the number of seats in the General Council was reduced to eleven, one for each of the constituencies in Tahiti and Moorea. The other islands—Tuamotu, Marquesas, Mangareva, and the Australs—were henceforth to be represented by special delegates appointed by and directly responsible to the governor. The reason which was given for this reform was that these islands, with their backward and primitive populations compared with Tahiti and Moorea, had in the past been shamefully neglected by their representatives, all of whom had been French merchants residing in Papeete. That this was indeed the case is proved by the budget figures. While the combined revenues of the more backward islands were greater than those of Tahiti and Moorea, the council had only rarely allocated more than one-tenth of the colony's annual budget to them, the other nine-tenths being devoted to house-building, harbour improvements, and road works in Papeete.[190] Thus Governor Gallet's reform was not as undemocratic as at first sight it might appear to be, and there can be no doubt that in proposing it his only intention was to put an end to a glaring injustice.

It so happened that the islands which the governor's reform thus deprived of their right to vote had returned as many as six of the eleven Catholic members of the council. On the other hand, in Tahiti and Moorea, which retained their vote, the Protestants were traditionally very strong. The new elections on November 19, 1899, could therefore have only one result; the Catholic Party won only four seats (all in Papeete), against seven Protestant seats.[191] Cardella gave instructions to increase the December issue of *Les Guêpes* from four to six pages and devote it to a vigorous protest against the governor's scandalously undemocratic and anti-French policy. This attack was continued in the succeeding numbers.

Unfortunately for the Catholic Party it had few good writers, which Cardella gave out as the main reason why his press campaign was a failure. By far the ablest polemicist in the colony, it seemed, was Paul Gauguin, who in the meantime had continued to harass the authorities both in his own monthly and occasionally also in *Les Guêpes*. While he had little personal regard for Gauguin, Cardella perceived that the party needed his talents, and so in January 1900 he offered him the editorship of the paper, at a payment to be based on merit.[102] Gauguin for his part was in sore need of help at this time, as he had used up all his canvas and paints and was again short of money. Contrary to his expectations in view of the fairly good sales in 1898, he had not received a centime from Paris since January 1899. The reason why nothing had come from Chaudet became apparent when the mail-boat arrived in January 1900; Chaudet was dead and the gallery closed. The sales of *Le Sourire* had never given more than 50 francs a month,[103] and so Gauguin was not only penniless, he was heavily in debt. The Catholic Party's enemies were his enemies, and he greatly needed an outlet for his pent-up anger. He therefore at once accepted Cardella's offer and began to pour out vituperative articles for the February issue of *Les Guêpes*. Altogether he seems to have written no fewer than six of the seven articles in this number, managing to find something malicious to say about nearly all of Cardella's political adversaries.

The article which must have given his new master the greatest satisfaction was a sweeping condemnation of the Protestant missionaries. By taking as his starting-point a recent administrative decree he managed at the same time to make Governor Gallet look ridiculous. The decree was unnecessary, indeed incomprehensible, for its aim was to suppress "vagrancy," of which there was none in the islands. The most likely explanation for this mysterious edict is that it was simply one of those numerous laws made by the central government in Paris for the mother country which quite often were automatically promulgated also in the colonies, where conditions were totally different. However that may be, Gauguin did not miss this marvellous opportunity to castigate "the proconsul's dictatorial methods" and to point out, that in fact there was only one category of people in the islands to whom the epithet "vagrant" could be applied: the Protestant missionaries. And against them stern measures were well justified, he continued; for these criminal individuals, who were "masquerading as religious puritans," not only put the money they "exacted" from the natives into their own pockets, but also had the audacity to make anti-French propaganda. Almost overcome by his own indignation, Gauguin concluded furiously: "Surely it is there that we have the true and dangerous vagrancy, to which our leaders seem so willingly to turn a blind eye. That is the suggestion we wish to make, but with little hope that it will be considered, knowing full well that when the wind blows from London or Geneva the fight against the Catholic religion is for certain individuals their foremost duty." A more complete reversal of the opinions expressed with the same eloquence and vehemence in his long essay on the modern spirit and the Catholic Church, three years earlier, can hardly be imagined.

The party's enemy number one, the governor, helped to make Gauguin's début as editor of Les Guêpes particularly noteworthy. Ignoring all the earlier attacks, Gallet pressed on with his reforms and in the middle of February reorganized the Papeete Chamber of Commerce on the same lines as the General Council. Rising to the occasion, Gauguin proved himself worthy of the confidence which had been placed in him and five days later, at record speed, produced a single-page supplement headlined, in the biggest available type, across the front: CHAMBER OF COMMERCE DISSOLVED! Fortunately, the text was more inspired than the headline; referring to Gallet as "Mr Meddlesome," Gauguin insinuated that the governor was actuated solely by vindictiveness against the leaders of the Catholic Party. The article concluded with this warning: "Mr Meddlesome would be wise to ponder on the old proverb that a pitcher which goes too often to the well gets broken."

As there had been neither time nor space to develop his theme adequately in the supplement, Gauguin also devoted the entire ordinary issue for March to demonstrating the contemptible character of the governor's motives. Nearly the whole of the front page was taken up by a signed editorial, describing Gallet's reforms as "a tissue of illogical contradictions," and their author as "an arbitrary despot." Yet almost in the same breath Gauguin, using highly original metaphors, inconsistently declared that the governor "only frightened sparrows, and resembled a man singing in the night from fear in order to keep himself from feeling lonely." In a sort of second leader on page two, Gauguin indicated the nature of the governor's deadly crimes with greater clarity, saying that he was bent on destroying "all progress, all freedom, and all the colony's trade."

In issue after issue Gauguin continued to harass the Catholic Party's real and imagined adversaries with similar attacks. I do not think that there can be two opinions about these articles: they are extremely boring and repetitive. Only twice did he leave the dreary subject of local politics. The first time this happened he simply enlivened an issue with the following short anecdote:

"When I am tight (please excuse me for this), I become a joker, and so one day, walking past the monumental French Academy, I got the strange idea of popping into the door-keeper's lodge. With the solemn look required by the circumstances I said to the venerable Cerberus:

" 'Is Monsieur Zola in?'

"To which he replied with a still more solemn look:

" 'Monsieur Zola will never enter Our House.' "

The second time, he dealt at length with a still frequently debated topic of more universal interest: Whether our technological achievements have brought us greater happiness. Since Gauguin for once seems to have been thoroughly sincere, it is well worth quoting this self-revealing article at some length:

"We are told that in the course of the past century we have spread our civilization, have made yet further progress, etc. Admitting this to be true, why so proudly use the word 'we' in this case? It tempts one to ask 'Who are *you?*' Like me, you are nothing. Completing some costly humanistic studies, we appear in the world like caterpillars metamorphosed into butterflies; brilliant people, shining from head to foot, able to talk on any subject. Which in short, alas, means that we are terrible fools.

"Everything is created by the exceptional man. God alone makes the genius; and the genius makes the earth move. Which is why a great artist said at the funeral of Pasteur: 'How long will it take nature to create another brain like that?'

"From the reign of Menes down to the Christian era, in that barbarous epoch when no one dreamt of trying to educate the people, what happened to Egypt? From one end to the other she became one huge monument, which appears as if created not by men but by giants, by gods.

"The Eiffel Tower, for example, does that really represent progress, when compared with the Temple of Jerusalem? But we have veloci- pedes and motor cars, someone objects. Of course, and undeniably they are new. But how many things and how many manufacturing secrets have been lost? Such as the hardening of bronze, a metal far stronger than our modern improved steel. And in philosophy there were Buddha, the Greeks, divine Plato, and finally Jesus. Do Luther and Calvin constitute progress?

"But *we* are civilized beings! Yes, yesterday slings and arrows were used, and today we have guns and cannons. And the barbaric hordes who in the past would have travelled on foot or on horseback now take the train or a steamer. Where, then, are the changes?

"Only when our society lives in blissful peace, when it benefits from the work of intellectuals, and when there is fair distribution for the workman and for the talented, then only can it be called a civilized society."

As he earned much more from editing *Les Guêpes* for the Catho- lic Party than by the far more exacting and time-consuming work of writing, illustrating, duplicating, and distributing his own *Le Sourire*, Gauguin discontinued this paper with the April issue and concen- trated all his energies on *Les Guêpes*. One of the many advantages of editing such a non-illustrated publication of four pages, which came out only once a month, was that it did not necessitate moving back into the town. In fact, knowing how indispensable he was to the Catholic Party, he would often tell his employers and associates to come out to him in Punaauia when there was some important matter to be discussed, instead of harnessing his horse and driving into Pa- peete himself. Happy to be at long last an honoured and respected member of society, he gladly overlooked the vulgarity and poor edu- cation of his new friends and frequently gave small parties for them.[194] After Cardella, the most powerful man in the party was the previously mentioned merchant, Raoulx, who happened also to be the island's biggest rum distiller and importer of French wines and liqueurs, and who as a rule, therefore, generously provided the drinks. Gauguin's companion at the time of his employment in the Public Works Department, the Breton ex-soldier Pierre Levergos, now lived in Punaauia, and occasionally he got invited to these parties. As a re- sult, we have the following reminiscence which is particularly val- uable for the psychological insight which it provides: "Gauguin at this time seemed to be rich, being always well stocked with spirits and every sort of tinned goods. Nearly every Sunday he would invite a few friends to a *tamara'a* (a meal cooked in the Tahitian way in an earth oven). The meal was always very carefully prepared and everything would pass off quietly and decently during dinner. After dinner, however, some new guests would arrive and the party would really warm up and usually would go on through the night. Gauguin liked to amuse himself persuading his guests to make fools of themselves (such as getting the women to undress). Although he drank copiously, he never seemed to get drunk himself, and always kept himself under control."[195]

The climax of Gauguin's political career came on September 23, 1900, when he spoke at a public meeting organized in one of the Papeete parks by the Catholic Party. The purpose of the meeting was to protest against the continued Chinese invasion of the colony. For some years, nearly every ship had brought with it a number of Chinese immigrants, sometimes as many as a dozen, and they had usually been allowed by the French authorities to stay, as they always claimed, rightly or wrongly, to be related to one or other of the Chinese families long established in Papeete—who would invariably welcome and look after the new arrivals. The industry and fellow-feeling of the Chinese had in course of time made them dangerous rivals to the French merchants, who were anxious, therefore, that further immigration should be prohibited. The meeting had been announced weeks in advance by means of posters and leaflets, and the town's entire population was there when it opened at half-past eight in the evening. (Many had probably come straight from one or other of the numerous Chinese restaurants.) Victor Raoulx, who was billed as one of the speakers, was voted chairman by show of hands, and Gauguin, who was to be the other speaker, was elected vice-chairman. Gauguin spoke first. His own report of this speech, the only political speech he ever made, is taken from the October issue of *Les Guêpes:*

"Gentlemen!

"I want to thank you first of all for responding to our appeal and attending this meeting. I see before me no ordinary gathering such as can be seen anywhere at any time, but a united family, a group of friends met here together far from our homeland, resolved by our labour and courage—as our country requires of us—to secure the welfare of ourselves and of the colony, each one of us equally proud to be French. It is chiefly as a Frenchman—a name very dear to my heart—

that (setting aside my reticence) I venture to claim your attention
for a few minutes now. I am a newcomer and by profession an artist,
and so I cannot delve into details which other more qualified speakers
to come after me will discuss. All I want to do, therefore, is to speak,
in general terms, of a serious problem (this well-known Chinese problem), so serious because it is endangering the whole life of Tahiti. In
the hope that it is not already too late, it is your duty to help in solving it by the adoption at this meeting of a carefully worked-out, vigorously worded, and well-based resolution.

"The statisticians tell us that there are no fewer than twelve million Chinese circulating about the Pacific and gradually obtaining
control over the trade of the South Seas. Does not the barbaric invasion of Attila, described by the history books with such horror, pale
in comparison?

"Unless measures are taken, Tahiti will soon be lost. Gentlemen,
do you really want to be buried before you die? No, of course you do
not; and it is a sufficient reason for your refusal to cite the example of
our illustrious ancestors, who purchased our liberty with their blood.

"Besides the current problem connected with the Chinese invasion
of our beautiful colony, another will of course arise. I refer to the new
generation, which will be half-Chinese and half-Tahitian. Indeed, it
will be more than half-Chinese, for the Chinese features, physical
and mental, always predominate. Children are registered at birth as
French citizens, and thus in time will have the same voting rights as
we have ourselves. This yellow blot on our country's flag makes me
blush with shame. Viewed from a moral standpoint—a standpoint
certain persons have seen fit to adopt now for some time—to permit
such a monstrosity is a crime.

"I try to persuade myself, while conceding to you the right to believe the opposite, that the authorities seek our welfare and act for the
colony's good, for its prosperity now and in the future. But unfortunately they are engaged in political struggles, of the kind which lead
to a colony's downfall, or are so burdened with work as to lack the
time for acquainting themselves with the problems. But there are
many people who are familiar with colonial problems and have had
long experience of colonial affairs, and who through the medium of a
press campaign, from a sheer sense of duty, having no desire for reward, and actuated solely by the urge to promote the just cause of the
hard-working settlers, have drawn the attention of our administration

to the danger inherent in the Chinese invasion and requested from it the protection to which they believe themselves entitled. All these efforts, however, have been *in vain*.

"Perhaps there are those who think that these protests are made by a few cranks, by people who complain for the pleasure of complaining, and who do not represent public opinion. It is for this reason that, faced with complete and absolute silence on the part of the administration, it was our duty to appeal to all true patriots to lend us their support; for the task of saving the colony is yours, gentlemen.

"By making your opinion known and signing the petition which will be circulated, it will be brought to the attention of people in France that there is a French colony in a far-off part of the earth where there are Frenchmen worthy of that name who do not want to become Chinese and who, for that reason, can no longer be ignored without the acceptance of a dreadful responsibility."

Who Gauguin's enemies were will have emerged clearly, I hope, from the quoted extracts from *Les Guêpes*. But whose interests was he defending? Was it exclusively the French traders? The questions have to be asked in the light of the statement so frequently made that Gauguin's principal aim in writing and editing this paper was to improve the lot of the poor oppressed natives. I shall confine myself to two short quotations from two widely read books about Gauguin, Raymond Cogniat's and Lawrence and Elizabeth Hanson's.[196] The former says unequivocally that the French settlers "considered Gauguin a kind of traitor because he took sides with the natives against them. A feeling of unrestricted justice and morality was set against class morality; conflict was inevitable." Mr and Mrs Hanson say, even more indignantly: "The French residents, who Gauguin believed hopefully would be driven to investigate charges and to protest against the treatment of the islanders, merely sniggered at this latest absurdity of the mad painter who had gone native. They read with pleasure but did nothing."

Though fairly confident of the result before I started, I have made a thorough search of every issue of *Les Guêpes* edited by Gauguin to find out if there is any truth in these generally accepted statements. Let me say, first, that the research was not easy. Unlike *Le Sourire* (which has even been published in a facsimile edition), *Les Guêpes* does not exist anywhere in a complete edition, not even in the French National Library, and it was only after several years of searching that

I finally succeeded in tracking down twenty-three of the twenty-five numbers which Gauguin either edited or wrote for.

A careful study of these reveals that native questions are discussed altogether four times. The first case is the report just quoted of Gauguin's speech attacking Chinese immigration. While he rightly represents uncontrolled Chinese immigration as a danger, he is obviously thinking of the financial losses facing the French traders rather than the shameful exploitation of the natives. In the second case, Gauguin severely criticizes the useless and one-sided education provided for the natives. But he suggests that the faults could soon be put right by entrusting their education to the Catholic missionaries instead of leaving it in the hands of native Protestants, who besides being inefficient were brazen enough to meddle in politics and make propaganda for the wrong party. A brief extract will suffice to show the general trend of thought: "Who elects these individuals who are so proud of their majority? After being rejected everywhere in the colony, they have been elected by the natives, whom they evidently regard as barbarous since they ask for schools to civilize them—with the help of native pastors who cannot speak a word of French—schools we taxpayers are called on to subsidize.

"Is it not obvious how ridiculous the Government is to rely on individuals who so completely lack any common sense, and who make us pay for educating those who lead us? A policy so muddled must inevitably lead to financial and moral disaster, provoke hatred of us Europeans by the natives, and encourage them to fleece us with impunity."[197]

The third case is an article given up entirely to a discussion of the means whereby the natives can be prevented from robbing the settlers. Gauguin's proposed solution to this problem, of which, as we have seen, he had had personal experience, is ruthless: "To station a resident European French gendarme in every district would, to be sure, be expensive. But the measure would be useful, and the settlers demand it."[198] Most revealing of all, however, is the fourth case, where an ironical article in which Gauguin comments on a proposal by a Protestant missionary in the General Council, intended to stop the fearful drunkenness among natives in country districts by withdrawing the licences of tavern-keepers—all of whom were, of course, French. With great indignation Gauguin argues that "such a withdrawal would only encourage the natives to drink even more. Unable to drink regularly every day, they would gradually develop such a thirst that they would come riding into Papeete to buy spirits by the bottle. In short, a measure aimed at the tavern-keepers, as this is, would fail in its intended effect and would only create dangerous congestion on the roads, while removing the source of income from a whole class of people."[199]

The sad but incontrovertible conclusion is that from first to last Gauguin served only the vested interests of his reactionary employers and sought with great loyalty to further their often dubious ends. It may be objected that of course he did not believe half of what he wrote; but that is a poor excuse. That his real motives were revenge on his personal enemies and the need to earn money did not escape his adversaries' attention. In fact, one of them expressed very eloquently what they all thought in a letter protesting against Gauguin's journalistic activities. The letter said: "You, Monsieur Gauguin, have chosen to spread lies and calumny about innocent people for gain. To exploit the good faith of his fellow-men and shamefully abuse the public trust is a strange employment for an artist."[200]

Today, fifty years after the event, it is difficult to feel the same moral indignation, especially as all these press campaigns were entirely without result. There is more reason to lament that an artist of Gauguin's greatness should have had no other means of obtaining a living than to become a paid mud-slinger, and in so doing be prevented from painting for nearly two years.

---→

45. A native woman does her ironing (with a coal-heated British iron of Victorian model), as she does all her other domestic work, seated on the floor, even though she may be well enough off to live in a splendid European-style house with a shining metal roof.

46. The narrow Atuona valley on Hivaoa island in the Marquesas, photographed from the rocky headland that was usually the destination of Gauguin's evening walks. The village is still as well hidden behind the palm-trees as it was in Gauguin's time.

47

48

X

THE HOUSE OF PLEASURE

GAUGUIN was rescued from the servitude he had descended into and enabled to start painting again by Ambroise Vollard, the young Paris art dealer who in the winter of 1893–94 had done him the more doubtful service of providing the "Javanese" girl Anna. Vollard had become extremely successful since then, by reason of his astonishing skill in investing in the right artists early on. For example, he had organized the first Cézanne exhibition, in 1895.

Vollard is usually made out to be a rogue and an unprincipled profiteer, and Gauguin no less often called him a thief and a liar, when he did not refer to him as a "crafty cheat" or an "alligator of the worst sort." Vollard undoubtedly had many unattractive characteristics, prominent among them being his reluctance to give a straight answer

47. *The native "reception committee" awaiting Gauguin on the shore was very similar to this, and demonstrated by the clothing that unhappily the missionaries had reached the Marquesas long before him.*

48. *With its many prison-like houses of stone, its schools and well laid-out streets, Atuona was by far the most civilized village in the whole island group.*

49. *Gauguin's favourite model, the red-haired Tohotaua, photographed in "The House of Pleasure" by his friend, the commercial traveller Louis Grelet, as she posed for a picture which is now in the Folkwang Museum at Essen in Germany.*

or a firm undertaking. He certainly exploited Gauguin shamelessly at the end of 1899 when he took advantage of his embarrassed situation to acquire nine pictures for the small sum of 1,000 francs. Yet when he offered to handle Gauguin's pictures after the death of Chaudet the following year the terms suggested were rather liberal in view of the continued lack of interest among the picture-buying public. He even offered to pay a regular monthly advance of 300 francs against a guaranteed purchase of at least twenty-five unseen pictures a year at 200 francs each. Furthermore, he undertook to supply at his own cost all the painting materials that Gauguin required. Yet, strange to say, he did not stipulate that he should have the sole agency, but allowed Gauguin to sell anywhere else if he painted more than twenty-five pictures a year. This was the sort of arrangement Gauguin had always desired, and he promptly signed the contract. Though in his letters he continued to complain bitterly of the shameless manner in which Vollard was exploiting him, his satisfaction at the time is shown by the fact that simultaneously he declined an offer by a wealthy Rumanian prince who wished to secure his whole production on precisely the same terms. In fact, the only serious criticism that can be made of Vollard is that he was at first incorrigibly slow and dilatory in remitting the agreed monthly payments. But in all fairness it has to be added that Gauguin, too, failed to meet his obligations during the first year, because his illness and his journalism had prevented him from painting.[201] However, in February 1901 Vollard made up for his earlier remissness by sending Gauguin the full amount due to him. Soon afterwards, he agreed to Gauguin's urgent request to raise the advance to 350 francs a month and the price of the pictures to 250 francs.

Gauguin at once decided to carry out his old intention of moving to the Marquesas Islands. As he ironically expressed it himself: "It was time to push off to some more primitive place with fewer colonial officials." A similar but more detailed explanation was: "I am certain that in the Marquesas, where models are easy to find (while in Tahiti it is getting more and more difficult), and where in addition there are landscapes to discover—new and more primitive sources of inspiration, in fact—I can do fine things. My creative powers were beginning to flag here, and moreover the art public was getting too familiar with Tahiti. Poeple are so stupid that when they have seen these pictures with their new and *terrible* features they will find my Tahitian paintings comprehensible and charming. My Breton paintings are now as rose-water because of my Tahitian paintings, and these will become *eau de cologne* after my Marquesan ones."

According to his good friends and neighbours, Pierre Levergos and Fortuné Teissier, the hope of finding new "models" was a much more compelling motive than Gauguin cared to admit in his letters. "Gauguin wanted me to go with him to the Marquesas as his cook," Levergos says. "But as my duties would also have included nursing the sores on his legs, the sight of which made me ill, I declined the offer. It was in fact the sores which made him leave Tahiti, because no women there would sleep with him any more. The women of the Marquesas were poorer and more savage, and he would have better opportunities there, he said."[202] Teissier confirms this statement with his recollection that Gauguin "one day returned triumphant from Papeete; he had heard that in the Marquesas you could still buy a girl model for a handful of sweets! He ordered a sackful, and with this honeyed 'barter' sought the last corner (of the archipelago)."[203]

It is easy to understand in the circumstances why Gauguin did not complain when Pau'ura, who by now was twenty and no longer fresh, flatly refused to leave her home district again for a future which was even more uncertain than when she had accompanied him reluctantly to Papeete in 1898. The future of his two-year-old son, Émile, concerned him even less, for he believed, rightly, that Pau'ura would have little difficulty in finding adoptive parents for him if, contrary to what he expected, she did not want to bring the boy up herself.[204]

Feeling sure that in the Marquesas Islands he would find what he looked for, Gauguin at once offered his property for sale, and the price of 5,000 francs which he asked for it being very reasonable soon found a buyer. The sale had been arranged when an unexpected complication arose. The lawyer who had been engaged to seal the contract found out that Gauguin was married and that his wife was still alive. There being no marriage settlement, she was formally the part-owner of the property, which thus could not be sold without her written consent. Gauguin had not heard from Mette since receiving the brief announcement of Aline's death four years before, and he had every reason to suppose that she was even more ill-disposed towards him now than she had ever been. He therefore instructed Daniel cautiously to write to Mette requesting the necessary authority, and enclosed the draft of a very diplomatic letter to her. Mette's failure to write to him after 1897 was partly due to the bitter and wounding reply which he had sent her after Aline's death; another serious reason for her silence was the publication in *La Revue Blanche* in October and November that year of *Noa Noa*. Few wives take pleasure at the sight of frank and enraptured accounts of their husbands' affairs with thirteen-year-old native girls, printed in well-known magazines with large circulations. Moreover, Mette is known to have been extremely jealous of Gauguin's Tahitian "models" and to have hated him for preferring such unworthy creatures to herself. The French author Victor Segalen, who dined together with Mette at Daniel de Monfreid's some years later, says that "when she wondered which of the women with bare bosoms and bare stomachs whose pictures hung on the walls of Fayet and de Monfreid had supplanted her in his affections, she could not find words and grimaces strong enough to express her scorn and disdain. With furious whisks of her napkin, she would lash out indignantly and annihilate all the odious *vahine* she saw in her imagination surrounding him."[205]

It is true that over three years had now elapsed since the account of Gauguin's love-life with Teha'amana-Tehura had been published in *La Revue Blanche*, but unfortunately *Noa Noa* had appeared in book form at the beginning of 1901, and Mette must have looked on this with even greater disfavour. Gauguin, too, was dissatisfied, though for a different reason: the book had come out six years too late and unillustrated. In the belief that Morice would never have either the time or the energy to see the venture through, Gauguin had long ago pasted a number of loose drawings and woodcuts on to the blank pages of the half-finished manuscript which he had copied hastily in Paris in the spring of 1895 and taken with him to Tahiti. This, incidentally, is the version of *Noa Noa*, alike incomplete and amplified, which is now usually reprinted and translated, though the now nearly forgotten edition of 1901, with Morice's introduction and verses, in fact comes closest to Gauguin's original conception of the book. To give full realization to his intention all that is necessay is to reprint this edition together with the ten woodcuts Gauguin made specially for it in the winter of 1893–94.

Although Mette, as we have seen, hardly felt well disposed towards her husband, she nevertheless sent him the required authorization—through Daniel and without a covering letter. Long before this, however, Gauguin, who had doubted her willingness to help him, had discovered a loophole in the law. This enabled him to sell his property after advertising the intention to do so a month in advance by means of an announcement in the Papeete registry office, without any objections—naturally enough—from Copenhagen. It should be said in fairness to Gauguin that he himself referred to this procedure as "a wretched trick," one he would not have resorted to if he had not been in so great a hurry to leave. The purchaser was able to take advantage of his impatience; when the deal at last went through on August 7, 1901, Gauguin had been beaten down to 4,500 francs. The shrewd buyer was a Swedish ex-seaman named Axel Edvard Nordman. After long employment as a salesman by a Papeete firm, he considered himself at 55 of pensionable age, and wished to retire from the "turmoil" of the busy town to a quiet place in the country. Taking possession of the house after Gauguin's departure, he found to his annoyance that it was full of old lumber. This little detail has been given to me by his son, Oscar Nordman, now a retired businessman in his turn, and the reason he remembers it so well is that among the "lumber," which on his father's instructions he burnt at the time, were hundreds of sketches, many woodcarvings, and several dusty rolls of pictures, which, had he kept them, would in time have made him a multi-millionaire. One of the few works of art that escaped destruction was a wooden panel, which most appropriately is now in the Swedish National Museum in Stockholm.

The day on which he settled with Nordman, Gauguin paid off the 600 francs, plus 203.95 francs in interest, which he still owed to the Agricultural Bank on the mortgage.[206] Before the end of the month he also brought another business matter to a close, when he edited his last number of Les Guêpes. His journalistic career seemingly ended in a blaze of glory, for, shortly before, the detested Gallet had returned, suddenly and precipitately, to France and had been succeeded by a new governor. To everyone in the colony it looked as if this replacement was a result of Gauguin's press campaign, and he was the first to claim the credit for it in several inflated articles. (The real reason, discovered by the colony long after, was Gallet's failing health, which had forced him to apply for early retirement.) The new governor, Édouard Petit, was in every respect Gallet's exact opposite; when he arrived on February 21, 1901, he was seen to be a lean and mild-mannered intellectual. The leaders of the Catholic Party firmly believed that his name answered to his character, and that they would soon succeed in convincing him of the rightness of their cause.[207] An even greater triumph for Gauguin, in its way, was the announcement which Cardella and Coulon felt obliged to insert in a prominent place in the paper's August number. The announcement informed readers that "in future the paper will only appear as and when the special need for it arises." It was a clear indication by the party leaders of their inability to produce a successful paper without Gauguin's help.

The chief reason why, among the more than a hundred islands in French Oceania, Gauguin chose the Marquesas was, as we have seen, identical with the one which in 1892 had led him to approach Governor Lacascade about the vacant post of magistrate there: he firmly believed that they were the only islands where the native culture and artistic traditions had survived. When for the second time he had wanted to settle in the Marquesas, on returning to Tahiti in 1895, his plans had taken such definite shape that he knew exactly where he would go; it was to Hivaoa, the second largest island in the group. Now that he could finally realize his ambition he held firmly, at first, to the belief that this was the most suitable island. But at the last moment he must have received more information, for just before leaving Papeete he changed his destination to Fatuiva, "a small island almost at the cannibal stage."

Once again he had been badly misinformed; or, perhaps more likely, had relied too heavily on his vivid imagination when piecing together a picture of his new island paradise with the help of such scraps of information as he seems to have bothered to gather—exactly as he had done before his first visit to the South Seas. Life in the Marquesas was certainly in its way more savage than in Tahiti. But not because the natives there had been more successful in preserving their ancient customs and traditions; on the contrary, they had almost completely lost their ancient culture, while at the same time they had acquired only a tithe of the Western artifacts, ideas, and institutions their Tahitian kinsmen had been blessed with. In short, they lived in a kind of cultural vacuum, where sheer anarchy often reigned. This tragic situation was principally the creation of European and American whalers, numbering thousands, who had made frequent and prolonged calls at the islands in the first half of the nineteenth century in search of fresh food and amusement. In return for liberal hospitality, more especially by the women, the natives received not only such prized things as nails, axes, beads, cast-off clothes, muskets, gunpowder, and spirits, but also the less welcome gifts of venereal disease, smallpox, tuberculosis, leprosy, and epidemics of all kinds, which every time wrought terrible havoc. The miserable natives did not even have time to recover between the visits, because the whaleboat captains used to leave sick sailors ashore, who perpetuated the diseases and spread them to even the remotest valleys.

In the Society Islands and Hawaii, which were also frequented by whalers, there were happily both self-sacrificing missionaries and strong native rulers to afford the populations a measure of protection against these harmful intruders. The Marquesas unfortunately lacked not only protectors but even unity, as they were split up among small tribes often at war with one another. A single small island, the size, say, of Jersey, might be divided among ten different tribes. This disastrous political cleavage was largely a consequence of the peculiar local topography: the islands are all of them very rugged, and each tribe was confined in its own narrow valley. The marooned sailors who got well again would invariably apply their restored energies to teaching the natives how to handle firearms, and the efficiency of these new weapons soon led to the deaths of practically all the chiefs and priests, who gallantly used to lead their troops into battle. Robbed of its leaders, the entire social and political system fell to pieces.

By the time the Marquesas were incorporated into the French colonial empire, in 1842, the population, which had numbered 80,000 when the whalers had first begun to visit them, had fallen to about 20,000. The French Government annexed these desolate islands purely for strategic reasons. Its administrative measures were therefore restricted to the stationing here and there of a few gendarmes, whose difficult task was to abolish feuds, murders, and drunkenness by building prisons and confining the worst offenders. Catholic missionaries of the Sacred Heart congregation strove with great energy and optimism to render a more positive contribution by converting and educating the children. But fifty years later the results were still meagre. Even those few children who completed their schooling soon forgot what little they had learnt. No more effective were the heroic efforts of a Catholic bishop who wrote, printed, and published "a cycle of moral poems intended mainly for a Marquesan princess but suitable also for the moral education of other young girls." By the time Gauguin decided to move there, the population had dropped to 3,500 and was still declining fast. The apathetic survivors were inspired by only one ambition, which was to be allowed to drink themselves to death as fast as possible. When the authorities placed a ban on the sale of claret and liquor, the natives applied their remaining energies to making wine from oranges and distilling spirits. As their numbers by now were very small and the dense forests provided them with excellent hideouts, the unfortunate gendarmes who still served as the sole representatives of colonial rule were lucky if they managed to catch an occasional miserable culprit. Thus by about 1900 it seemed fairly obvious to everybody that it was only a matter of time before the race would die out altogether.[208] The only solution to the depopulation problem the colonial administration could think of was to replace the doomed natives with French immigrants. However, the few Frenchmen who emigrated to the South Seas invariably settled in Tahiti with its pleasanter life, and of the two hundred non-natives who were living in the group in 1901 only about fifty were French. The number of Chinese was nearly the same and the majority of the whites were absconded American, German, and British sailors. The only trading companies of any importance were German and British. Before leaving Papeete, incidentally, Gauguin arranged for the German firm to act as his bankers, and from then on Vollard's monthly payments were made through the firm's head office in Hamburg.

The most positive proposal for resettling the Marquesas Islands so far had come from Léonce Brault, the Papeete lawyer and newspaper editor who, since Gallet's reform, had been the appointed representative for the Marquesas Islands. He believed that the deplorable reluctance of Frenchmen to settle in the Marquesas was closely connected with prohibition, and said in the course of a speech in the colony's Chamber of Commerce: "To prohibit the sale of wine in a French territory is a colossal absurdity, which we shall not cease to protest against. It is the Government's duty, of course, to combat drunkenness. But to ban the drinking of wine for that reason is to overshoot the target, and moreover is highly damaging to French exports. It is making a French colony uninhabitable by Frenchmen and forcing them to yield their place to tea-drinking foreigners."[209]

It should perhaps be added that it was only the natives who were forbidden to import wine and liquor or buy them on visiting schooners; so the alleged sufferings of the French settlers, nearly all of whom were traders, were mostly financial. Regarding the business methods of this class of people, an exasperated gendarme, who had been stationed in the islands for many years, made this outspoken statement: "The traders, both white and Chinese, robbed the natives appallingly. All the kanakas at this time were illiterate, and when they brought in 150 kilograms of a product the scale would point to 100. If the price was, say, 40 centimes a kilo, the traders would multiply 100 by 30, instead of 150 by 40."[210]

Just as in June 1891 on his first arrival in Papeete, the sudden confrontation of Gauguin's dream picture with reality resulted in bitter disappointment. The only difference was that this time he became disillusioned more quickly, sooner even than he would have done had he realized his plans in 1892 and 1895. Since 1899 the service between Tahiti and the Marquesas had been maintained by a Government-subsidized steamer of 554 tons, which in fact belonged to a New Zealand company though the vessel had temporarily been given a French name, *Croix du Sud*. More than once in the columns of *Les Guêpes* Gauguin had attacked the disgraceful favouring of a foreign company by the governor, but had failed in this case as in others—fortunately for himself, as it now proved—to influence the governor's dispositions. By local standards the *Croix du Sud* was exceptionally large as well as fast. While it took the small copra schooners at best ten days to do the 750 miles between the Marquesas and Tahiti, the *Croix du Sud* made the voyage regularly without fail in five days, even including several half-calls at atolls in the Tuamotu group—a record, incidentally, that has never since been beaten by any other ship.

But even a voyage on the *Croix du Sud* had its discomforts. Douglas Hall, the junior member of the cheerful two-man team from Oxford who made the trip shortly before Gauguin, for instance, could not refrain from the following minor reservations: "Goodness, how we did roll and pitch about in this little steamer, and what a superfluous amount of ants, rats, cockroaches, and other free passengers she carried. My berth was about a foot too short for me, so I had to sleep in the saloon, and I used to be awakened every night by the cockroaches biting my toe-nails and getting into my hair. I think we must have also eaten about half-a-pound weight of ants, of which the sugar and everything else they could get into was full. . . . One night we thought we would like to catch a few of the superfluous cockroaches in the cabin, as, what with the increased stench from the copra . . . and the heat and one thing or another, it was too unbearable for words, so we put a large bowl of molasses in the middle of the cabin. Next morning we counted five hundred cockroaches captured, and that did not empty the bowl."[211]

Thanks to the pride felt by the authorities in their splendid modern steamship (though in fact she was British), her voyages were always reported in detail in the local *Journal Officiel*. For this reason, we now know for certain that Gauguin was on board the *Croix du Sud* when she steamed out of the lagoon at Papeete on September 10, 1901. As is customary in the South Seas even today, the cargo consisted chiefly of flour, biscuits, corned beef, soap, spirits, claret, and missionaries.[212] In a corner of the hold were Gauguin's furniture and three easels. The journey cost him 250 francs—130 francs for a first-class ticket and the rest in freight.

The *Croix du Sud* arrived at Taiohae on Nukuhiva island, her first port of call in the Marquesas, on September 15 according to schedule. The appearance and composition of the "reception committee" waiting on the stone jetty must have convinced Gauguin at once that conditions there were less primitive than he had imagined them; the party consisted of a uniformed gendarme wearing a white topee, several besotted traders, some black-gowned missionaries, and a crowd of native men in trousers and bush shirts and native women in long shapeless dresses. It is worth mentioning in passing that it was on this very island, about four miles to the east of Taiohae, that Herman Melville, as described in his book *Typee*, had found sixty years earlier exactly what Gauguin was looking for, namely a simple and happy life among free and unspoilt savages proud of their native culture. Although Melville is now seen to be the greatest of all the writers on the South Seas, one looks in vain for any reference to his works, or quotations from them, in Gauguin's books and letters. Since Gauguin would unquestionably have agreed absolutely with his precursor's eulogy of the primitive life and his wholesale condemnation of every agent of Western civilization, one must conclude that he had never read any of Melville's books, a fact not so remarkable, however, as at first sight it appears, as Melville had been quite forgotten at the turn of the century and *Typee*, moreover, had never been translated into French.

The *Croix du Sud* called at only one other place in the Marquesas group—at Atuona on Hivaoa island[213]—where she arrived early in the morning of September 16. Travellers who, like Gauguin, were bound for the "cannibal" island of Fatuiva thus had to disembark at Atuona and proceed from there by one of the small cutters which cruised about the islands buying up copra for the German firm. The village of Atuona is situated in a very shallow bay which is swept by the easterly trade winds, and so every vessel, then as now, had to anchor in the adjacent Tahauku creek, which is more sheltered (site 1 on map 3, page 259). The crowd that stood waiting when Gauguin managed to jump on to the steep and rocky shore from the bobbing ship's boat differed from the crowd at Taiohae in one respect only; it included a young

Annamese prince, who, welcoming Gauguin in impeccable French, offered to show him the village.

This extraordinary guide, whose name was Nguyen Van Cam but who was usually known as Ky Dong, had been deported from the newly acquired French colony of Indochina three years before for "revolutionary" activity. Owing to a lucky mistake by one of the many offices of the Colonial Department, however, he had arrived in the South Seas instead of on Devil's Island in French Guiana as intended. As he had seemed to thrive only too well during his first exile in Tahiti, the authorities there had deported him to the Marquesas and found employment for him as a male nurse, an arrangement which, in view of his utter lack of qualifications, would appear to have been a punishment inflicted on his patients rather than on him. Like many another nationalist in French colonies, before and since, he had acquired most of his revolutionary ideas while studying at a French *lycée*, where he had also come to appreciate French art, music, and literature.[214] The thoroughness with which he had pursued his French studies is witnessed by the fact that he even wrote poetry in French. Ky Dong's works include a "guaranteed true" poem in alexandrine measure describing Gauguin's arrival in the Marquesas.[215] The poem has 1,500 lines, so all I can do here is to say that it deals with the amusing complications that arose when the women of Atuona heard of the arrival of the rich French bachelor Paul. As a nurse, Ky Dong naturally dwells at length on Gauguin's numerous open sores and eruptions, which even made some of the case-hardened native women hesitate. The comic effects of Ky Dong's poem derive from one revealing source, being invariably connected with Gauguin's habit of losing his spectacles and having difficulty in distinguishing between pretty young girls and ugly scarecrows.

As courtesy and policy prescribed, Gauguin called soon after disembarking on the two representatives of French rule—the gendarme Charpillet and the military doctor Buisson. He had known them both in Tahiti, where he had always found them friendly, as indeed they were now. But their reception paled beside the enthusiastic welcome accorded to him by a dozen or so French merchants and planters and a like number of nuns and schoolteachers who were permanently resident in the village. The reason is not far to seek; they had all been regular readers of *Les Guêpes*. One of the planters, a former gendarme named Reiner, had also represented the Catholic Party on the colony's

General Council until losing his seat as a result of Gallet's reform in 1899. The other representative had been Ambroise Millaud, Cardella's manager at the pharmacy; so that Gauguin may well have carried a letter of introduction to Reiner from either Cardella or Millaud.

With its five hundred inhabitants, two mission stations (there being also a small Calvinist congregation), five or six shops, and two Chinese bakeries, Atuona was undoubtedly the most civilized place in the entire Marquesas group. Gauguin must by now have realized, however, that there were no longer any cannibal Edens left in the group. Why bother to go on to Fatuiva, then? Especially since Atuona offered so many advantages—precisely because it was so civilized. First of all, it was clear that he had friends there; whereas in most of the other valleys and islands he would not have found anyone who could speak French. Even the few Tahitian words and phrases which he knew would have been useless to him there, because the Marquesan language is as different from Tahitian as, say, French is from Italian, or Dutch from German. Then again, Atuona was the only place, with the exception of Taiohae, which had direct boat connection with Tahiti, a point of some importance in view of the remittances from Europe. And finally, it was the residence of the only doctor in the islands. Gauguin therefore at once decided to stay there, and with Ky Dong's help obtained a room in the house of a Chinese half-caste, one Matikaua.

In the main street in the centre of the village there was a vacant site, of about an acre, which appealed to Gauguin as a suitable place for his new home because of his inability to walk very far owing to his bad foot. The best stocked store in the village, which was run by a young American named Ben Varney, was very conveniently situated on the opposite side of the street. It turned out that the plot belonged to the Catholic mission, which had become the island's biggest landowner, chiefly through encouraging natives when they died to bequeath a piece of their land to it—and as previously stated they died rather fast. The bishop, who alone could transact business on behalf of the mission, happened in the middle of September to be visiting the neighbouring island of Tahuata. Gauguin had therefore to await his return. He made good use of the interval of waiting by attending mass every morning in company with the gendarme and the doctor. Accordingly, the bishop when he returned had no hesitation about granting the request of such a devout and right-thinking man, though he demanded the somewhat un-Christian price of 650 francs for the plot. Luckily for Gauguin, he could afford it, and the sales contract was duly signed on September 27.[216] It had been drawn up by the gendarme, who besides his various duties as policeman, tax-collector, prison director, harbour captain, and public works engineer, also served as notary public.

To enable him to move again into a house of his own as quickly as possible, Gauguin engaged the best two carpenters in the village, Tioka and Kekela, and gave them as many assistants as they asked for. With the stimulus of a liberal supply of free claret, they managed to complete the house in about a month. This was something of an achievement, since it was a two-storey building, forty feet by eighteen feet, of a type they had never seen before, though there were a number of two-storey houses in Tahiti.[217] In contrast to these houses, with their metal roofs, wooden walls, and verandahs with fancy balustrades surrounding both floors, Gauguin's unique construction was an elevated oblong house with a heat-insulating roof of palm-leaves and walls of loosely plaited bamboo canes to let in the air, which rested on two wooden cubes, one at either end. The two cubes were a wood-carving shop and a kitchen, both fitted with locks and bolts as they contained tools, implements, pots and pans, and other valuable articles coveted by thieves. Instead of enclosing the space between workshop and kitchen, Gauguin left it open on both sides, thus obtaining an extremely cool and airy dining-room. His only surviving friend, Louis Grelet, who at twenty-two was a commercial traveller when he called on Gauguin at Atuona for the first time in order to offer him his goods, consisting chiefly of brandy and liqueurs, has helped to provide the sketch on page 255, and has also furnished me with the following excellent description of the upper storey: "This was eight feet above the ground and was reached by means of an outside staircase near to one of the gables. The staircase led to a small ante-room, containing only a single piece of furniture, a rickety wooden bed, which he had decorated with carved figures and scrolls. . . . A thin wall separated this room from the studio, which gave the impression of being rather large and was an absolute lumber-room, without any sort of order. A small harmonium stood in the middle of the floor, the easels being placed in front of a large window at the far end of the room. Although Gauguin had two chests of drawers, they were too small to hold all his belongings, so he had had shelves made from ordinary wooden planks put up round the walls. In native fashion he kept all his valuables in strong chests, which were padlocked. On the walls were some reproductions of paintings and forty-five pornographic photographs which he had bought at Port Said on the way out from France. Besides the harmonium, Gauguin had a mandolin and a guitar, but could not play any of the instruments properly. His favourite tunes were Schumann's *Berceuse* and Handel's *Reverie.*"[218]

Below the window on the far side of the studio Gauguin had a well dug, and this at once supplied him with fresh water. He soon devised an excellent means of quenching his thirst while painting, without leaving his place at the window: he kept a jug constantly cooled in the well, and used to hoist it up with the help of a fishing rod.[219]

An inspiration which friends and neighbours found much less attractive was his elaborate decoration of the doorway. With meticulous care, he carved five wooden panels about sixteen inches wide and ranging in length from five to eight feet. One of these, which was inscribed "Be mysterious," he placed on the left of the door, and another, inscribed "Be loving and you will be happy," on the right, horizontally and level with the threshold. The three remaining panels he arranged round the door, two vertically at the sides and one horizontally as a lintel above the door. On the lintel were inscribed, in large letters, MAISON DU JOUIR—"House of Enjoyment;" or, in view of the special kind of enjoyment which is associated with the French word *jouir,* "House of Pleasure."

The name was very appropriate; for drawn by Gauguin's generous bumpers of rum and claret, large crowds of natives used to come every evening, gape at the pornographic pictures on the walls, and spend half the night singing and playing. One of the women would, of course, stay all the night. Practically all these women, however, were well past their prime and were rather worn and haggard, so that Gauguin, who had by this time developed a distinct Lolita complex, hesitated to ask any of them to stay with him permanently. The restricted choice was not due to a greater solicitude for their teenage daughters on the part of Marquesan parents than by Tahitian parents, any more than it was due to a stricter moral outlook (on the contrary, rather), but to the strange attitude, from the native point of view, of the Catholic missionaries, who had decreed that girls in their early teens were children and had induced their parents with the help of threats and bribes to send them to a convent school.

Gauguin's "House of Pleasure" at Atuona

The ground floor was occupied by a woodcarving studio on the left and a kitchen on the right. The airy room without side walls in the middle served as dining-room and in the last year of Gauguin's life also as coach-house for his trap. One floor up there was a small bedroom on the left and a large painting studio on the right. The entrance was surrounded by painted wooden panels. From the far studio window with the help of a fishing rod Gauguin used to haul up a water bottle hung to cool in the well.

As the days elapsed, Gauguin gazed ever more wistfully at the groups of fresh young girls who passed his house chaperoned by one or more black-gowned nuns. It was not long before he had found out that the missionaries were in error in asserting that all parents were legally bound to send their children to the school, even though it was classed as a state school; for under French law, which also applied in the distant Marquesas, only children living within a radius of two and a half miles from a school were compelled to attend. Gauguin soon managed to persuade a native couple, who lived in the Hekeani valley six miles east of the village, to take their fourteen-year-old daughter, Vaeoho, from the mission school and allow her to share his life of bliss in the House of Pleasure. His magnificent "wedding present" to Vaeoho and her parents consisted of six yards of cotton cloth, seven yards of chintz, eight yards of muslin, ten yards of calico, three dozen ribbons, a dozen pieces of lace, four reels of thread, and a sewing-machine, which last alone cost him 200 francs at Varney's store. We also know from the storekeeper's account book, which has survived, that this new love affair was negotiated on November 18, 1901. Vaeoho must have been well content with this unexpected development in her European education, because she willingly stayed with Gauguin. The household was supplemented with two cheerful but lazy servants, the cook Kahui and gardener Matahava, each of whom was paid ten francs a month and was barely worth it.

It was not the first time that Gauguin had initiated a new period in the South Seas with reckless spending; but this time, fortunately, there were no embarrassing financial repercussions, because he could now rely on the guaranteed monthly payments by Vollard. When, therefore, he discontinued his studio parties soon after finding Vaeoho and began in earnest to paint again, he was able to do so with greater concentration and peace of mind than ever before. It was not too early, for he was now over 53 and the many battles he had fought to attain this objective had taken their heavy toll.

The native culture was dead and the natives were themselves dying out. But here and there among the survivors an occasional man or woman confirmed the old reputation of the Marquesans for being the handsomest people in the South Seas. (Their chief difference from the Tahitians was that they were taller and slimmer, as well as definitely long-headed.) What is more, many natives were still tattooed, from the roots of their hair to their toe-nails, with extremely intricate geometrical patterns. By dint of persistent searching and questioning, Gauguin, too, could occasionally persuade a native to bring out some family heirloom, such as an elegantly carved wooden bowl, or an ear-plug delicately cut from whalebone. Again, the scenery was far wilder than in Tahiti. Thus, on the whole Gauguin was well pleased with his new existence. Following his usual custom, he worked almost entirely indoors. Exactly as in Tahiti, the natives had plenty of time and gladly sat for him in his House of Pleasure, and would receive as rewards, besides the satisfaction of their curiosity, small gifts such as a piece of cloth, a bottle of scent, or a few tins of food from Varney's store.

Gauguin's favourite model was not, as one would be inclined to expect, Vaeoho, but a red-haired woman from the neighbouring island of Tahuata named Tohotaua. It is a surprising fact that there were some red-haired natives in the islands when they were first discovered, the result of some mysterious racial intermingling in prehistoric times, and Tohotaua is unanimously reported to have belonged to a family with this curious strain in its genetic heritage. One of the pictures for which this woman posed is *Barbaric Tales* (which is now in the Folkwang Museum in Essen). In this picture Gauguin produced one of his most enigmatic works, in which he achieved his effect by contrasting her perfect, nude body with a memory picture of his also red-haired, though hunchbacked and repulsively ugly, friend of the Brittany years, Meijer de Haan. However we interpret the symbolism in this painting, on one point we can be sure: there is no ground for seeking a prototype of the red-haired woman of this picture in the works of Botticelli, as many commentators have done. Old memories are present also in another picture for which Tohotaua was the model, a half-length portrait of her holding a fan; very similar, therefore, to the picture of Teha'amana painted in 1893. This picture, too, is in the Folkwang Museum at Essen; but instead of a reproduction of the painting I have chosen to include among the illustrations a photograph of Tohotaua taken by Louis Grelet while posing for it in Gauguin's studio (Fig. 49). Tohotaua had married a man from Atuona, named Haapuani, who besides being the most accomplished dancer in the village was its most feared magician, generally credited with the ability to work black magic on anybody. Gauguin was no less fascinated by this man than by his wife and he got him to pose, wearing a red cloak, for a well-known picture (now in the Musée des Beaux-Arts at Liége) which is appropriately titled *The Enchanter* or *The Sorcerer*, but is sometimes absurdly called *In Tahiti*, though it is clearly dated 1902.

Although Gauguin's friendship with the pretty Tohotaua was what must properly be called intimate, no complications with her husband arose, because of the couple's truly Marquesan outlook which favoured polyandry. This marriage form, extremely rare elsewhere on the earth, had in fact always been the preferred one in the Marquesas, and many unions of this type survived until fairly recent times. Another friend of Tohotaua and Haapuani, who ten years after Gauguin's death lived for several months at Atuona, has this revealing anecdote to tell: "Haabuani, master of ceremonies at the dances, the best carver and drum-beater of all Atuona, who was of pure Marquesan blood, but spoke French fluently and earnestly defended the doctrine of the Pope's infallibility—even coming to actual blows with a defiant Protestant upon my very *paepae* (house terrace)—explained his attitude:

" 'If I have a friend and he temporarily desires my wife, Toho, I am glad if she is willing. But my enemy shall not have that privilege with my consent. I would be glad to have you look upon her with favour.' "[220]

Of the score of pictures dating from the first remarkably productive months of 1902, several compare favourably with the best of those which Gauguin painted in 1892, in his idyllic *Noa Noa* days in Mataiea with Teha'amana. The most familiar of these are *And the Gold*

Map of Atuona

1. Landing place for passengers
2. Landing place for cargoes
3. Gauguin's plot and "House of Pleasure"
4. Catholic church and small square
5. Residence of Catholic bishop
6. Catholic boarding school for girls
7. Catholic elementary school for boys
8. Protestant church and school
9. Residence of Pastor Vernier
10. House of deacon Kekela
11. Military doctor's house and clinic
12. Gendarme's residence and office
13. Store kept by Ben Varney
14. House of Chinese half-caste Matikaua
15. Store kept by Émile Frébault
16. Chinese Ayu's bakery and restaurant
17. Hut of Gauguin's friend Tioka
18. House of the Annamese prince, Ky Dong
19. The Chinese Lam-keu's store
20. Small group of native huts
21. Small group of native huts
22. Small group of native huts
23. Cemetery with Gauguin's grave

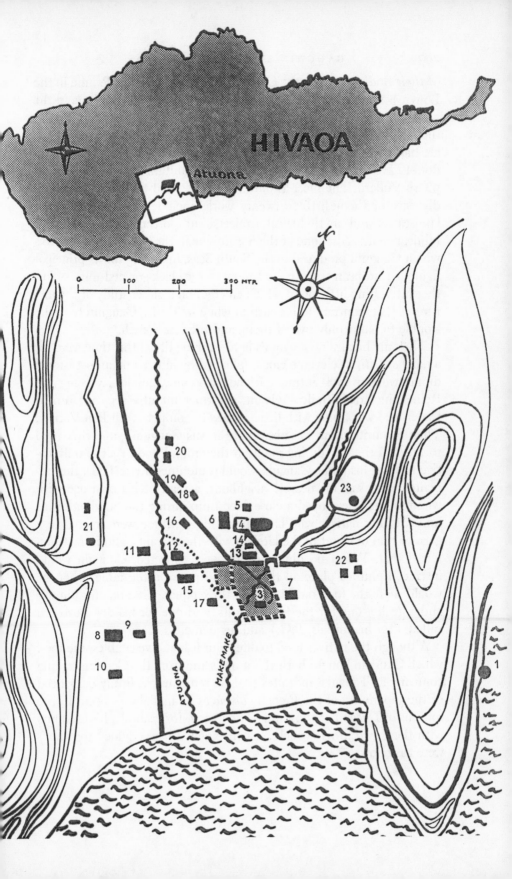

of their Bodies (now in the Gauguin room of the Jeu de Paume in the Louvre) and the two versions of *Horsemen on the Beach* (one in the possession of the Greek shipowner Stavros Niarchos, the other in the Folkwang Museum). Some other works of this period, however, are hardly more than unsuccessful sketches, which Gauguin would no doubt have destroyed but for the need to maintain the contracted supply to Vollard. The most astonishing thing about these pictures is the diversity of themes; these twenty works include not only the usual landscapes and mythological subjects but portraits, still lifes, and biblical scenes. Also, one of them is unique in the whole body of works which Gauguin produced in the South Seas, in having for its principal figure a European woman, and moreover a black-gowned nun. A further interesting little point which emerges on a closer study of the pictures is that, contrary to his custom when in Tahiti, Gauguin took the trouble to name only two of them, and then in French.

The only breaks in Gauguin's hard-working life at this time were for a daily *apéritif* at eleven o'clock, followed by lunch, and an occasional dinner with his most intimate friends, who now, besides Ky Dong and Reiner, included Émile Frébault, a former infantry sergeant turned trader who was trying with little success to compete with Ben Varney. Their favourite drink was absinth, as it was Gauguin's, and they used to meet in the airy dining-room on the ground floor. As the only native to sit at his table, Gauguin would sometimes invite Tioka the carpenter, who was his nearest neighbour, a man of his own age with whom he had developed a close friendship during the building of his house. Other natives who had earned his gratitude were treated to a glass of rum or claret in the kitchen with the servants, and in fact preferred that. When no dinner guests were expected, Gauguin would instruct Kahui to place all the pots and pans on the table, when he would share the food out himself in three equal parts: one for himself and Vaeoho, one for the two servants, and one for his dog Pego (so called after his initials, P.G.) and his nameless cat.[221]

Although the natives used to offer him fish and vegetables, the food which Gauguin bought both at Varney's and from the German trading company at Tahauka indicates that he remained as firmly convinced of the superiority of the French *cuisine* as he had always been. In the months of December 1901 and March 1902, for example, his accounts with these two firms (which for convenience I have added together) were as follows:[222]

December 1901

Dec. 2	32 litres of claret	35.20 francs
	20 kilos of potatoes	12.00
	5 kilos of onions	3.50
	6 tins of tripe	7.80
Dec. 4	1 tin of preserved butter	2.50
Dec. 12	1 sack of rice	13.00
	½ kilo of starch	0.40
Dec. 16	1 tin of preserved butter	2.50
	3 tins of asparagus	6.00
	2 tins of beans	5.00
	1 bag of salt	0.45
	1 bottle of tomato sauce	2.00
	2 packets of tea	2.00
	2 tins of anchovies	4.00
	1 litre of vinegar	3.00
Dec. 18	10 kilos of potatoes	5.00
	5 kilos of onions	3.50
	32 litres of claret	35.20
Dec. 26	18 litres of claret	19.80
	16 litres of rum	56.00
	6 tins of preserved butter	14.40
	6 tins of asparagus	10.80
	12 kilos of sugar	15.60
	1 sack of rice	13.00
	16½ litres of claret	18.15
	5 kilos of onions	3.50
	2 kilos of garlics	3.00
	4 tins of asparagus	7.20
	1 litre of olive oil	5.00

Total 309.50

March 1902

March	3	20	kilos of potatoes	12.00
		12	tins of sardines	8.60
		5	kilos of onions	3.50
		4	kilos of garlics	6.00
		10	tins of asparagus	18.00
		12	kilos of sugar	15.60
March	10	1	sack of rice	12.00
		3	packets of tea	4.50
		6	bottles of tomato sauce	12.00
		5	tins of butter	7.50
March	12	3	cheeses	24.00
		2	tins of asparagus	3.60
		5.6	kilos of dried cod	9.24
		1.9	kilo of cheese	11.40
March	22	12	tins of tripe	28.80
		1.4	kilo of sausages	13.30
		24	tins of sardines	17.00
		24	tins of peas	31.20
		2	litres of absinth	15.40
March	27	1	tin of cocoa	3.50
		1	kilo of tobacco	13.00
		10	packets of cigarettes	6.50

Total 276.64

These purchases, which will doubtless have been supplemented by others from Frébault and some of the Chinese dealers, whose accounts have not survived, give a very good idea of the deserved affluence to which Gauguin had at long last attained. That his material prosperity was matched by happiness and a peace of mind rarely before experienced is attested by his satisfied statement to Daniel in March 1902: "You can't imagine the tranquil life I have here in my solitude, completely alone, surrounded by foliage. I badly needed this rest, well away from all those colonial officials in Tahiti. I praise my decision daily."

XI

DESPERATE PLEA

GAUGUIN's letter had barely been dispatched when his new-found bliss was intruded upon by a visit from the very sort of person he would have wanted to avoid. About the middle of March, a French cruiser steamed into Tahauku Bay with the new governor and his staff. The praiseworthy purpose of Governor Petit's visit was to make a personal survey of the affairs and problems of the Marquesas.[223] He was already intimately acquainted with the islands, as he had spent half a year there in 1881–82, as a purser in the French Navy. His previous travels in the South Seas are well described in the two books, *En Océanie* and *Au Loin*, which he published under the pen-name of Aylic Marin.[224]

The French traders and planters naturally seized on this welcome opportunity to air some of their grievances, and of course chose as their spokesman the well-known patriot Gauguin. The complaint he was charged with submitting, ironically enough, was substantially the same anomaly as had led the harshly criticized Governor Gallet to introduce his reform two years before—that the considerable sums paid into the colonial budget in taxes, stamp duties, and imposts by the residents of the Marquesas and other outlying islands were spent largely on public works and development in Papeete, the capital. The wording of the hastily drafted petition was high-flown and bombastic, down to its turgid conclusion, which ran: "Nurtured in the Christian spirit, we have so far obediently submitted, though we tell ourselves in our hearts that God has clearly forsaken us."[225] The governor's staff naturally enough included the head of the colony's judicial system; that is to say, Gauguin's principal enemy, Édouard Charlier. The governor was therefore well briefed when Gauguin also asked for a private interview, and he refused flatly to receive him. Gauguin's protest took a very logical but rather dangerous form; when the demand for payment of tax for the year 1902 arrived soon after, he refused to pay the sum of forty-four francs due and stated his reason for doing so in a letter to the Marquesan administrator. The latter briefly replied:[226]

"Taiohae, April 5, 1902

"Sir,

"I have to acknowledge the receipt of your letter of the 25th of March, 1902. With regard to your request, I can only submit this to the governor. In my capacity of Government representative in these islands it is my duty to ensure that all laws and decrees are respected without discussion. Pending the governor's decision concerning your objection, I must insist, therefore, that you carry out your lawful obligations to the full.

I am, Yours truly,
Maurice de la Loge de Saint-Brisson."

Another old enemy reappeared to give him trouble at about the same time as Charlier—Gauguin's long-latent disease. As before, the chief symptoms were persistent pains in the leg, palpitations, and general debility. Up to now, he had at least been able with the aid of a stout stick to take a daily stroll round the village, or down to the beach to shoot sea-birds, a pastime which he not only found amusing but which also provided a little variety in his diet.[227] Soon his bad ankle began to give him such great pain again that he stopped going out altogether. To try to ride, as everyone else in the island did, would have been out of the question. In order, therefore, to avoid becoming an

———————————————————————→

50. *Typical representatives of the old and the new order: a native chief in an unusually decorative costume and a French gendarme in ordinary service dress.*

51. *The mightiest man of all was His Reverence Bishop Joseph Martin, who strongly disapproved of Gauguin's immoral ways and anarchist opinions.*

53

absolute captive in his "House of Pleasure," he asked the American trader Ben Varney to order a two-wheeled trap from Papeete.

Unfortunately, Dr Buisson, who was the only doctor in the whole group, had been recalled in February 1902 to Papeete, where in the opinion of the authorities his services were more necessary, and it was extremely uncertain whether he would be replaced.[228] As Gauguin was soon to find out, if he did not already know, the poet-prince Ky Dong, who so suddenly found himself in charge of the islands' health service, knew more about literature than about medicine. Gauguin, therefore, sent for the only person in the village who was able to help him, the young and dedicated head of the French Calvinist mission, Paul Vernier, who in addition to theology had studied medicine both in France and at Edinburgh.

Less than two years before, Gauguin had published in *Les Guêpes* a highly offensive article about this missionary, the general tone of which is indicated by the following extract: "With boundless abnegation, Paul Louis Vernier has settled on a small isolated island—three days' distant from Tahiti, where his father lives, and eight days from San Francisco—in a splendid new house built of timber imported from America. 'I live here with my loving young wife and lovely baby,' he writes in a letter which the Evangelical journal has found interesting enough to publish, 'and it is from here that I shall now begin my fight against savagery, which will be a stupendous fight because the Catholic missionaries are absolutely unscrupulous. I am weak and yet young, but I trust that God will hear my prayers and take note of my sufferings.' Reading this letter I almost wept, and then had a vague vision of Dante leading Virgil to Hell. At this my soul was uplifted."[229]

---

52. A *sick, tired, and marked man, unable to paint any longer without spectacles: Gauguin's last self-portrait begun by Ky Dong and painted in 1902 when Gauguin was 54.*

53. *Gauguin's nearest neighbour, the American Ben Varney (on horseback), and the native carpenter and Protestant deacon Kekela in front of Varney's store.*

54. *One of Gauguin's last pictures, painted at the beginning of 1903, also includes the crucifix in the cemetery where he was buried only a few months later.*

Despite this sharp attack on him, Vernier responded with Christian charity to Gauguin's summons and generously gave him both medicine and good advice. It is hardly a detraction to observe that Vernier's willingness to associate with Gauguin can up to a point be explained by the circumstance that he had lost his beloved wife the year before and was at the time extremely unhappy, as well as lonely among his more or less hostile Catholic compatriots.[230] When paying his sick visits, therefore, he would stay to discuss literature, art, music, and ethnology. Gauguin, of course, was delighted to have somebody to talk with whose interests went further than the latest gossip or dirty joke. Their cheerful and willing messenger was Gauguin's good friend and neighbour, Tioka the native carpenter, who as it happened was a member of Pastor Vernier's small congregation, and indeed had proved himself so firm in the faith that, shortly before, he had been made a deacon.

This unorthodox choice of companions of course was frowned on from the start by the Catholic bishop. By ceasing to attend church a few weeks after his arrival, and by his goings-on with the girls, Gauguin had already given great offence. But at least the girls had been Catholics, and had from time to time obtained absolution. Furthermore, Gauguin had undoubtedly lived a decent and respectable domestic life since finding Vaeoho, for which reason the bishop had turned a blind eye on the ill-matched couple's scandalous neglect of civil and ecclesiastical formalities. Truth to tell, if he had insisted on the marriage ceremony in the case of every white man in the Marquesas he would at once have lost his most zealous parishioners and generous benefactors. A strong contributory reason for the bishop's passivity up to now was the fact that he had been heavily engaged in attacking a far greater evil—Pastor Vernier's heresies. About the time of Gauguin's arrival, the dispute had entered a particularly critical stage when Vernier had converted a dozen Catholic natives in Hanaiapa, a small valley on the north coast of Hivaoa. Bishop Martin had made the counterattack in person, and eventually had managed to lead the lost sheep back into the proper fold at the beginning of January 1901. Returning from Hanaiapa on the day of victory, however, he had met with an accident when his horse had slipped on a steep hill and thrown him. The bishop's right shoulder had been dislocated and his whole arm paralysed, and as his condition had got worse instead of better he had reluctantly embarked, a few weeks later, on the *Croix du Sud* in order to obtain medical attention in Papeete. There he had been compelled to stay for a whole month, and had arrived back just in time for Governor Petit's visit to Atuona in mid-March.[231] The unfortunate episode had naturally made the bishop and his Catholic missionaries more uncompromising than ever in their attitude to Pastor Vernier, the man chiefly responsible for it.

The indignant mood which prevailed in the Catholic mission is indicated by the fact that a jubilee celebration which had long been planned, and eventually took place on June 8, 1902, turned into a demonstration against the diabolical machinations of the heretical Vernier. To Gauguin (who now had his trap—at a cost of 515 francs with harness[232]—and so was able to get about the village again) the occasion was interesting for another reason. This is how the missionary who took part in the jubilee celebration describes it: "The faithful were summoned to service early in the morning by the pealing of the church bells and the sound of drums and trumpets. The church was not big enough to hold them all. A monumental altar between five and six metres high, which was also to be used for the evening service, had been erected, therefore, in the nunnery garden. . . . I say without the slightest hesitation that this was the most solemn open-air mass that has ever been celebrated in the Marquesas. After the reading of the text for the day, Father David in well-chosen words said that this service, like the evening one, should be seen as a vigorous and warranted protest not only against those who deny the presence of Jesus Christ at the Eucharist, but also against those who believe in that doctrine but remain passive. It is to be hoped that his eloquent rebuke will prove to be effective; for these apostles of 'free thinking' have even come here, to the ends of the earth, to proclaim the freedom to believe what suits us—always assuming, of course, that, like them, we do not believe in the presence of Jesus Christ at the Eucharist, which their own leader, Luther, confesses to having received from the father of all lies, Satan himself . . . ! This is the error we are protesting against.

"At two o'clock the entire population once again demonstrated in the same splendid manner by taking part in the solemn procession of the Host. The procession was led by the bearer of the Crucifix, who was followed by the standard-bearers, and they by the bearer of the Host who walked under a canopy. The same choirs as earlier in the morning sang all through the procession, alternating with the brass band of the boys' school. Bishop Martin walked piously behind the Host, which was carried by one of the missionaries. From start to finish, the conduct of those taking part was impeccable and even edifying. For our Marquesan 'savages' realize the need to behave decently when taking part in a procession, or otherwise to stay away. Least of all would they contemplate the absurdity of creating a disturbance in order to stop a church procession; such ideas are born only in the minds of 'progressives,' whose so-called freedom has only the one object of depriving their opponents of their freedom. . . .

"The evening was set aside for a ceremony the memory of which. will endure in the mission for ever. Our Holy Father in Rome had ordered a Jubilee and celebration of the end of the century and Bishop Martin had decided to erect a commemorative monument to the glory of our Saviour Jesus here in Atuona; and the pious zeal of the congregation in thus obtaining the special absolution of the jubilee shows how appropriate this measure of His Reverence was. There arrived for this purpose from Paris a group of figures representing Christ on the cross, St John pointing with his arm to Heaven, and a St Magdalen with eyes turned to the sky and an expression of unutterable grief on her face. All three figures, which are in cast iron, are life size. . . . They stand on an oblong stone pedestal, with five steps, which has a total volume of seventy cubic metres. Suitable stones are here as rare as sculptors, and we also had to find stones that could be shaped with our available tools. Some first-rate stones were found on Vaitahu, and inferior ones at Hanaupe and Taaoa. Others were furnished by the people of Atuona. God will reward those who in the sweat of their brows procured this building material, as He also will Goteve Tiko, the gifted worker who knew how to turn them to the best account. . . . The bishop in blessing the monument promised a hundred days' remission of sins for every devout prayer offered on the spot. The first artistic monument to be erected on a public site in the Marquesas is thus very appropriately a Crucifix with our Saviour who rules the world from His Heaven above."[233]

It would have been very interesting and entertaining to have Gauguin's opinion of this extraordinary monument, which still stands on the same site, and which in the banality and vapidity of its three chocolate-coloured figures beats even the ubiquitous painted plaster saints that are the only works of art usually found in Catholic churches in the South Seas. Unfortunately, however, there is a gap in Gauguin's correspondence from the end of May to the end of August 1902, because on May 27 the splendid *Croix du Sud* met with the fate which every ship in French Polynesia sooner or later experiences; she ran aground on a coral reef in the Tuamotus and became a total wreck.[234] It was three months before the service could be resumed by another vessel, and by that time Gauguin had other and more important things to write about than the Catholic jubilee celebrations. However, one of his books contains a sarcastic attack on Europeans for their inability to appreciate native art, which shows indirectly that he would certainly have preferred a monument in native Marquesan style. The idea of commissioning Gauguin to execute the first public work of art in the Marquesas would have been too preposterous, of course, for it to have occurred to anyone. . . .

In the light of the fierce animosity which prevailed between the rival missions at Atuona, it is not as strange as at first it would appear that the Catholic bishop, after conniving for over six months at Gauguin's "immoral life," should suddenly frown on him for openly associating with the Calvinist missionary Vernier. The point of open warfare, however, was not reached until Bastille Day on July 14. Even in the Marquesas, this was the biggest occasion of the year and was duly celebrated as it was in Tahiti, with dancing, singing, and music contests on a big scale, attended by every native of Hivaoa and neighbouring islands who could climb into a boat. The person responsible for the official arrangements at Atuona, of course, was the official representative of the Republic, that is to say, Charpillet, the gendarme. As in Tahiti, prizes of money were awarded to the best choirs and dancing teams. It was therefore important that there should be a discriminating and impartial judge, and in Charpillet's opinion the person best qualified for this task was Gauguin—a fact which might indicate that the mutual relations of these two remained close and cordial. They may well have been so, but another possibility is suggested by certain passages in the excellent account given by David Hall of the national celebrations at Atuona the year before:

"The feasting began about eleven o'clock, and I was introduced to all the white population of these islands—about twenty men, including half-a-dozen gendarmes. Except these latter, they were the most broken-down, disreputable-looking lot of beachcombers I ever set eyes on; but when you think that some live as solitary traders on lonely islands, with never a soul to talk to except natives, and no communication whatever with the outside world, it is not to be wondered at that they lose their self-respect and so often take to drink. They had, most of them, brought their wives with them, who were dressed up 'to kill.' A very good dinner was prepared for us, washed down with plenty of cheap red wine and topped up with coarse brandy. After dinner, as might be expected whenever Frenchmen are gathered together, the speech-making was great, and compliments flew round like snowflakes.

"Then the real business of the day began, and each 'valley' came up in turn and formed in four long parallel lines—two of men and two of women, about twenty in each row—in front of our dining-place, and danced for all they were worth. Each 'valley' danced separately, and was headed by a sort of *maître de danse*, habited in some old cast-off naval uniform, given him perhaps years ago by some passing ship, or failing this, in the best imitation they could make of one, constructed out of coloured cotton and yellow braid.

"In the meantime, all the rival dancers whose turn had not yet come crowded round, and expressed their opinions pretty freely. They were good enough to make me chairman of the committee to decide which were the best dancers. I thought I saw a smile on Varney's face when I accepted, and soon discovered the reason, as I found myself in a position a shade worse than that of a referee at a football match. Not only did all the natives crowd around me and point out the beauties of the dancing of their particular 'valley,' but each individual gendarme would come and sit by me and explain how I *must* give the first prize to his 'valley,' or I should be perpetrating the grossest piece of injustice. The gendarmes were the most excited of all. Two of them eventually fell out, and started pummelling each other's heads, and had to be sternly put under arrest by the brigadier.

". . . They danced all that afternoon, while we sat and watched, and the majority of the whites steadily soaked in as much brandy and wine as they could hold, so that by the time dinner was served in the evening, they were all three parts drunk; and after dinner I could not find a sober member of my committee with whom to consult regarding the distribution of prizes.

"In the evening the singing competition commenced, and each 'valley' in turn sat round in a big circle, cross-legged on the ground, and sang their peculiar and rather mournful *raris*; and a pretty, picturesque sight it was, all lit up with great flaming bamboo torches.

"There must have been two or three thousand natives gathered together here in Atuona. Its normal population is not more than five hundred. Needless to say, when one considers the marked peculiarities of the Marquesans, later on in the night the scene beggared description.

"When I got back to my house, about two o'clock in the morning, I found half-a-dozen men and girls in proud possession of it, and rolled up, prepared to sleep there for the night; even my bed was not sacred, as two of them were fast asleep on that, and nothing I could say would induce any of them to leave. Finally, in sheer desperation, I had to send for a gendarme, who soon bundled them out.

"These gendarmes are a very fine class of men, generally picked from amongst the best of the old soldiers of the *Garde Républicaine* in Paris; and the way they shift a crowd of natives by carefully stamping on their bare feet would do credit to a New York policeman. I slept little that night, as my house was in the thick of the row; and as I had no fastening to my door—in fact, scarcely any door at all—natives kept continually strolling in, and several of them after all did sleep there.

"I forgot to mention that there is great rivalry on this island between the Catholic and the Protestant missions, and that was particularly shown at these festivities. Each mission sent a party of dancers from amongst their converts to compete for the prizes, and the only way I was able to satisfy them both (I say 'I,' because my committee were all so jealous of each other, and also so very far from sober, that they would only accept a decision from me, a stranger) was by giving each faction a first prize, and even then the two ascetic-looking Jesuit priests regarded me with far from friendly glances."[235]

Gauguin tried hard to get out of the embarrassing situation which his own thoughtlessness or ignorance had led him into at the time of the 1902 celebrations in exactly the same way; that is, by presenting two first prizes in the singing contest, one to the Catholic choir for its excellent rendering of the *Hymn to Joan of Arc* and another to the Calvinist choir for the magnificent singing of the *Marseillaise*.[236] It was an expedient which satisfied nobody, least of all the Catholic bishop.

Unfortunately, it was not long before the bishop had occasion to criticize Gauguin for something much more serious than mere prejudice. About this time, Gauguin's settled domestic life with Vaeoho came to an end when like her predecessors she found that she was pregnant, though with the difference that in her case it had taken less time; by the fourteenth of July she was already seven months gone. Neither of the partners took this very seriously, but a problem arose when at the end of the celebrations she went home to her parents to have her baby among friends and relatives, leaving Gauguin on his own. (Her baby girl was duly born in her home valley of Hekeani on September 14, 1902.[237]) The problem sprang chiefly from the bishop's determination to prevent any of the other girls at the mission school from entering Gauguin's centre of advanced learning. This is Gauguin's sardonic comment on the ban: "The bishop is an old rabbit, while I am a very tough and sometimes hoarse old cock. If I say the rabbit started it I shall be telling the truth. To want to make me take the oath of chastity is really a bit thick."

To Gauguin's misfortune, it was the beginning of the summer holidays and most of the girls had already gone home to their parents in other remote valleys, or on other and even remoter islands. The few girls who lived in Atuona went in such fear of the bishop by now that the furthest they dared go was to visit the "House of Pleasure" when it grew dark and leave at sunrise. Gauguin avenged himself by carving two figures about two feet high out of wooden blocks and setting them up in front of the steps leading to his house, where they were quickly recognized by everybody in the village. The right-hand figure, inscribed on the base *Père Paillard* (Father Lechery), exactly resembled the bishop except for the pair of horns on its head. The left-hand figure, which was inscribed *Thérèse*, was that of a native woman, almost completely nude, whose equally recognizable features were those of one of the bishop's servants who bore the same name, and who, according to unsubstantiated gossip, had been his mistress until her hasty marriage to a native catechist.[238] The bishop's horns have undoubtedly, therefore, a coarser meaning than the one usually suggested—that he was diabolic. It was probably at the same time that Gauguin carved a third, somewhat larger figure out of wood, a hideously ugly man clasping his hands round his huge belly, which he inscribed *Saint Orang*, a name that has given rise to a good deal of futile speculation. It is fairly obvious that the latter half of the second word has been omitted and that it should be *Orang-Utang*. Who was it Gauguin was calling a holy orang-utang in Atuona? The answer to this question becomes easy when it is known that Bishop Martin's right-hand man at the mission at this time was a priest with the unusual name of Orens Saint-Cricq, who moreover was far from handsome.[239] But the Catholic missionaries, too, could be witty; thenceforward they always referred to Gauguin as "Coquin," an onomatope meaning "blackguard."

At the beginning of the new term, Gauguin struck an even heavier blow at the mission by driving down to the beach and, statute book in hand, explaining to parents as they got off the boats from other valleys and islands that they were not bound to send their children to school as they had been told they were. The number of pupils in each class fell as a result by about half. Even many children who lived in Atuona, and who therefore were obliged to attend, stayed away. As an inevitable consequence of this fresh turn of events, Gauguin made himself a new enemy in the otherwise good-natured Charpillet; not only because Charpillet was a practising Catholic but because the heated dispute between Gauguin and the mission as to which children were or were not obliged to attend school gave him a good deal of extra work. Charpillet's first reaction was rather ludicrous; he summonsed Gauguin for being without lights on his trap one evening after dark, though as Gauguin's was the only vehicle in the whole of the Marquesas it can hardly have been a danger to traffic. Soon, however, Charpillet resorted to something far more drastic; on August 28 he wrote a long report to the administrator of the group who resided at Taiohae on Nukuhiva island, and accused of Gauguin of:

(1) inciting certain named persons to keep their children from attending school in Atuona; and

(2) inciting certain named natives to withhold payment of their taxes.

Figures which he attached showed that the revenue from taxes had fallen to 13,000 francs from the sum of 20,000 francs the year before. Charpillet's report concluded as follows: "In addition to these nuisances, Monsieur Gauguin has occasioned others of a secondary nature; for example, by his morals, which are those of a disciple of Epicurus and set the natives an example they certainly did not need."[240]

Gauguin was saved by a stroke of good luck. That zealous guardian of the law, Maurice de la Loge de Saint-Brisson, had just been succeeded by an old friend of his, François Picqenot, who had been transferred from Papeete as a punishment for "insubordination."[241] The new administrator was thus able to understand a man who, like Gauguin, sometimes rebelled. That he remained well disposed to Gauguin until towards the end is proved not only by his own assurance after Gauguin's death that "although I did not share all Gauguin's opinions, we had excellent relations,"[242] but also by his actions. One of the first of these was to try in his reply to Charpillet to calm him down. With regard to non-attendance at school, he went so far as to advise against taking any action, on the ground that in most cases Gauguin undoubtedly had the law on his side. However, to tolerate the non-payment of taxes would be to go too far, and so he authorized Charpillet to distrain on Gauguin if all else failed.

As Gauguin was soon to realize, he had given rise to all this agitation and made enemies for himself to no purpose. By September, his health had worsened to such an extent that he no longer had either the desire or the energy to look for a successor to Vaeoho, and before long his pains grew so unbearable that he had to fall back again on morphine injections in order to get a little sleep. Soon, when he had increased the dosage a number of times and was afraid of increasing it any more, he gave Varney his syringe so as to avoid further temptation and had recourse to laudanum, which however made him perpetually drowsy. Under these conditions, of course, he painted "little and that badly." This, surely, is also the appropriate point at which to quote Émile Frébault's statement that Gauguin often "after the light was gone would sit at the organ in his studio and make one cry with his music."[243]

One of the few persons who were allowed into his studio during this depressing period was Ky Dong. One day, after failing in every other attempt to cheer his friend up, Ky Dong sat down at one of the easels and began to paint. Gauguin's interest was aroused, as was the intention, and before long he had limped across to the easel to inspect the result. Ky Dong was painting his portrait. Without a word, Gauguin picked up a mirror and, thrusting his friend aside, took the brush and finished the portrait himself. The picture which it reveals with brutal realism is of a man, grey-haired, lined, and suffering, gazing at the viewer with tired eyes through his thin-rimmed spectacles (Fig. 52). Understandably enough, some of the experts have for stylistic reasons long doubted the authenticity of this unsigned and undated portrait, which is now in the Kunstmuseum at Basle, but the difference in style from every other picture by Gauguin is sufficiently explained by its genesis.[244]

Gauguin for a time almost convinced himself that a skilled specialist would be able to cure him if he were to return to Europe, and even decided where he would settle after his recovery. This, surprisingly, was in Spain. However, he may well have been correct in his belief that behind the conventional pictures of bullfighting, beautiful señoritas and flamenco dancers was hidden another, more interesting, and entirely unknown Spain. When Daniel de Monfreid learnt of these ideas he explained tactfully that any hope of recovery was illusory. With prophetic insight, Daniel also saw a compelling reason for staying in the South Seas: "In returning you will risk damaging that process of incubation which is taking place in the public's appreciation of you. At present you are a unique and legendary artist, sending to us from the remote South Seas disconcerting and inimitable works which are the definitive creations of a great man who, in a way, has already gone from the world. Your enemies—and like all who upset the mediocrities you have many enemies—are silent; they dare not attack you, do not even think of it. You are so far away. You should not return. . . . You are already as unassailable as all the great dead; you already belong to *the history of art*."

By the time he had received Daniel's reply, Gauguin had long since come to the same conclusion, and with poignant resignation was trying to console himself that "even if I am unable to recover my health, it would not be so disastrous so long as the pains would stop for a little. My brain keeps on working, and I shall resume my work so as to try in all soberness to complete what I have begun. In fact, that is the only reason why I refrain in my more desperate moments from blowing my brains out."

As so often before when he was unable to paint, Gauguin spent the time writing. Most of what he wrote inevitably reflected his understandable pain, bitterness, and frustration. It included two long essays for publication, in which he attacked his chief enemies, on the island and elsewhere. Two-thirds of the longer essay was no more than a transcript of his confused work, *The Modern Spirit and Catholicism*, which he had written at the end of 1897 in an even blacker period of his life, when contemplating suicide. But once launched on the subject of the Catholic Church's tyranny, now again very topical, he added twenty more pages. His long experience as a journalist and editor in the meantime is plain to see in this addition, the style being far more vivid and direct.[245] He chose as his starting-point a personal recollection from 1888, which is immediately arresting: "Witnessing an execution, the present author saw a group of people advancing in the early light towards the guillotine. Observing one of these with *a pale complexion, head hanging, dejected, in short very ignoble in appearance*, he felt a sort of instinctive repulsion. He was wrong. This ignoble face was the chaplain's; truly an actor of the highest order, since for his emoluments he thus simulated great suffering!

"At his side was a young man, who, despite the shackles on his hands and feet, walked determinedly, with a courageous, almost smiling expression on his face. He inclined his head over the edge of the

lever, and said: 'What is that?' At the same time he motioned with
his head towards a box in front of him, next to the knife. 'That's the
basket for the head.' 'And that,' indicating a large box on the right.
'That's the box for your body.' 'Let's get on with it,' he cried. That
was all. With a sinister noise the collar fell into place; then the knife
dropped. The red gleams of dawn suffused the sky; the red blood
flowed over the paving-stones. Some gentlemen in dress-coats were
seen—the *police*. The chaplain also wore a black coat; the cassock
fraternizing with justice. There were, too, the troops, the sergeants;
the curious driven outside the enclosure. The outer barrier was en-
riched with a quite special crowd—prostitutes, pimps, and ex-gaol-
birds. And they were shouting: 'Long live the assassin; down with
justice!' . . . All this helps to provide a good time for the spectators,
who laugh at the sufferer's grimaces and *pretend, all of them, to be
virtuous*; for do they not go to church, or even say mass? After numerous thefts with the help of *the law, the prime school for felony*, they
arrive at their retirement believing in the Church's gospel, the gospel
which conveniently makes reason and every effort to think unnecessary. *Far from righteousness, a long way from fraternity, far from
charity!*

"Such are the reasons which have made the present writer so often
insist on the texts of the gospels, incessantly repeat them, forcing
himself to make them understandable in the hope of bettering the
world, with no idea of recompense other than the satisfaction of a
duty done. On the one hand, love of beauty and reason; on the other,
hatred of this despotic and pernicious Church; hatred of superstition,
which is so opposed to progress and the happiness of man."

Clearly actuated again by painful personal experience, Gauguin
with equal fervour condemned another gross social injustice, in these
terms: "If, then, this institution of marriage, which is *no more than
a sale*, is *declared to be the only recognized moral means of sexual
union*, it follows that morality is excluded in the case of those who
have no wish to, or who cannot, marry. For *love*, for wholesome
emotion, there is no longer any room. . . . Treated thus, the woman
descends into servility, condemned to marry, *fortune permitting*, or
else to remain a virgin, that unwholesome and unnatural monstrosity
so contrary to nature and so repugnant to true sentiment, which is
love. . . . If ever a society was cruel and barbarous, surely it is modern society; this hypocritical society which in the name of *Christian
morality* thus orders the fate of women and causes so much suffering.

"Console yourselves, poor young women; the priest is there waiting to lead you to Paradise; from St Lazare, from prison, from the guillotine, it is a short way to Heaven, and the priest will accompany you there.

"But we cry out: The woman who is after all our mother, our daughter, our sister, *is entitled to earn her daily bread*; is entitled to love the man who pleases her; is entitled to dispose of her body and of her beauty; is entitled to procreate with the *possibility* of raising her child, without passing through the hands of the priest and the lawyer; is entitled to as much esteem as the woman who *only sells herself in marriage*. . . . Moreover, marriage is responsible for creating, from the cradle up, two quite distinct classes, the legitimate and the natural child, the latter condemned to everlasting censure, victim of the fault, a pretended *fault invented* by the Church, in accordance with the Church's commandment: 'Thy body shall only be sold in matrimony.' "

This, however, was nothing in comparison with another crime which Gauguin believed the Catholic Church to be guilty of: "All these disorders in the colonies leading to war have been *recognized* for several years as without question religious in origin, showing the danger of sending out missions—an ever-growing danger which the states are powerless to avoid. China is beginning to close her borders to missionaries; is in fact murdering them. And Europe is angered to the point of proceeding to shed blood to no avail in support of these missions. Is no-one aware of the immoral injustice in this state of affairs? That this constitutes an attack on the freedom of the conscience? Let us suppress these missions to China, and peace will follow at once."

Echoing even more strongly the anarchist opinions of many of the artists and writers with whom he had consorted in Paris at that remote time during the winter of 1890–91 when he was still young and hopeful, Gauguin next devoted a page to a wholesale condemnation of the State. He admitted that the army might still be able to preserve the existing order for some time to come. But in the end the whole bureaucratic machinery and power monopoly would be swept away irresistibly when the down-trodden people rose up in anger. As the true foundations for the new "good and rational" society to be constructed on the ruins of the old, Gauguin, with a simplicity not wholly admirable, proposed "reason, humanity, fraternity and charity," and assured his readers that "outside this gospel there is no salvation."

Realizing, apparently, even while rewriting and expanding this long and obscure essay that no publisher would ever print it, Gauguin decided to make other use of it; he persuaded the trader Émile Frébault, the only one of his intimate friends who was on good terms with the Catholic mission, to pass it on, casually and to all appearance innocently, to the bishop himself. The latter, preserving an equally straight face, graciously returned the compliment by lending Frébault a handsome, gilt-edged volume describing the triumphant progress of the Catholic missions. The book quickly found its way to Gauguin as intended. This strange epistolary duel reached its conclusion when Gauguin returned it through the same channel together with his critical commentaries.[246]

The other essay was much shorter, and more readable and interesting. Although Gauguin could not altogether resist the temptation to include miscellaneous recollections, it consisted mainly of a witty and well-documented attack on the French art critics, full of concrete examples of their incredible blindness to the great revolution which was taking place in French painting. The title of this critique of the critics caught perfectly the book's highly personal style; it was *Racontars de Rapin*—Gossipings of a Dauber. In great hope he sent the manuscript off to the *Mercure de France*. It took fifty years for it to get published.

Gauguin next dashed off three long angry letters. The first, and most vigorously worded, was an open letter to Governor Petit, which he forwarded to Cardella and Coulon for inclusion in an issue of a new paper, the *Indépendant*, which they planned to publish.[247] To the intense disappointment of the Catholic Party, Governor Petit had pursued the same independent and largely pro-native policy as his predecessor Gallet, and the party was preparing, therefore, to launch an all-out attack on him. Gauguin's biting letter opened with the following sarcastic account of Petit's inspection of the Marquesas Islands six months previously: "There was every reason to hope and believe that you came here to obtain information about local conditions, and that, guided by this information, you would then govern the colony judiciously and to the extent possible bring about much-desired reforms. . . . The hopes and expectations vanished with the smoke from the warship's funnels. You called upon the bishop of the mission and were called upon in turn at Government House by the gendarme. Clearly exhausted by this extremely hard work, you rested by taking photographs; for example, of beautiful girls with firm breasts and sleek stomachs, splashing in a stream. . . . Whereas it would have been so interesting and useful if instead you had endeavoured to cast aside the lofty airs which you have paraded since your arrival in Tahiti (in order, it seems, to avoid any real encounter with the settlers) and had been willing to consult the only persons able to give you any information, namely those who live in the Marquesas and who try with their intelligence, labour, and investment to colonize them. If you had done this, you would have found that we are not a sort of menial like your stablemen (as, to judge from your behaviour to us, you would seem to think), as also many other things of which you are, or appear to be, ignorant."

The letter's character of indignant protest on behalf of the neglected settlers was somewhat dimmed towards the end of it where it became only too apparent that what most irritated Gauguin was the lack of mail and food supplies during the three months which had followed the loss of the *Croix du Sud:* "We are often short of supplies, without bread, rice, biscuits, salt, and potatoes, the only civilized riches we receive being idiotic decrees. It is no exaggeration to say that we should never be left without food in this way if the islands were a penal settlement. Our families at home in France are very worried at the absence of any news from us. Our correspondents think that we must have met with accidents, and will neither risk completing business deals they have initiated nor remit any money to us without confirmation that we are still alive. In the absence of ships for exporting their goods or replenishing their stocks, the traders have nothing to do but sit idle in their empty stores on the verge of ruin. . . . 'But,' you may argue in your own excuse, 'the loss of the *Croix du Sud* is a rare and isolated occurrence.' No, *Monsieur le Gouverneur*, it is such an easily predictable accident that the insurance companies refuse to insure vessels which sail through the Tuamotus except at exorbitant premiums. In any case, the objection does not make the neglect any better. For, supposing that you did not happen to have a warship available, what has prevented you from sending us a schooner with a cargo of food, especially flour? As I have already said, you would not have treated convicts in a penal colony like this! I hear the objection 'But there is no money available;' and reply: 'How can you be short of money when we have paid huge taxes and got nothing back?' "

The second letter was to the colony's General Council, whose president now was his old foe, Auguste Goupil, and it consisted of "some observations on the decree relating to stray pigs."[248] Gauguin's main point here was that the existing legislation, based on conditions in France, was quite unsuitable for the Marquesas Islands, and only led to "daily killings just for the pleasure of killing, without any profit except that the administration receives a couple of francs each time." His very sensible conclusion was: "Why not put pigs, like horses, in the category of domestic animals, which may not be killed except for utilitarian reasons?" The General Council decided to pass the letter to the office of the local colonial administration, where it still lies.

Gauguin's third polemical letter differed from the other two in being a private letter. Written at the beginning of December 1902, it was addressed to the head of the *gendarmerie* in Papeete.[249] Although the motive, even more clearly in this letter than in the others, was the same—wounded vanity and animosity—the complaint was none the less justified. The chief point of criticism was Charpillet's practice of making the prisoners in the Government gaol do their penal servitude for his personal benefit by growing vegetables, chopping wood, and performing other domestic tasks. Even worse, when there were no prisoners available Charpillet had made the native gaoler do the same work. Gauguin had hardly posted this letter when Charpillet was recalled; not because of the criticism but simply because he was due for a routine transfer to another island. As Gauguin reluctantly admitted, Charpillet at least "had a modicum of education and treated us settlers courteously." His successor, Jean-Pierre Claverie, who arrived on December 4 and took over officially on December 16, was on the contrary coarse and oafish, seeming to take delight in behaving as aggressively as possible. Moreover, he was prejudiced against Gauguin from the start, having served, seven years earlier, in Mataiea, where the missionaries had pestered him with complaints until, after long and troublesome spying, he had managed to catch Gauguin bathing in a state of nature and had fined him for public indecency.[250]

Claverie showed his character in his very first act after arrival, which was to criticize angrily his predecessor's leniency. Next he gave an exhibition of the right way to deal with interfering cranks by demonstratively turning his back on Gauguin in front of the assembled citizens at their first meeting in Atuona. Unable to counterattack there and then, Gauguin bided his time and once more retired into his shell; that is to say, he shut himself up in his "House of Pleasure" and began frantically to fill page after page of a large and thick notebook. "It gives relief," was his own simple and candid explanation.

The notebook developed into a sort of diary, where, in chronological order, he recorded his actions and observations, interspersed, without order or system, with miscellaneous recollections. The excellent title which he gave to this well-known work, in English usually called *Paul Gauguin's Intimate Journals*, was *Avant et Après*—Before and After. The implied dividing line was his first voyage to Tahiti in 1891.

Gauguin's first opportunity to hit back at Claverie and arouse general resentment against him came in the middle of January 1903. It was triggered off by a natural disaster of rare occurrence in this part of the Pacific; on the evening of January 13 a cyclone swept through the islands from the north. Because Atuona happens to be situated on the south coast of Hivaoa behind lofty mountains, it was fairly well sheltered from the violent winds. But there was no escaping the accompanying deluge, and by midnight the two rivers in the valley were flooded in all directions. Soon after, the western river, which is named after the valley, became blocked by boulders and uprooted trees at its mouth and, diverted from its course, joined up with the other river, the Makemake, just below Gauguin's house (see dotted line on the map of Atuona, page 259). In doing so it swept away both Tioka's hut and the *gendarmerie*, where Madame Claverie was alone in the house, her husband being on a tour of inspection in another valley; she just managed to escape with her life and the cash-box. At the same time, Gauguin's private bridge across the Makemake river was destroyed, cutting him off from the rest of the village and forcing him to spend a very wet and unpleasant night in his draughty house without a light.

When day dawned at long last, the water was still so deep that he dared not try wading or swimming to safety. The only persons in sight were two native men on the verandah of Varney's store who pretended not to hear his cries for help. However, Gauguin knew by experience how to attract the attention of natives: he brought some bottles of rum and waved them vigorously. As he had expected, the men at once plunged into the water and carried him out on their backs. Thanks to its exceptional height, his "House of Pleasure" withstood the floods, and when they finally subsided the next day the damage proved to be very small. The only casualty in Atuona was one child drowned, and the damage wrought there was negligible compared to the devastation in some other valleys in the group, to say nothing of the disaster which the cyclone caused in the low-lying coral islands of the Tuamotu archipelago, where 517 people were drowned.[251]

Nevertheless, the cyclone had other and more lasting consequences for the natives of Atuona, as it completely destroyed the breadfruit, banana, yam, and sweet potato crops on which they depended. Gauguin requested Claverie to postpone the ten days of annual road work due from all inhabitants of the Marquesas (or the payment of twenty francs in lieu of it) until fresh supplies of food could be obtained; but, perhaps because the request had come from such a contemptible quarter, the gendarme sharply turned it down. Gauguin wisely limited his protest to ordering his cook, Kahui, to refuse either to do any road work or pay the fine.[252] That he was genuinely actuated by sympathy is clear from the fact that at the same time he made a generous gift by legal deed of a part of his property (the small square in the northwest corner marked by broken lines on the map on page 259) to his neighbour Tioka, who was reluctant to rebuild his devastated home on his own low-lying land.

Gauguin did not have to wait long for Claverie to expose himself; the gendarme's competence had already been put to its first serious test, and by the end of January it was apparent that he had miserably failed. The occasion was a *crime passionel*, which had led to a woman's death. The drama had taken place in Charpillet's time, and Gauguin, assisted by Tioka, Reiner, Varney, and Ky Dong, who all mixed freely with the natives and knew the language, had from the start patiently accumulated a mass of evidence and hearsay about it. The most important piece of evidence was provided by Ky Dong, who as the official nurse had treated the victim for several weeks before her death, and who swore that besides two obvious knife wounds the woman had suffered extensive injuries to the vagina. Following an extremely amateurish and superficial investigation, Charpillet had hastily arrested the victim's husband, a runaway Negro sailor, though all the evidence pointed to her native lover as the culprit; with the connivance of the other natives in the valley, he had frightened her into remaining silent.[253] Claverie made his predecessor's mistake worse by concentrating on collecting evidence to incriminate the prisoner and flatly refusing to listen to Gauguin.

The post of magistrate in the Marquesas, for which Gauguin had unsuccessfully applied during his first stay in Tahiti, was still vacant, the authorities having decided it was sufficient to send a magistrate from Papeete "as and when required." The need for a more qualified investigator of this lurid crime at length became apparent in Papeete, and on February 5, 1903, a young magistrate named Horville duly arrived by a splendid, newly chartered steamship, which was proudly and promisingly called *Excelsior*.[254] Gauguin had drawn up, well beforehand, a long report covering the known facts in the murder case, and denouncing Claverie, in no uncertain terms, for the disgracefully inefficient manner in which he had handled the case. This document he immediately passed to the magistrate. But to his understandable indignation, day followed day and Horville still made no move to interrogate him or any of the persons named who could give valuable information. It was plain to see that he was satisfied with the investigations made by Charpillet and Claverie and intended to refer the case to the court in Papeete, the only court which had the jurisdiction to try a murder case. Meanwhile, in quick succession, he tried a number of minor cases which were within his competence to deal with. One of the pending cases was, in Gauguin's view, based on a false charge. It concerned a group of twenty-nine natives in the Hanaiapa valley, on the island's north coast, whose alleged offence was drunkenness. The charge had been brought by a half-caste, one Maurice, who had frequently been fined not only for this very offence but for far graver ones, which included perjury and false witnessing. All twenty-nine natives, including men and women, swore they were innocent and accused Maurice of seeking revenge for personal injuries. Gauguin was just as well informed about this case as about the other, because several of the accused had, as Protestants, spoken to Pastor Vernier, and one knew enough French to confide in Gauguin direct.

Doubly eager to stroke a blow for justice because it seemed that at the same time he would be hitting Claverie, Gauguin resolved to act as counsel for the defence of the twenty-nine accused, which he was fully entitled to do. The proceedings opened badly for him when he appeared in court dressed in his ordinary everyday clothes, which consisted of a striped and rather soiled cotton vest and a flowered loincloth, and squatted native fashion on the floor, with his sored and swollen legs crossed in front of him. The magistrate refused to accept a counsel who exhibited such obvious contempt of court; and Gauguin, muttering to himself, limped off home and put on a pair of trousers while the magistrate waited. However, all his efforts were nullified by Claverie, who suddenly called a fresh witness in the case, namely Tumahuna, the native chief of the Hanaiapa valley. While admitting that he had not *seen* any of the drunks, Tumahuna declared that he had *heard* them, and that they had created such a disturbance all through the night that there could be no room for doubt that they were drunk. This sufficed to get each of the twenty-nine accused a sentence of five days' imprisonment and a fine of a hundred francs. Loudly and angrily, Gauguin objected that the legal paragraph the magistrate had cited was not applicable. The magistrate retorted that if he was not satisfied he could appeal to the court in Papeete, and, when Gauguin persisted in his protests, ordered the other gendarme, who functioned as usher, to expel him. Gauguin threatened to knock the man down if he dared to lay hands on him, but in the end withdrew of his own accord. But before doing so, he promised his twenty-nine clients that he would certainly lodge an appeal, and make himself responsible for the costs.

A few hours later, one of the oldest French settlers in the island, a Basque called Guilletoue, whose occupation was hunting and slaughtering wild cattle, and who knew both the natives of Hanaiapa and the language better than anyone else, reported to Gauguin that Chief Tumahuna at the time of the alleged carousal had been in another valley five miles away. Guilletoue promised to report this vital evidence of Tumahuna's perjury without delay to Claverie. But when Gauguin triumphantly presented himself in the gendarme's office soon after in order to satisfy himself that Claverie had taken down Guilletoue's statement, Claverie to his utter amazement said he knew nothing about it. At the last moment, Guilletoue had had second thoughts and, fearing the consequences of siding with Gauguin, had gone off into the mountains. At this point, Reiner and Varney volunteered the statement that they had heard Guilletoue's account of Tumahuna's part in the affair as Gauguin had described it. When several more days had elapsed and Claverie had still failed to summon either Guilletoue or Tumahuna, Gauguin limped, fuming with rage, to the *gendarmerie* and demanded an explanation. Claverie replied arrogantly that he did not take his orders from Gauguin. There ensued a "violent argument," which so upset Gauguin that after arriving home he suffered a haemorrhage of the lungs.[255]

To Gauguin's intense satisfaction, at any rate to begin with, the island received a visit a few weeks later, on March 10, 1903, to be exact, by two inspectors; these were officials who were sent out at intervals of a few years from Paris to inspect the administration of the colony. Gauguin quickly drew up another long complaint, not only reiterating his criticism of Claverie's manner of performing his duties, but attacking just as strongly the recipient of his earlier complaints, the magistrate Horville.[256] "For economical reasons," he began, "representatives of the law are sent here only about once every eighteen months. When, therefore, the magistrate arrives he gets very busy trying the many cases which have accumulated in the course of the year, knowing nothing either of the natives or of the cases other than is contained in the dossiers provided for him by the gendarme. Seeing a tattooed face, he says to himself: 'He must be a cannibal bandit.' Especially since the gendarme tells him he is. Or the gendarme will draw up a charge, based on a simple denunciation, accusing some thirty persons who have been playing and dancing, and also in some cases drinking orange wine. The thirty persons are each fined a hundred francs (a hundred francs here is equal to 500 francs anywhere else); that is to say, 3,000 francs in all, plus costs. . . . I think that I should also point out to you that this 3,000 francs plus costs exceeds the yield of the entire valley in a whole year, and that even so most of the valley does not belong to these natives. . . . The magistrate arrives, and he stays, not at a hotel but *of his own accord* with the gendarme, sharing his meals and meeting no other person but this man, who at the same time is the person furnishing him with all the dossiers in every case, along with appropriate comments. . . . 'That man, and that,' and in the end 'all of them,' according to the gendarme, 'are ruffians.' Whereupon he will add: 'You see, sir, unless we are severe, we shall all be murdered.' The magistrate is entirely convinced."

For the most, however, Gauguin correctly ascribed the abuses to the absurd procedure of trying to govern a population of primitive and ignorant natives in a remote South Sea island under French laws and ordinances: "At the inquiry the accused is interrogated through an interpreter who is unfamiliar with the nuances of the language, especially judicial language, which is very difficult to translate into the primitive native tongue, except perhaps by means of paraphrases. A native is asked, for example, if he has been drinking. The answer is No, and so the interpreter says, 'He says he has never drunk.' Which statement causes the magistrate to exclaim: 'But he has had a previous conviction for drunkenness!' The natives are very reserved in the presence of Europeans, who seem to them so much superior and better informed. They also remember the cannon of the past, and have been intimidated by the gendarme, other magistrates, etc., before ever they appear in court. They therefore prefer to confess even when innocent, knowing that to deny the offence is to incur a bigger penalty. In short, it is the terrorist method."

After enumerating the mistakes and injustices committed by Claverie and Horville, Gauguin concluded by setting out the following very reasonable and well-justified requirements:

(1) that magistrates in future should not lodge with the gendarme;

(2) that magistrates should seek to carry out independent inquiries and should check the gendarme's statements by interrogating other people;

(3) that fines should be reduced to a level more in line with native incomes.

Unfortunately, the inspectors were in as big a hurry as Governor Petit had been the year before. They talked to Claverie on the day of their arrival, attended a reception at the Catholic mission the next day as guests of honour of the bishop, and left again that same afternoon at five o'clock. They had no time, therefore, to receive either Gauguin or his letters of complaint.[257] On the other hand they could hardly avoid hearing plenty of complaints about him. To judge from the report which the senior inspector, André Salles, made to the Colonial Department, the complaints come mostly from Claverie and the bishop, for the report contained the following passage: "The Marquesan natives continually indulge in drunken orgies in remote parts of the valleys. On such occasions, groups of forty–fifty persons fill the largest containers in their village with orange wine, and sometimes even use a canoe for the purpose. The men and women, completely nude, will then drink and drink, fight and copulate. The gendarmes know that it is very dangerous to arrive in the middle of such a feast. The painter Gauguin, who lives in Atuona and defends all the native vices, sees in these savage scenes no more than a simple amusement necessary to the well-being of the natives; the settler Guilletoue of Hanaiapa, on the other hand, writes to me to say that he can no longer move about without a drawn revolver in his hand.

"Simply to try to repress these abuses does no good; what we must also do is influence the children, so as to make them detest the savage behaviour of their parents. Only schools, including boarding schools, can achieve this twofold purpose. The successive administrators and doctors and missionaries stationed in the Marquesas understood this very well at an early date. They therefore assembled all, or nearly all, the children of this group in the existing schools. The natives had become resigned to committing their girls and boys to the care of the nuns of St Joseph de Cluny and the friars of the *Instruction Chrétienne,* and undertook to furnish them, regularly once a week, with the required supplies of native food.

"All this has changed in the last two years. A sick painter of the Impressionist school, Monsieur Gauguin, has settled at Atuona, in what he calls his 'House of Pleasure.' From the start he made it his business to set the natives against the established authorities, inciting them to refuse payment of their taxes and stop sending their children to school. To the latter end, though an invalid who has difficulty in walking, he has even gone down to the shore in order to persuade people from Tahuata to return to their island with their children. This is corroborated by reports from the *gendarmerie.*

"The purpose has been achieved. Four or five years ago, the Catholic schools at Atuona and Puamau had over 300 pupils. Now there are only 70. At the convent school (in Atuona) in September of last year there were 60 girls. I have seen only 35 there."[258]

The inspector's report, of course, was a direct encouragement to the governor and the head of the colony's *gendarmerie* to suppress this dangerous anarchist, and they promptly gave Claverie to understand that he could rely on their sanction and support for whatever measures he might choose to take. By this time Claverie knew exactly how to deal with his troublesome adversary. At the beginning of February, Gauguin had requested an investigation into certain rumours current in Atuona to the effect that Claverie's subordinate on the neighbouring island of Tahuata, the gendarme Étienne Guichenay, had both accepted bribes and been guilty of smuggling during a recent visit by American whalers. To protect the interests of local French traders, the law prohibited foreign ships (and certain French vessels) from selling goods to natives or making payment in kind during their visits. On the occasion in question it appeared that the whalers had done exceptionally brisk business and that many natives had gone over from Atuona to Tahuata and returned unmolested with large quantities of goods. It seems highly likely that it was Gauguin's friends, Frébault and Varney, who had inspired him to write his accusatory letter, being reluctant to take action on insufficient evidence themselves. As the magistrate Horville had completely ignored his previous complaints, Gauguin wrote this time to the administrator, Picquenot, who was on the point of visiting Hivaoa, Tahuata, and Fatuiva. Picquenot bravely promised to look into the matter, but being unable to find Guichenay during his short call at Tahuata could only leave a letter for him, requesting an explanation. On returning to Tahuata a day or two later, Picquenot was handed a reply from Guichenay, who strangely enough had gone into the interior again on urgent business. In this reply, Guichenay indignantly denied Gauguin's accusations and stated categorically that no goods had been landed from the whaler except for a few small articles given to him by the captains. He was able to prove that he had paid duty on these gifts by enclosing a receipt duly signed by the local customs officer—who was none other than Guichenay himself. Picquenot, who had no legal powers, once more displayed his friendly feelings towards Gauguin by calling on him at Atuona and privately advising him to withdraw his accusations, adding that Claverie was so furious at what he considered to be an unwarranted interference in his duties that he would have recourse to any pretext, however flimsy, to do him serious harm. Gauguin wisely took Picquenot's advice and immediately retracted his accusations in writing.[259]

Meanwhile, however, Guichenay had forwarded Picquenot's letter, with Gauguin's original request for an investigation, to Claverie, who decided after consulting his superior in Papeete to sue Gauguin for libelling a gendarme in the course of his official duties. In a summons dated March 27, 1903, Gauguin was ordered to appear in court in Atuona on the thirty-first. There the magistrate, Horville, dismissed his request for a thorough and impartial inquiry into Guichenay's actions, as well as his plea for more time in which to prepare his de-

————————————————————————→

55. *Gauguin's daughter by Vaeoho, born on September 14, 1902, now lives the quiet life of a native in a secluded valley on Hivaoa island. The only artistic activity which has ever held any attraction for her is making patchwork quilts, neither better nor worse than those which other Marquesan women make.*

56. *Pau'ura's son, Émile, photographed when about fifty in his Tahitian home, with his wife and some of his large family. He is holding an album with a self-portrait of his father, painted when Paul Gauguin was fifty. There is undoubtedly some resemblance.*

57. *Émile has recently exploited the curiosity of tourists and makes childish drawings like this, which he sells for a dollar or two. The picture illustrated here represents Tahitian ghosts, and can therefore be said to be a counterpart to his father's* Manao Tupapau.

56

57

fence, and accepting the statement of the public prosecutor—Claverie —fined Gauguin 500 francs and sentenced him to three months' imprisonment.[260] The injustice of this hastily pronounced judgment is rendered even greater by the fact—which Gauguin found out afterwards—that the legal provision under which it was passed applied only to libellous statements in print.

Gauguin, with every reason to feel deeply indignant, from then on concentrated all his efforts on obtaining redress. His first action was to dispatch a formal request for a new trial to the court of appeal in Papeete by the next mail-boat, on April 2. At the same time he wrote to his former political enemy in Papeete, the newspaper editor and lawyer Léonce Brault, who happened to be one of the new appointed representatives of the Marquesas Islands, and asked him to plead his cause.[261] While he awaited news of the date on which the hearing would take place, he began another long letter to the chief of the colony's *gendarmerie*. As he had done on many an occasion before, he also wrote to Charles Morice and asked him to influence public opinion in France by means of some outspoken newspaper articles about the scandalous conditions prevailing in the Marquesas. But after writing half a page, he turned from old habit to artistic matters, and among other things passed the following accurate judgment on his own work: "You were wrong to say I was mistaken when I called myself a savage. And every civilized person knows that this is true; for what astonishes and baffles them in my art is this very fact—that I am a savage in spite of myself. Indeed, that is why it is inimitable. . . . Everything I have ever learnt from anybody else has always been an impediment to me. Hence I can say: Nobody ever taught me anything. It is true that I know little! But I prefer the little I have created

---

58. *The Tahitians and Marquesans, now as in the past, principally express their exuberant* joie de vivre *in dancing, singing, and music-making. The only difference since the days of Gauguin's gay parties in "The House of Pleasure" is that the guitar has taken the place of the accordion as the most popular instrument.*

59. *Such black Polynesian pigs have been made familiar by Gauguin's pictures. They run loose and make themselves a nuisance all over the islands, rooting up crops and always gathering round the natives as soon as they start breaking coconuts to make copra.*

which is truly mine. And who knows, that little, when it has been turned to good account by others, will one day perhaps grow into something big?"

With all these trials and tribulations, Gauguin unfortunately had had little time for painting, and had got so badly in arrears with his deliveries to Vollard that he was afraid the dealer would stop his monthly payments. Furthermore, his account with the German trading company now showed a debit of 1,400 francs, instead of a credit of about that amount which it would require to travel to Papeete and get justice. Rummaging in his chests and drawers, therefore, he managed to find nine old pictures, dating mostly from 1899 but including also a Breton landscape, which he had kept in some cases for sentimental reasons and in others simply because he thought the works inferior. These nine pictures he dispatched to Vollard together with one of the four which he had succeeded in painting that year.[262] The other three he sent to a rich collector whom Daniel de Monfreid had discovered, along with an urgent appeal for 1,500 francs in cash by return. Of the four pictures painted in 1903, one represented his horse under the mango-tree before his studio window, two were village scenes showing the cemetery in the background, and the fourth was a version, much smaller, of his spiritual testament, from 1897, *Where do we come from? What are we? Where are we going?*

At this time, when more than ever he needed to be fit, Gauguin's health began to deteriorate again. As before, he sent for Vernier, but the pastor could do little more than change his bandages and advise caution in the use of laudanum. This was good advice, but as the pains in his leg got rapidly worse he was unable to follow it. When the laudanum no longer seemed to afford relief, Gauguin even begged Varney to give him back the morphine and syringe he had committed to his care with instructions never to return them. Varney at first loyally refused, but growing tired of Gauguin's persistent pleas in the end gave way.[263] Thanks to the relief provided by the morphine, Gauguin managed to finish his letter to the chief of the *gendarmerie* in Papeete in time to catch the next mail-steamer on April 28. The closely written letter of thirteen foolscap pages was both an eloquent defence and an angry attack.

The turning-point, according to this important unpublished document, had been the arrival of Claverie. Before then Gauguin said: "Infirm, working at my art, and not knowing a word of the Marquesan language, I had lived a solitary life here in the islands, well away from the road, rarely seeing more than a couple of people." But then: "From the very start (of Claverie's regime) I have been exposed to continual victimization, and whenever I have raised objections have been violently abused, and that in public places before both Europeans and natives. My life is becoming intolerable, a struggle like that described by Balzac in *Nos Paysans*."

After recounting the violent quarrel with Claverie following the sentencing of the twenty-nine natives of Hanaiapa, Gauguin went on: "That is why it becomes necessary to inform you, sir, that although they carry out many administrative duties your gendarmes are here to deal with crime and offences against the law and that settlers should never be treated as though they were at their beck and call like soldiers. I think that in this respect you have enough sense of justice not to side with your gendarmes. If I am treated in the same way again, I shall ask you *to make* the insolent scoundrel fight a duel with me.

"The natives are lucky to have me as their protector, for so far the settlers, who are all poor, earning their living as traders, have always been afraid to antagonize the gendarmes and so have kept silent. Therefore, the gendarmes, being free from control (you are so far away and unlikely to be correctly informed), are absolute masters. . . . I am being condemned merely for defending these poor defenceless people. Animals at least have a society to protect them."

This was followed by a long and excellent summary of all the abuses he had had to contend with, concluding with these words: "However, I would like to inform you that I shall go to Tahiti to defend myself, and that my lawyer will have much to tell. . . . Even should I be sent to prison, which I would regard as shameful (it is a thing unknown in my family), I shall always hold my head high, proud of my well-earned reputation. Nor shall I permit anyone to say anything derogatory to my honour outside the court-room, however exalted his rank."[264]

The defiant tone and lucid style convey a false impression of the state of Gauguin's mind and health, for in fact the letter was a product of great effort and much rewriting, as is shown by the many drafts and notes which have survived. In reality, he was quite exhausted, and in order to get a complete rest he shut himself up again in his house as soon as the steamer had left and did not invite anyone to visit him for a whole week. Then, early in the morning of May 8, he sent for Pastor Vernier. Climbing the steep steps of the silent "House of Pleasure," Vernier found its owner lying on the bed. Gauguin asked weakly whether it was day or night, and complained of pains "all over." He added that he had had two fainting fits. But soon he turned abruptly to the discussion of art and literature, especially Flaubert's novel *Salammbô*. As on previous occasions, it seemed to do him good just to have someone to talk to, for the aching soon stopped. Gauguin had, as usual, no idea where his two servants were. But this did not seem to worry him very much, and after a while Vernier left him to return to his interrupted schoolteaching.[265]

At eleven o'clock Gauguin's grateful friend Tioka, who had proved himself to be much more useful and dependable than his paid servants, called to see him again, announcing his arrival, in accordance with native etiquette, by shouting "Koke, Koke" from a distance. After waiting in vain for permission to enter, he hesitatingly climbed the stairs, to find Gauguin lying on the edge of the bed with one leg hanging over the side. When he took hold of him and rebuked him for foolishly trying to get up, there was no response. Suddenly it flashed across Tioka's mind that his friend might be dead. To make sure, he resorted to a traditional Marquesan method and bit his head. Gauguin remained silent and motionless. Tioka in a shrill voice intoned a death lament. Standing on a small table was an empty bottle that had contained laudanum or morphine. Perhaps Gauguin had taken an overdose. Deliberately, some villagers said; by mistake, others thought. Perhaps the bottle had been empty for a long time. We can only guess.[266]

Gauguin's two lazy and shiftless servants eventually appeared, and hastened to spread the news in the village. A quarter of an hour later the musty little bedroom was full of inquisitive villagers. The crowd of more or less sincere mourners was soon joined not only by Pastor Vernier—who attempted artificial respiration—but surprisingly by the bishop, who was accompanied by two friars from the nearby school for boys. However, the bishop had an excellent reason for paying this final visit to a fallen foe: as Gauguin had been baptized into the Catholic Church, he was entitled to burial in consecrated ground. Claverie, too, was present in an official capacity: to see that Gauguin, in death as in life, duly conformed to the regulations. Without delay he ascertained that the first two persons to arrive on the scene were Tioka and Frébault, filled in a death certificate and asked them to sign it. Punctilious as ever he even added the following words, which have definitely a reproachful ring: "He was married and a father, but the name of his wife is unknown."

As in most tropical countries, the existing regulations prescribed burial within twenty-four hours. To Claverie's intense annoyance, however, the last round was Gauguin's: it was about two o'clock on the following day—three hours late—when the rough and hastily carpentered coffin was lowered into the red volcanic earth of the Catholic cemetery on the hill of Hueakihi a quarter of a mile to the north of Atuona. Apart from the four paid native pall-bearers, the only villager who had taken the trouble to climb the steep hill in the heat of the day was Émile Frébault.[267] There was no funeral oration. The only epitaph the Catholic Mission cared to compose was the following bitter note in a letter written by Bishop Martin to his superiors in France three weeks later: "The only noteworthy event here has been the sudden death of a contemptible individual named Gauguin, a reputed artist but an enemy of God and everything that is decent."[268]

At the same time another official personage in the Marquesas, Picquenot the administrator, in a report to his superiors concluded, a little more sadly: "I have requested all creditors of the deceased to submit duplicate statements of their accounts, but am already convinced that the liabilities will considerably exceed the assets, as the few pictures left by the late painter, who belonged to the decadent school, have little prospect of finding purchasers."

LIST OF NOTES

To avoid needless burdening of the text no numerical references are given to quotations from Gauguin's own well-known writings and letters, *except* when I have felt obliged to correct the hitherto generally accepted date.

The following abbreviations have been used:

Annales	Annales des Sacrés Coeurs
Annuaire	Annuaire de Tahiti et dépendances
BO	Bulletin Officiel des Établissements Français de l'Océanie
BSEO	Bulletin de la Société des Etudes Océaniennes
JO	Journal Officiel des Établissements Français de l'Océanie
JME	Journal des Missions Évangéliques
MF	Mercure de France
MT	Le Messager de Tahiti
Répertoire	O'Reilly, Patrick–Teissier, Raoul: Tahitiens, Répertoire bio-bibliographique de la Polynésie Française.

1. A reference to Vincent van Gogh shows clearly that this letter (No 68) was written in Arles and not, as stated by Malingue, in Pont-Aven.

2. *Exposition Universelle,* the official weekly, especially Nos 24 and 25, 3/8 and 10/8 1889, contain good descriptions and illustrations of the French colonial pavilions and the Javanese village. The Tahitian section is described in great detail in the Tahitian JO 6/2 1890.

3. MT 16/11 1889.

4. This letter (No 106) was certainly not written in June 1890, as suggested by Malingue, but in autumn 1889, as shown both by its contents and by Gauguin's

references to his articles for *Le Moderniste* in the latter year.

5. Merete Bodelsen has convincingly shown (1957: 202) that this letter (No 82) must have been written in November and not in June 1889, which is the date given by Malingue.

6. Loti, Part I, Chapter XXIII, and Part II, Chapter X.

7. That this hitherto unidentified handbook is Henrique, L. et al.: *Les colonies françaises*, Paris, 1889, is conclusively proved by the fact that three letters by Gauguin contain literal quotations from it. (See notes 10, 11 and 12 for references to these letters.) The quotations on this and the following pages are taken from Henrique, L. et al.: 24–5, 48.

8. Veene: 305–23. The "lecture by van der Veene" referred to by Gauguin in his letter to F. J. Willumsen was thus known to him only through this brief quotation in the handbook.

9. Basing himself on several articles which appeared in French newspapers between 1891 and 1895, Perruchot (43–4) claims that Gauguin visited Tahiti already in 1867, when he was second mate on the ship *Chili*, and that his nostalgia for the island forcefully contributed to his decision in 1890. Although this seems extremely unlikely even on purely logical grounds, considering the complete lack of any statement to this effect in Gauguin's own letters and books, I have, in order to ascertain the facts, gone through the Tahitian shipping register for 1867. No visit of a ship by that name is recorded.

10. Willumsen: 73–4; Lövgren, 1959: 163–5.

11. Redon: 193.

12. Dorra: 197–8.

13. Redon: 194–5.

14. Joyant: I, 118.

15. Morice, 1920: 25–6.

16. Rotonchamp: 84–5.

17. Marks-Vandenbroucke: 34.

18. Alexandre: 154.

19. Dolent: 43.

20. Maszkowski: 24.

21. Willumsen: 74; Rewald, 1961: 286–7.

22. Judith Gérard's unpublished memoirs and letter LIV to Daniel.

23. *Écho de Paris* 16/2 1891; *Le Figaro* 18/2 1891.

24. MF March 1891.

25. Huyghe: 1949: 95–6.
26. Rostrup: 78; Pola Gauguin: 142.
27. This equally revealing letter, No 99, also was evidently written *after* Gauguin's return from Copenhagen, and not in January as the editor indicates.
28. Rey: 49.
29. Morice, 1920: 29–30.
30. Rotonchamp: 89–90.
31. MF May 1891: 318–20.
32. Annuaire 1891: 181–3.
33. The information about the *Océanien* is from the archives of the French shipping company, Messageries Maritimes, in Paris. A good description of such a voyage and the conditions on board such a vessel at this time is given in the article by Charles Degras, listed among the sources.
34. JO 28/5 1885; Cotteau: 279.
35. JO 11/6 1891.
36. Cotteau: 279–80.
37. The exact date and time of arrival is found in JO 11/6 1891. The voyage out from France had thus taken 70 days and not 63 as stated by Gauguin in the famous opening lines of his own travel account, *Noa Noa.*
38. Jénot: 11–8; and oral information by Alexandre Drollet.
39. Adams: 478. An account of the Tahitian portion of the voyage round the world of Henry Adams and John La Farge will be found in the introduction by Marie-Thérèse and Bengt Danielsson to *Mémoires d'Arii Taimai.*
40. Répertoire: 247–8.
41. JO 11/6 1891.
42. The exact date of this letter (No 125, dated June 4 by Malingue) is easily determined since it was written "the third day after our arrival."
43. JO 16/6 and 18/6 1891; JME 1891: 387–9.
44. Répertoire: 186; Salles's report of May 15, 1903.
45. Pallander: 299.
46. Claverie: 130–3. Another, excellent account of these dance evenings is given in Mativet: 44–6, 92–3.
47. Desfontaines: 118.
48. Claverie: 133–5.
49. Agostini, 1905: 31–2.
50. Letter No 126, wrongly dated by Malingue. That it must have been written on June 29 is shown both by the words "twenty days have now passed since I arrived" and the fact that the mail ship referred to

reached Tahiti on this date.

51. The subsequent account is based on the programme in JO 11/6 1891, notices in MT 11/7 and 18/7 1891, Jénot: 124, and oral information by Alexandre Drollet.

52. Pallander: 288–9.

53. Pallander: 295–7.

54. Oral information from Susannah's cousin, M. Tony Bambridge, and from M. Henri Bodin.

55. Loti, Part II, Chapter XX.

56. Courtet: 215–6.

57. Hall-Osborne: 53–4.

58. Garnier: 353.

59. Courtet: 208.

60. This accident has been thought by all previous biographers to have occurred in March 1892, because Gauguin does not mention it in his correspondence until that month. His statement that up to this time he had had *no relapse* and the fact that he had been taking digitalis "from time to time," however, reveal clearly that it was not a recent event. Definite proof that the haemorrhage actually occurred in August 1891 is furnished by Jénot: 125, and by oral information from Alexandre Drollet.

61. Pola Gauguin: 158.

62. Annuaire 1891: 147; and oral information from Alexandre Drollet.

63. No 430 in Wildenstein's catalogue, listed by Gauguin in his *Carnet de Tahiti* (2V) as *Le Bûcheron de Pia*. Since the name of the district, Paea, is commonly pronounced Paia, the picture called *Paysage de Paia soir*, in the same list, must also have been painted there. Further evidence of his stay in Paea is his account in *Noa Noa* of a sunset behind Moorea, which he must have written while he was Gaston Pia's guest, as this island is not visible from Mataiea on the south coast where he moved shortly afterwards.

64. Répertoire: 453; Agostini 1905: 83.

65. Oral information from Anani's son and from M. Puto'ura a Ta'iterefa'ato'a, churchwarden in Mataiea. The bamboo hut disappeared some years later, and when I first visited the site in 1953 it was completely covered with thick bushes. Surprisingly enough, however, Anani's house was still standing and was not pulled down until 1957.

66. Dorival, 1951: 118 and ill. Nos 15–6.
67. No 491 in Wildenstein's catalogue.
68. Various advertisements in *Le Messager de Tahiti* for 1891–3.
69. Information given by Gauguin himself in a long autobiographical letter to Bonnemaison, lieutenant of the gendarmes, in 1903.
70. Intentionally or unintentionally, Gauguin's chronology in *Noa Noa* (appendix of the first draft, not published until 1954) is very confused in this case. There can be no doubt, however, that this incident occurred at the beginning of 1892, for a notice in BO No 1, 1892, shows that it was precisely at this time that the post of magistrate (and administrator) of the Marquesas became vacant. From BO No 3, we also learn that the post was eventually filled on March 1, 1892. Consequently, the disappointed Gauguin wrote (letter No 130) shortly afterwards (at the beginning of May, and not in July, as Malingue mistakenly indicates) to Mette: "The two administrators of the Marquesas and Raiatea have just de-parted on leave and their substitutes have arrived."
71. MT 5/3 1892.
72. It should be added that the mail box mentioned in this quotation was not installed on the coach until October 4, 1892. (Annuaire 1897: 168.) Up to that time all residents in the districts were thus obliged to go to Papeete and collect their mail at the post office there.
73. Courtet: 193–6.
74. Répertoire: 439, Ginies; and oral information by Alexandre Drollet, who was present when Gauguin painted this picture. Aristide Suhas is buried at Tipaerui just outside Papeete, and the inscription on his grave is still fully legible.
75. Répertoire: 16; obituary in *Les Guêpes* 18/7 1901; and oral information from Mme May Wilmot, Captain Arnaud's adopted daughter. Information about Captain Arnaud's voyages during this period is found in JO 24/3 and 7/4 1892.
76. Gray, in his recent catalogue of *Sculpture and Ceramics of Paul Gauguin*, relies to a very large extent for his interpretations on

the well-known anthropological work *Ancient Tahiti* by Teuira Henry, which is an unsound method. Most of the customs and beliefs described in this work, based on notes from the 1820s and 1830s, had disappeared several generations before Gauguin's arrival and the book was not published until 1928. Gauguin could not have consulted Teuira Henry either, as she lived in Honolulu from 1890 to 1905.

77. The introduction to *Mémoires d'Arii Taimai* by Marie-Thérèse and Bengt Danielsson contains a full account of her literary collaboration with R. L. Stevenson and Henry Adams.

78. The Arioi society is described in Danielsson: *Love in the South Seas*, ch. 8.

79. JO 12/5 1892; and Gauguin's original receipt in the possession of Dr Pierre Cassiau. In all probability it was at this time that Gauguin made the excursion into the nearby Punaruu valley described in *Noa Noa* in the middle of his long account of his life in Mataiea.

80. Maugham, 1949: 130–1.

Although Wildenstein (or rather Raymond Cogniat) quotes Maugham's account in his *Catalogue*: 227–8, which clearly indicates that this undated glass painting was found in Anani's house, 25 miles from Papeete, and therefore must have been executed during the period to which I ascribe it, he places it without any explanation among the works painted by Gauguin in 1896, when he lived on the west coast of Tahiti only eight miles from Papeete.

81. A notice in JO 2/6 1892 shows that Captain Arnaud returned from Mangareva on May 29 and that the mail schooner arrived on June 1.

82. Oral information from Mme May Wilmot. According to the same informant, Gauguin also, at an unspecified date, painted a portrait of Captain Arnaud which has now disappeared.

83. Rey: 55.

84. Death certificate in the registry at Papeete and oral information by Teha'amana's subsequent husband Ma'ari a Teheiura and son Teheura a Ro'o.

85. That this letter (No 129) was written considerably later than June, the date attributed to it by Malingue, is clearly shown by Gauguin's words that his dispatch on May 14 of "a sample picture" was made "three months ago."

86. Second draft of *Noa Noa*, 1893–95, in collaboration with Charles Morice, facsimile edition, 1947: 48–50. The English translation here has been made direct from the Tahitian original: the French translation by Gauguin and Morice is very inaccurate. It is also rather revealing that Gauguin reprinted this song, and none other, from *Noa Noa* when he became editor of *Les Guêpes* (see No 15, 1900).

87. Rostrup: 79–82.

88. This letter (No 128), dated May 1892 by Malingue, must instead have been written in September 1892, for the simple reason that Gauguin says he has "eleven months of effective work" behind him, a period which evidently began when he settled in Mataiea in October 1891. Another certain indication is the number of pictures painted at the time he wrote this

letter—44. In May 1892 he had painted only 32.

89. That this letter (No XII), too, was written in September 1892 (and not on March 31) is evident both from the number of pictures painted at this time and the reference to the dispatch of a picture on May 14, the reception of which Gauguin had now had time to learn of.

90. Gray No 98.

91. Gauguin's account of such a fishing expedition tallies with Courtet: 211–5 and Desfontaines: 157–63. The best and fullest account of Tahitian tunny fishing is by Charles Nordhoff. The fishing always takes place in October, which thus makes it possible to date this episode, as given here in Gauguin's original version from the facsimile edition of the first draft of *Noa Noa*.

92. Oral information from Mme Teraiehoa Lequerré, born 1875, and M. Puto'-ura a Ta'iterofa'ato'a, born 1877. Both lived in Mataiea in Gauguin's time and belonged to the same group of young people as Teha'amana.

93. For the date of this letter see note 89.

94. Rey: 53–5.
95. MT 15/10 1892.
96. JO 15/12 1892.
97. Moerenhout: 1, 428.
98. Répertoire: 432. Spitz later included the picture in a portfolio published in Paris. The American scholar Richard Field has recently analysed Gauguin's sources of inspiration and methods of work in this and similar cases.
99. Written not, as Malingue suggests, at the beginning of April but at the beginning of February 1893, as is shown by a comparison with the easily datable letter X to Daniel de Monfreid.
100. Mette's letter did not reach Tahiti some time in April or May, as Malingue suggests (No 136), but more than a month earlier, since these 700 francs were dispatched on February 10 (Loize, 1951: 94) and the mail schooner arrived on March 21.
101. MT 22/4 1893.
102. The biographical data about Madame Charbonnier have been supplied by Mlle France Brault and M. Pierre Levergos. Information about the genesis of the glass-painting has been given both by the British painter Stephen Haweis, who bought it in 1913 from Madame Charbonnier (Haweis: 124), and by Frederick O'Brien, 1920: 226–7 and 1922: 446–7. Usually, on the few occasions when it has been reproduced, only the upper portions have been shown, often with the two halves reversed. There is a complete reproduction in Wildenstein's catalogue (No 509) under the heading *Paris* (!), together with the strange, erroneous statement that it was "painted by Gauguin for his Tahitian hut." It is very clearly dated 1893, and the title Gauguin gave to it is *Rupe Tahiti*, the first words of a very popular song at that time, meaning "Beautiful Tahiti."
103. Rey: 51–3.
104. Letter, dated July 2, 1893, from Tati Salmon to Henry Adams.
105. That Gauguin did indeed leave Tahiti in the *Duchaffault* at this late date, and not in the *Durance* on May 1, as hitherto believed, is proved by his account in the supplement to the first draft of *Noa Noa* and by a notice in JO 22/6 1893.

106. The information about Gauguin's return voyage is taken from the report of the ship's commander, Poydenot.

107. Newspaper notice pasted in *Cahier pour Aline*: 42 and letter dated October 3, 1893, by Camille Pissarro to his son Lucien.

108. Personal communication by Mr Jïrí Mucha who is now preparing a life of his father. Modigliani later had a studio in the same house.

109. All Gauguin's letters from this period must have been written at least a week later than the dates indicated by Malingue, since the *Armand Béhic* did not reach Marseilles until August 30. (See note 106.)

110. Rostrup: 79–82; Pola Gauguin: 183–6; Sutton, 1956: 91–2; and Strömbom: 48.

111. The only extant invitation card, No 112 in Alfred Dupont's autograph collection, sold in 1958, shows that the generally accepted chronology needs revision as indicated.

112. The two wooden sculptures were in all probability Nos 94 and 97 in Gray's catalogue, considering that photographs of these were reproduced in an article by Roger Marx about the exhibition in *La Revue Encyclopédique* for February 1, 1894. A complete list of the paintings exhibited is found, for instance, in Rotonchamps: 136–8.

113. Morice, 1920: 31–2.

114. Letter, dated November 23, 1893, from Camille to Lucien Pissarro.

115. Gauguin himself collected the newspaper reviews quoted. They are pasted in at the end of *Cahier pour Aline*. Other reviews that I have been able to discover appeared in Clemenceau's paper *La Justice* on November 12 (by Gustave Geffroy) and in the January issue of *Le Figaro Illustré*.

116. Rotonchamps: 141–2; and oral information from Dr Gerda Kjellberg, Stockholm. In addition, an article by Arthur Möller in the Swedish weekly *Vecko-Journalen* is illustrated with an excellent photograph of the singular building.

117. Leclercq, 1895: 121; and Judith Gérard's memoirs. A little-known photograph of William Molard at the bark-cloth-covered packing-case desk in Gauguin's studio is reproduced by Kjell-

berg between pages 56 and 57.

118. Kjellberg: 40–2. Ida Ericson was born in 1853 and William Molard in 1862.

119. Judith Gérard's memoirs.

120. Judith Gérard: Julien Leclercq.

121. Without adducing any evidence, Malingue dates this letter February 5, 1894, but it was certainly written at the beginning of January, when, as we know thanks to Daniel de Monfreid's carefully kept diary (Loize, 1951: 19), Gauguin was seriously ill.

122. Once more Loize's patient researches (1951: 19, 58) permit us to correct a wrongly dated letter, in this case No XVII to de Monfreid, which undoubtedly was written on February 22 instead of in Septemper 1893.

123. Vollard: 199–202. That this event did not take place until late in February is shown by Daniel de Monfreid's diary.

124. Wildenstein No 506–7; Gray No 109; and Judith Gérard's manuscript: Absence de Gauguin.

125. Wildenstein No 508. The correct title is clearly visible on a photograph supplied by the French firm

Giraudon. Gauguin's splitting up of the words in two groups shows also that the order among them is the one I have chosen, which moreover is in accordance with Tahitian sentence structure.

126. Personal communication by Judith's son, M. Gilles Gérard-Arlberg.

127. Edwards: 4–5.

128. Gauguin's first independent draft was discovered in the early 1950s by the French historian and author Jean Loize, and has been published only in a small facsimile edition in 1954 and an English translation in 1962. In the latter edition Teha'amana's name is unfortunately throughout misprinted Tehaurana.

129. Huyghe, 1951.

130. Loti, Part I, Chapter XLIII.

131. Moerenhout: I, 434.

132. He was right, for several of the sculptures were recently sold for close on 300,000 francs.

133. Mortimer Menpes: 931; and Redon: 196.

134. Dorothy Menpes: 139, 141.

135. O'Conor catalogue: 1–2; Sutton, 1960 and Bell: 163–7.

136. Shortly before his death Séguin published in the magazine *Occident* an account of his association with Gauguin in the summer of 1894. Sutton, 1964, supplements it with several letters by Séguin which throw an interesting light on his character.

137. Most accounts of the affray at Concarneau and the proceedings at Quimper are highly imaginative and embellished. My version is based on the only existing primary material: Gauguin's own letters, Filiger's letter to Blois, written a few days after the brawl, and René Maurice's article reproducing the judgment and contemporary newspaper reports.

138. Gauguin's reference to the sentence as having been passed "last Thursday" shows clearly that this letter (No 152) was written during the last week of August and not in September.

139. Written on September 20, as shown by Loize, 1951: 98.

140. The evidence for Gauguin's intention to settle in Samoa though indirect is strong, for he not only asked Molard (letter No 152) to buy him a Samoan dictionary but also inscribed an engraving that he gave to O'Conor *in English:* "For my friend O'Conor, one man of Samoa." (O'Conor catalogue No 17.)

141. Perruchot: 287–8.

142. Ahlström, ch. 6. Although Strindberg was very proficient in French, he wrote this letter in Swedish and asked William Molard to translate it (Information supplied by Strindberg's publisher, Albert Bonnier, Stockholm).

143. In the letter about the sale (No 158) there is a copying error: "464 fr 80 *dans* ma poche" instead of "464 fr 80 *de* ma poche."

144. Loize, 1951: 25; and Perruchot: 293–4. The symptoms summarily described by his friends do not in any way conflict with my hypothesis in Chapter IV that Gauguin had contracted syphilis already before 1891. Furthermore—if true—his utterance when warned on this occasion, in January 1895, of the risk of being infected, "At my age, there is nothing more one can catch," only becomes intelligible if one supposes that Gauguin was previously syphilitic.

145. Gray No 113; Bodelsen, 1964: 146–52; and Morice, 1896: 4. Most art historians have overlooked the undated, very important article by Morice because of the erroneous assumption that it was published in 1891. Morice's assertion that Gauguin was 48 years old, however, proves that the article was written in 1896. The same *oviri* figure reappears in a painting (Wildenstein No 570) from 1898, *Rave te hiti ramu*.

146. This is one of the statements quoted by Perruchot: 43, which seemingly proves that Gauguin had been to Tahiti before 1891. The contrary evidence adduced in note 9, however, is in my opinion enough to indicate that the interviewer must have misunderstood Gauguin—if the latter did not deliberately mislead him.

147. This manuscript has been published in two facsimile editions, the later one in 1947 by the Jan Förlag, Stockholm. The illustrations are, however, later additions. The most important contribution towards the solution of the many intricate problems connected with the genesis of *Noa Noa* has been made by Loize, 1962.

148. Mager, 1902, gives an excellent account of such a voyage via Auckland. The information concerning the voyage of the *Australien* is taken from Captain Didier's report in the archives of the Compagnie des Messageries Maritimes, Paris. The date of the *Richmond's* arrival is to be found in JO 12/9 1895. Letter No 159 (dated "end of June" by Malingue) must accordingly be re-dated end of August.

149. MT 10–25/8, 1895; and Agostini, 1905: 111–2.

150. Pallander: 289–90.

151. Letter No 160, dated July by Malingue.

152. Répertoire: 86–7, 342. The lasting esteem Gauguin had for this friend and amateur poet is clearly shown by his praise for Olivaint's *Fleurs de corail* in *Les Guêpes*, No 15, 1900.

153. Lemasson, 1950; Agostini, 1905; and oral information from M. Alexandre Drollet.

154. JO 20/11 1895.

155. Séguin: 160.

156. Sutton, 1961: 173.

157. Oral information by M. Ma'ari a Teheiura.

158. Unpublished correspondence between Julien Leclercq and William Molard (appendix to Judith Gérard: Julien Leclercq, Un satellite de Gauguin), shows that Gauguin also left many paintings in the latter's care before his departure and that these were soon passed on to Vollard for sale on a commission basis.

159. Oral information by M. Henri Teissier and Mme A.-C. Brillant.

160. Unpublished letter in Alfred Dupont's autograph collection (item 115), sold at auction in Paris on December 3, 1958.

161. Répertoire: 186; and oral information by Auguste Goupil's daughter, Mme Madeleine Sigogne, born 1882. Jeanne, born in 1887, whose Tahitian name was Vaite, died in 1943. Renée Hamon reproduces a picture of Jeanne Goupil, taken in 1938.

162. Wragge: 262–3.

163. Répertoire: 31, Michel Béchu.

164. Ramsden in newspaper article; and oral information by Pau'ura's cousin, M. Poara'i a Tai.

165. Sold by auction at Hôtel Drouot, Paris, June 5, 1962.

166. Hall-Osborne: 54–5.

167. The campaign is fully described, *inter alia*, by Caillot, 1909, and Agostini, 1905. Morice complied with Gauguin's request and succeeded in getting a fictitious interview into the November 1897 issue of the radical cultural journal *La Revue Blanche* in connection with the publication of *Noa Noa* in serial form.

168. Deed of conveyance in the land registry, Papeete.

169. Lemasson, No 2 1950: 19.

170. The manuscript was bought after Gauguin's death by M. Alexandre Drollet. It is now in the City Art Museum of St Louis, USA.

171. Gauguin says expressly in a letter to Daniel (No XL), written in February 1898, that he made his attempt at suicide about one month earlier, "as soon as the mail-boat arrived." As the shipping list shows the arrival date as December 30, 1897, this important event, which most of Gauguin's biographers place at the end of January or beginning of February 1898, can be dated with far greater exactitude.

172. Lemasson No 2 1950: 19; BO No 12 1895: 260.
173. BO No 1 1898: 37.
174. The regulations referred to are paragraphs 17 and 19. (See BO No 12 1895: 266-7.) The deed of loan, now in the Papeete Museum, was published by Jacquier, 1957, but without the supplementary papers showing the dates of Gauguin's reimbursements.
175. Oral information by Mme Teraiehoa Lequerré.
176. Agostini, 1905: 28-31.
177. BO No 1, 4, 5 1898; Répertoire: 20; Dorsenne: 134-5; Lemasson No 3: 32; and oral information by Jules Auffray's daughter, Mlle Hélène Auffray. This rather unusual sort of work for a draughtsman is not the only reason why later generations of civil servants have failed, in spite of eager searching, to discover the slightest little sketch or marginal drawing by Gauguin in the office files. Another good reason for this meagre result is a cyclone, which in 1906 levelled the offices to the ground and swept the files out to sea.
178. Letter from Picquenot to Daniel de Monfreid. Oral information from M. Pierre Levergos and Mme Teraiehoa Lequerré.
179. Leblond, Revue Universelle: 536-7; Dorsenne: 139; Répertoire: 86; and oral information by Mme A.-C. Brillant.
180. Répertoire: 318-9; and oral information from Ambroise Millaud's daughter, Mme Marcelle Peltier.
181. Deed of loan in Papeete Museum; and Register of Papeete Hospital for 1898.
182. Birth certificate in Papeete registry office dated April 21, 1899, and signed by Paul Gauguin who, however, could not formally recognize the child since he was still married to Mette. While his first child with Mette was baptized Emil in Danish style, the identical name of the boy borne by Pau'ura, was spelt Émile in the French manner.
183. The above account of the events is based on the version given by Gauguin himself in this open letter, supplemented by information from Leblond, Revue Universelle: 537; Lemasson, No 2 1950: 19; and oral information by Mme A.-C. Brillant.

184. Original belonging to Mme Elizabeth Montrose, Papeete.

185. This copy is now in the Louvre, Paris, Cabinet des dessins, R.F. 28: 844.

186. Répertoire: 74–5, 102; and oral information from Mme Marcelle Peltier.

187. This was not Cardella's and Raoulx's first venture into journalism, for they had in 1884–9 jointly owned and published the *Messager de Tahiti* which, however, through mismanagement eventually passed into the hands of their adversary, Léonce Brault. See Répertoire: 56, 395.

188. Mativet: 108.

189. ˙La Croix 14/12 1899.

190. BO No 10 1899: 199–206.

191. BO No 12 1899: 327.

192. Cardella did not have the same faith in his new collaborator's artistic genius; the contemporary portrait of him which still hangs in Papeete's town hall is *not* painted by Gauguin.

193. This is the sum Gauguin mentions himself in letter LIX to Daniel, without specifying whether he meant French or Chilean francs, both of which were used in Tahiti at this time, with a rate of exchange of roughly two Chilean

francs to one French. As the advertisement reproduced as Fig. 39 shows, *Le Sourire* sold for 1.50 francs, Chilean money. If we are to believe Gauguin, he must thus have sold between 30 and 35 copies of each issue at least, and as much as double this if his "monthly income of 50 francs" was calculated in French currency.

194. Gauguin on these occasions often made menus and illustrated them with humorous drawings. Eleven of these have been preserved and were published in 1950 with an introduction by Robert Rey. Basing himself on stylistic comparisons with drawings in one of Gauguin's sketchbooks, René Huyghe, 1952: 115, concludes with remarkable exactness that these menus were executed "between December 1899 and June 1901."

195. Written report of a conversation, kindly lent by M. Yves Martin, Papeete.

196. Cogniat: *Gauguin:* 72; Lawrence and Elizabeth Hanson: *The Noble Savage:* 255. The editor of the facsimile edition of *Le Sourire,* L. J. Bouge, in his introduction makes the

same preposterous claim that Gauguin's main purpose when publishing this paper was to defend the Tahitians, although nothing in the issues reproduced supports this opinion.

197. *Les Guêpes* February 1901: 1.

198. *Les Guêpes* December 1900: 50.

199. *Les Guêpes* December 1900: 49.

200. Open letter from schoolmaster Georges Dormoy in *Les Guêpes* August 1901: 3. The only impartial contemporary visitor to the island who noticed the existence of the paper is Douglas Hall, and he dismisses it (Hall-Osborne: 75) with the scornful remark that it "chiefly confines itself to scurrilous abuse of the Governor and the Government generally."

201. The only year for which no paintings are listed in Wildenstein's *Catalogue* is 1900.

202. Written note by Pierre Levergos in M. Guillaume Le Bronnec's possession.

203. Keable: 771.

204. As Gauguin had foreseen, Pau'ura and her family took good care of the boy, who is still alive and doing very well indeed. After he had lived completely in the Tahitian manner in Punaauia until the age of about fifty, the unavoidable happened: he found it more profitable to move to Papeete and let tourists take photographs of him for a small fee. Soon he also began to make childish drawings of the kind reproduced as Fig. 57, which sold so well that unscrupulous "promoters" are now helping him both to manufacture and sell drawings and oil paintings on a large scale.

205. Loize 1951: 164.

206. Deed of loan in Papeete Museum.

207. Répertoire: 357–8; *Les Guêpes* February 1901: 1–2.

208. The history, culture, and geography of the Marquesas Islands are more fully described in my book *Forgotten Islands of the South Seas*.

209. Minutes of meeting held April 13, 1901.

210. Guillot: 63.

211. Hall-Osborne: 81.

212. JO 21/11 1901.

213. Hivaoa is generally called Dominique in the Gauguin literature. This name,

however, given to the island by its Spanish discoverer in 1595, is never used in French Polynesia and is quite unknown to the natives. Two other gross errors frequently made are the horrible misspellings Atuana and Hivahoa for Atuona and Hivaoa.

214. Répertoire: 470–1; BO No 5 1899, No 1 1900 and No 7 1900; and decree signed by the French Governor General in Hanoi on January 24, 1898. (In the possession of M. Raoul Teissier, Papeete.)

215. Manuscript belonging to Ky Dong's son, M. Pierre Van Cam; and oral information by him.

216. Jacquier, 1957: 13.

217. There is no existing photograph of this house and the drawing which accompanies Le Bronnec's article in the *Gazette des Beaux-Arts*: 196 is unfortunately quite wrong—for which, however, he cannot be held responsible, since he did not do it. Another good description of the house is found in O'Brien, 1919: 149, in the form of an interview with Gauguin's neighbour and friend, "the old settler Bau-

fré"—who of course was Frébault under an easily recognizable disguise. An excellent check on the exactness of the measurements given by M. Le Bronnec and M. Louis Grelet is made possible by the preservation in the Louvre of the panels which stretched along the entire width of one short end of the house. Their total length is exactly 18 feet!

218. Letter from M. Louis Grelet, dated March 1, 1960. The two inventories made after Gauguin's death and published by Jacquier, 1957: 25–43, constitute the most detailed and exact record of Gauguin's possessions at this time.

219. Numerous writers have stated that it was instead a bottle of absinth that Gauguin used to cool in the well; this seems highly doubtful on logical grounds, since it is precisely the addition of cool water that gives an absinth drink its freshness. Significantly, the two persons interrogated, who personally visited Gauguin's "House of Pleasure," Timo and M. Louis Grelet, both affirm that the absinth bottle al-

ways stood on the table in the dining room.

220. O'Brien, 1919: 109; Le Bronnec, 1956: 196–7; and letter from M. Louis Grelet, dated March 1, 1960.

221. Oral information from Timo, slightly different from the version in Le Bronnec, 1956: 199.

222. Jacquier, 1957: 17–23; and Varney's complete ledger.

223. That Petit visited the Marquesas in mid-March and not in October 1902, as believed by Chassé and Perruchot, is indicated by JO 6/3 1902 and Petit's report of May 11, 1903, page 16.

224. The portions describing his experiences in the Marquesas are found in *Au loin*: 155–299.

225. Loize, 1951: 120.

226. Government archives in Papeete.

227. Gauguin's rifle, whose butt was beautifully carved (Gray No 141), remained longer in the islands than any other object of art from his hand. It was only in 1938 that it was discovered and acquired by the well-known Norwegian anthropologist, writer, and explorer, Thor Heyerdahl.

228. JO 6/3 1902.

229. *Les Guêpes* July 1900: 30; and JME June 1900: 509–14.

230. Répertoire: 479; and JME August 1903: 134–6, September 1903: 207–8.

231. Annales November 1902: 354–5.

232. Varney's complete ledger. The trap arrived and was debited on May 24, 1902.

233. Annales November 1903: 342–51.

234. Governor Petit's report of June 26, 1902.

235. Hall-Osborne: 139–46.

236. Chassé, 1955: 109.

237. Le Bronnec, 1956: 192; and birth certificate at the registry office, Papeete.

238. Chassé, 1955: 104–5, 109–10.

239. Répertoire: 416; and Annales March and November 1900. Father Orens' real name was Isidore but he took this new name, borne by a previous missionary at Atuona, upon his arrival.

240. Loize, 1953: 11.

241. JO 7/11 1901; BO No 7 1902: 329.

242. Letter from Picquenot to Molard after Gauguin's death.

243. Borel, 1942; letter, dated March 1, 1960, from M. Louis Grelet; and O'Brien, 1919: 148.

244. Schmidt: 251–261. M. Grelet, to whom Ky Dong gave this portrait in 1905, has supplied the information about its genesis. It is furthermore confirmed by Ky Dong's son. The note quoted in Le Bronnec, 1956: 193–4 is confused and misleading; the only correct statement being that the picture was painted in 1902.

245. That the last twenty pages were added at this time is proved not only by the sudden change in style but still more conclusively by the references to the massacres in China, which did not begin until 1900 and were still going on when Gauguin decided to rewrite the manuscript.

246. Gauguin gives this information himself in *Avant et Après*. That the go-between was Frébault is confirmed by both M. Louis Grelet and Timo. The book was Vol. I of J. B. Piolet, ed.: *Les Missions Catholiques Françaises au XIXe Siècle*. Paris, n.d.

247. Gauguin also sent a copy of the letter to the *Mercure de France* which, however, did not publish it until after his death, with several omissions and misprints. (MF August 1904: 569–73). M. Louis Grelet has recently found a letter to him, written by his brother in October 1902, which contains the following interesting passage: "Gauguin is still waging war against the bishop. He has also written a fulminating letter to the Governor; I don't know if it will be published and I for my part doubt it, but Gauguin is sure it will."

248. JO 11–15/12 1902.

249. Unpublished letter to Lieutenant Bonnemaison, dated December 1902.

250. Annuaire 1891: 167, 1903: 177; Chassé, 1955: 111; and oral information from M. Raoul Teissier.

---

60. *In the Marquesas, which have neither roads nor bridges, everyone still rides a horse, from the bishop down to the smallest native boy; but rivers often become so swollen and bridle paths so slippery after heavy rain that even the sure-footed Marquesan horses cannot cross from valley to valley.*

251. JO 12–13/2 1903; Annales July 1903: 211; and letter from M. Guillaume Le Bronnec, dated May 18, 1960.

252. BSEO 133–4: 216–8.

253. Oral information from Timo and Bishop Le Cadre. Gauguin's own summary of the facts he had been able to ascertain were included in *Avant et Après*.

254. JO 23/10 1902 and 12–13/2 1903.

255. The most complete and detailed account of this episode is given in a recently discovered letter, dated July 26, 1903, from Reiner to the lawyer Léonce Brault. Other important sources are Gauguin's letter to Horville, published by Loize, 1953: 12; and the account of one of the accused men in Le Bronnec, 1956: 197–8.

256. JO 24/3 1903. Gauguin's letter of protest is included in *Avant et Après*.

257. BSEO 133–4: 218.

258. Salles's report to the Colonial Department, dated April 4, 1903; and manuscript by the missionary Roulon.

259. The recently discovered letters from Gauguin to the lawyer Léonce Brault (BSEO 133–4) make it possible to reconstruct the events in detail. The only published character sketch of Guichenay by a contemporary visitor to the Marquesas, to my knowledge, is one by Douglas Hall, whose impressions were rather unfavourable (Hall-Osborne: 157–62).

260. Court verdict in files of Department of Justice, Papeete. Gauguin wrongly states in several letters that he was fined 1,000 francs. Governor Petit openly admits in his report of May 11, 1903, that he was behind the judgment against Gauguin and had long wished to deport him from the colony, for which, how-

61. *After being long overgrown with weeds and then for many years disfigured by an ugly slab of cement, Gauguin's grave has recently been marked by this slightly better stone cover. His nearest neighbour in the cemetery is the man who in life was his bitterest enemy; since 1912, Bishop Martin has lain buried in the large white vault next to the crucifix.*

ever, he lacked the legal authority.

261. BSEO 133–4: 223–8; and annulment of this appeal, dated September 19, 1903, in the archives of the Tribunal Supérieur de Papeete.

262. With the help of the list given by Rotonchamp: 221–2, the nine old pictures can easily be identified with the following numbers in Wildenstein's Catalogue: 524, 578, 581, 584, 586, 587, 589, 591, 593. The new picture dispatched to Vollard was evidently No 637, the other new ones Nos 635, 636 and 638.

263. M. Louis Grelet, as quoted by Borel, 1942: 16. When I enquired what he had replied to a letter from Pastor Vernier (recently published by Bompard: 188) expressing certain doubts on this point, M. Grelet sent me the following statement, dated March 1, 1960: "I can answer categorically that Varney had returned the morphine kit to him (Gauguin) some weeks before his death. It was in my own and my brother's presence that Gauguin had originally given the box to Varney

and told him not to hand it back to him on any pretext. Varney replied: 'But throw it into the sea then!' To which Gauguin said: 'No, I may need it later in an emergency.'"

264. Original letter in the archives of the *Gendarmerie Nationale* in Papeete. The various drafts have been found by Loize (1953: 11).

265. Letter from Vernier to Daniel de Monfreid, dated March 8, 1904 and reproduced by Rotonchamp: 223–7.

266. Bishop Le Cadre still believed in 1951 when I interviewed him that Gauguin had committed suicide. (Danielsson, 1957: 131.) The foremost champion of the hypothesis that Gauguin was murdered was the art historian Charles Kunstler (See *Le Journal des Arts*, No 85, 1934). Two other myths which die hard assert that the last picture painted by Gauguin was a Breton landscape in snow and that the natives of Atuona on May 8 cried "Gauguin is dead; we are lost!" The former myth originated in an article by Victor Ségalen in the June 1904 number

of the *Mercure de France*. But Ségalen never met Gauguin and did not stay long enough in Atuona to carry out any research. Moreover, a careful reading of his article reveals that it was no more than a guess. The latter very touching legend is based on a complete mistranslation of a Marquesan phrase in Vernier's letter to Daniel de Monfreid in 1904 (Rotonchamp: 225). Correctly spelt the lament reads: *Ua mate Koke, ua pe te enata*, and quite simply means "Gauguin is dead; it's all over with the fellow." The interpretation becomes even more prosaic if we retain the basic meaning of the verb *pe*, which is "to rot."

267. The letter by Pastor Vernier to Daniel de Monfreid, already referred to, also contains an account of the subsequent events up to and including the burial. It is of course very critical of the Catholic missionaries. Bishop Le Cadre's unsigned account of the same event, published in the catalogue of the Gauguin exhibition at the Louvre in 1949, is very similar in spite of its equally polemical tone. Additional information is supplied by O'Brien, 1919: 148, 1920: 228–32 and Le Bronnec, 1956: 194. With the help of Father Amerigo Cools, the archivist of the congregation of the Sacred Heart in Rome, I have been able to ascertain that the priest who buried Gauguin was a recently arrived young missionary by the name of Victorin Saltel.

268. Archives of the congregation of the Sacred Heart 47-7, according to a personal communication of January 24, 1965, from the archivist. Picquenot's report quoted in the final paragraph is now in the Papeete Museum.

LIST OF SOURCES

Gladly leaving the enormous task of compiling a complete Gauguin bibliography to the specialists, I shall here confine myself to listing the documents and informants that have supplied me with useful facts concerning the period of Gauguin's life dealt with in this book.

Adams, Henry: *Letters 1858–1891*. Edited by F. C. Chauncey. Boston, 1930.
—— *Memoirs of Arii Taimai*, Paris, 1901.
Agostini, Jules: *L'Océanie Française, Les Iles sous le Vent*. Paris, 1897.
—— *Folk-lore de Tahiti et des îles voisines*. Paris, 1900.
—— *Tahiti*. Paris, 1905.
Ahlström, Stellan: *Strindbergs erövring av Paris*. Stockholm 1956.
Alazard, Ildefonse: Les Iles Marquises. In P. Piolet: *Les missions catholiques françaises au XIXe siècle*. Paris, 1902.
Alexandre, Arsène: *Paul Gauguin, sa vie et le sens de son oeuvre*. Paris, 1930.
Annales des Sacrés-Coeurs. Monthly Catholic missionary review. Paris, 1891–1903.
Annuaire de Tahiti et dépendances. Official handbook, published annually. Papeete, 1891–1903.
Auffray, Hélène, Papeete: Oral information.
Aurier, Albert: Le symbolisme en peinture, Paul Gauguin. *Mercure de France*. Paris, March 1891.
Baessler, Arthur: *Neue Südsee-Bilder*. Berlin, 1900.
Bell, Clive: *Old friends*. London, 1956.

Bernard, Émile: *Souvenirs inédits sur l'artiste Paul Gauguin et ses compagnons.* Lorient 1939.

Bodelsen, Merete: Unpublished Letter by Theo van Gogh. *Burlington Magazine*, London, June 1957.

—— Gauguin and the Marquesan God. *Gazette des Beaux-Arts.* Paris, March 1961.

—— *Gauguin's Ceramics*, London, 1964.

Bodin, Henri, Papeete: Oral information.

Bompard, Pierre: *Ma mission Paul Gauguin aux Marquises.* Paris, 1962.

Borel, Pierre: Une canaque de sang royal connut le secret de la mort de Paul Gauguin. *Paris-Soir*, July 28, 1939.

—— Les derniers jours et la mort mystérieuse de Paul Gauguin. *Pro Arte et Libris.* Geneva, September 1942.

Bouge, L. J.: Traduction et interprétation des titres en langue tahitienne inscrits sur les oeuvres océaniennes de Paul Gauguin. *Gazette des Beaux-Arts.* Paris, January–April 1956.

Bovis, Edmond de: Etat de la Société Tahitienne à l'arrivée des Européens. *Revue coloniale*, No 14. Paris, 1855.

Bracconi, Pierre: La Colonisation française à Tahiti. *Questions diplomatiques et coloniales*, No 224. Paris, 1906.

Brault, France, Papeete: Oral information.

Brillant, Augustine-Célestine, Punaauia: Oral information.

Bulletin de la Société des Études Océaniennes. Quarterly review devoted to anthropological and historical studies, published in Papeete since 1917.

Bulletin Officiel des Établissements Français de l'Océanie. Monthly publication listing all government decrees, appointments and mutations. Papeete, 1891–1903.

Cabanne, Pierre: *Charles Filiger.* Introduction to exhibition of works by Filiger at Reid Gallery. London, 1963.

Cachin, Françoise: Un défenseur oublié de l'art moderne (Octave Mirbeau). *L'Oeil.* Paris, June 1962.

Caillot, Eugène: *Les polynésiens orientaux au contact de la civilisation.* Paris, 1909.

—— *Histoire de la Polynésie orientale.* Paris, 1910.

Cassiau, Louise, née Goupil, Papeete: Oral information.

Chambre de Commerce des Établissements Français de l'Océanie. Minutes of meetings. Papeete, 1891–1903.

Chassé, Charles: *Le mouvement symboliste dans l'art du XIXe siècle*. Paris, 1947.

— *Gauguin et son temps*. Paris, 1955.

— Le sort de Gauguin est lié au krach de 1882. *Connaissance des arts*. Paris, February 1959.

Chéronnet, Louis: P. Gauguin à Tahiti. *France-Illustration*, No 173. Paris 1949.

Claverie, Paul: *Pages détachées*. Paris, 1894.

Cochin, Jean: Letters, dated June 8, July 14 and August 14, 1944, describing a meeting with Paul Gauguin at Atuona March 10–11, 1903. In the possession of Father Patrick O'Reilly, Paris.

Conseil Général des Établissements Français de l'Océanie. Minutes of meetings, Papeete, 1891–1903.

Cotteau, Edmond: *En Océanie*. Paris, 1888.

Courtet, E.: Autour de l'Ile de Tahiti. *Société de Géographie de l'Est*, Vol. XXI, Nancy, 1899.

Danielsson, Bengt: *Love in the South Seas*, London, 1956.

— *Forgotten Islands of the South Seas*, 1957.

— Sanningen om Gauguin, *Vecko-Journalen*, Nos 44–46, Stockholm, 1964.

— När Gauguin censurerades i Stockholm, *Svenska Dagbladet*, November 11, Stockholm, 1964.

Danielsson, Bengt and Marie-Thérèse: Introduction to Mémoires d'Arii Taimai, *Publications de la Société des Océanistes*, No 12, Paris, 1964.

Daulte, François: L'art de "transposer" le sujet chez Gauguin. *Connaissance des Arts*. Paris, February 1959.

Delesemme, Paul: *Charles Morice*. Paris, 1958.

Desfontaines, Jules: *Les îles enchantées de la Polynésie*. Nantes, 1891.

Desgras, Charles: Carnet de bord. *Courrier des Messageries Maritimes*. Paris, January–February 1963.

Didier, G., Commander: Report concerning the voyage of the *Australien* from Marseilles to Nouméa, July 3–August 10, 1895. Archives of the Messageries Maritimes, Paris.

Dolent, Jean: *Maitre de sa joie*. Paris, 1902.

Dorival, Bernard: Sources of the Art of Gauguin from Java, Egypt and Ancient Greece. *Burlington Magazine*. London, April 1951.

— *Carnet de Tahiti de Paul Gauguin*. Paris, 1954.

Dorra, Henri: The first Eves in Gauguin's Eden. *Gazette des Beaux-Arts*. Paris, March 1953.

—— Émile Bernard et Paul Gauguin. *Gazette des Beaux-Arts*. Paris, April 1955.

Dorsenne, Jean: *La vie sentimentale de Paul Gauguin*. Paris, 1927.

Drollet, Alexandre, Papeete: Oral information.

Dupont, Alfred: *Précieux authographes*. Catalogue of letters sold at the Hôtel Drouot, December 3–4. Paris, 1958.

Edwards, Hugh: *Gauguin prints*. Chicago, 1959.

Esposition Universelle de 1889. Official weekly, published in Paris from October 15, 1888 to February 19, 1890.

Field, Richard: Plagiaire ou Créateur? In *Gauguin*. Collection Génies et Réalités. Paris, 1960.

Filiger, Charles: Letter to J. Blois, written at the end of May 1894. In Auriant: XII Lettres inédites de Charles Filiger. *Maintenant*, No 6. Paris, July 1947.

Fontainas, André: Art Moderne, Exposition Gauguin. *Mercure de France*. Paris, January 1899.

Frankenstein, Alfred: *Angels over the altar*. Honolulu, 1961.

Gann, Louise Gebhard: Gauguin's Image of Himself. *International Studio*. London, May, 1925.

Garnier, Jules: *Voyage autour du monde*. Paris, 1871.

Gauguin, Paul: *Ancien culte mahorie* (1892). Paris, 1951.

—— *Cahier pour Aline* (1893). Paris, 1963.

—— *Noa Noa* (1893–94). Facsimile edition of the first draft. Paris, 1954.

—— Armand Séguin. *Mercure de France*. Paris, February 1895.

—— Sous deux latitudes. *Essais d'Art Libre*. Paris, February–April 1894.

—— A propos de Sèvres et du dernier four. *Le Soir*. Paris, April 23, 1895.

—— Les peintres français à Berlin. *Le Soir*. Paris, May 1, 1895.

—— L'esprit moderne et le catholicisme (1897). Manuscript in the possession of the City Art Museum, St Louis, USA.

—— *Le Sourire* (August 1899–April 1900). Facsimile edition. Paris, 1952.

—— *Racontar de rapin* (1902). Paris, 1951.

—— *Avant et Après* (1903). Facsimile edition. Copenhagen, 1951.

—— *Lettres de Gauguin, à sa femme et à ses amis*. Edited by Maurice Malingue. Second edition. Paris, 1949.

—— *Lettres de Gauguin à Daniel de Montfreid*. Edited by Annie Joly-Ségalen and with a preface by Victor Ségalen. Paris, 1950.

—— *Letters to Ambroise Vollard and André Fontainas.* San Francisco, 1943.

—— Letter to J. F. Willumsen. *Les Marges.* Paris, March 15, 1918.

—— Letter to Schuffenecker, dated April 10, 1896. See Dupont, Alfred, No 115.

—— Letter to Schuffenecker, written sometime in 1896. See Dupont, Alfred, No 116.

—— Letter to Armand Séguin, dated January 15, 1897, sold at an auction at the Hôtel Drouot in Paris, June 5, 1962.

—— Draft of a collective letter to the governor, June 1899. Copy in the author's possession.

—— Letter to the Conseil Général des Établissements Français de l'Océanie, November 1902. *Procès-verbaux du Conseil Général,* Année 1902.

—— Letter to Lieutenant Bonnemaison, head of the Géndarmerie National in the French Oceanic Settlements, December 1902. Government archives, Papeete.

—— Letter to Lieutenant Bonnemaison, head of the Géndarmerie National in the French Oceanic Settlements, April 1903. Government archives, Papeete.

—— Letters to lawyer Léonce Brault, dated February, March 6, March 26, April, and April 27, 1903. In the possession of the lawyer's widow Jane Brault, Papeete.

—— Receipt for a payment of 36.75 francs, made by lawyer Auguste Goupil, dated May 18, 1892. In the possession of Dr Pierre Cassiau, Papeete.

—— Various documents concerning the loan of 1897 from the Agricultural Bank and its repayments. Papeete Museum.

—— Death certificate, No 14, Atuona, May 8, 1903. Government registry, Papeete.

—— Annulment, dated September 19, 1903, of an appeal to the Tribunal Supérieur against the condemnation of March 31, 1903, due to the appelant's death.

Gauguin, Paul—Morice, Charles: *Noa Noa.* Facsimile edition of the manuscript of 1895 in Gauguin's handwriting with illustrations added later. Stockholm, 1947.

—— *Noa Noa. La Revue Blanche.* Paris, October 15 and November 15, 1897.

—— *Noa Noa.* Paris, 1901.

Gauguin, Pola: *Mette og Paul Gauguin,* Copenhagen, 1959.

Geffroy, Gustave: La Bretagne du Sud. *Le Tour du Monde,* Vol X. Paris, 1904.

Gérard, Judith: Mémoires. Manuscript. In the possession of Dr Gerda Kjellberg, Stockholm.

—— Absence de Gauguin. Manuscript with information about Gauguin's friends. In the possession of Dr Gerda Kjellberg, Stockholm.

—— Julien Leclercq, un satellite de Gauguin. Manuscript in the possession of Dr Gerda Kjellberg, Stockholm.

Gérard-Arlberg, Gilles: Nr 6, rue Vercingétorix. *Konstrevy,* No 2. Stockholm, 1958.

Ginies, Louis: Histoire d'un portrait inconnu de Gauguin. *Marseille Matin.* Marseille, December 21, 1937.

Goldwater, Robert: A Unique Gauguin, Marquesan Elements in a Woodcut. *Magazine of Art.* London, January 1937.

Goupil, Auguste: Les îles Tahiti. In Alfred Rambaud: *La France coloniale.* Paris, 1886.

Gray, Christopher: *Sculpture and Ceramics of Paul Gauguin.* Baltimore, 1963.

Grelet, Louis, Omoa, Fatuiva, Marquesas Islands: Letters to the author, dated March 1 and May 9, 1960.

Guillot, François: *Souvenirs d'un colonial en Océanie.* Annecy, 1935.

Hall, Douglas—Osborne, Albert: *Sunshine and surf.* London, 1901.

Hammacher, A. M.: *Les amis de van Gogh.* Paris, 1960.

Hamon, René: *Gauguin, le solitaire du Pacifique,* Paris, 1939.

Haweis, Stephen: Paul Gauguin, artist. *International Studio.* London, May 1921.

Henrique, L. et al.: *Les colonies françaises, Tahiti, Iles sous-le-vent.* Paris, 1889.

Huguenin, Paul: *Raiatéa, la sacrée.* Neuchâtel, 1902.

Huguet: Les îles Sous-le-Vent, l'Expédition de Raiatea. *A travers le Monde,* Nos 11 and 13. Paris, March, 1898.

Huyghe, René: *Gauguin, créateur de la peinture moderne.* Preface to the centenary exhibition held in the Orangerie annex of the Louvre. Paris, 1949.

—— *La clef de Noa Noa.* Concluding essay at the end of Gauguin's *Ancien culte mahorie.* Paris, 1951.

—— *Le carnet de Paul Gauguin.* Paris, 1952.

Jacquier, Henri: *Dossier de la succession Paul Gauguin.* Papeete, 1957.

—— Une correspondance inédite de Paul Gauguin. *Bulletin de la Société des Études Océaniennes*, No 133–134. Papeete, December 1960–March 1961.

Jaworska, Wladyslawa: Gauguin—Slewinski—Makowski. *Sztuka i Krytyka*, No 3–4. Warszawa, 1957.

Jénot: Le premier séjour de Gauguin à Tahiti. *Gazette des Beaux-Arts*. Paris, January–April 1956.

Journal des Missions Évangéliques. Monthly review published by the French Calvinist missionary society. Paris, 1891–1903.

Journal Officiel des Établissements Français de l'Océanie. Weekly paper containing not only decrees but also articles of a general interest, statistics and the dates of the arrival and departure of all ships calling at Papeete. Papeete, 1891–1903.

Joyant, Maurice: *Henri de Toulouse-Lautrec*. Paris, 1926.

Järv, Harry: Gauguins elaka tidskrift. *Biblis*. Stockholm, 1964.

Keable, Robert: From the House of Gauguin. *Century*, Vol 106. New York, September 1923.

Kede, Svante: *Otaheiti*. Stockholm, 1933.

Kjellberg, Gerda: *Hänt och sant*. Stockholm, 1951.

La Farge, John: *Reminiscences of the South Seas*. New York, 1912.

Lebeau, Henri: *Otahiti*. Paris, 1911.

Leblond, Marius-Ary: La vie anarchiste d'un artiste. *La dépêche de Toulouse*. Toulouse, October 1, 1903.

—— Gauguin en Océanie. *Revue Universelle*, Paris, October 15, 1903.

Le Bronnec, Guillaume, Atuona, Hivaoa. Oral information and letters to the author, dated September 6, 1957, May 18 and August 2, 1960.

—— La vie de Gauguin aux Marquises. *Bulletin de la Société des Études Océaniennes*, No 106. Papeete, March 1954.

—— Les dernières années. *Gazette des Beaux-Arts*. Paris, January–April 1956.

Lecadre, David, Catholic Bishop in the Marquesas Islands: Oral information.

Leclercq, Julien: *Strophes d'Amant*. Paris, 1891.

—— Exposition Paul Gauguin. *Mercure de France*. Paris, November 1894.

—— *La physionomie, d'après les principes d'Eugène Ledos*. Paris, 1896.

—— *Le caractère et la main, histoire et documents*. Paris, n.d.

Lemasson, Henry: *Notice sur les Établissements Français de l'Océanie*. Paris, 1900.

—— Paul Gauguin vu par un de ses contemporains à Tahiti. Encyclopédie de la France et d'Outre-Mer, Nos 2 and 3. Paris, February 1950.

Le Messager de Tahiti. Weekly newspaper. Papeete, 1891–1903.

Les Guêpes. Monthly political paper, published regularly from March 1899 to August 1901. Last issues published in 1902. Copies consulted are in the possession of Mitchell Library, Sydney, Papeete Museum, M. Henri Thirel and M. Raoul Teissier, Papeete, Bibliothèque Nationale, Paris, and Dr John Rewald, New York.

Levergos, Pierre: Oral information and unpublished notes in the possession of M. Yves Martin, Papeete.

Loize, Jean: Gauguin écrivain ou les sept visages de Noa Noa. *Journal de la Société des Océanistes*, No 5. Paris, December 1949.

—— Les amitiés du peintre Georges Daniel de Monfreid et ses reliques de Gauguin. Paris, 1951.

—— Il faut réhabiliter Gauguin, *Arts*, No 410, Paris, May 1953.

—— *The real Noa Noa and the illustrated copy*. Postscript to the English translation of the first draft of *Noa Noa*, London, 1962.

Loos, Viggo: Swedenborg, Baudelaire och Gauguin. *Svenska Dagbladet*. Stockholm, July 28, 1956.

Loti, Pierre: *Le mariage de Loti*. Paris, 1880.

Lövgren, Sven: Myten om Gauguin. *Dagens Nyheter*. Stockholm, July 17, 1952.

—— Gauguin och Noa Noa. *Dagens Nyheter*. Stockholm, May 19, 1953.

—— *The Genesis of Modernism*. Stockholm, 1959.

Mager, Henri: *Cahiers coloniaux*. Paris, 1889.

—— Grandeur et décadence de Taïti. *Revue Française de l'étranger et des colonies*, Vol XXII. Paris, 1897.

—— *Le Monde Polynésien*. Paris, 1902.

Marks-Vandenbroucke, Ursula: Gauguin, ses origines et sa formation artistique. *Gazette des Beaux-Arts*. Paris, January–April 1956.

Massey, Gerald: *La Nouvelle genèse*. Paris, 1888.

Maszkowski, Karol: Chez Madame Charlotte. *Sztuki Piekne*, No II. Warszawa, 1925–26.

Mativet M. (Monchoisy): *La nouvelle Cythère*. Paris, 1888.

Maugham, Somerset: *A writer's notebook*. London, 1949.

—— *Purely for my pleasure*. London, 1962.

Maurice, René: Autour de Gauguin. *Nouvelle Revue de Bretagne*. Rennes, November–December 1953.

Menpes, Dorothy: *Brittany*. London, 1905.

Menpes, Mortimer: *Who was who, 1929–1940*. London, 1941.

Moerenhout, Jacques Antoine: *Voyage aux îles du Grand Océan*. Paris, 1837.

Montfreid, Daniel de: Letter to William Molard, dated September 1, 1901. In the author's possession.

—— Un grand artiste. *La dépêche de Toulouse*. Toulouse, October 10, 1903.

Morice, Charles: Exposition d'oeuvres récentes de Paul Gauguin. *Mercure de France*. Paris, December 1893.

—— Paul Gauguin. *Le Soir*. Paris, November 23, 1894.

—— L'atelier de Paul Gauguin. *Le Soir*. Paris, December 4, 1894.

—— Le départ de Paul Gauguin. *Le Soir*. Paris, June 28, 1895.

—— Paul Gauguin. *Les Hommes d'Aujourd'hui*, No 440. Paris, 1896.

—— Letter to Paul Gauguin dated March 5, 1897. In the possession of Mr Georges Taran, Papeete.

—— *Paul Gauguin*, Paris, 1920.

Mucha, Jiri, Prague: Oral information.

Myrica, Pierre de: Tahiti, Notes et Impressions. *Le Tour du Monde*, No 8. Paris, 1902.

Möller, Artur: Strindberg och Gauguin. *Vecko-Journalen*, No 42. Stockholm, 1919.

Neverman, Hans: Polynesien und Paul Gauguin. *Baessler-Archiv*, Vol IV. Berlin, 1956.

Nordhoff, Charles: Notes on the off-shore fishing of the Society Islands. *Journal of the Polynesian Society*, Vol 39. New Plymouth, N.Z., 1930.

Nordman, Axel Edvard: Deed concerning the purchase of the plot Atio at Punaauia. Vol 261: 1 Archives of the land bureau, Papeete.

Nordman, Oscar, Papeete: Oral information.

O'Brien, Frederick: *White Shadows in the South Seas*. New York, 1919.

—— Gauguin in the South Seas. *The Century*. New York, June 1920.

—— *Atolls in the sun*. London, 1922.

Océanie Française. Monthly political paper. Papeete, 1891–1903.

O'Conor catalogue. Collection of paintings and drawings sold at the Hôtel Drouot in Paris, February 6–7, 1956.

Olivaint, Maurice: Voyage à Tahiti. *Bulletin de la Société de Géographie d'Algar et de l'Afrique du Nord,* Vol 25. Alger, 1920.
—— *Fleurs de corail,* Paris, 1900.
—— *Sur les coraux.* Paris, 1924.
O'Reilly, Patrick: Charles Alfred Le Moine, peintre de la Polynésie Française. *Bulletin de la Société des Études Océaniennes,* No 126. Papeete, March 1959.
—— "Les amours d'un vieux peintre aux Marquises" ou Paul Gauguin héros d'une comédie en vers écrite de son vivant. *Journal de la Société des Océanistes,* No 18. Paris, December 1962.
O'Reilly, Patrick—Teissier, Raoul: Tahitiens, répertoire bio-bibliographique de la Polynésie Française. *Publications de la Société des Océanistes,* No 10. Paris, 1962.
Pallander, Edwin: *The Log of an Island Wanderer.* London 1901.
Peltier, Marcelle, née Millaud, Papeete: Oral information.
Perruchot, Henri: *Le vie de Gauguin.* Paris, 1961.
Petit, Édouard (pseudonym Aylic Marin): *En Océanie.* Paris, 1888.
—— *Au loin.* Paris, 1891.
—— Report, dated June 25, 1902, concerning the loss of the steamer *Croix du Sud* addressed to the Minister of Colonial Affairs. Archives Nationales, Paris.
—— Report, dated May 11, 1903, concerning the situation in the Marquesas Islands, addressed to the Minister of Colonial Affairs. Archives Nationales, Paris.
—— *Discours devant le Conseil Général, le 10 novembre 1903.* Papeete, 1903.
Piquenot, François: *Géographie physique et politique des Établissements Français de l'Océanie.* Paris, 1900.
—— Letter, dated June 18, 1903, to William Molard. Copy in the author's possession.
Pissarro, Camille: *Lettres à son fils Lucien,* Paris, 1950.
Poydenot, Commander: Report concerning the return voyage of the *Armand Béhic* from Nouméa to Marseille, July 16—August 30, 1893. Archives of the Messageries Maritimes, Paris.
Précaire, M. de: Rapport de mer sur le cyclone des îles Tuamotu. *Revue Coloniale.* Paris, May 1903.
Puig, René: *Paul Gauguin.* Perpignan, 1958.
Ramsden, Eric: Death of Gauguin's Tahitian mistress. *Pacific Islands Monthly.* Sydney, January 1944.
Redon, Odilon: *Lettres.* Paris, 1960.

Reeves, Edward: *Brown Men and Women, or the South Sea Islands in 1895 and 1896.* London, 1898.

Rewald, John: The genius and the dealer. *Art News.* New York, May 1959.

—— *Le Post-Impressionnisme.* Paris, 1961.

Rey, Robert: *Onze menus de Paul Gauguin.* Genève, 1950.

Ro'o, Teha'amana. Death certificate. Government registry, Papeete.

Rostrup, Haavard: *Gauguin og hans venner,* Copenhagen, 1956.

—— Gauguin et le Danemark. *Gazette des Beaux-Arts.* Paris, January–April 1956.

Rotonchamp, Jean de: *Paul Gauguin.* Paris, 1925.

Rott, Céline: *Moana, ou voyage sentimental chez lez Maoris et les Peaux-Rouges des Iles.* Paris, 1923.

Rousseau, Theodore, et al.: *Catalogue* of the Gauguin exhibition in the Art Institute of Chicago and the Metropolitan Museum of Art in New York, February 12–March 29 and April 21–May 31. Chicago, 1959.

Rugière, Paul: Tahiti et Gauguin. *Mercure de France.* Paris, November 1921.

Roulon, Henri Charles: Les Frères de Ploermel en Océanie. Manuscript. Archives of the Congregation of the Sacred Hearts, Rome.

Salles, André: Report, dated April 4, 1903, to the minister for Colonial Affairs concerning his voyage of inspection to the Marquesas Islands. Archives Nationales, Paris.

—— Report, dated May 15, 1903, to the minister for Colonial Affairs concerning the political situation in the French Oceanic Settlements. Archives Nationales, Paris.

Salmon, Tahiti: Letters to Henry Adams, 1892–1913. Massachusetts Historical Society Library, Boston, USA.

Schmidt, George: Paul Gauguins letztes Selbstbildnis? *Jahresbericht der öffentlichen Kunstsammlung.* Basel, 1945.

Ségalen, Victor: Cyclone des îles Tuamotu. *Armée et Marine.* Paris, April 12, 1903.

—— Gauguin dans son dernier décor. *Mercure de France.* Paris, June 1904.

Séguin, Armand: Paul Gauguin. *L'Occident.* Paris, January, February, March 1903.

Sérusier, Paul: *ABC de la peinture,* Paris, 1950.

Severson, T. B.: Description of Tahiti. *Overland Magazine.* San Francisco, June 1901.

Sigogne, Madeleine, née Goupil, Papeete: Oral information.

Simon, T. F.: Stefánik po Gauguinových stopàch na Tahiti. *Hollar*, No 1. Prague, 1937.

Spitz, Charles et al.: *Autour du Monde, Possessions Françaises en Océanie.*

Steinen, Karl van den: Reise nach den Marquesas Inseln. *Gesellschaft für Erdkunde*, Vol 25. Berlin, 1898.

Strömbom, Sixten: Konstnärsförbundets historia, Vol II. Stockholm, 1965.

Sutton, Denys: "La Perte du pucelage" by Paul Gauguin. *Burlington Magazine*. London, April 1949.

—— Notes on Paul Gauguin apropos a Recent Exhibition. *Burlington Magazine*. London, March 1956.

—— Roderic O'Conor. *The Studio*. London, November 1960.

—— Echos from Pont-Aven. *Apollo*. London, May 1964.

Sýkorová, Libuše: Gauguin woodcuts. Prague and London, 1963.

Tai, Émile, Punaauia, Tahiti: Oral information.

—— Birth certificate, Government registry, Papeete.

Tai, Pau'ura: Birth certificate, Government registry, Papeete.

Tai, Poara'i: Oral information.

Ta'iterefa'ato'a, Puto'ura, Mataiea, Tahiti: Oral information.

Tardieu, Eugène: Paul Gauguin. *L'Echo de Paris*. Paris, May 13, 1895.

Teheiura, Ma'ari, Mataiea, Tahiti: Oral information.

Teissier, Henri, Punaauia, Tahiti: Oral information.

Teissier, Raoul, Papeete: Oral information.

Teri'iero'oitera'i, Teri'iero, Papenoo, Tahiti: Oral information.

Van Cam, Nguyen, alias Ky Dong: Les amours d'un vieux peintre aux îles Marquises. Manuscript in the possession of his son, M. Pierre Van Cam, Papeete.

Van Cam, Pierre, Papeete: Oral information.

Varney, Benjamin: Ledger, containing Gauguin's account from October 1, 1901 to November 15, 1902. In the possession of M. Guillaume Le Bronnec, Atuona, Hivaoa.

Veene, Théophile van der: Conférence sur Tahiti. *Bulletin de la Société des Études coloniales et maritimes*. Paris, 1884.

Verkade, Willibrod: *Die Unruhe zu Gott*. Freiburg im Breisgau, 1933.

Vernaudon, Emile, Punaauia, Tahiti: Oral information.

Vernier, Paul: Letters to Louis Grelet concerning Gauguin's death, dated July 22 and October 8, 1948. In the possession of M. Louis Grelet, Fatuiva.

Villaret, Bernard: Les dernières années de Gauguin. *Revue de Paris*, Paris, February 1953.

Vollard, Ambroise: *Souvenirs d'un marchand de tableaux*. Paris, 1937.

Wildenstein, Georges: L'idéologie et l'esthétique dans deux tableaux-clés de Gauguin. *Gazette des Beaux-Arts*. Paris, January–April 1956.

—— *Gauguin, Catalogue*, Vol I. Paris, 1964.

Willumsen, J. F.: *Mine erindringer*. Copenhagen, 1953.

Wilmot May, Papeete: Oral information.

Wragge, Clement: *The Romance of the South Seas*. London, 1906.

INDEX

Absinth, 64, 73, 99, 161, 260, 310
Académie Colarossi, 45, 46
Academy of Art, 51, 132, 140, 141, 142, 150, 200; Gauguin attacks, 182
Adams, Henry, 62–63, 71, 94, 108
Adelaide, Australia, 58
Aden, 57
Agostini, Jules, 192–93, 217, 218–19
Aita Parari Te Tamari Vahine Judith, 166
A la zoologie de la femme (Strindberg), 177
Alcohol, use of, 88. *See also* Absinth; Drinking; Rum; Wine-drinking
Americans, the, 69–70, 189, 248, 252
Anani ("Orange," a native), 94, 95, 97, 110, 297
Anarchism (anarchists), 41, 138, 180, 277–78, 287
Ancien culte mahorie (Gauguin's notebook), 133, 134
And the Gold of their Bodies, 258–60
Angelus, The (Millet), 191
Angkor Wat, 29
Anglo-Americans, 70, 189, 248
Anna the "Javanese," 144, 164–66, 177; with Gauguin in Brittany, 171, 172, 174, 176
Aoni (Chinese store-keeper), 99
Ariioehau, 92. *See also* Tetuanui, Chief
Arii Taimai Salmon, 108
Arii Vahine, 198
Arioi society, 108–9, 166
Arlberg, Fritz, 159
Arles, 24, 49
Armand Béhic (steamer), 143–44, 145
Arnaud, Charles, 105–6, 109, 111–12
Art (arts and crafts), native, 84–85, 100
Art and artists, Gauguin on, 139, 153, 156–57, 182–84, 278
Atheneum Museum, Helsinki, 99
Atuona, 240, 241, 250 ff., 267 ff., 281 ff.;

Gauguin builds house in, 253–54 ff.; map of, 258
Auckland, New Zealand, 188
Audoye (French officer), 133
Auffray, Jules, 219–20
Au Loin (Petit), 263
Aurier, Albert, 150
Australia, 55, 57, 58
Australien (steamer), 188
Austral islands, 60, 231
Avant et Après (Gauguin), 281
Ayu (Chinese restaurant owner), 258

Balls. *See* Dancing
Bambridge, Susannah, 82
Bambridge, Thomas, 81–82
Bananas, 33, 48, 87, 91–99
Barbaric Tales, 257
Basle, Kunstmuseum in, 77, 274
Bastille Day, 78–81, 269–71
Bayerische Staatsgemäldesammlungen, Munich, 203
Beaux-Arts Musée, Liége, 257
Beer-drinking, 99–100
Berceuse (Schumann), 254
Bernard, Émile, 23–24, 28, 31–32, 34, 38, 198; breaks with Gauguin, 48–49, 53; Séguin resembles, 173
Bernard, Madeleine, 23, 48
Bibelots sauvages, 125–26
Bible reading, 83–84, 87
Bonnard, rue (Papeete), 76, 77
Bonnat, Léon-Joseph-Florentin, 136, 186
Bonnemaison, Lieutenant, 298
Bonnier, Mrs., 159
Book of the Beginnings, A (Massey), 210–11
Bordeaux, France, 55
Botticelli, Sandro, 158, 183, 257
Bouguereau, W. A., 182, 183, 186
Bourse, 19, 20, 21, 25, 138, 215–16
Boussod et Valadon art gallery, 25, 39–